Little Miss P

KEN KOYAMA

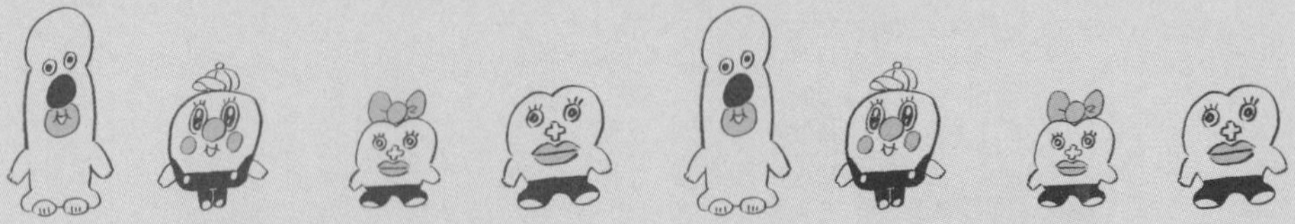

Little Miss P

CONTENTS

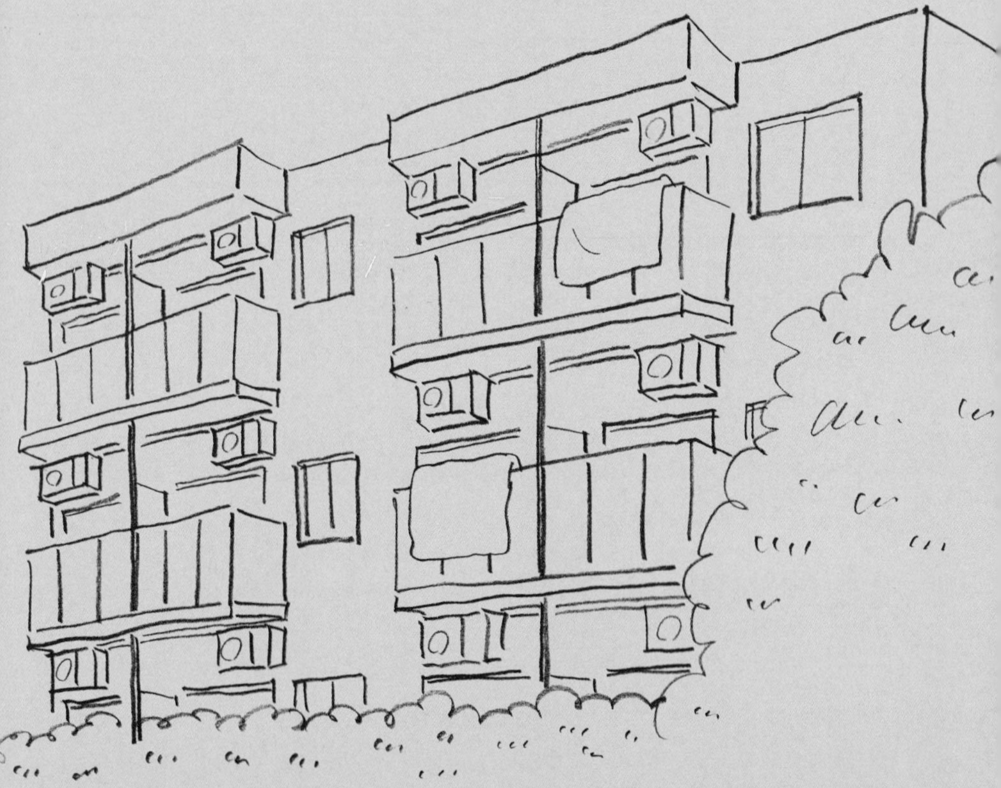

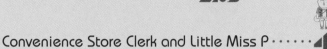

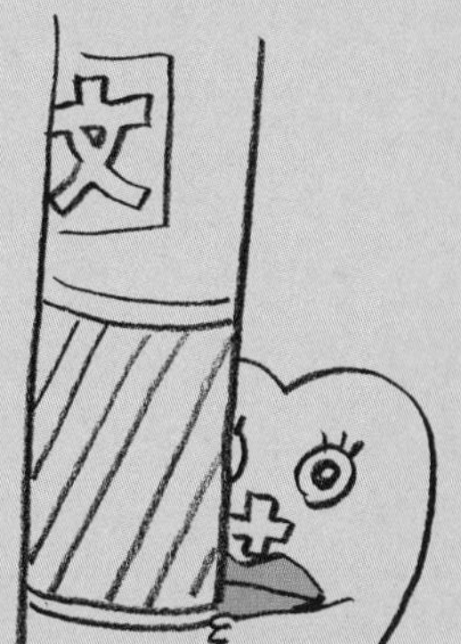
文

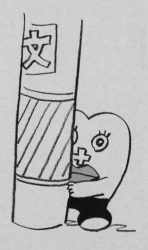

HOUSEWIFE AND LITTLE MISS P

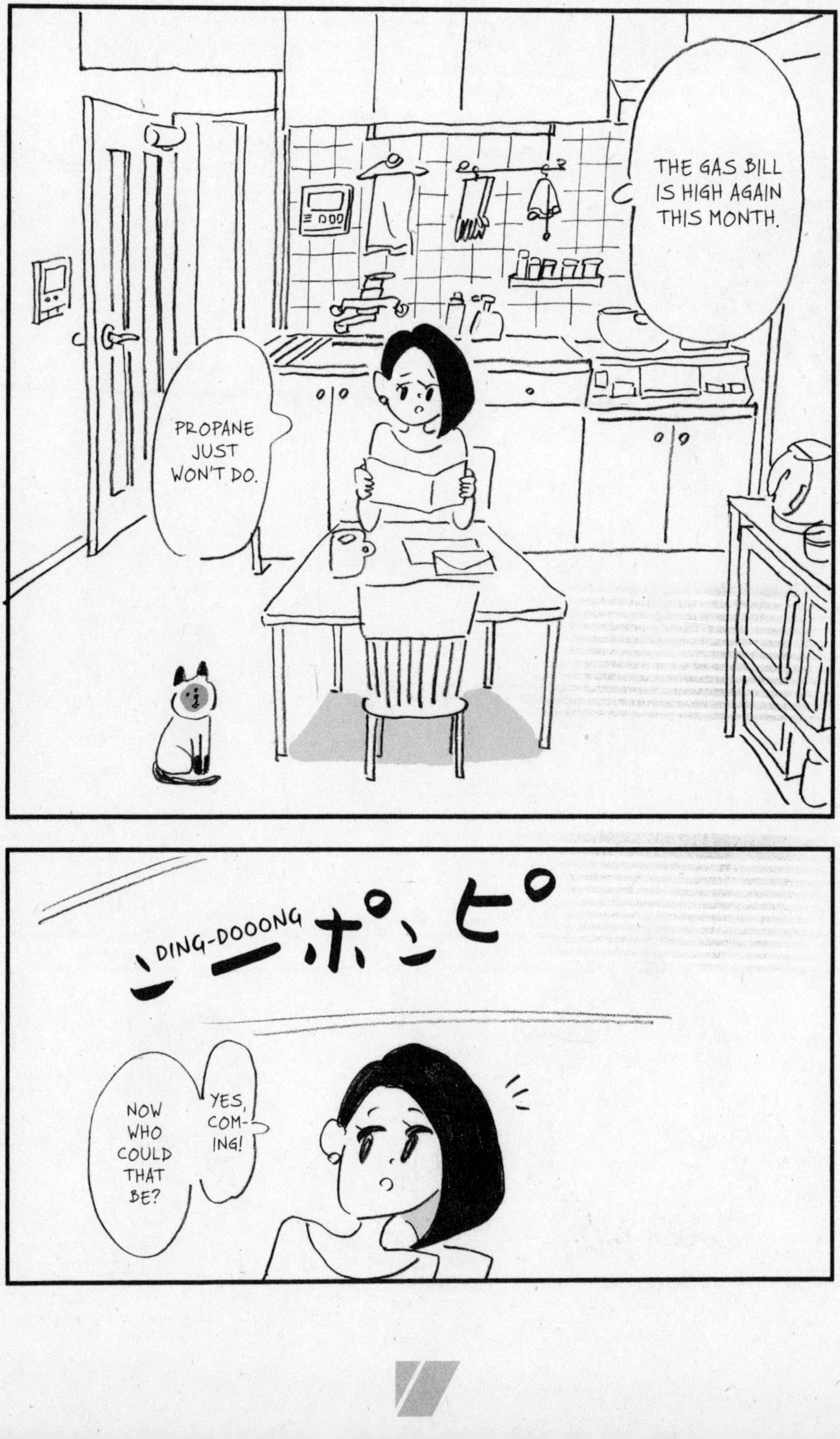
THE GAS BILL IS HIGH AGAIN THIS MONTH.
PROPANE JUST WON'T DO.
DING-DOOONG
ピンポーン
YES, COM-ING!
NOW WHO COULD THAT BE?

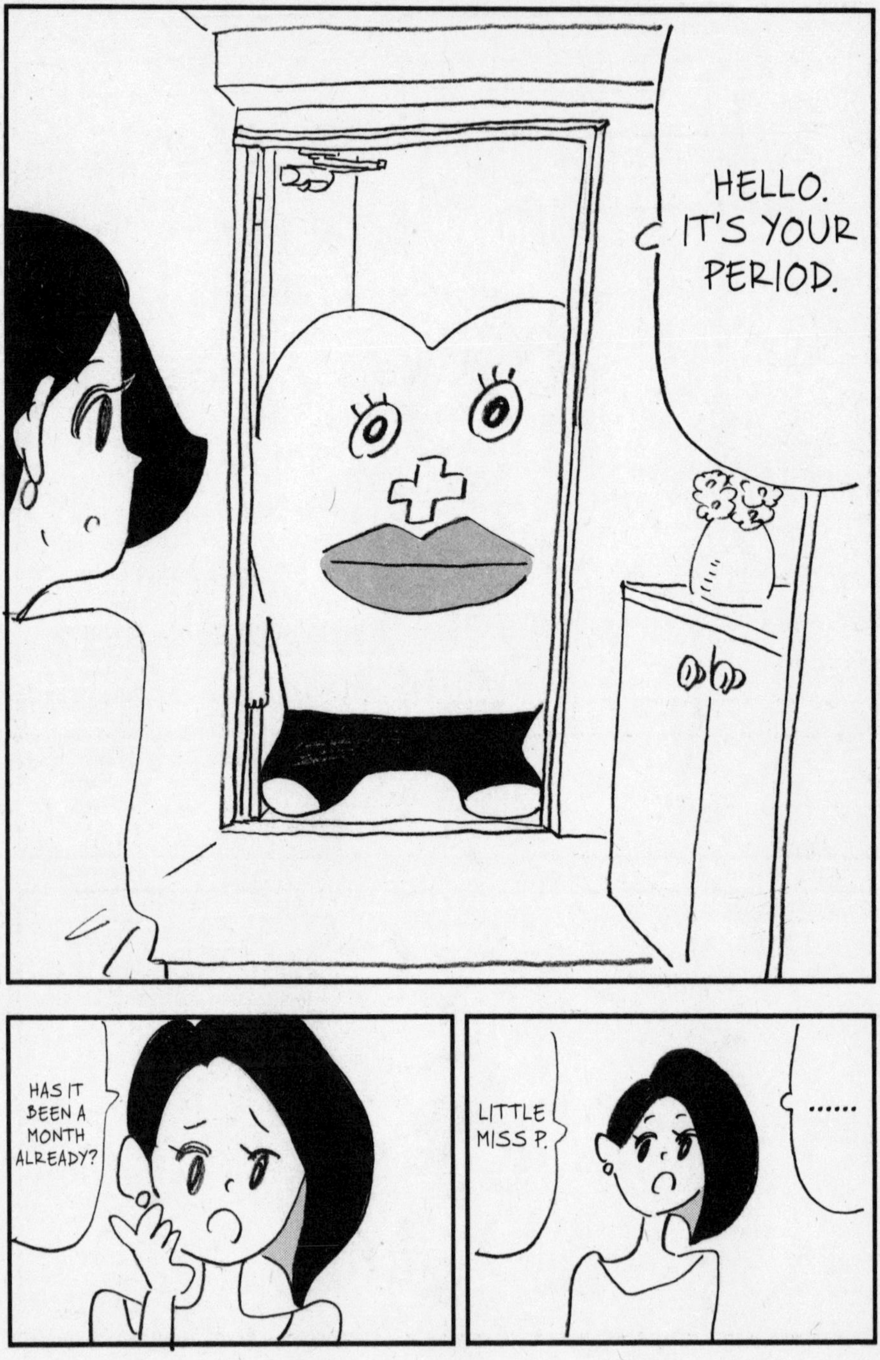
HELLO. IT'S YOUR PERIOD.
......
LITTLE MISS P.
HAS IT BEEN A MONTH ALREADY?

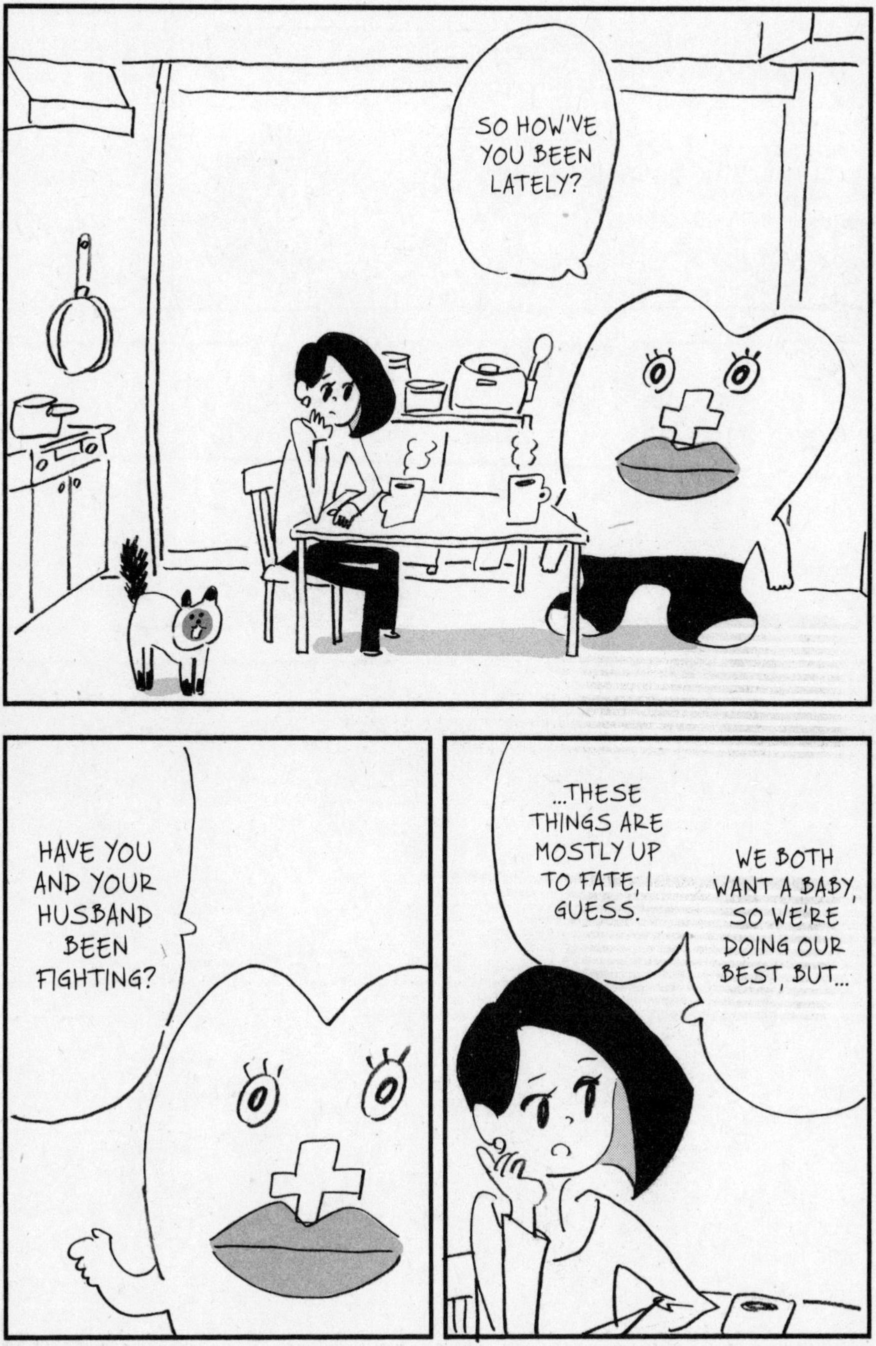
SO HOW'VE YOU BEEN LATELY?
WE BOTH WANT A BABY, SO WE'RE DOING OUR BEST, BUT...
...THESE THINGS ARE MOSTLY UP TO FATE, I GUESS.
HAVE YOU AND YOUR HUSBAND BEEN FIGHTING?

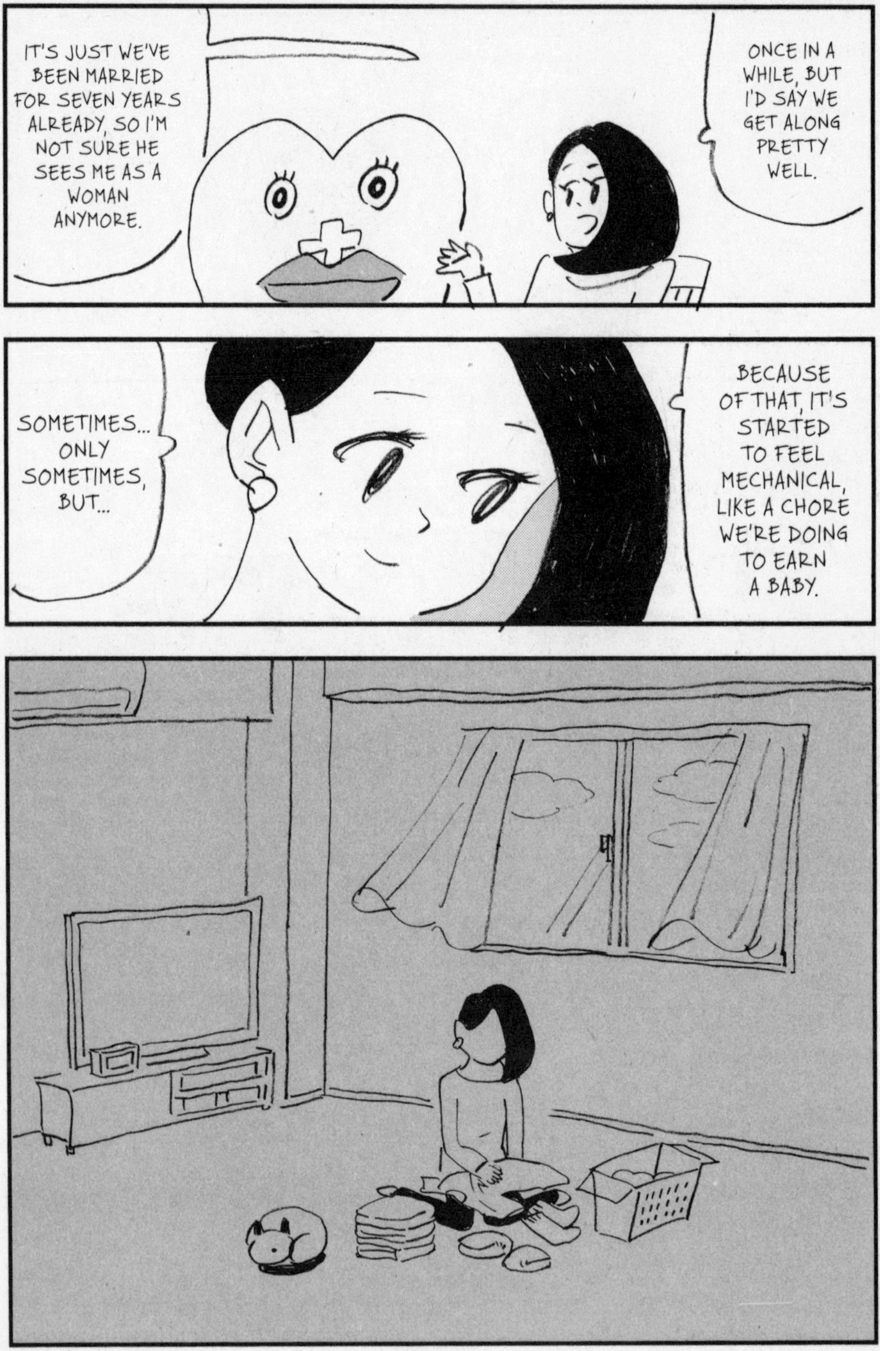
ONCE IN A WHILE, BUT I'D SAY WE GET ALONG PRETTY WELL.
IT'S JUST WE'VE BEEN MARRIED FOR SEVEN YEARS ALREADY, SO I'M NOT SURE HE SEES ME AS A WOMAN ANYMORE.
BECAUSE OF THAT, IT'S STARTED TO FEEL MECHANICAL, LIKE A CHORE WE'RE DOING TO EARN A BABY.
SOMETIMES... ONLY SOMETIMES, BUT...

...LATELY, I'VE BEEN THINKING IT WOULDN'T BE SO BAD TO GIVE UP.
AFTER ALL, THERE ARE ALL SORTS OF WAYS TO LIVE THESE DAYS.
THAT'S TRUE. ...WELL, IT'S ABOUT TIME FOR THE USUAL.
WHIRL WHIRL
EEEEEK! WAIT, WAIT, TIME OUT!
ドゴッ
WHUD
AAAAGH!

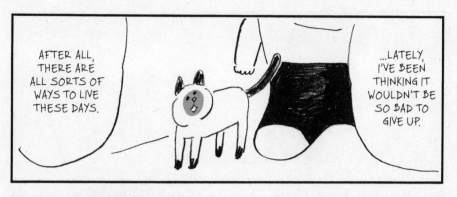

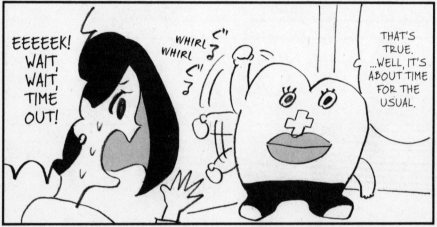

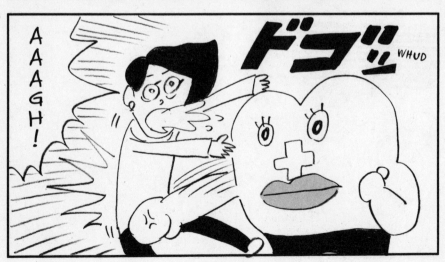

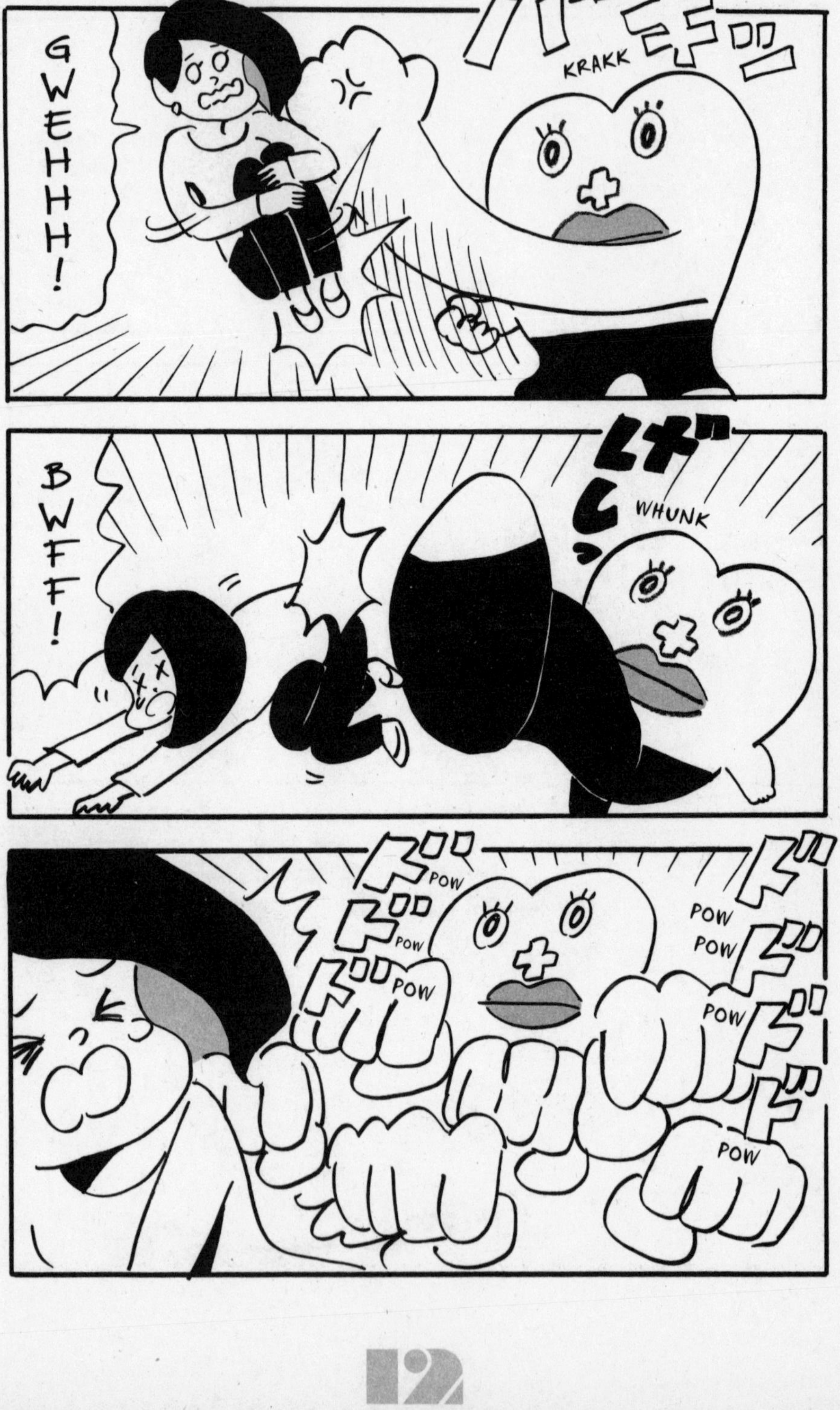
KRAKK
GWEHHHH!
WHUNK
BWFF!
POW
POW
POW
POW
POW
POW
POW

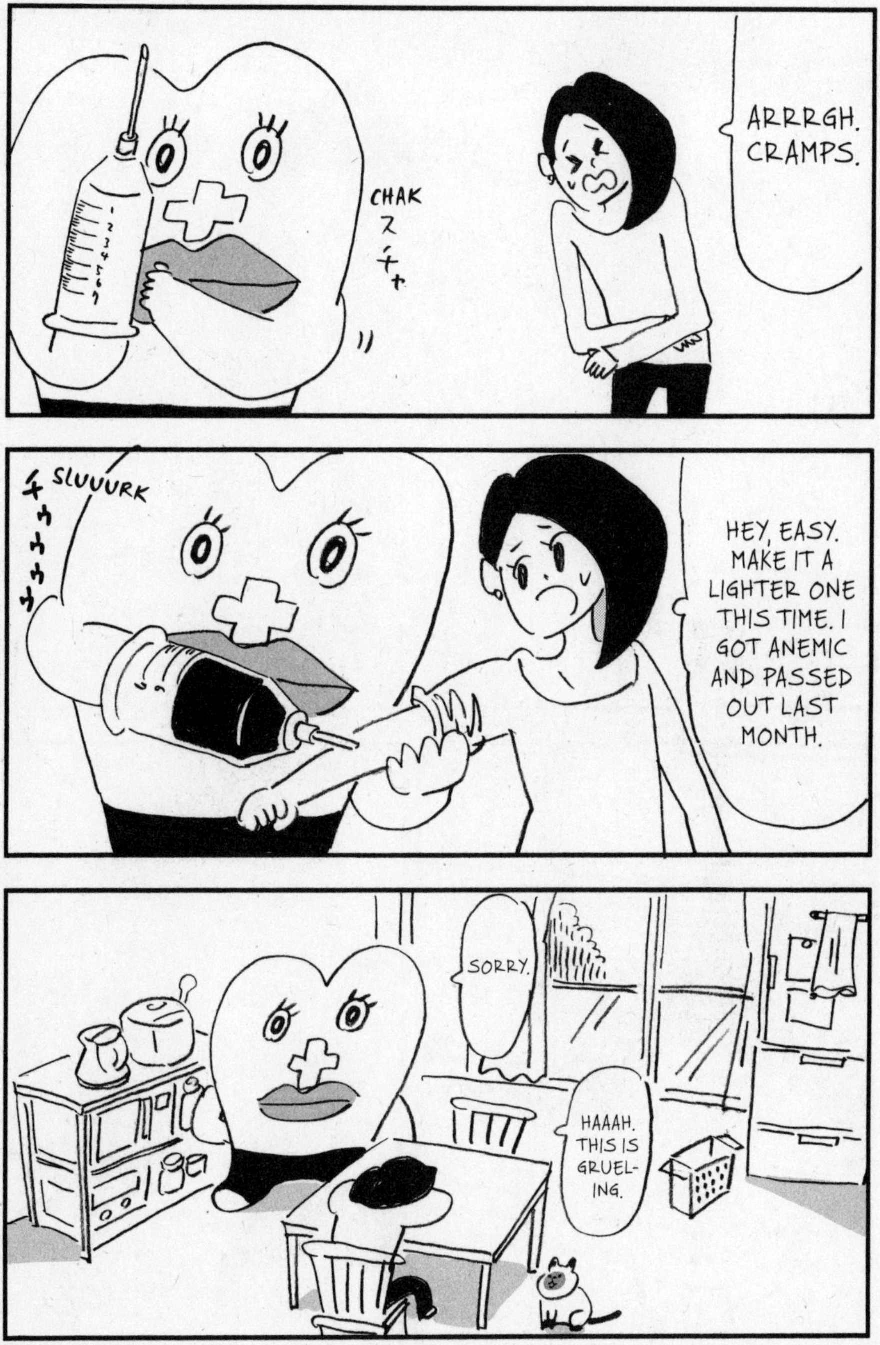
ARRRGH. CRAMPS.
CHAK
スチャ
HEY, EASY. MAKE IT A LIGHTER ONE THIS TIME. I GOT ANEMIC AND PASSED OUT LAST MONTH.
SLUUURK
チュううう
SORRY.
HAAAH. THIS IS GRUEL-ING.

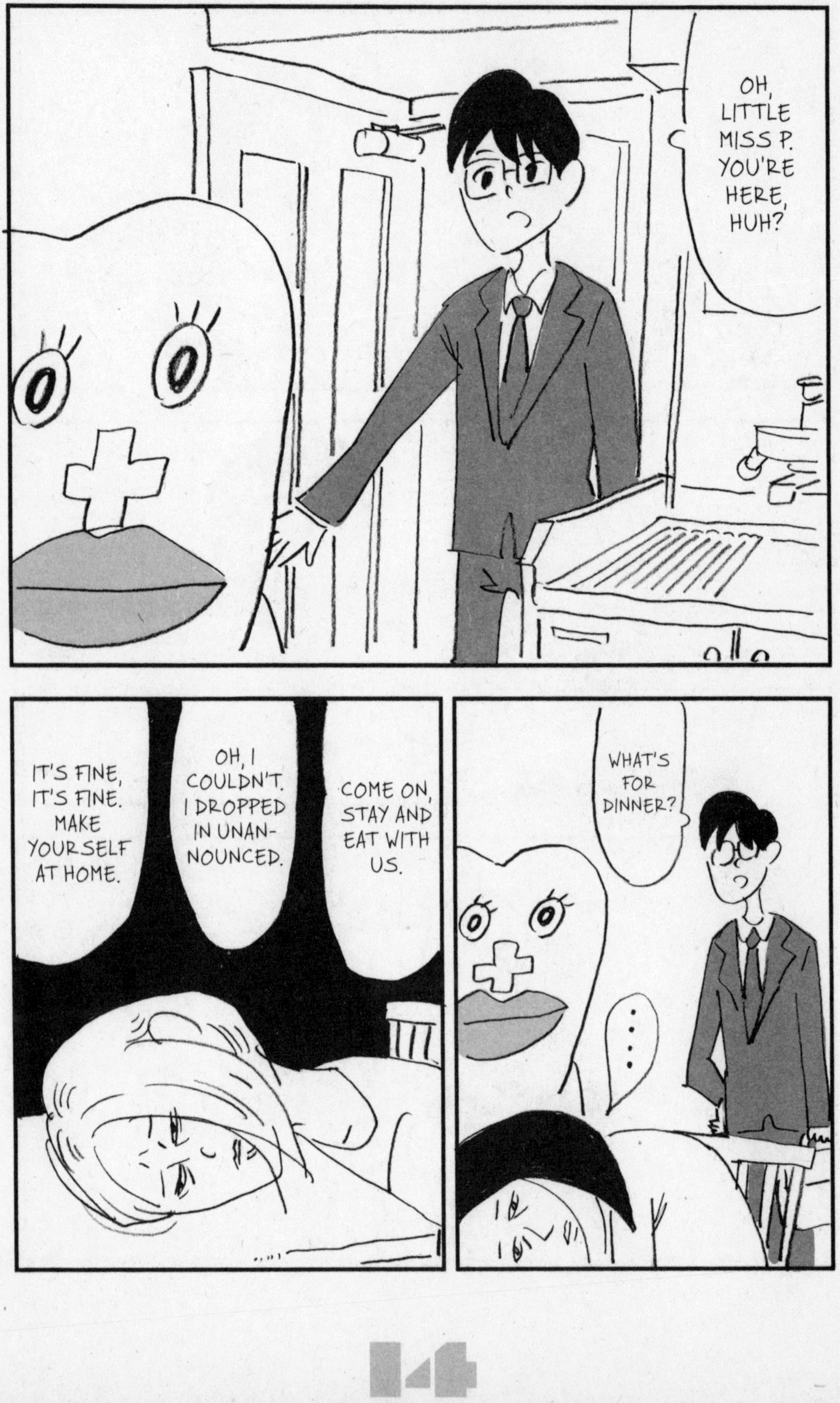
OH, LITTLE MISS P. YOU'RE HERE, HUH?
WHAT'S FOR DINNER?
....
COME ON, STAY AND EAT WITH US.
OH, I COULDN'T. I DROPPED IN UNAN-NOUNCED.
IT'S FINE, IT'S FINE. MAKE YOURSELF AT HOME.
...

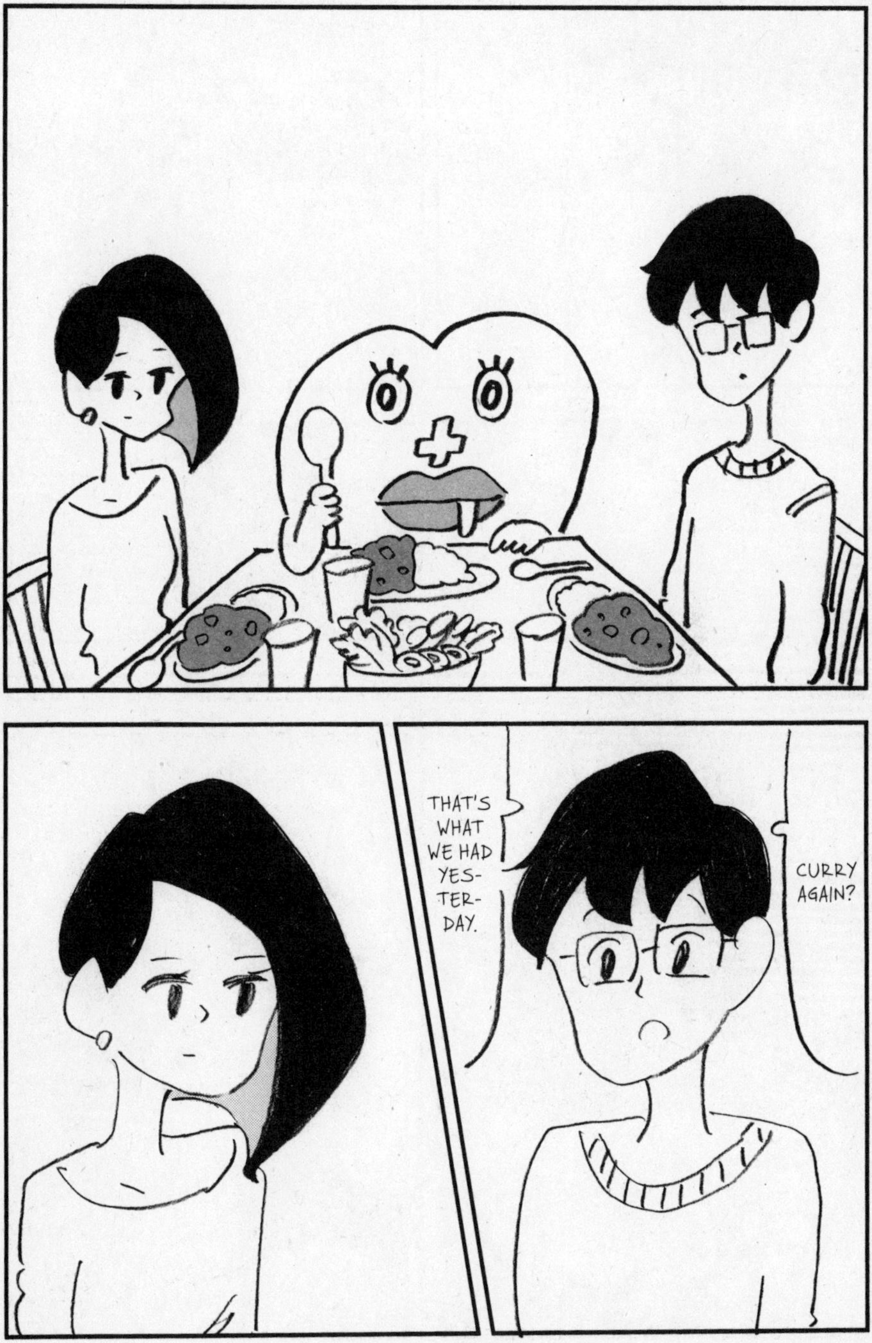
CURRY AGAIN?
THAT'S WHAT WE HAD YES-TER-DAY.

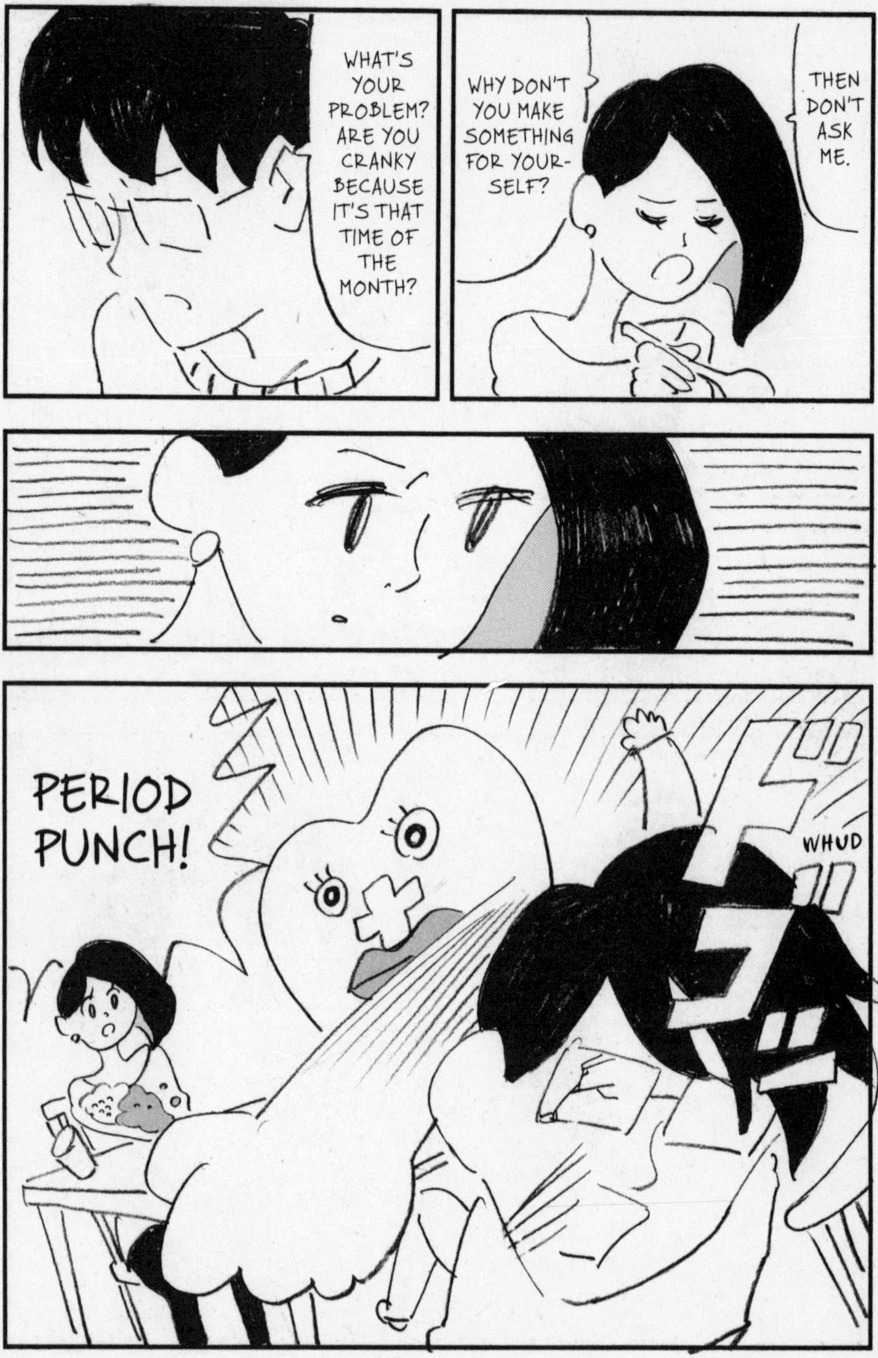
THEN DON'T ASK ME.
WHY DON'T YOU MAKE SOMETHING FOR YOUR-SELF?
WHAT'S YOUR PROBLEM? ARE YOU CRANKY BECAUSE IT'S THAT TIME OF THE MONTH?
WHUD
PERIOD PUNCH!

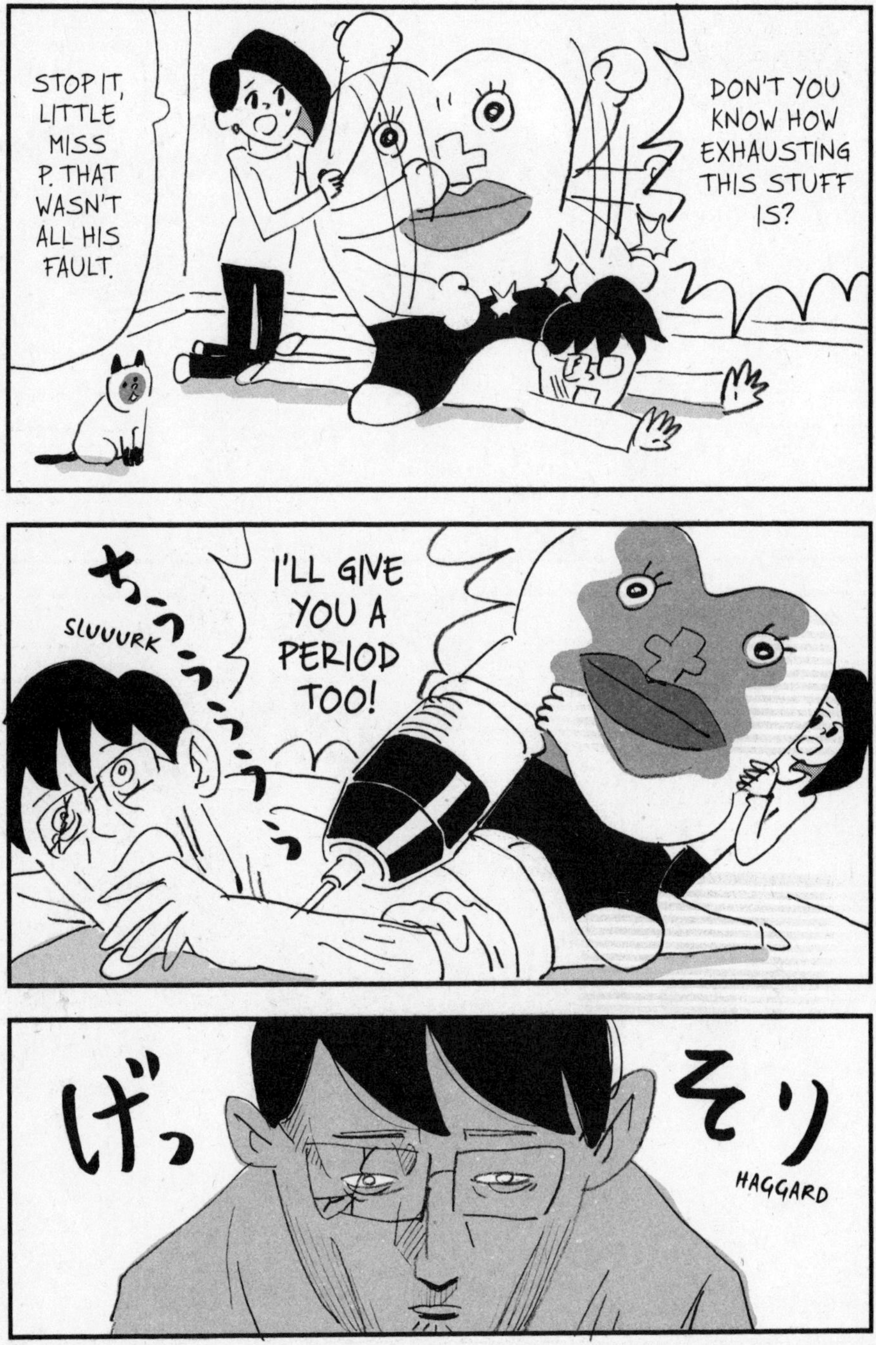
DON'T YOU KNOW HOW EXHAUSTING THIS STUFF IS?
STOP IT, LITTLE MISS P. THAT WASN'T ALL HIS FAULT.
I'LL GIVE YOU A PERIOD TOO!
SLUUURK
げっそり
HAGGARD

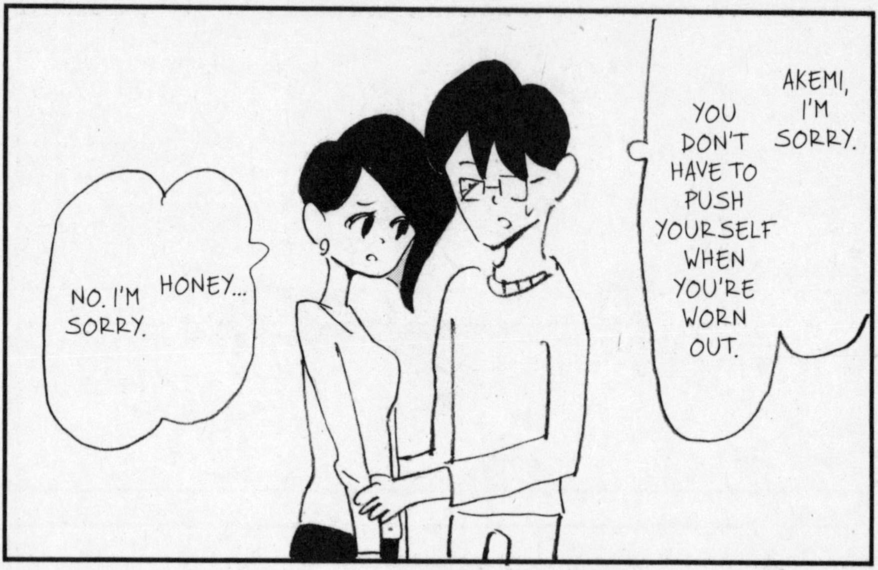
AKEMI, I'M SORRY.
YOU DON'T HAVE TO PUSH YOURSELF WHEN YOU'RE WORN OUT.
HONEY...
NO. I'M SORRY.

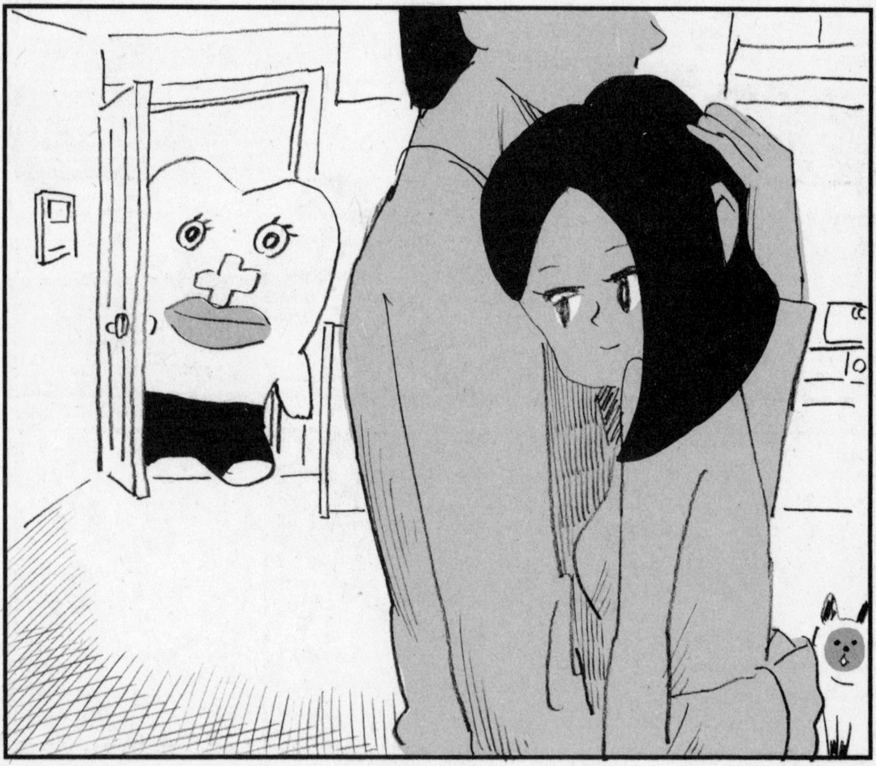

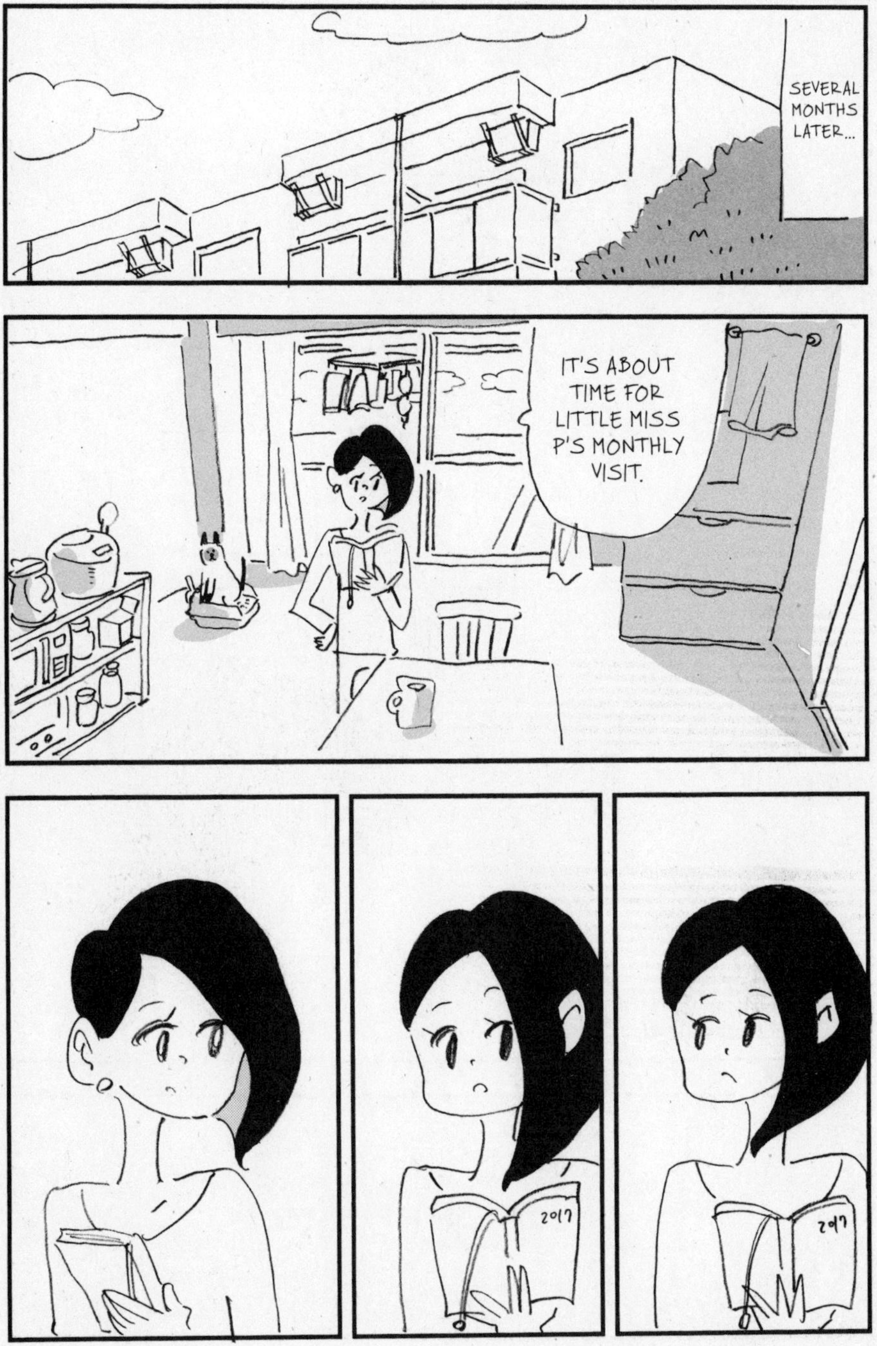
SEVERAL MONTHS LATER...
IT'S ABOUT TIME FOR LITTLE MISS P'S MONTHLY VISIT.
2017
2017

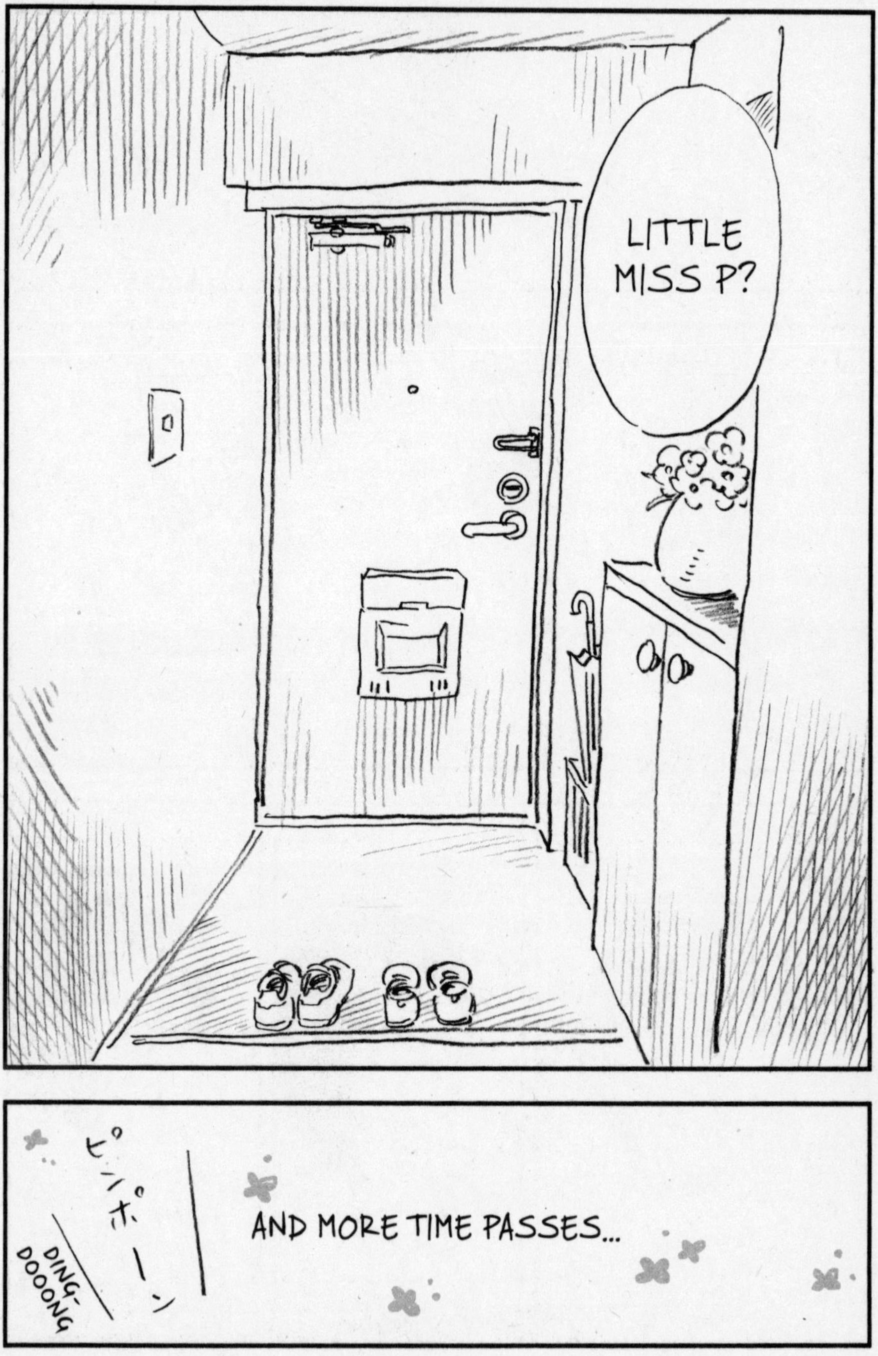
LITTLE MISS P?
AND MORE TIME PASSES...
ピンポーン
DING-DOOONG

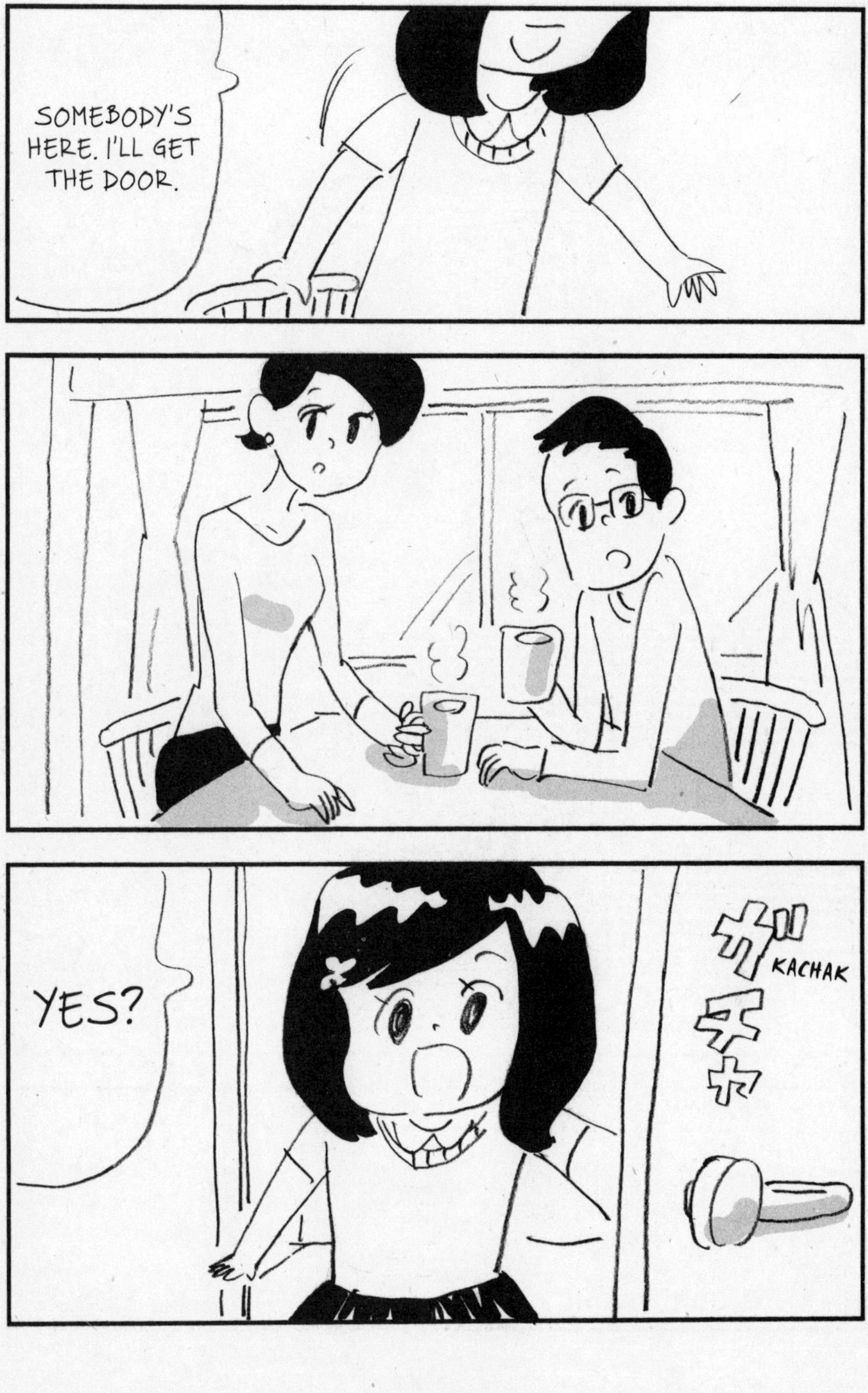
SOMEBODY'S HERE. I'LL GET THE DOOR.
ガチャ
KACHAK
YES?

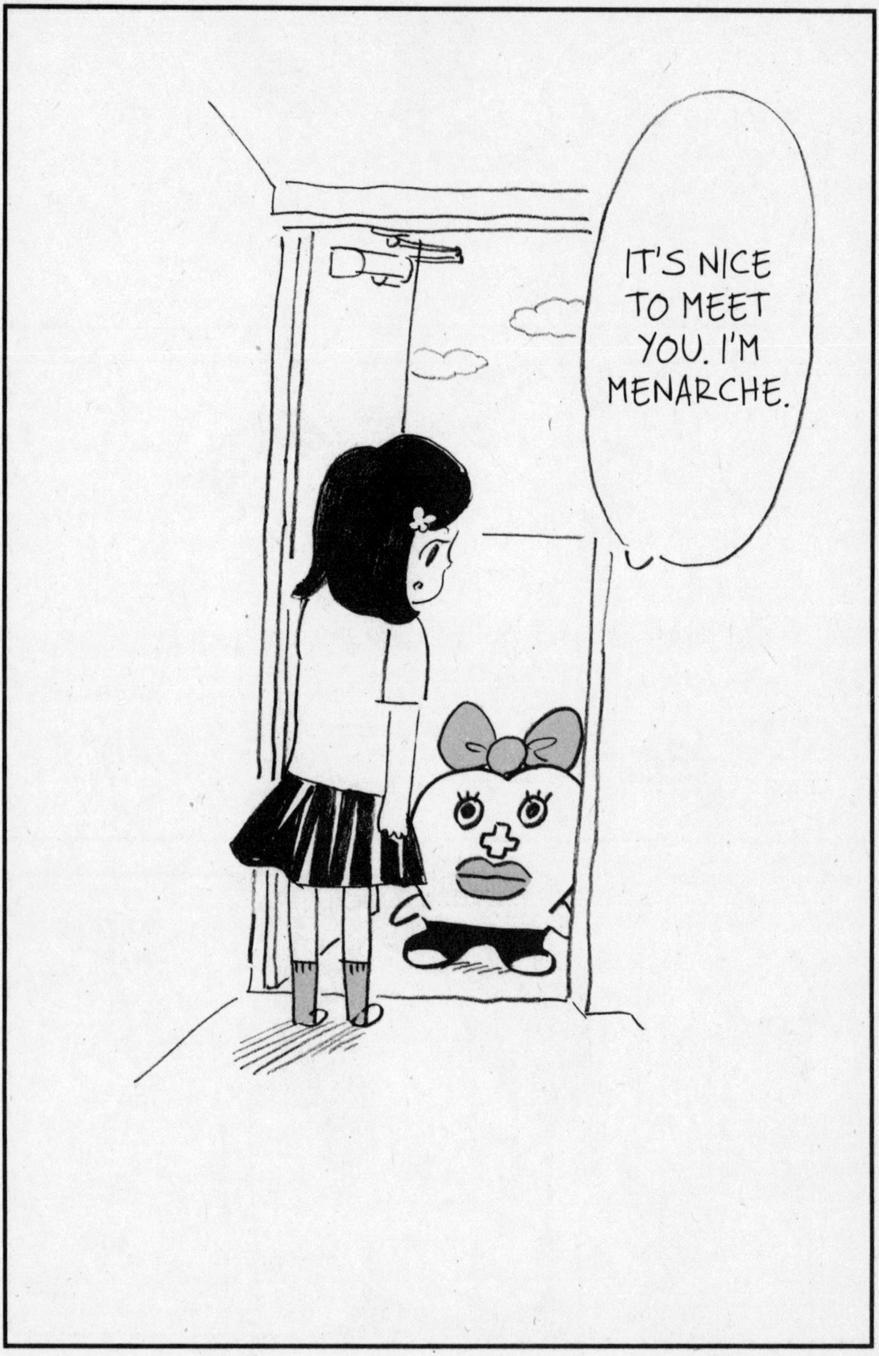
IT'S NICE TO MEET YOU. I'M MENARCHE.

WRITER AND LITTLE MISS P

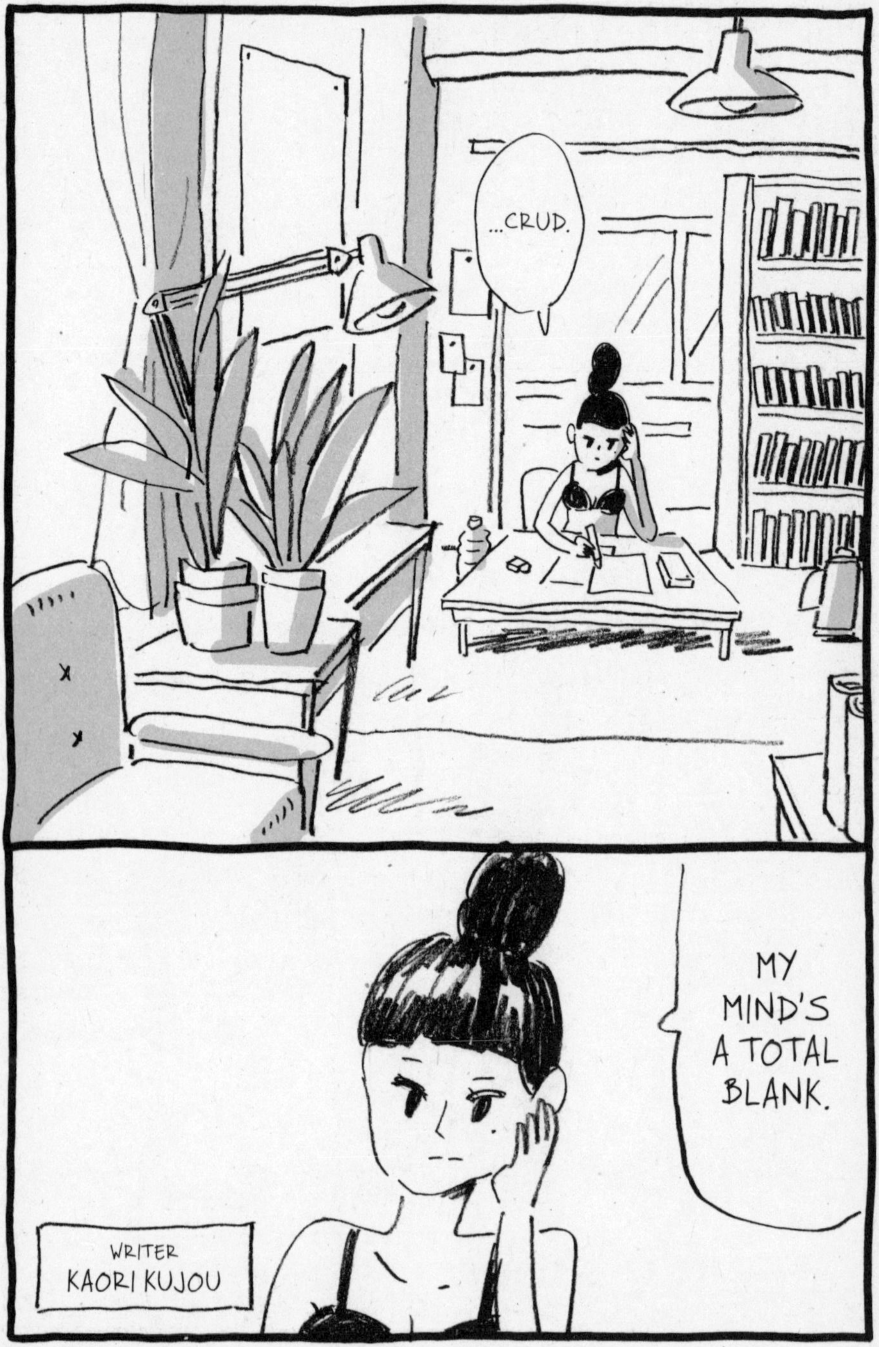
...CRUD.
MY MIND'S A TOTAL BLANK.
WRITER KAORI KUJOU

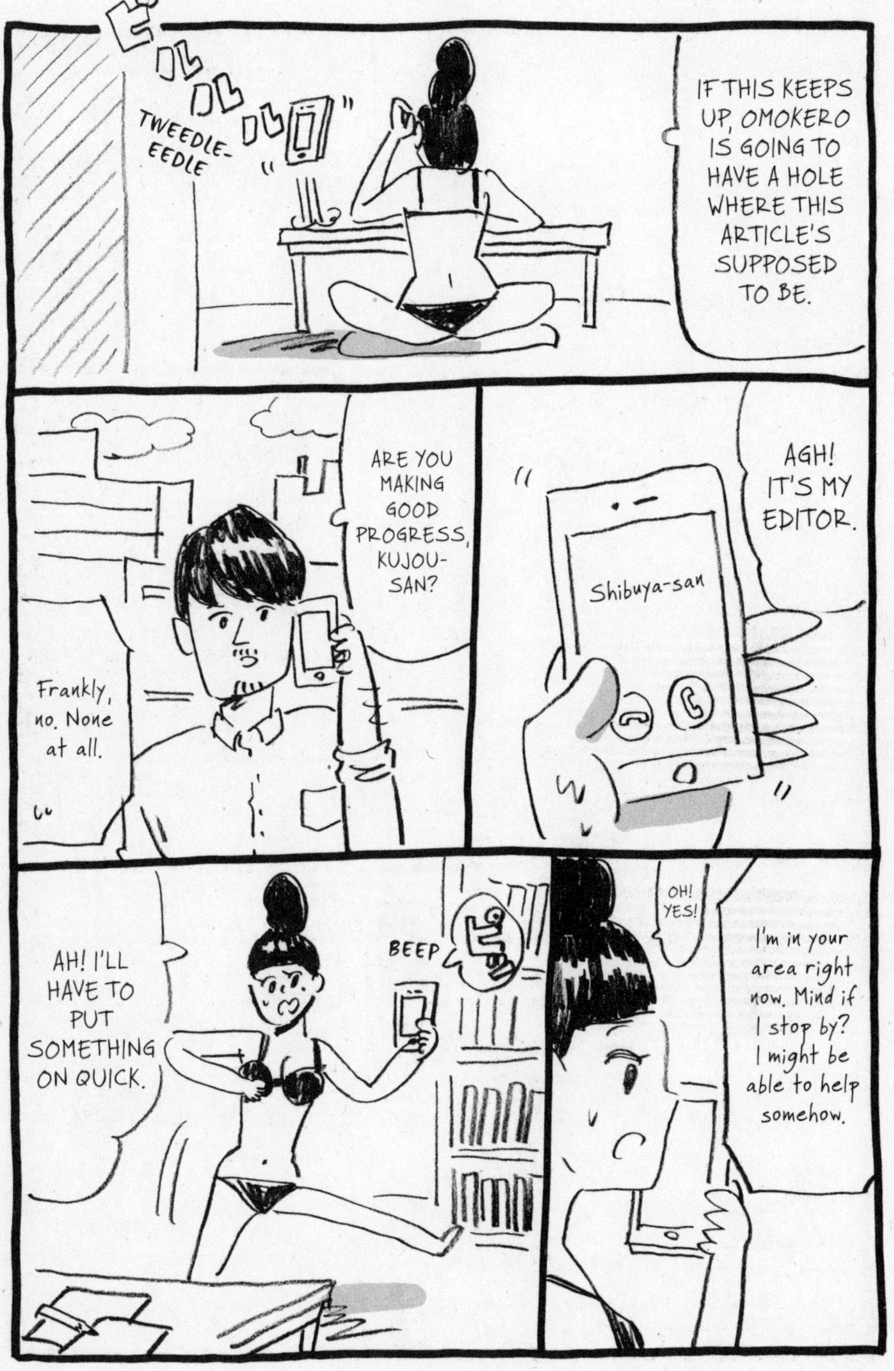
IF THIS KEEPS UP, OMOKERO IS GOING TO HAVE A HOLE WHERE THIS ARTICLE'S SUPPOSED TO BE.
TWEEDLE-EEDLE
AGH! IT'S MY EDITOR.
Shibuya-san
ARE YOU MAKING GOOD PROGRESS, KUJOU-SAN?
Frankly, no. None at all.
OH! YES!
I'm in your area right now. Mind if I stop by? I might be able to help somehow.
BEEP
AH! I'LL HAVE TO PUT SOMETHING ON QUICK.

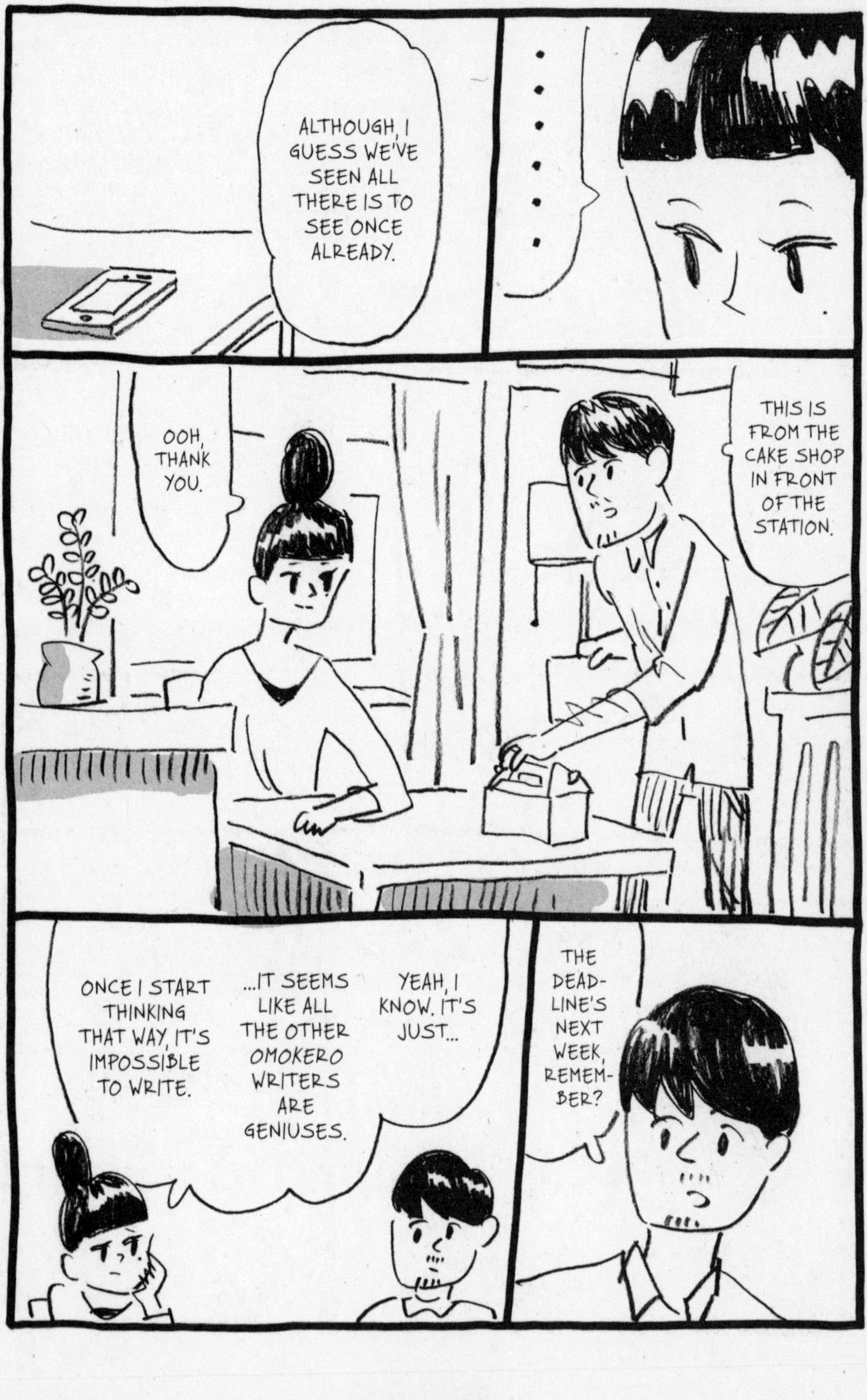

......
ALTHOUGH, I GUESS WE'VE SEEN ALL THERE IS TO SEE ONCE ALREADY.
THIS IS FROM THE CAKE SHOP IN FRONT OF THE STATION.
OOH, THANK YOU.
THE DEAD-LINE'S NEXT WEEK, REMEM-BER?
YEAH, I KNOW. IT'S JUST...
...IT SEEMS LIKE ALL THE OTHER OMOKERO WRITERS ARE GENIUSES.
ONCE I START THINKING THAT WAY, IT'S IMPOSSIBLE TO WRITE.

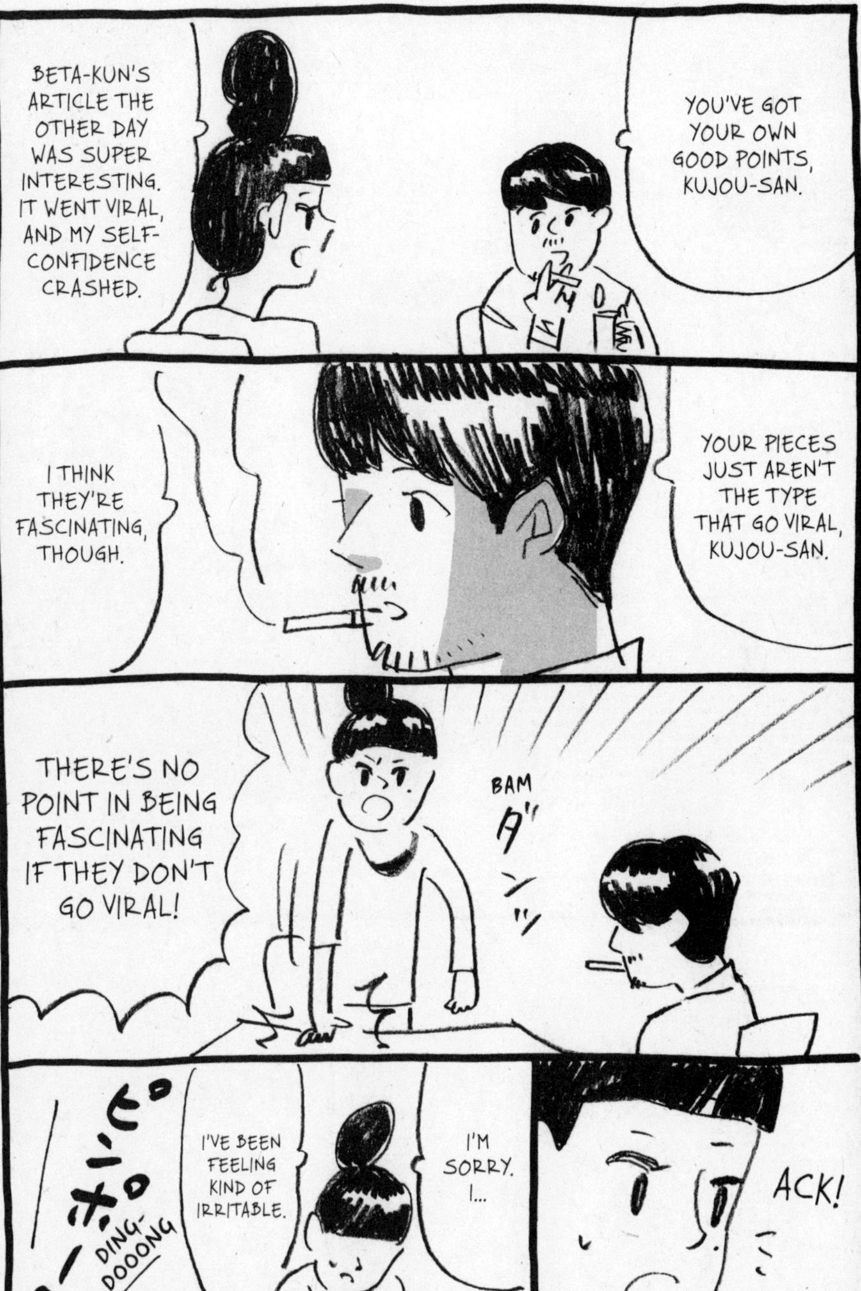
YOU'VE GOT YOUR OWN GOOD POINTS, KUJOU-SAN.
BETA-KUN'S ARTICLE THE OTHER DAY WAS SUPER INTERESTING. IT WENT VIRAL, AND MY SELF-CONFIDENCE CRASHED.
YOUR PIECES JUST AREN'T THE TYPE THAT GO VIRAL, KUJOU-SAN.
I THINK THEY'RE FASCINATING, THOUGH.
BAM
ダンッ
THERE'S NO POINT IN BEING FASCINATING IF THEY DON'T GO VIRAL!
ACK!
I'M SORRY. I...
I'VE BEEN FEELING KIND OF IRRITABLE.
ピンポーン
DING-DOOONG

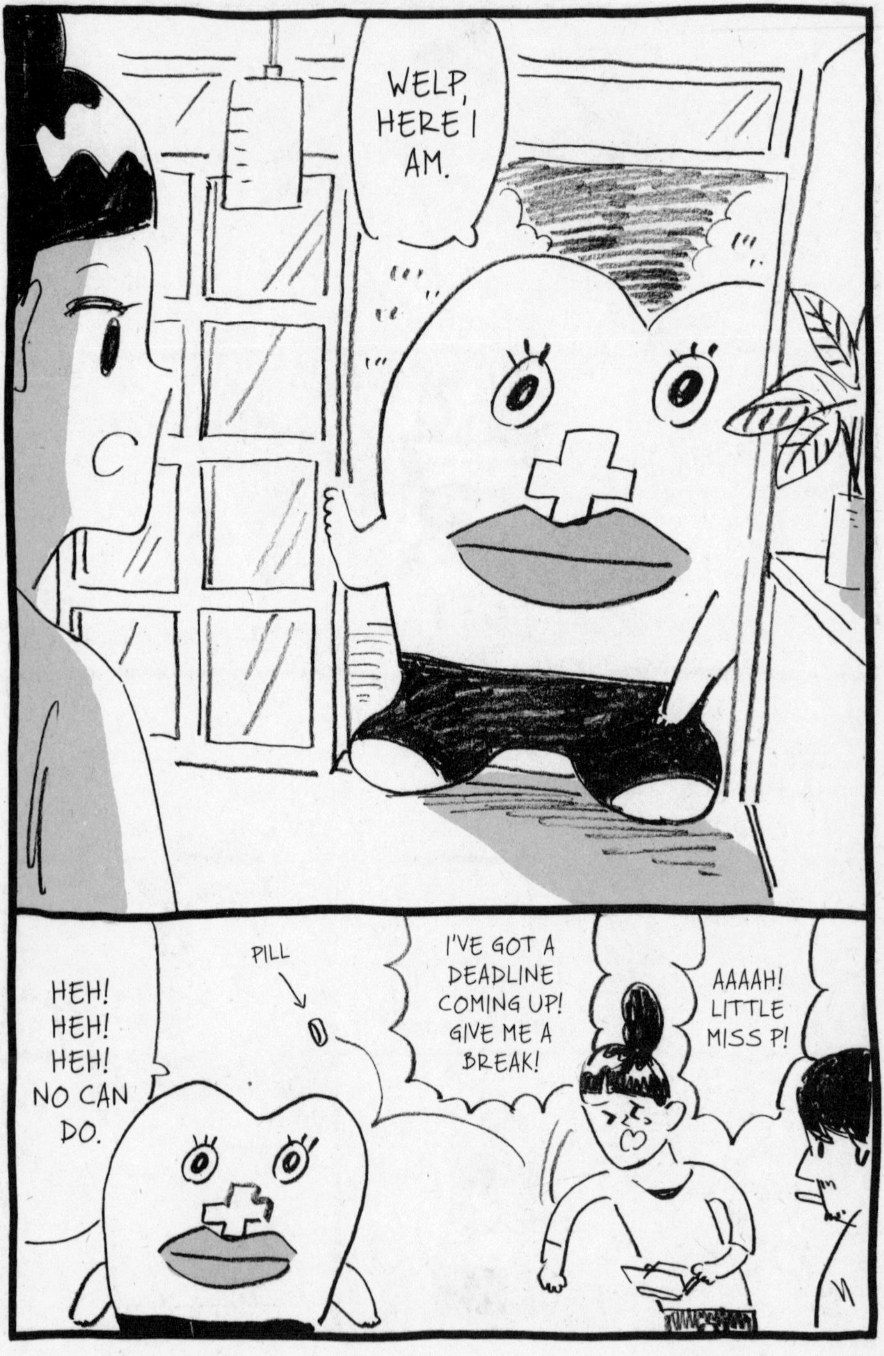
WELP, HERE I AM.
AAAAH! LITTLE MISS P!
I'VE GOT A DEADLINE COMING UP! GIVE ME A BREAK!
PILL
HEH! HEH! HEH! NO CAN DO.

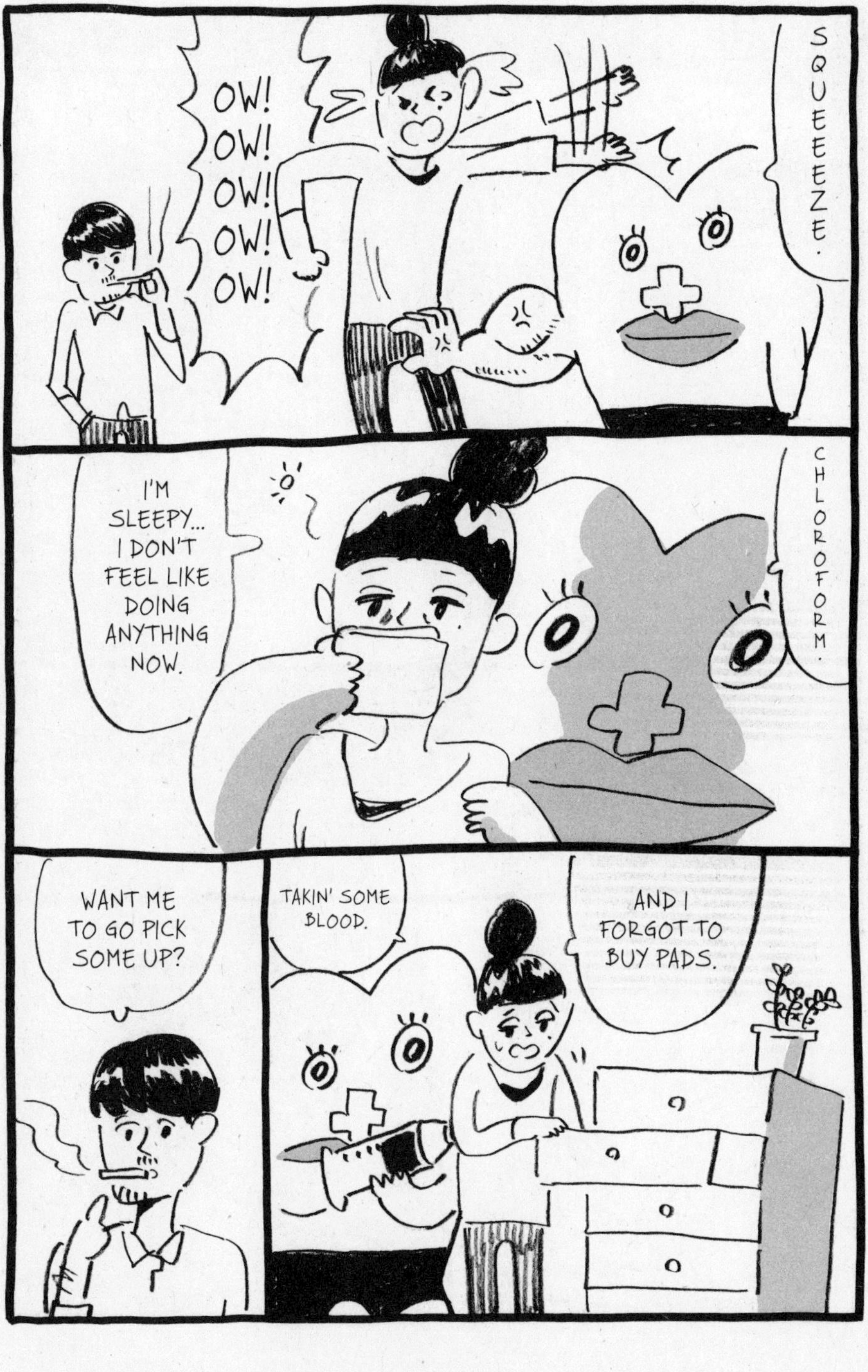
SQUEEEZE.
OW! OW! OW! OW! OW!
CHLOROFORM.
I'M SLEEPY... I DON'T FEEL LIKE DOING ANYTHING NOW.
AND I FORGOT TO BUY PADS.
TAKIN' SOME BLOOD.
WANT ME TO GO PICK SOME UP?

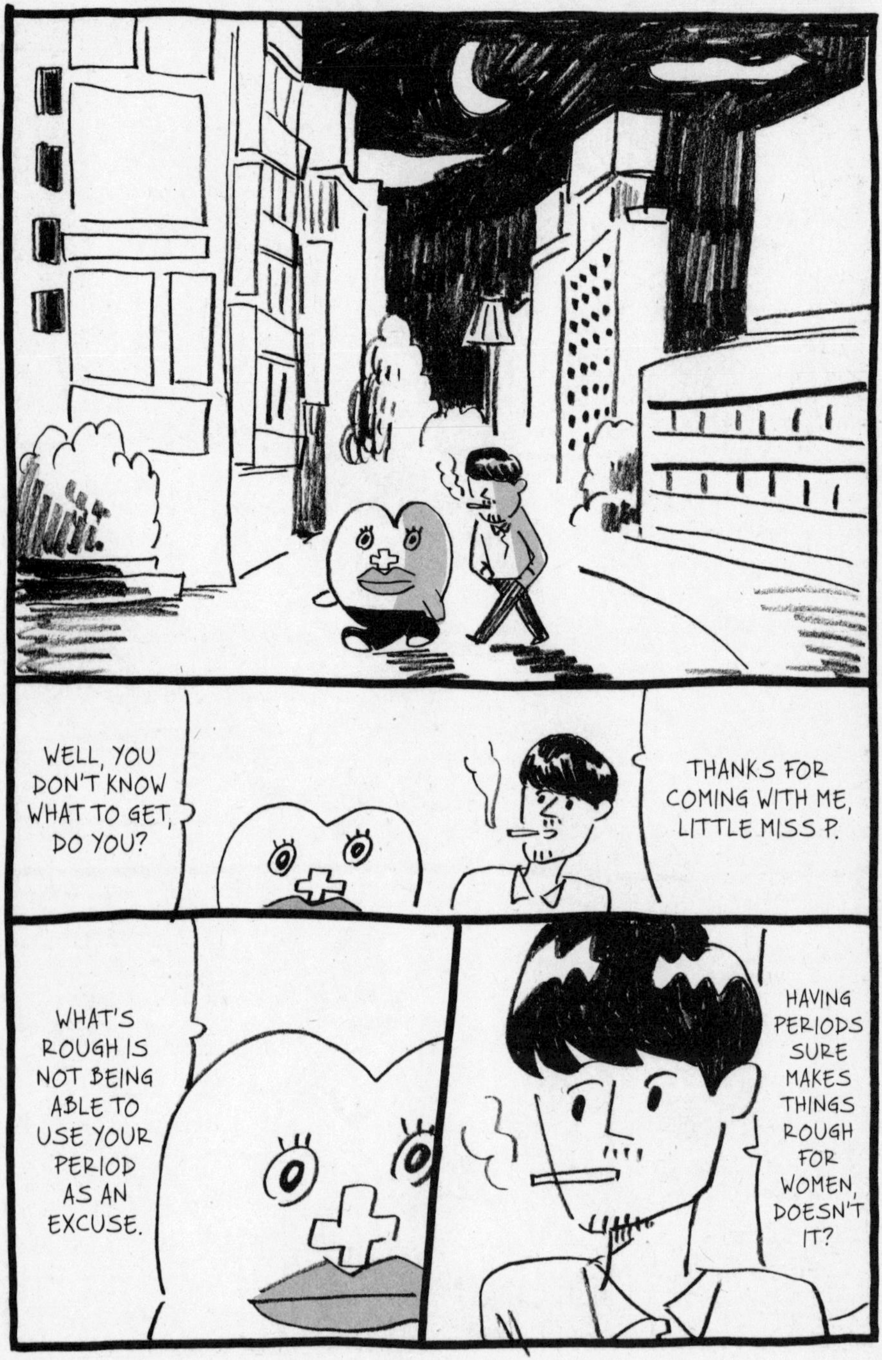
THANKS FOR COMING WITH ME, LITTLE MISS P.
WELL, YOU DON'T KNOW WHAT TO GET, DO YOU?
HAVING PERIODS SURE MAKES THINGS ROUGH FOR WOMEN, DOESN'T IT?
WHAT'S ROUGH IS NOT BEING ABLE TO USE YOUR PERIOD AS AN EXCUSE.

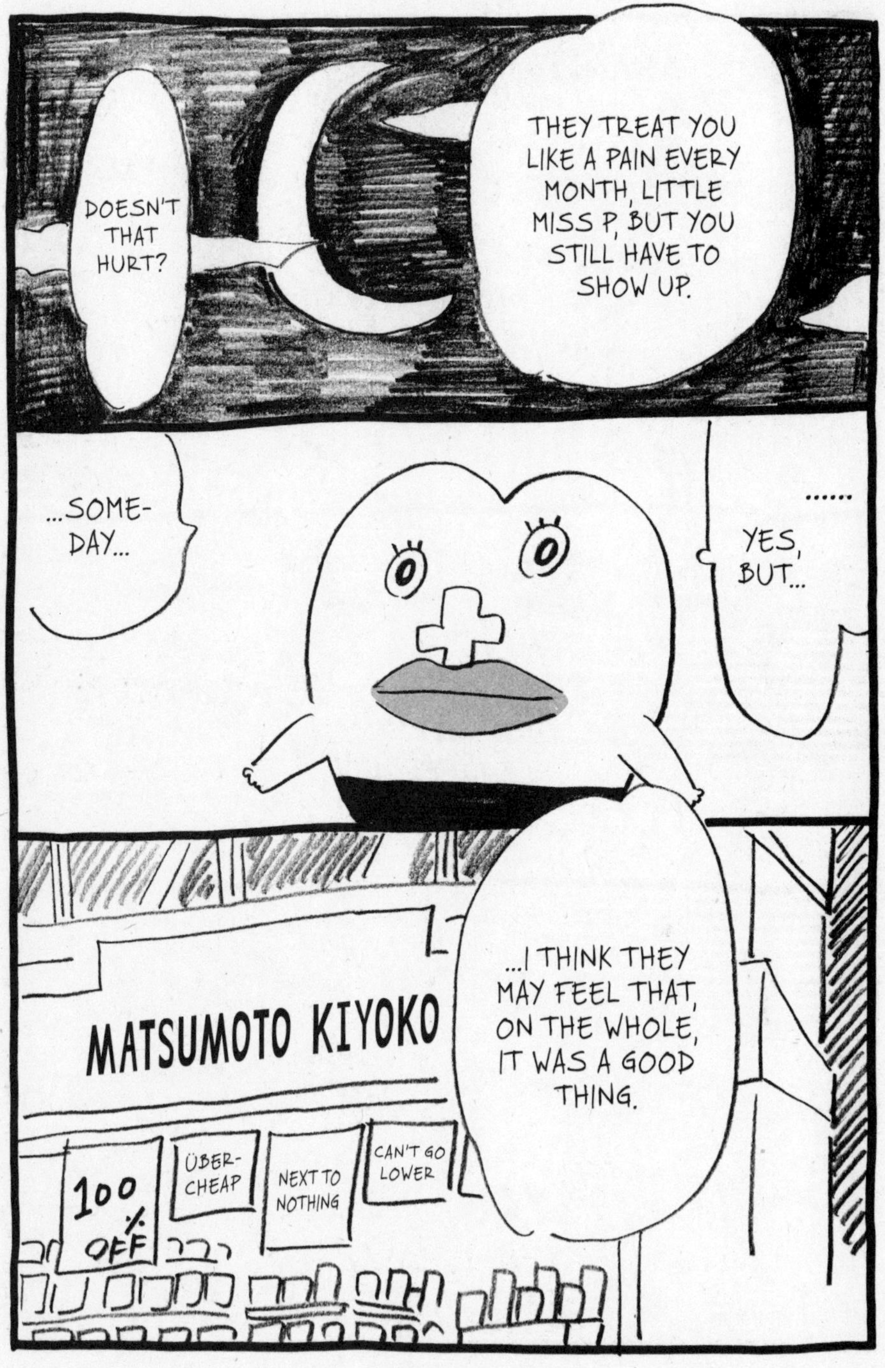
THEY TREAT YOU LIKE A PAIN EVERY MONTH, LITTLE MISS P, BUT YOU STILL HAVE TO SHOW UP.
DOESN'T THAT HURT?
...... YES, BUT...
...SOME-DAY...
...I THINK THEY MAY FEEL THAT, ON THE WHOLE, IT WAS A GOOD THING.
MATSUMOTO KIYOKO
CAN'T GO LOWER
NEXT TO NOTHING
ÜBER-CHEAP
100% OFF

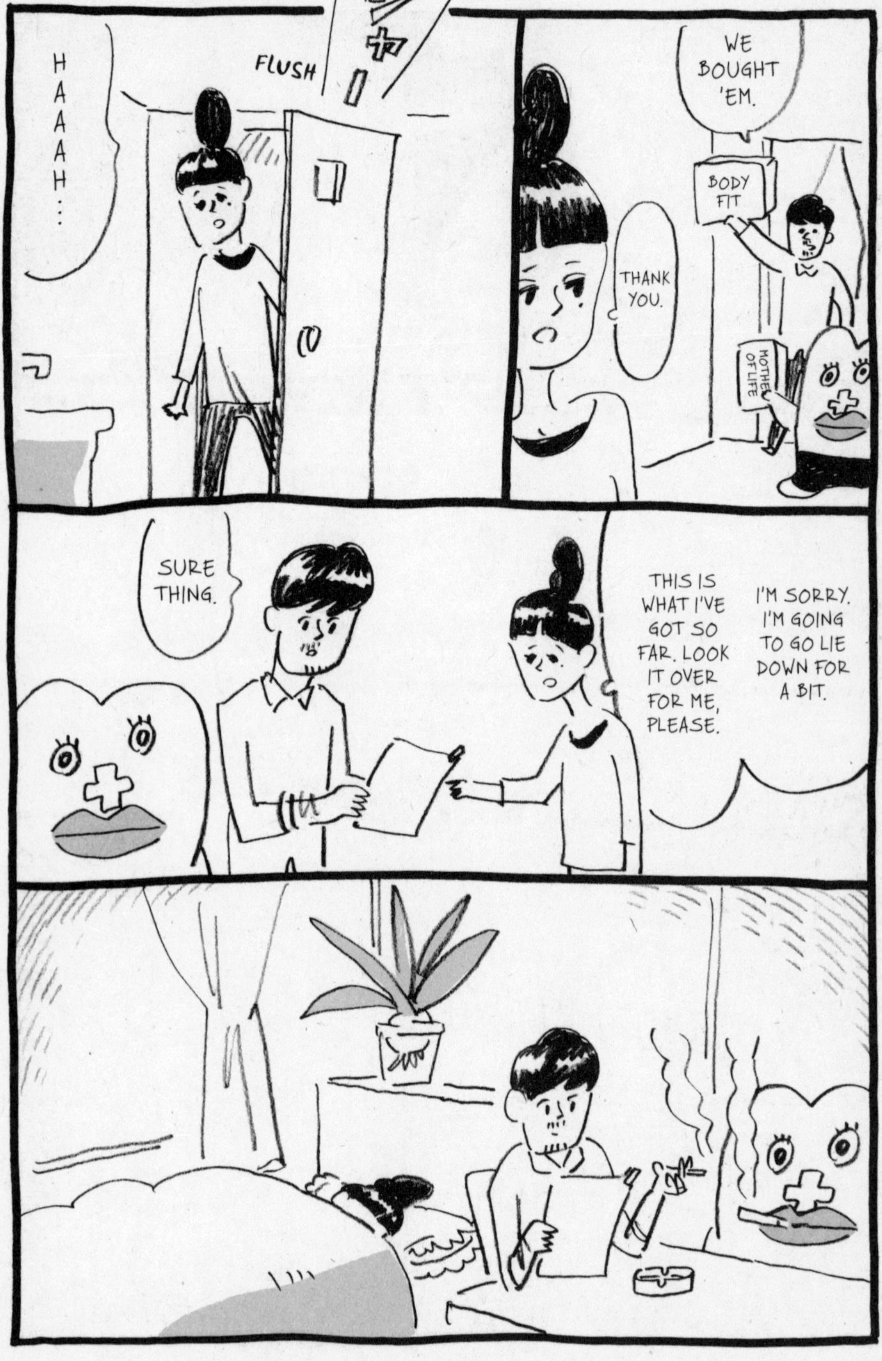
WE BOUGHT 'EM.
BODY FIT
MOTHER OF LIFE
THANK YOU.
ジャー
FLUSH
HAAAAH...
THIS IS WHAT I'VE GOT SO FAR. LOOK IT OVER FOR ME, PLEASE. I'M SORRY. I'M GOING TO GO LIE DOWN FOR A BIT.
SURE THING.

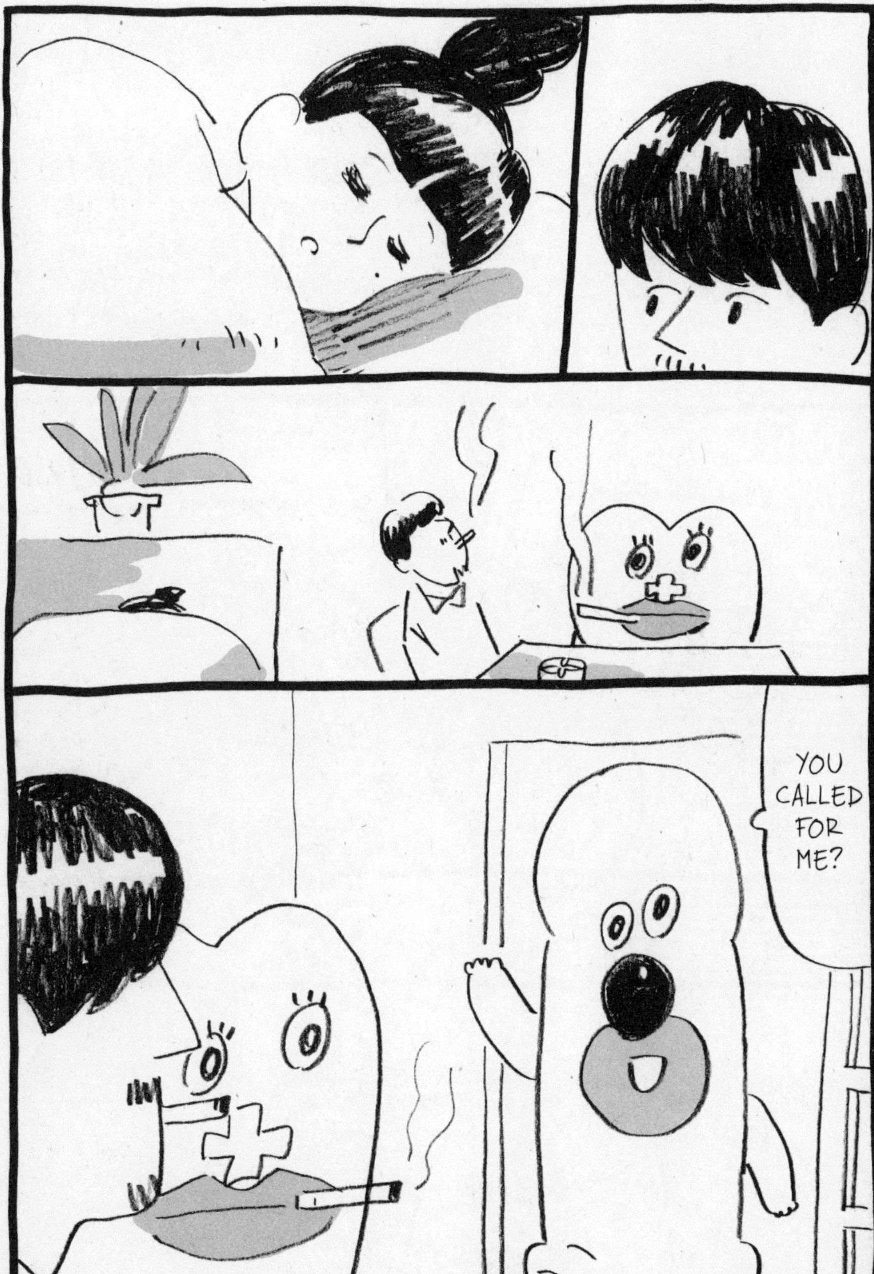
YOU CALLED FOR ME?

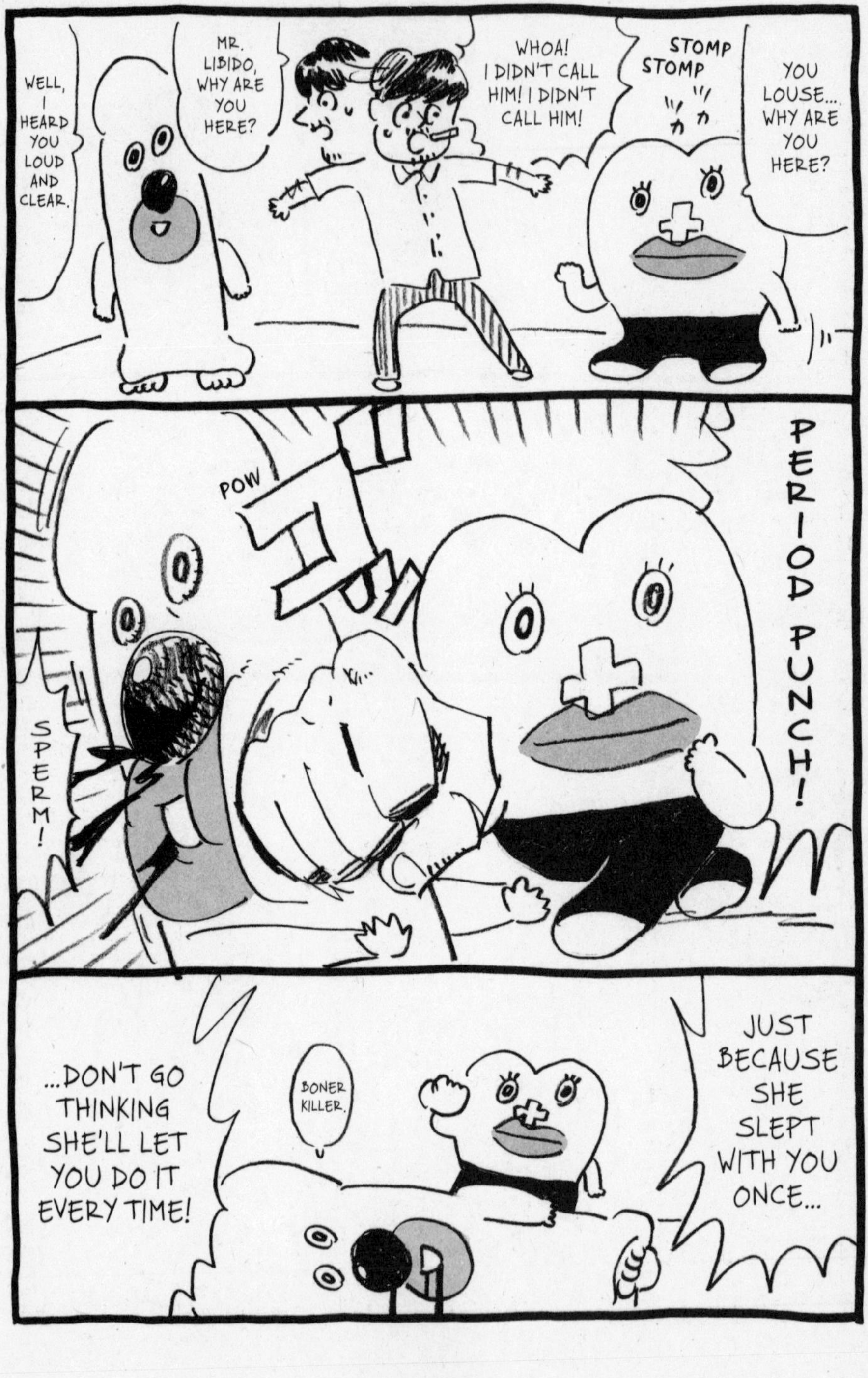
YOU LOUSE... WHY ARE YOU HERE?
STOMP STOMP
WHOA! I DIDN'T CALL HIM! I DIDN'T CALL HIM!
MR. LIBIDO, WHY ARE YOU HERE?
WELL, I HEARD YOU LOUD AND CLEAR.
PERIOD PUNCH!
POW
SPERM!
JUST BECAUSE SHE SLEPT WITH YOU ONCE...
BONER KILLER.
...DON'T GO THINKING SHE'LL LET YOU DO IT EVERY TIME!

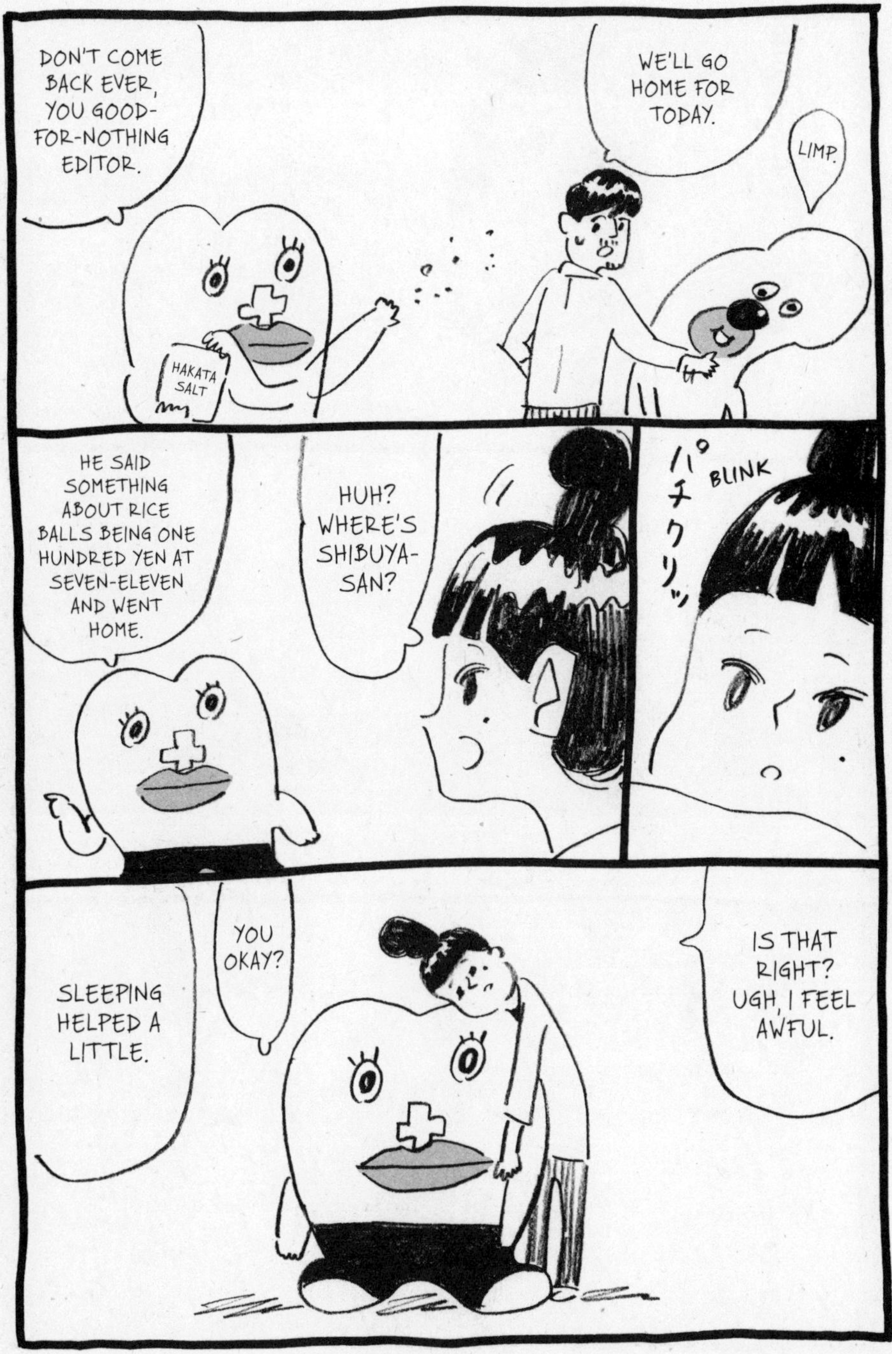

WE'LL GO HOME FOR TODAY.
LIMP.
DON'T COME BACK EVER, YOU GOOD-FOR-NOTHING EDITOR.
HAKATA SALT
パチクリッ
BLINK
HUH? WHERE'S SHIBUYA-SAN?
HE SAID SOMETHING ABOUT RICE BALLS BEING ONE HUNDRED YEN AT SEVEN-ELEVEN AND WENT HOME.
IS THAT RIGHT? UGH, I FEEL AWFUL.
YOU OKAY?
SLEEPING HELPED A LITTLE.

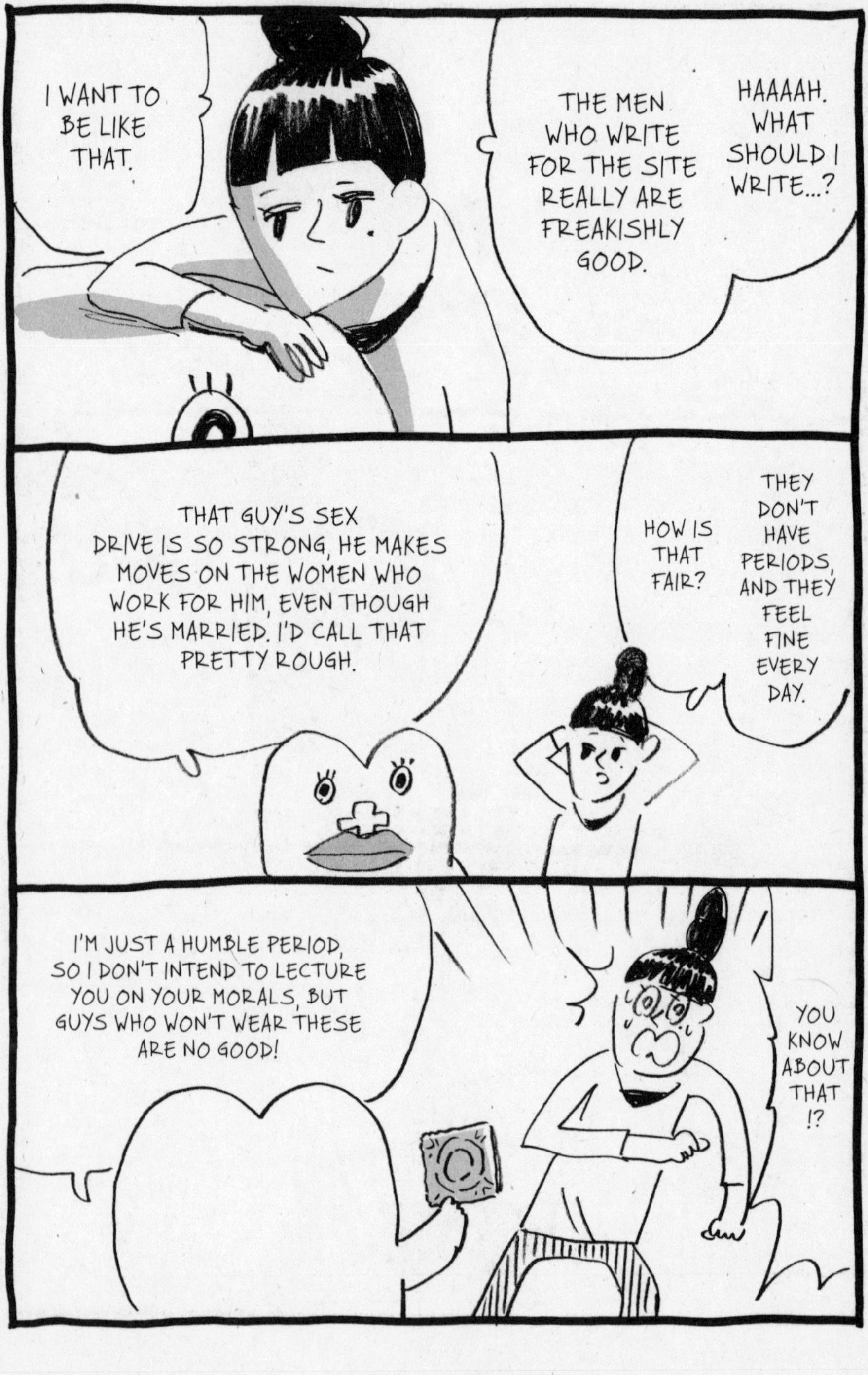
HAAAAH. WHAT SHOULD I WRITE...?
THE MEN WHO WRITE FOR THE SITE REALLY ARE FREAKISHLY GOOD.
I WANT TO BE LIKE THAT.
THEY DON'T HAVE PERIODS, AND THEY FEEL FINE EVERY DAY.
HOW IS THAT FAIR?
THAT GUY'S SEX DRIVE IS SO STRONG, HE MAKES MOVES ON THE WOMEN WHO WORK FOR HIM, EVEN THOUGH HE'S MARRIED. I'D CALL THAT PRETTY ROUGH.
I'M JUST A HUMBLE PERIOD, SO I DON'T INTEND TO LECTURE YOU ON YOUR MORALS, BUT GUYS WHO WON'T WEAR THESE ARE NO GOOD!
YOU KNOW ABOUT THAT!?

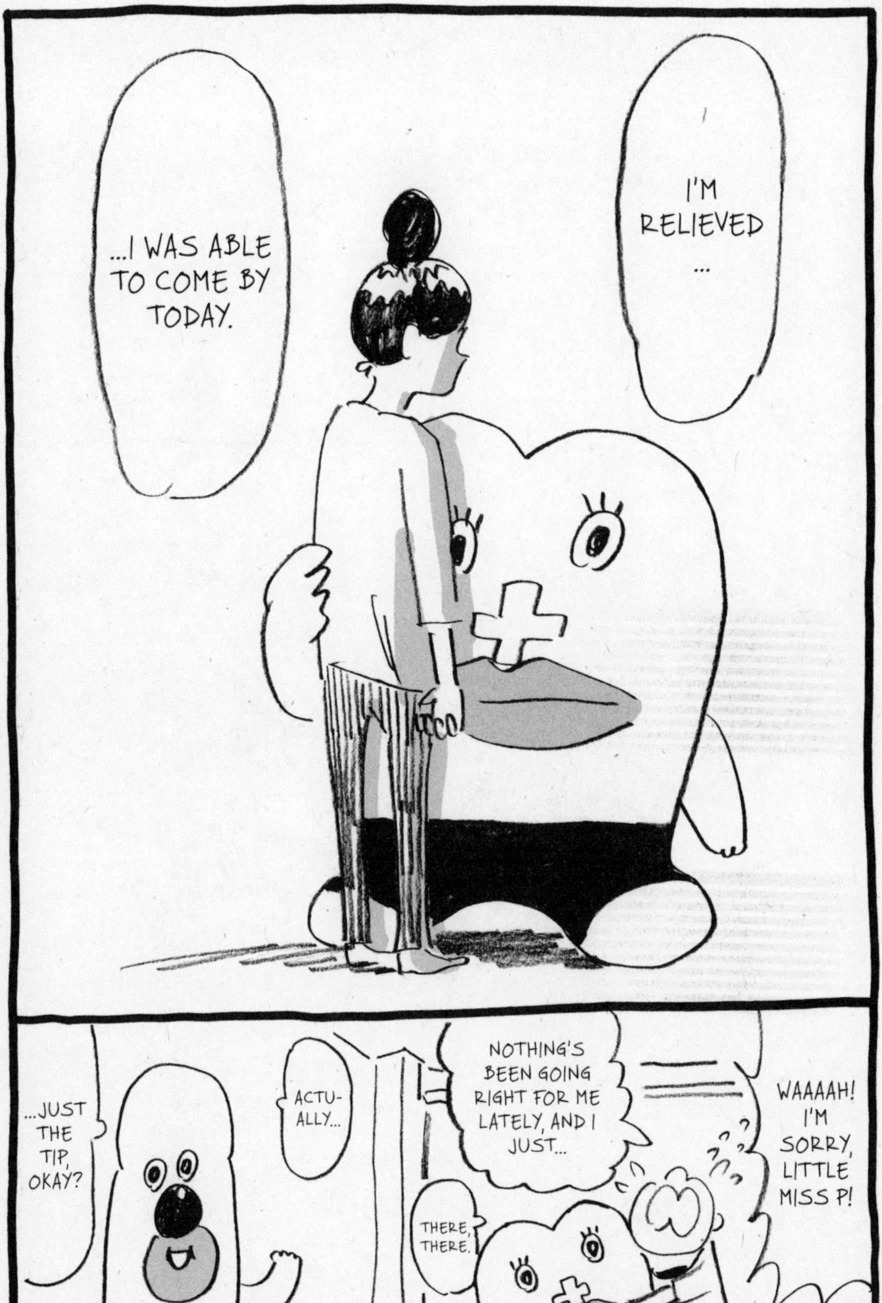
I'M RELIEVED ...
...I WAS ABLE TO COME BY TODAY.
WAAAAH! I'M SORRY, LITTLE MISS P!
NOTHING'S BEEN GOING RIGHT FOR ME LATELY, AND I JUST...
THERE, THERE.
ACTU-ALLY...
...JUST THE TIP, OKAY?

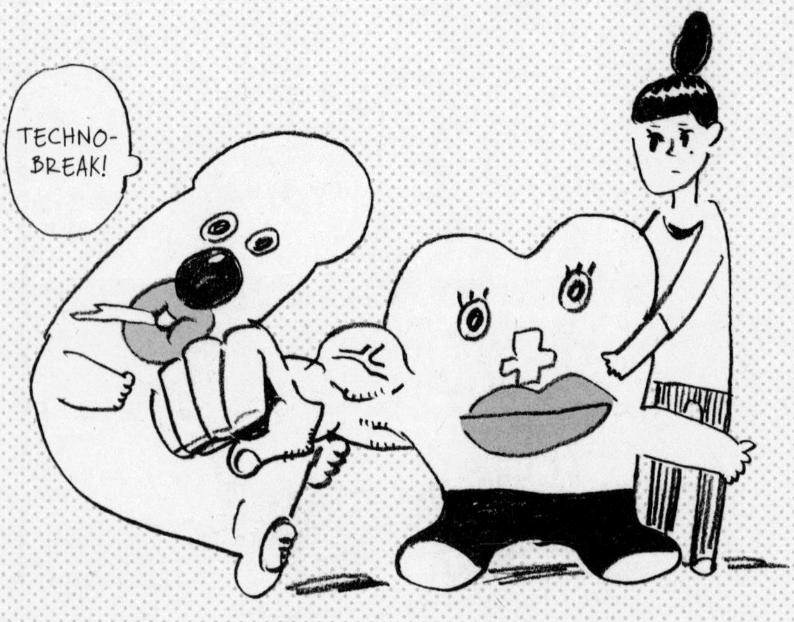
TECHNO-
BREAK!

CONVENIENCE STORE CLERK AND LITTLE MISS P

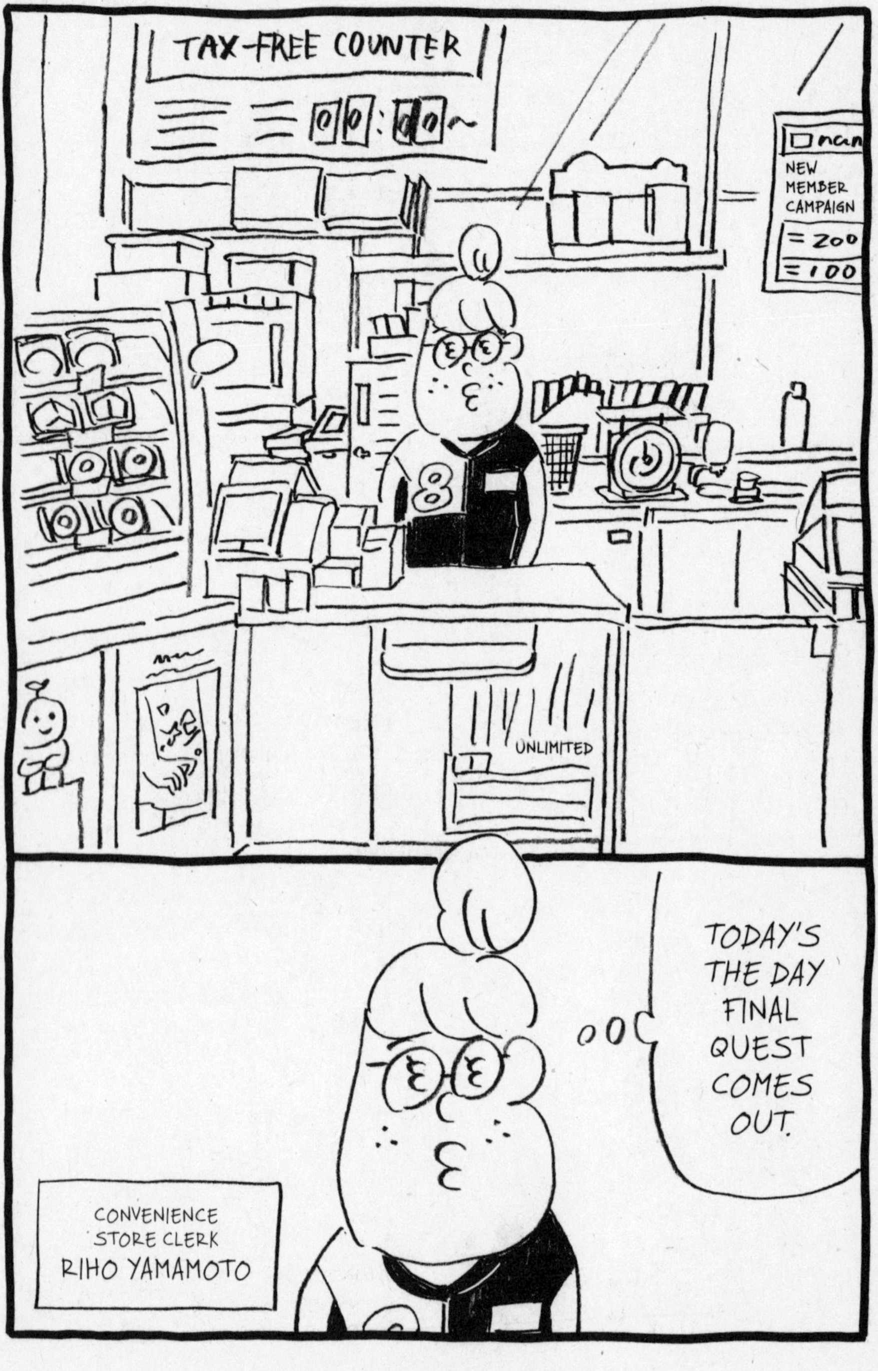
NEW MEMBER CAMPAIGN
=200
=100
TAX-FREE COUNTER
UNLIMITED
TODAY'S THE DAY FINAL QUEST COMES OUT.
CONVENIENCE STORE CLERK RIHO YAMAMOTO

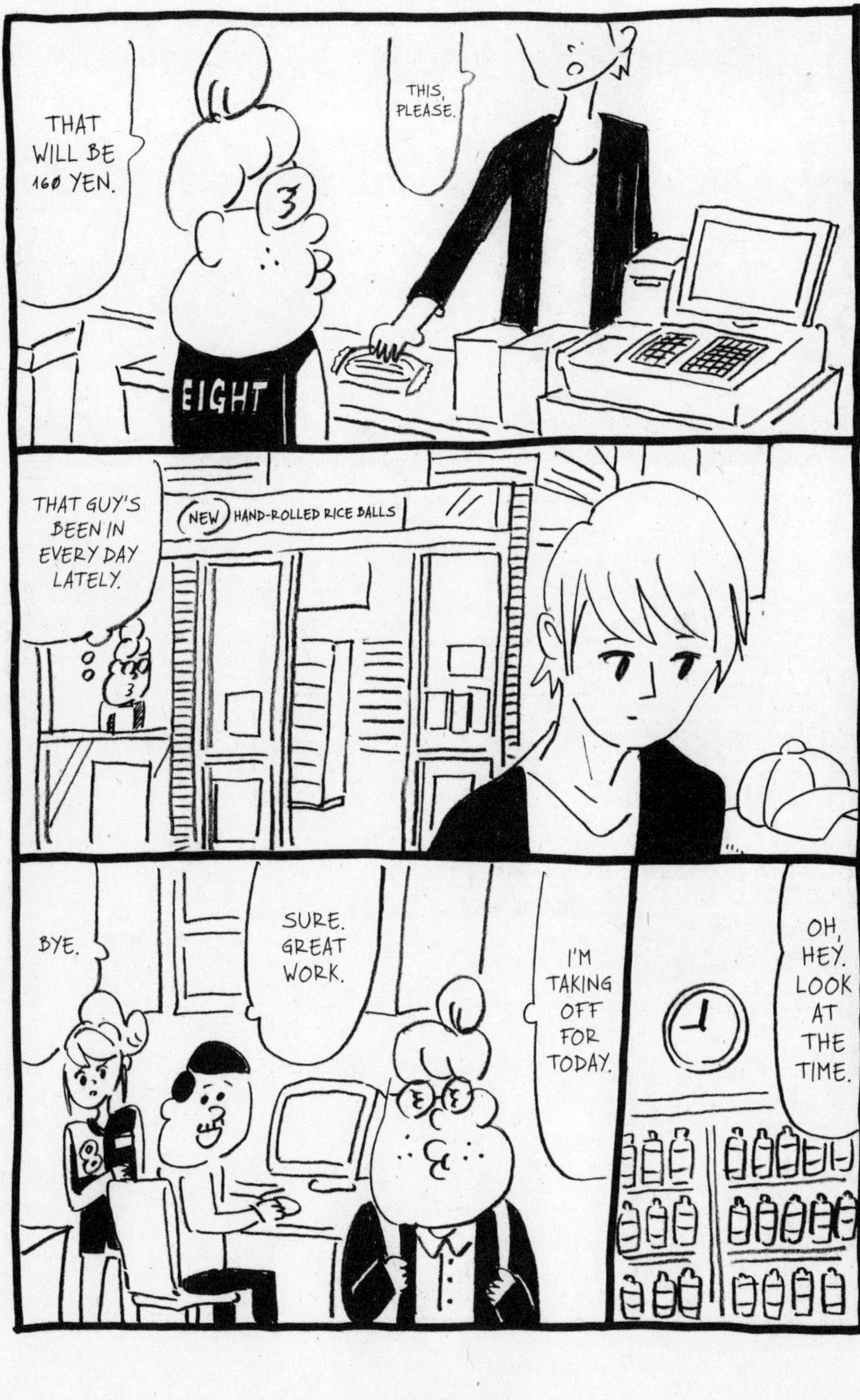
THIS, PLEASE.
THAT WILL BE 160 YEN.
NEW HAND-ROLLED RICE BALLS
THAT GUY'S BEEN IN EVERY DAY LATELY.
OH, HEY. LOOK AT THE TIME.
I'M TAKING OFF FOR TODAY.
SURE. GREAT WORK.
BYE.

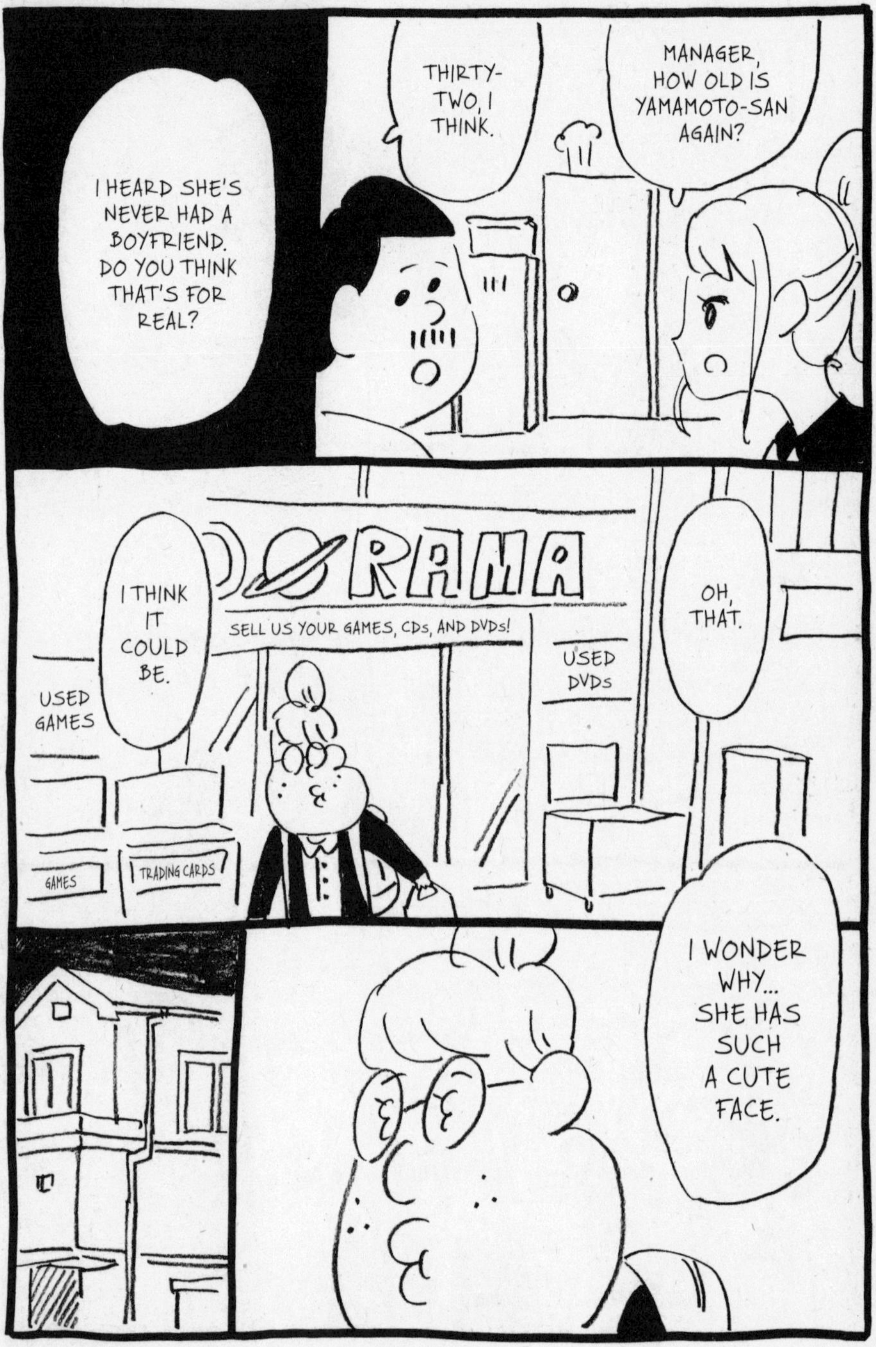
MANAGER, HOW OLD IS YAMAMOTO-SAN AGAIN?
THIRTY-TWO, I THINK.
I HEARD SHE'S NEVER HAD A BOYFRIEND. DO YOU THINK THAT'S FOR REAL?
OH, THAT.
RAMA
SELL US YOUR GAMES, CDs, AND DVDs!
USED DVDs
I THINK IT COULD BE.
USED GAMES
TRADING CARDS
GAMES
I WONDER WHY... SHE HAS SUCH A CUTE FACE.

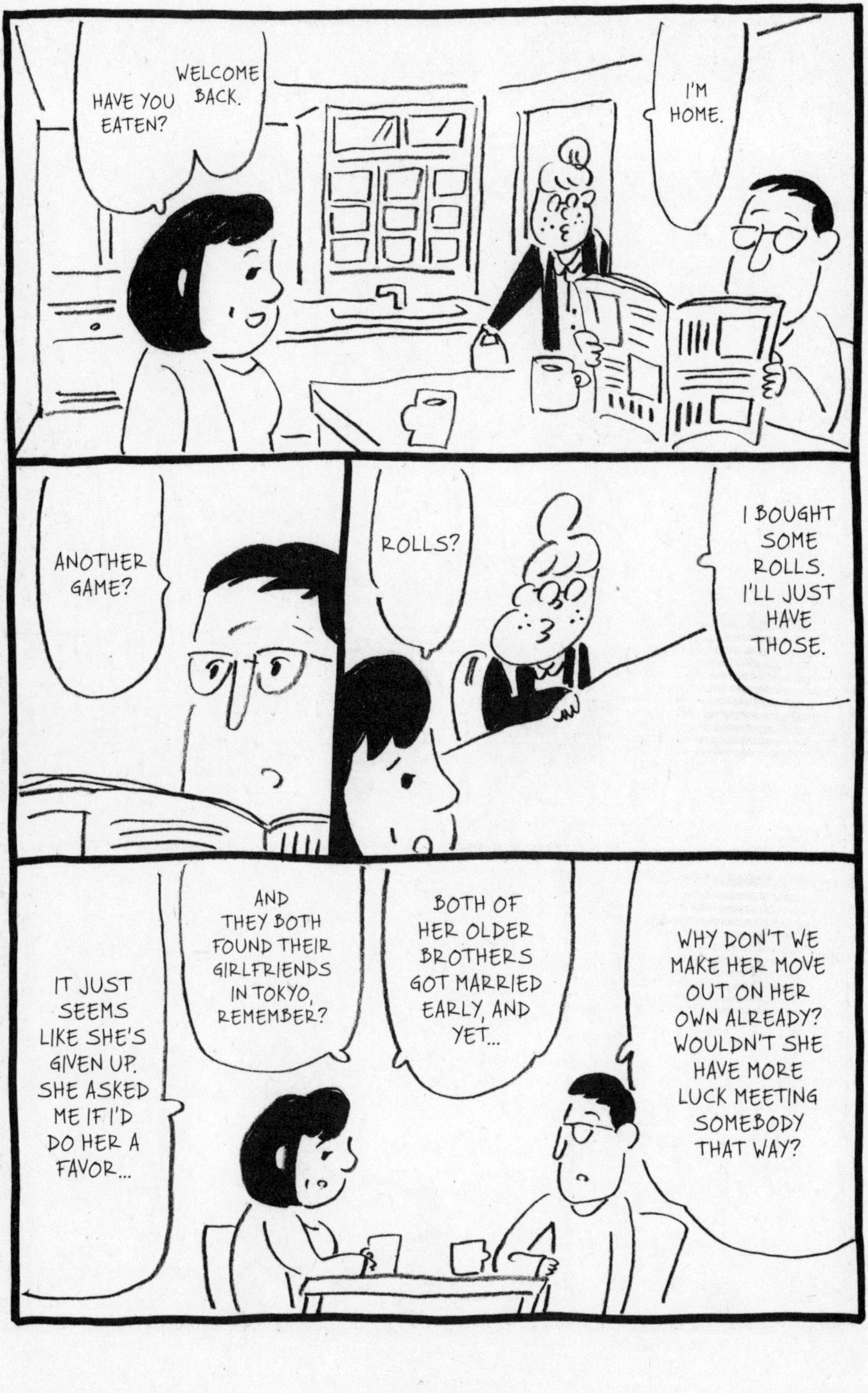
I'M HOME.
WELCOME BACK.
HAVE YOU EATEN?
I BOUGHT SOME ROLLS. I'LL JUST HAVE THOSE.
ROLLS?
ANOTHER GAME?
WHY DON'T WE MAKE HER MOVE OUT ON HER OWN ALREADY? WOULDN'T SHE HAVE MORE LUCK MEETING SOMEBODY THAT WAY?
BOTH OF HER OLDER BROTHERS GOT MARRIED EARLY, AND YET...
AND THEY BOTH FOUND THEIR GIRLFRIENDS IN TOKYO, REMEMBER?
IT JUST SEEMS LIKE SHE'S GIVEN UP. SHE ASKED ME IF I'D DO HER A FAVOR...

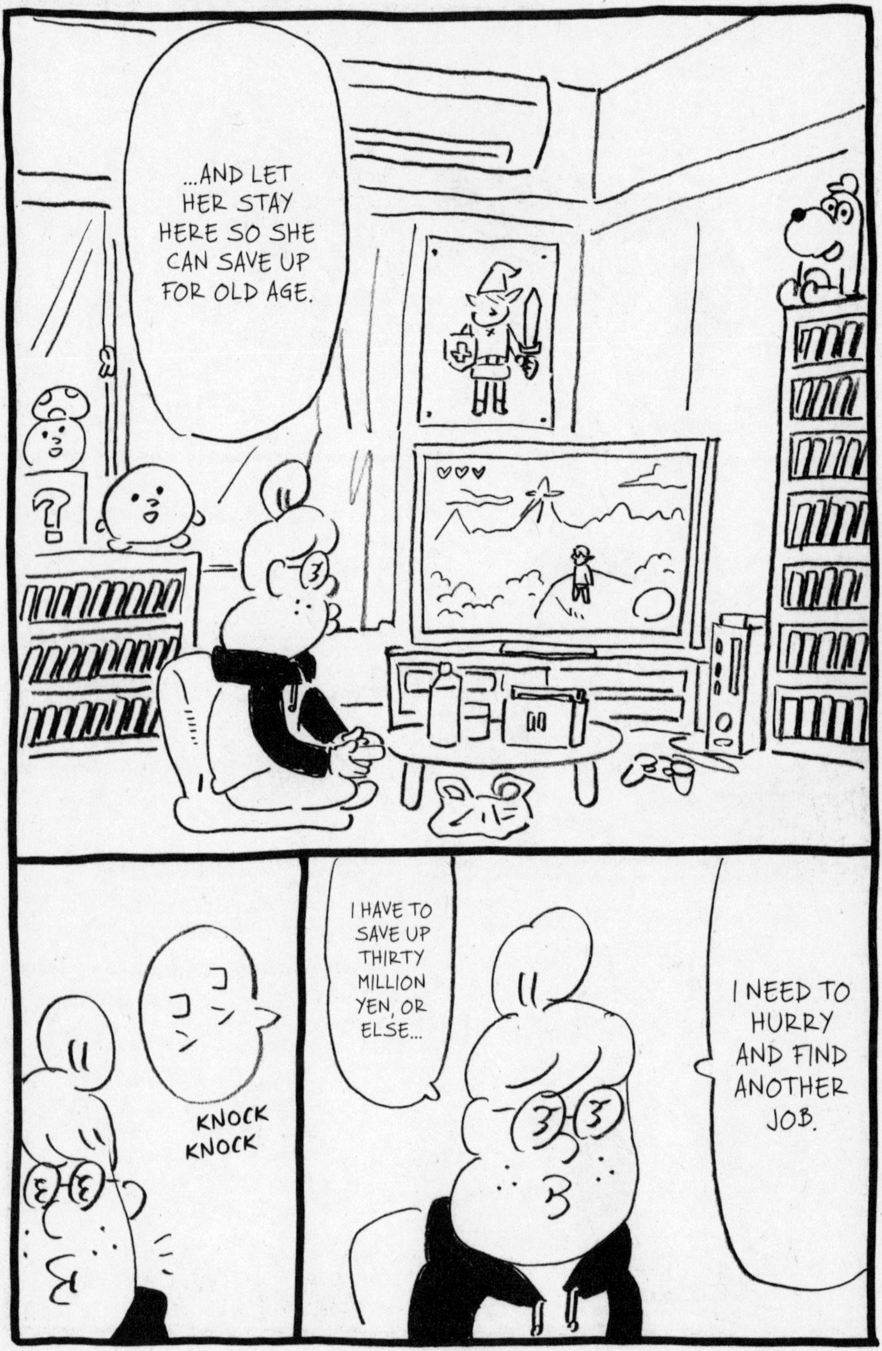
...AND LET HER STAY HERE SO SHE CAN SAVE UP FOR OLD AGE.
I NEED TO HURRY AND FIND ANOTHER JOB.
I HAVE TO SAVE UP THIRTY MILLION YEN, OR ELSE...
KNOCK KNOCK

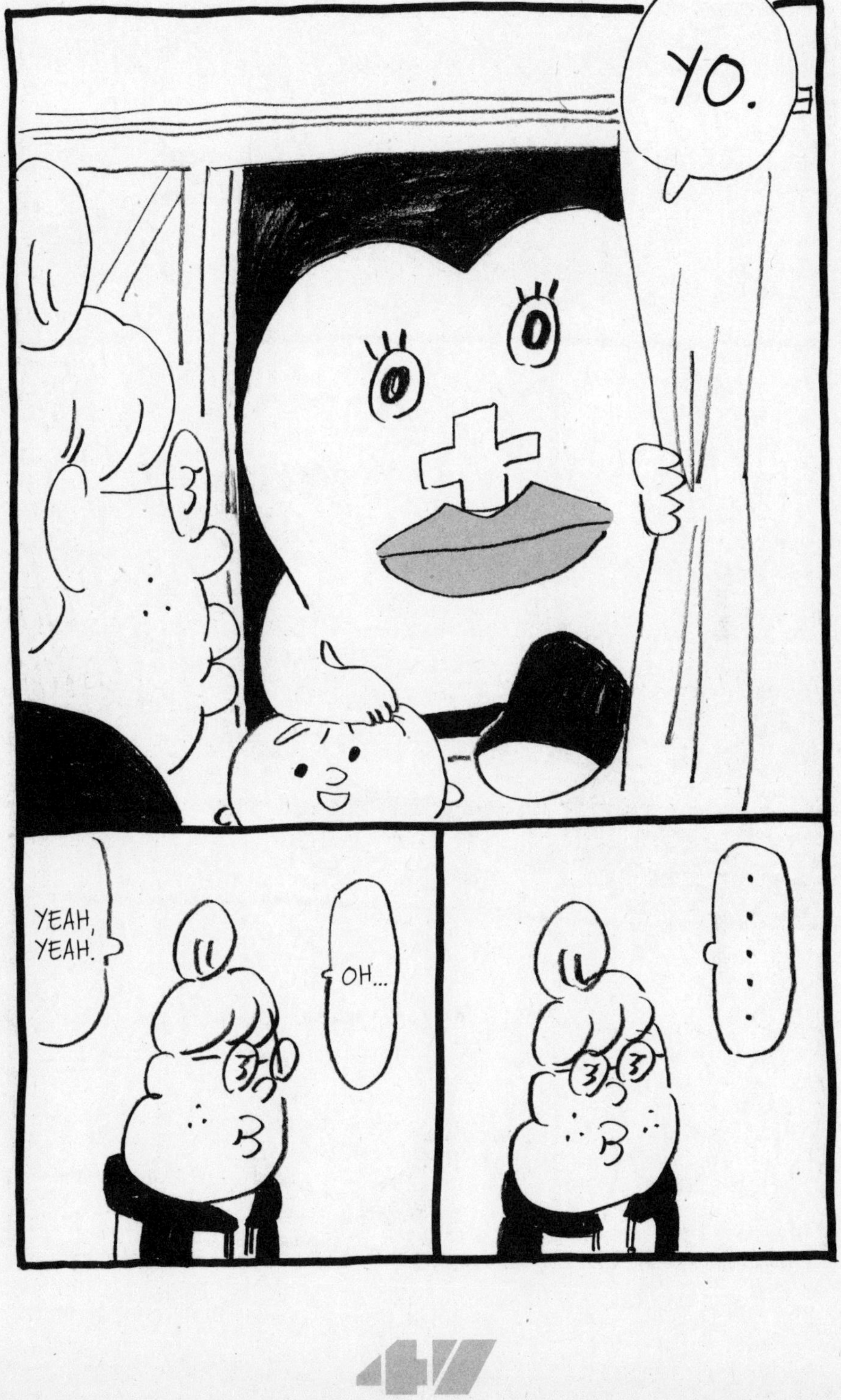
YO.
.....
OH...
YEAH, YEAH.

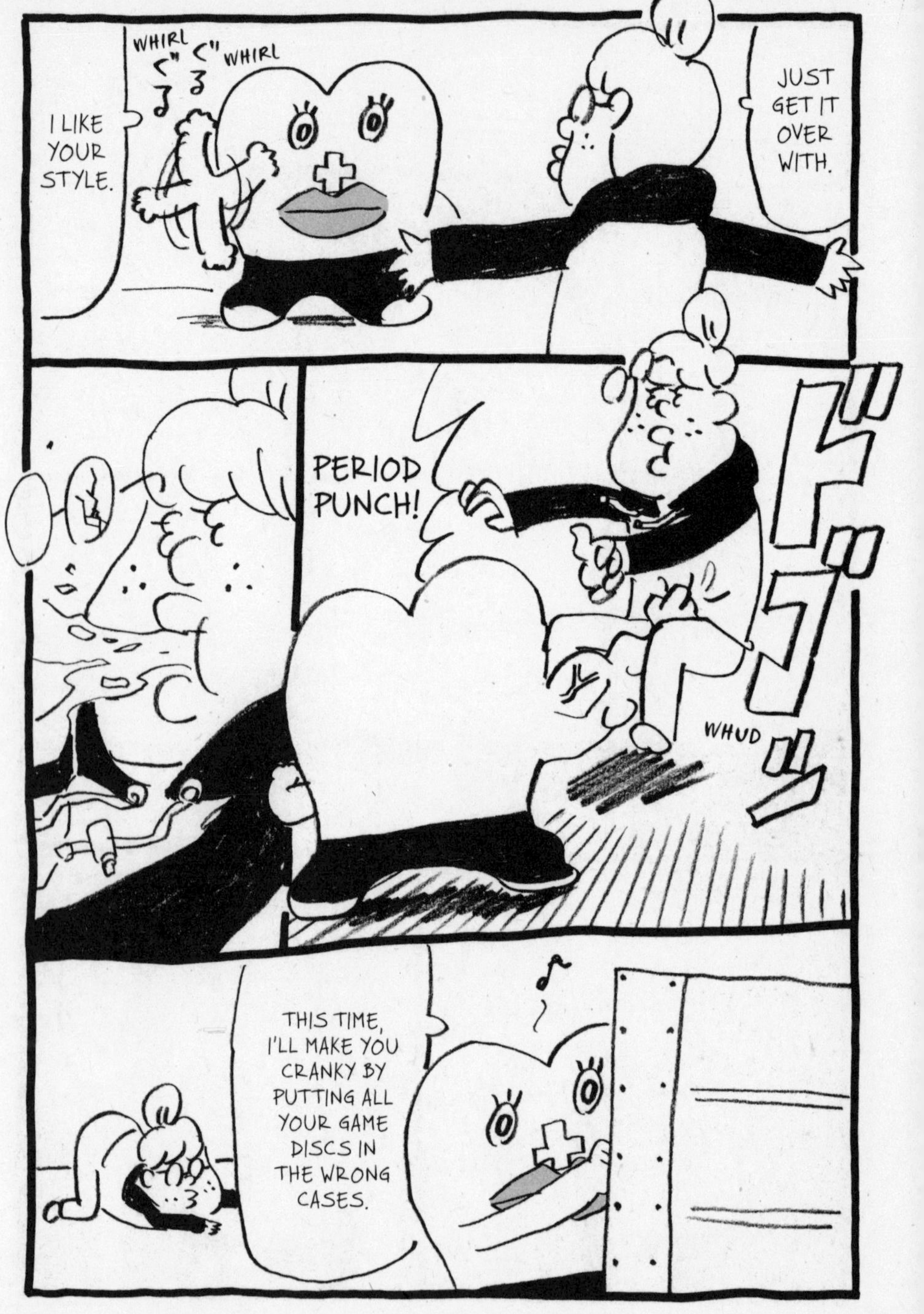
JUST GET IT OVER WITH.
WHIRL ぐるぐる WHIRL
I LIKE YOUR STYLE.
PERIOD PUNCH!
WHUD
THIS TIME, I'LL MAKE YOU CRANKY BY PUTTING ALL YOUR GAME DISCS IN THE WRONG CASES.

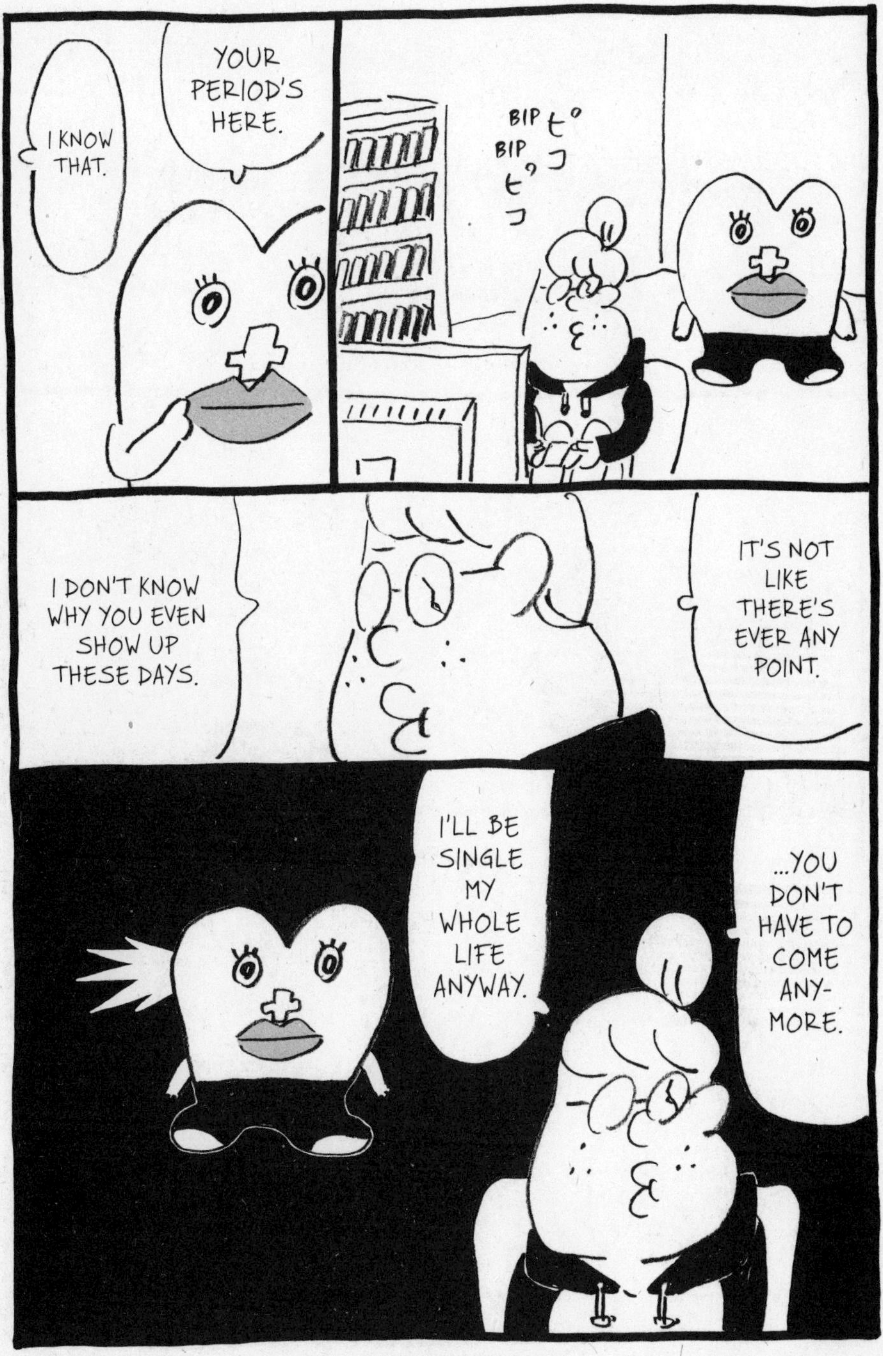
BIP BIP ピコピコ
YOUR PERIOD'S HERE.
I KNOW THAT.
IT'S NOT LIKE THERE'S EVER ANY POINT.
I DON'T KNOW WHY YOU EVEN SHOW UP THESE DAYS.
...YOU DON'T HAVE TO COME ANY-MORE.
I'LL BE SINGLE MY WHOLE LIFE ANYWAY.

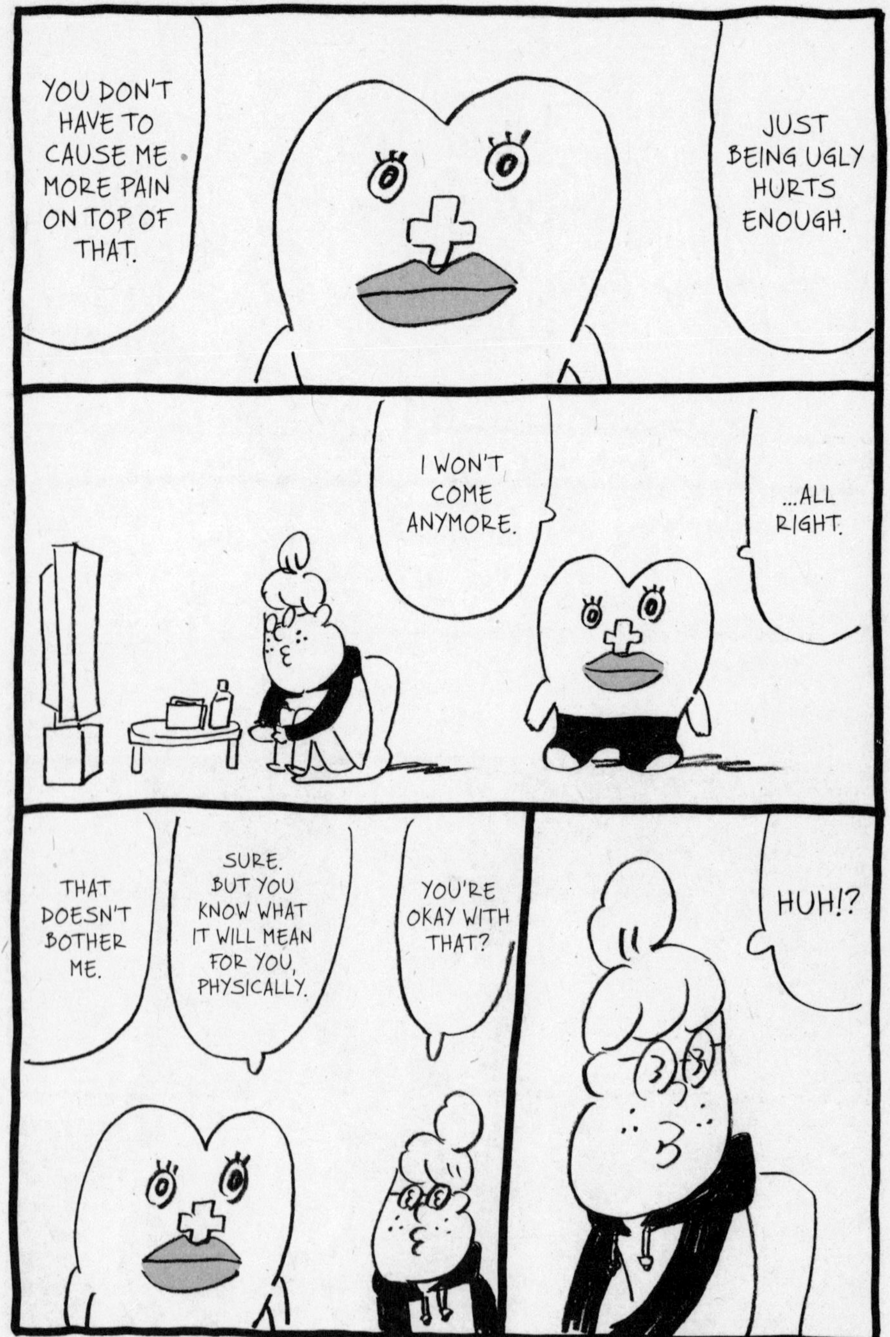
JUST BEING UGLY HURTS ENOUGH.
YOU DON'T HAVE TO CAUSE ME MORE PAIN ON TOP OF THAT.
...ALL RIGHT.
I WON'T COME ANYMORE.
HUH!?
YOU'RE OKAY WITH THAT?
SURE. BUT YOU KNOW WHAT IT WILL MEAN FOR YOU, PHYSICALLY.
THAT DOESN'T BOTHER ME.

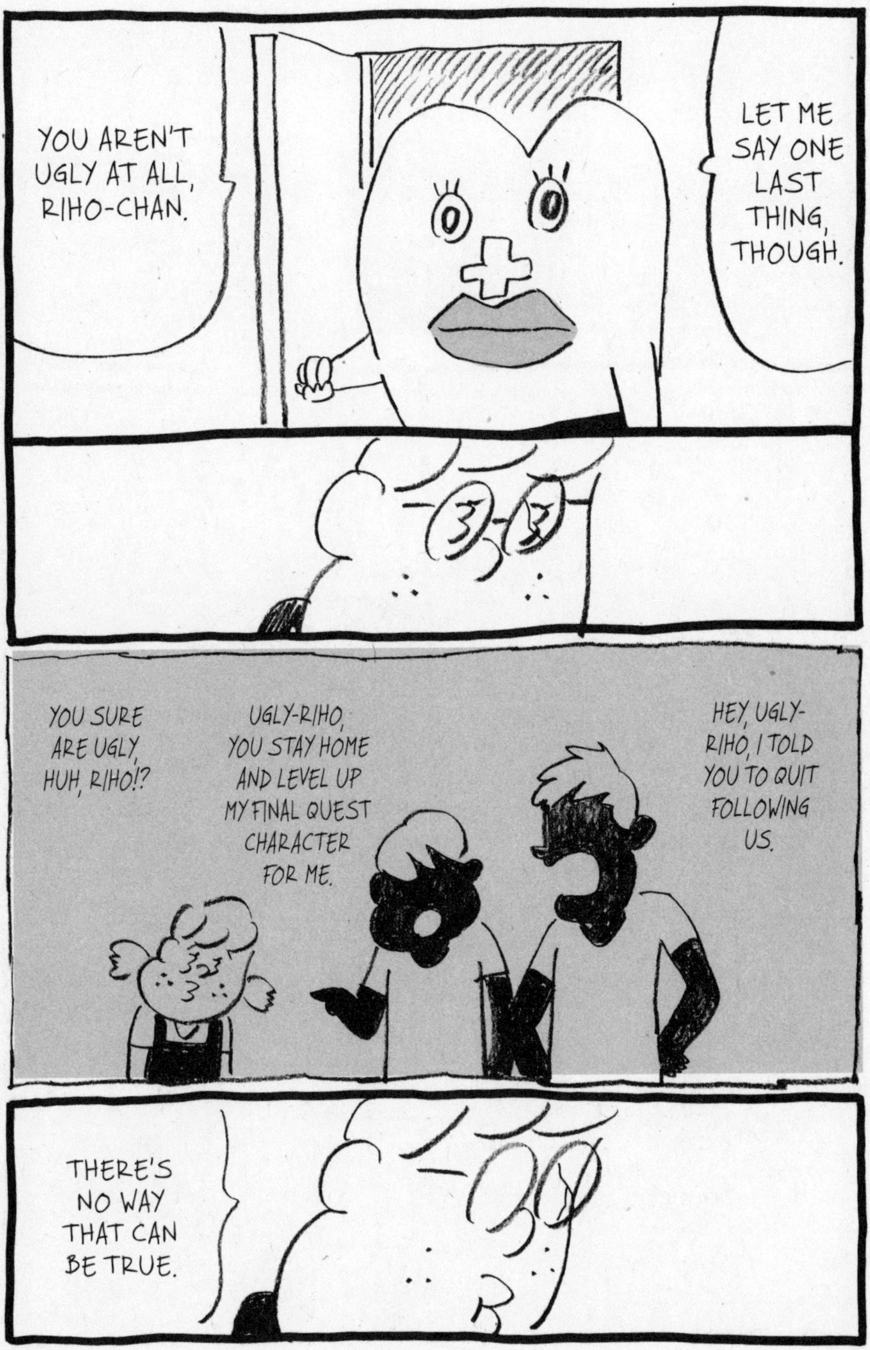
LET ME SAY ONE LAST THING, THOUGH.
YOU AREN'T UGLY AT ALL, RIHO-CHAN.
HEY, UGLY-RIHO, I TOLD YOU TO QUIT FOLLOWING US.
UGLY-RIHO, YOU STAY HOME AND LEVEL UP MY FINAL QUEST CHARACTER FOR ME.
YOU SURE ARE UGLY, HUH, RIHO!?
THERE'S NO WAY THAT CAN BE TRUE.

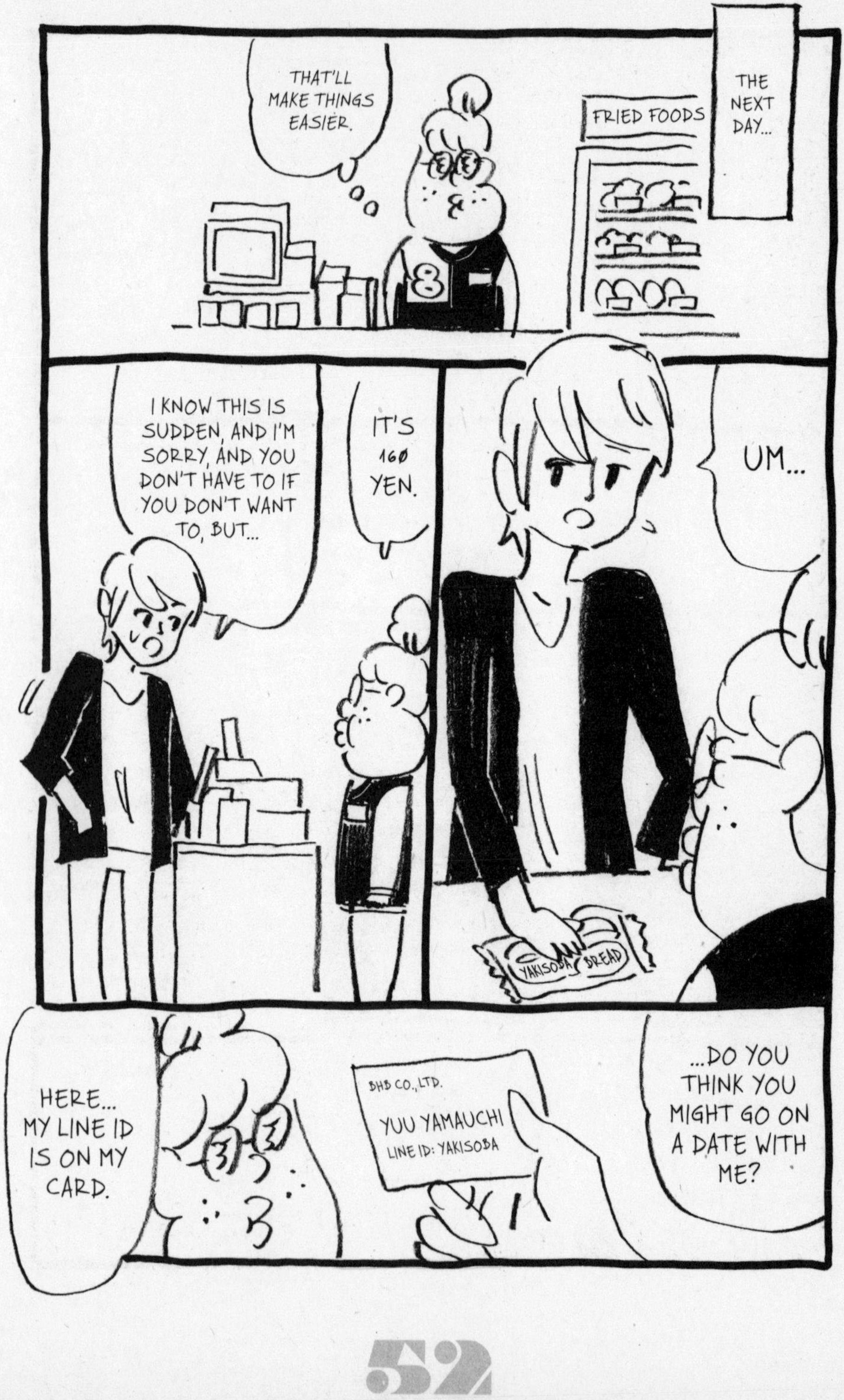
THE NEXT DAY...
FRIED FOODS
THAT'LL MAKE THINGS EASIER.
UM...
YAKISOBA BREAD
IT'S 160 YEN.
I KNOW THIS IS SUDDEN, AND I'M SORRY, AND YOU DON'T HAVE TO IF YOU DON'T WANT TO, BUT...
...DO YOU THINK YOU MIGHT GO ON A DATE WITH ME?
BHB CO., LTD.
YUU YAMAUCHI
LINE ID: YAKISOBA
HERE... MY LINE ID IS ON MY CARD.

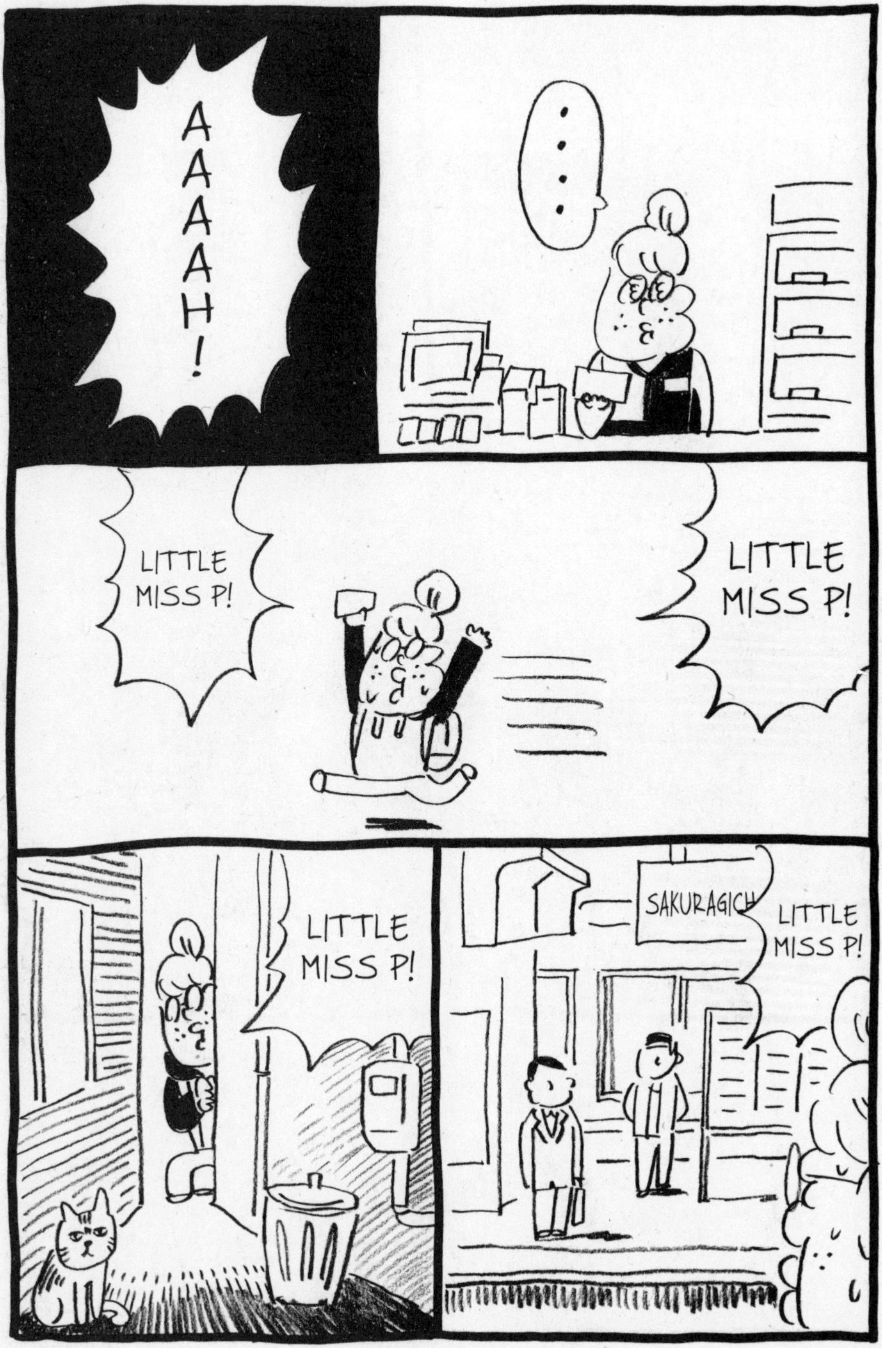
...
AAAAH!
LITTLE MISS P!
LITTLE MISS P!
SAKURAGICH
LITTLE MISS P!
LITTLE MISS P!

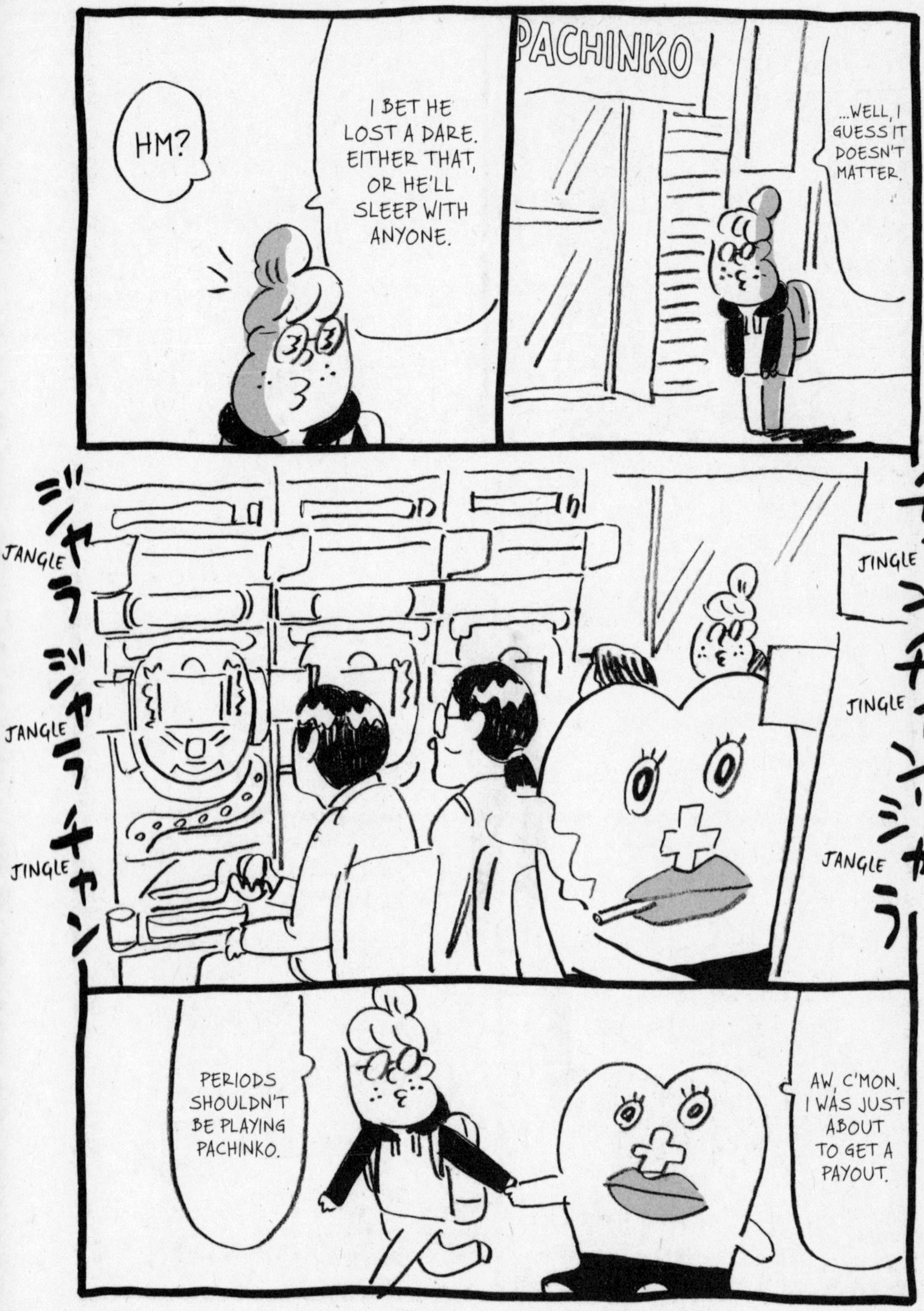
PACHINKO
...WELL, I GUESS IT DOESN'T MATTER.
I BET HE LOST A DARE. EITHER THAT, OR HE'LL SLEEP WITH ANYONE.
HM?
チャンチャンジャラ
JINGLE
JINGLE
JANGLE
ジャラジャラチャン
JANGLE
JANGLE
JINGLE
AW, C'MON. I WAS JUST ABOUT TO GET A PAYOUT.
PERIODS SHOULDN'T BE PLAYING PACHINKO.

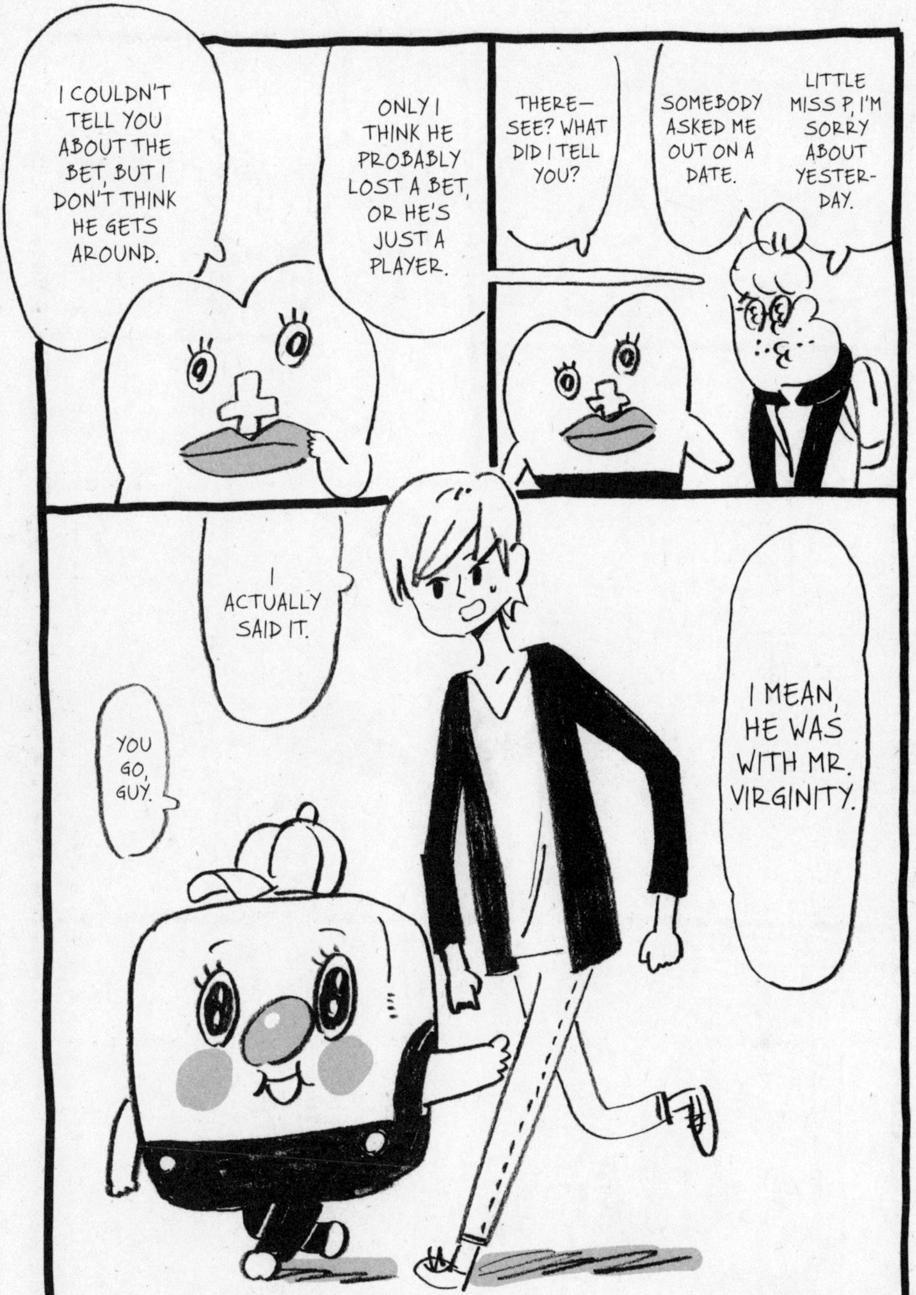
LITTLE MISS P, I'M SORRY ABOUT YESTER-DAY.
SOMEBODY ASKED ME OUT ON A DATE.
THERE— SEE? WHAT DID I TELL YOU?
ONLY I THINK HE PROBABLY LOST A BET, OR HE'S JUST A PLAYER.
I COULDN'T TELL YOU ABOUT THE BET, BUT I DON'T THINK HE GETS AROUND.
I MEAN, HE WAS WITH MR. VIRGINITY.
I ACTUALLY SAID IT.
YOU GO, GUY.

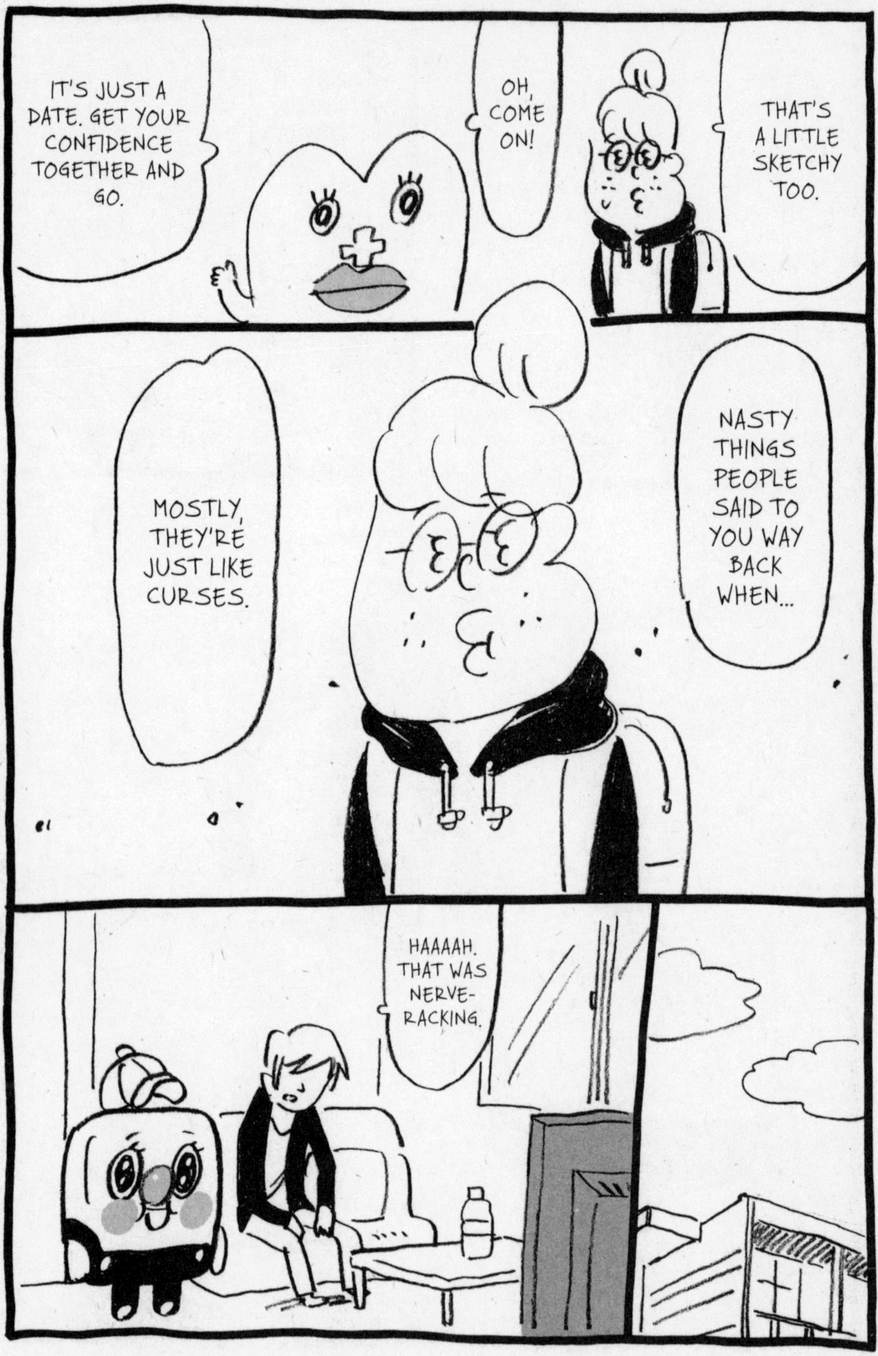
THAT'S A LITTLE SKETCHY TOO.
OH, COME ON!
IT'S JUST A DATE. GET YOUR CONFIDENCE TOGETHER AND GO.
NASTY THINGS PEOPLE SAID TO YOU WAY BACK WHEN...
MOSTLY, THEY'RE JUST LIKE CURSES.
HAAAAH. THAT WAS NERVE-RACKING.

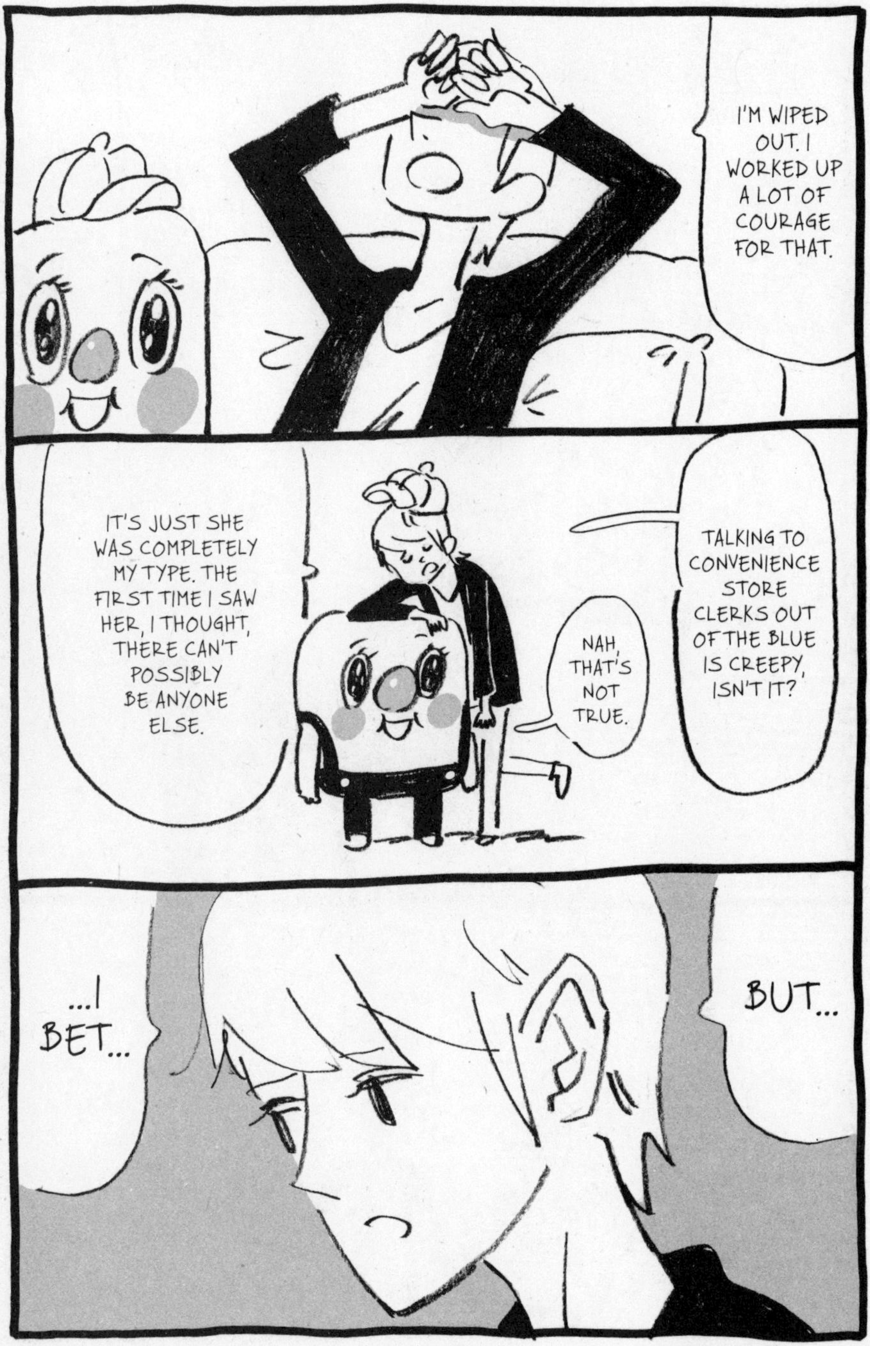
I'M WIPED OUT. I WORKED UP A LOT OF COURAGE FOR THAT.
TALKING TO CONVENIENCE STORE CLERKS OUT OF THE BLUE IS CREEPY, ISN'T IT?
NAH, THAT'S NOT TRUE.
IT'S JUST SHE WAS COMPLETELY MY TYPE. THE FIRST TIME I SAW HER, I THOUGHT, THERE CAN'T POSSIBLY BE ANYONE ELSE.
BUT...
...I BET...

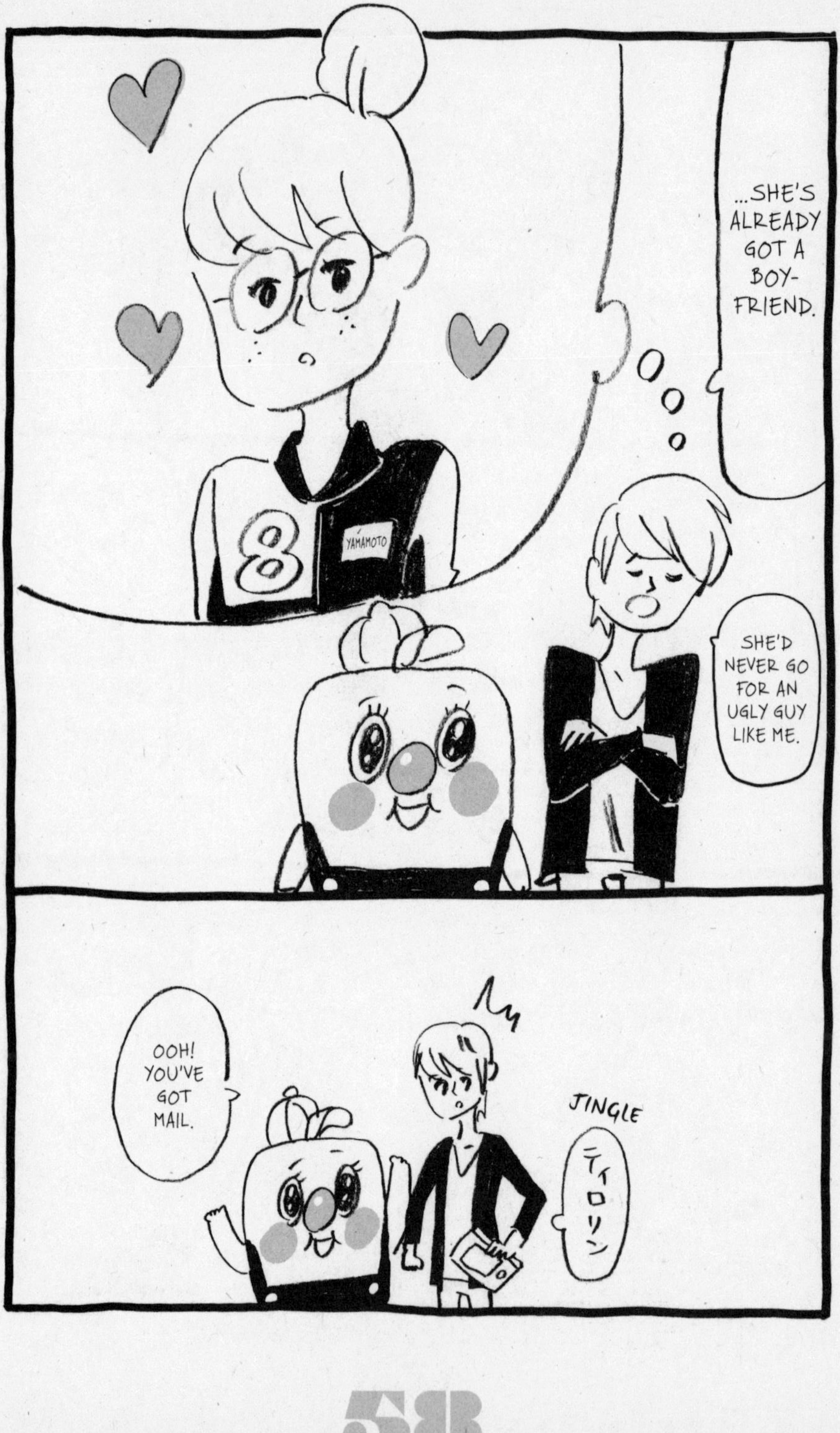
...SHE'S ALREADY GOT A BOY-FRIEND.
YAMAMOTO
8
SHE'D NEVER GO FOR AN UGLY GUY LIKE ME.
JINGLE
ティロリン
OOH! YOU'VE GOT MAIL.

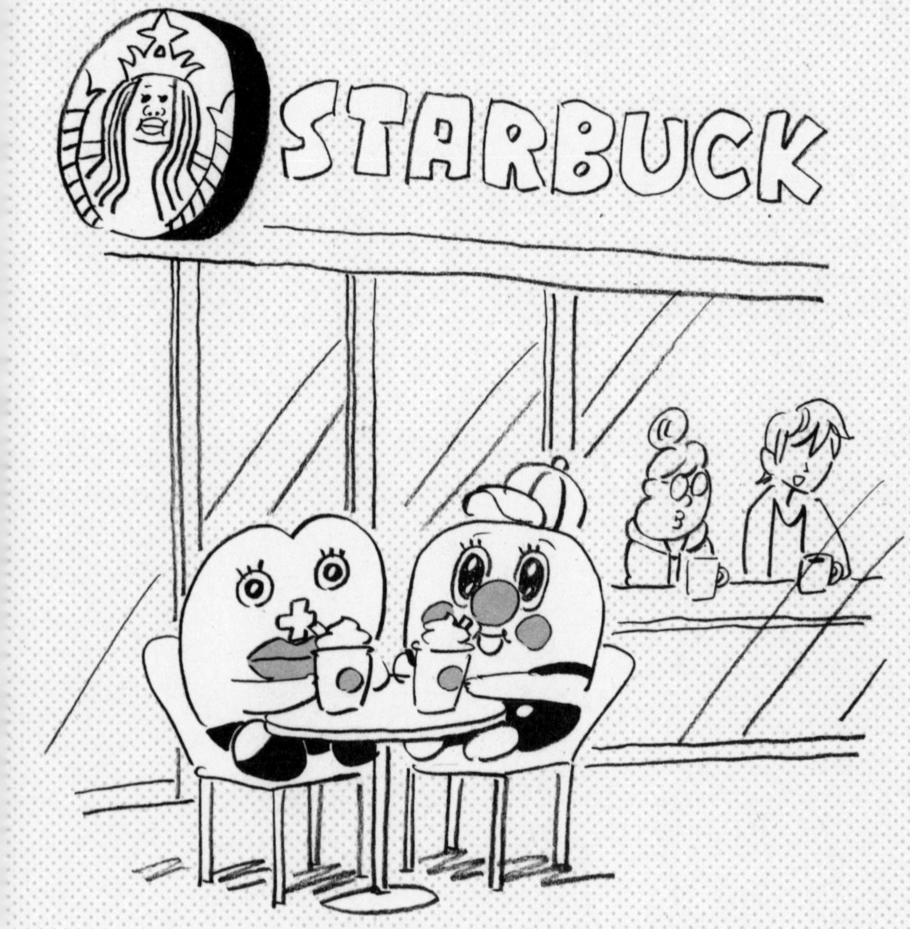
STARBUCK

SUPERHEROINE AND LITTLE MISS P

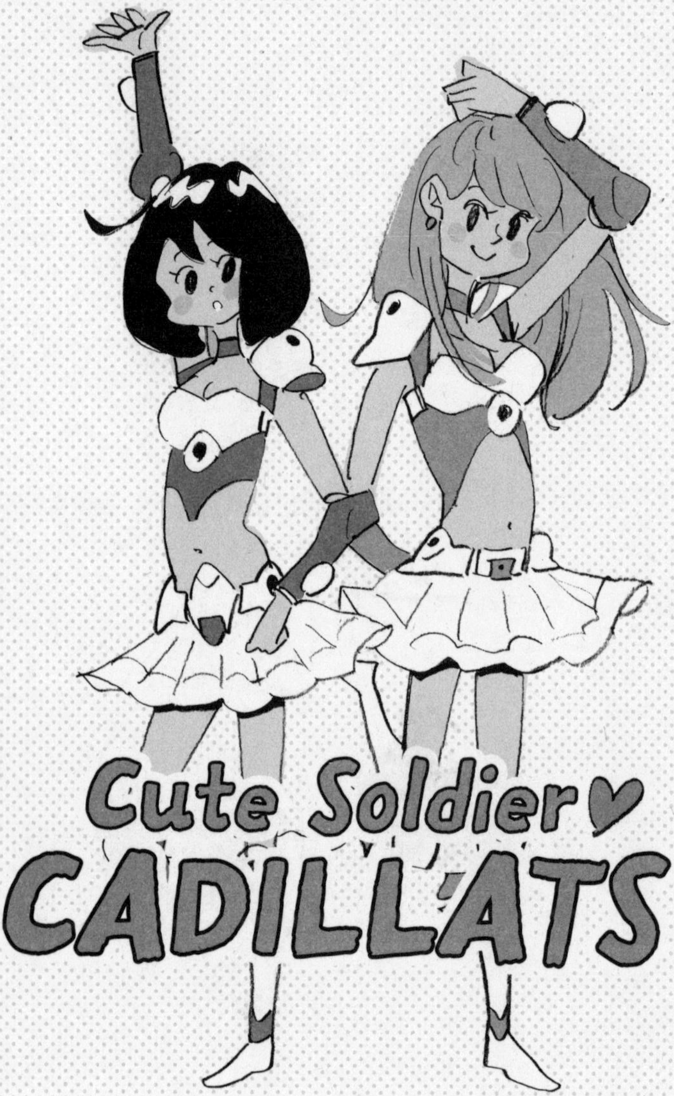
Cute Soldier♥
CADILLATS

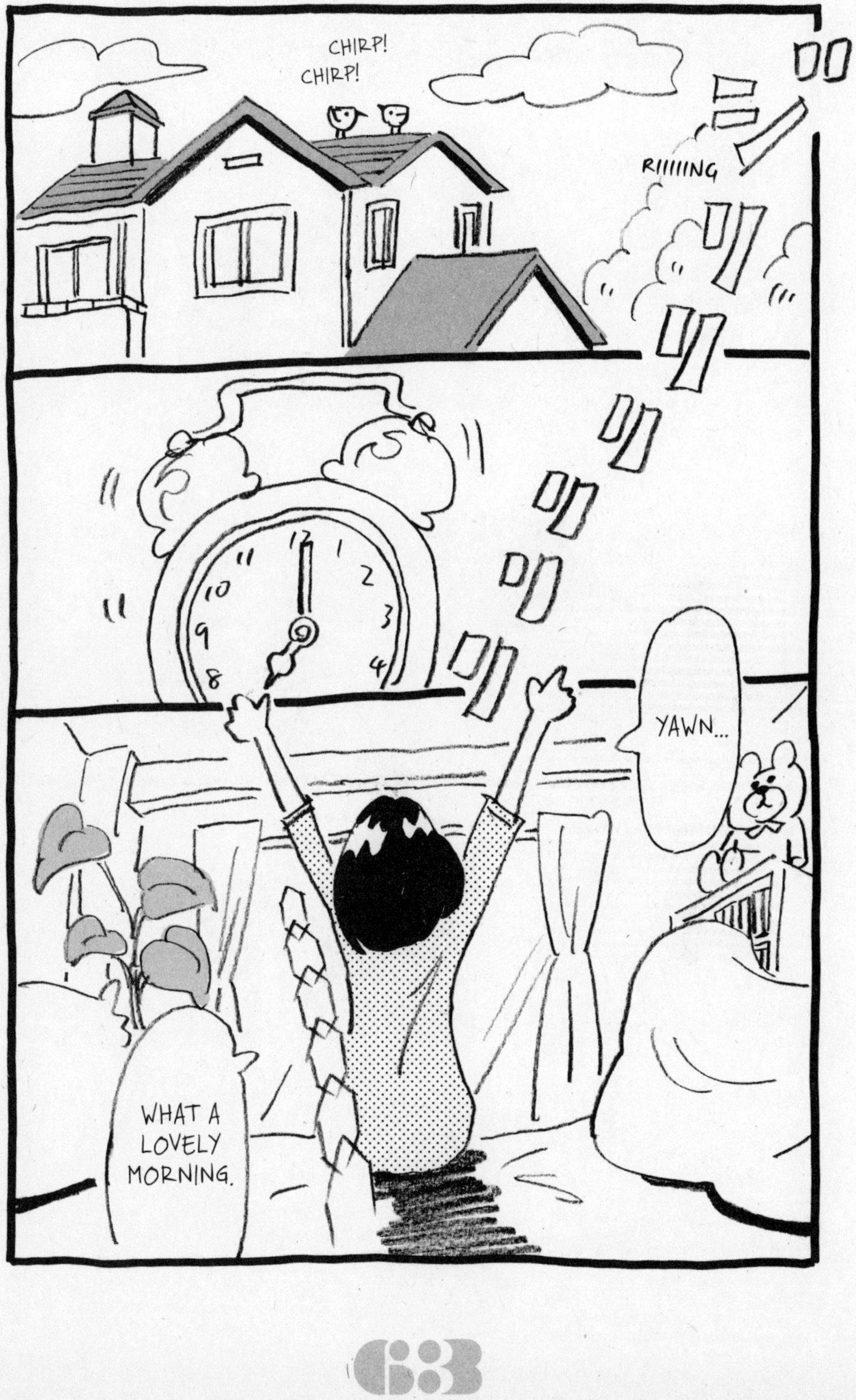
CHIRP!
CHIRP!
RIIIIING
YAWN...
WHAT A LOVELY MORNING.

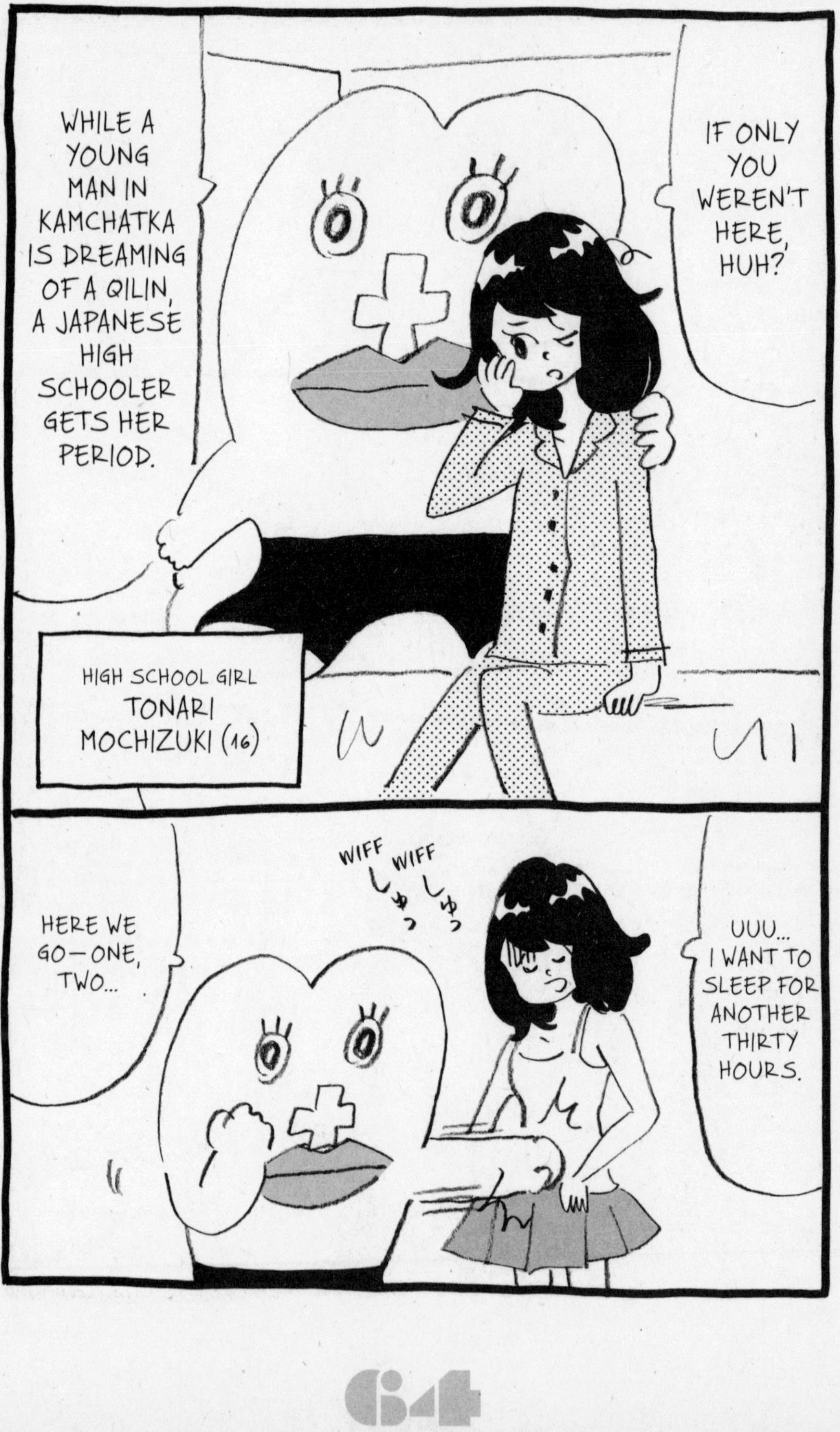
IF ONLY YOU WEREN'T HERE, HUH?
WHILE A YOUNG MAN IN KAMCHATKA IS DREAMING OF A QILIN, A JAPANESE HIGH SCHOOLER GETS HER PERIOD.
HIGH SCHOOL GIRL TONARI MOCHIZUKI (16)
UUU... I WANT TO SLEEP FOR ANOTHER THIRTY HOURS.
WIFF しゅっ
WIFF しゅっ
HERE WE GO—ONE, TWO...

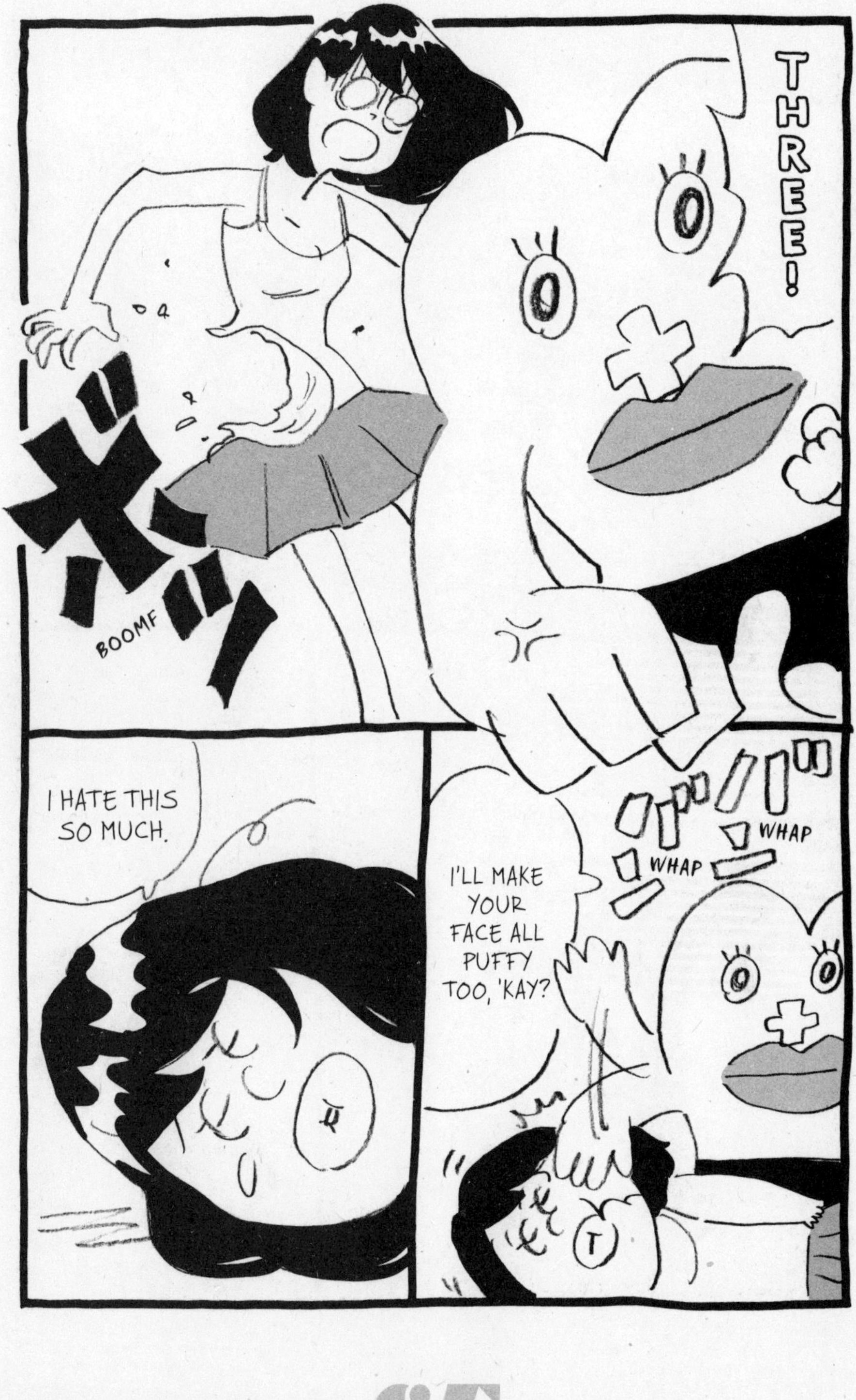
THREE!
BOOMF
WHAP
WHAP
I'LL MAKE YOUR FACE ALL PUFFY TOO, 'KAY?
I HATE THIS SO MUCH.

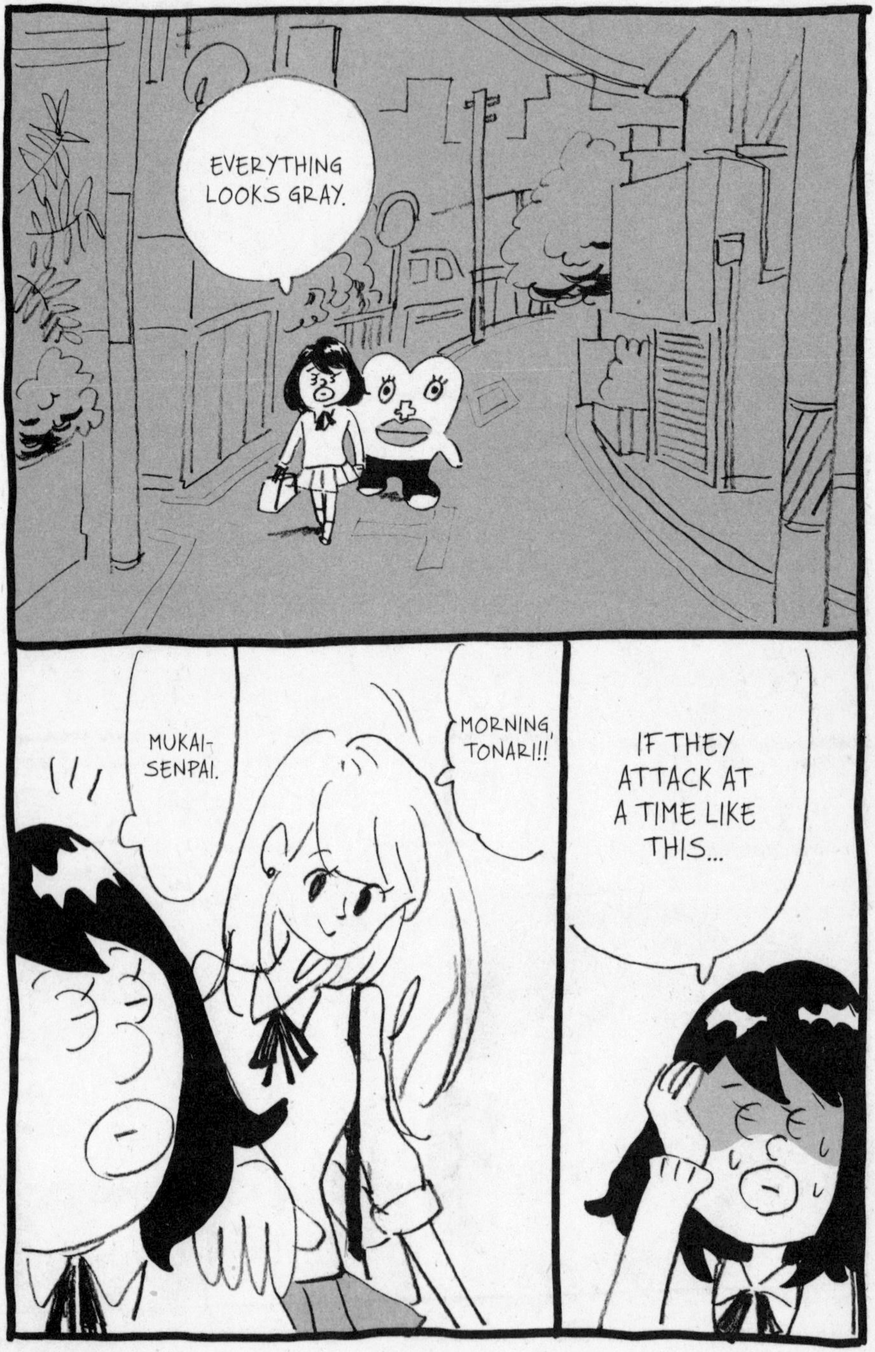
EVERYTHING LOOKS GRAY.
IF THEY ATTACK AT A TIME LIKE THIS...
MORNING, TONARI!!
MUKAI-SENPAI.

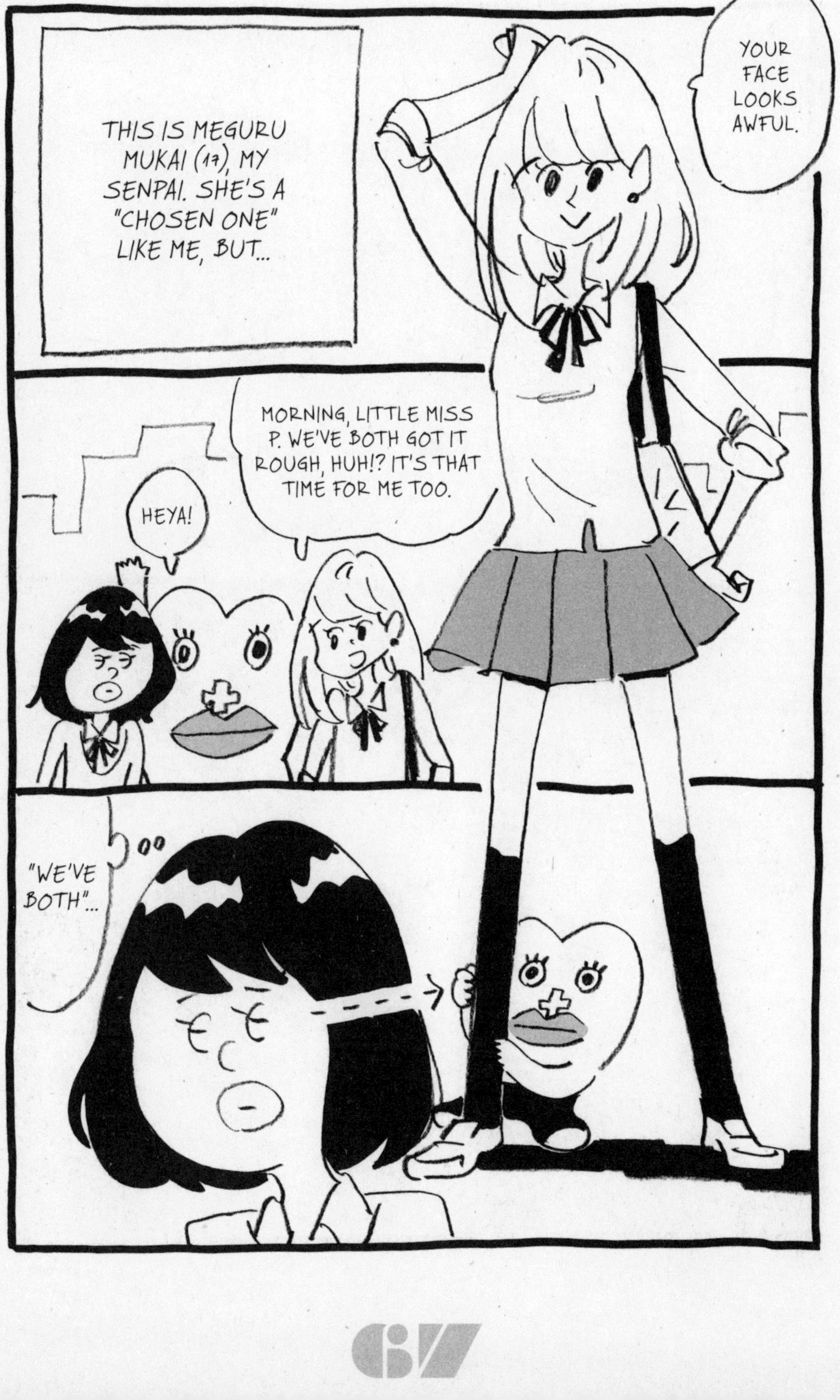
YOUR FACE LOOKS AWFUL.
THIS IS MEGURU MUKAI (17), MY SENPAI. SHE'S A "CHOSEN ONE" LIKE ME, BUT...
MORNING, LITTLE MISS P. WE'VE BOTH GOT IT ROUGH, HUH!? IT'S THAT TIME FOR ME TOO.
HEYA!
"WE'VE BOTH"...

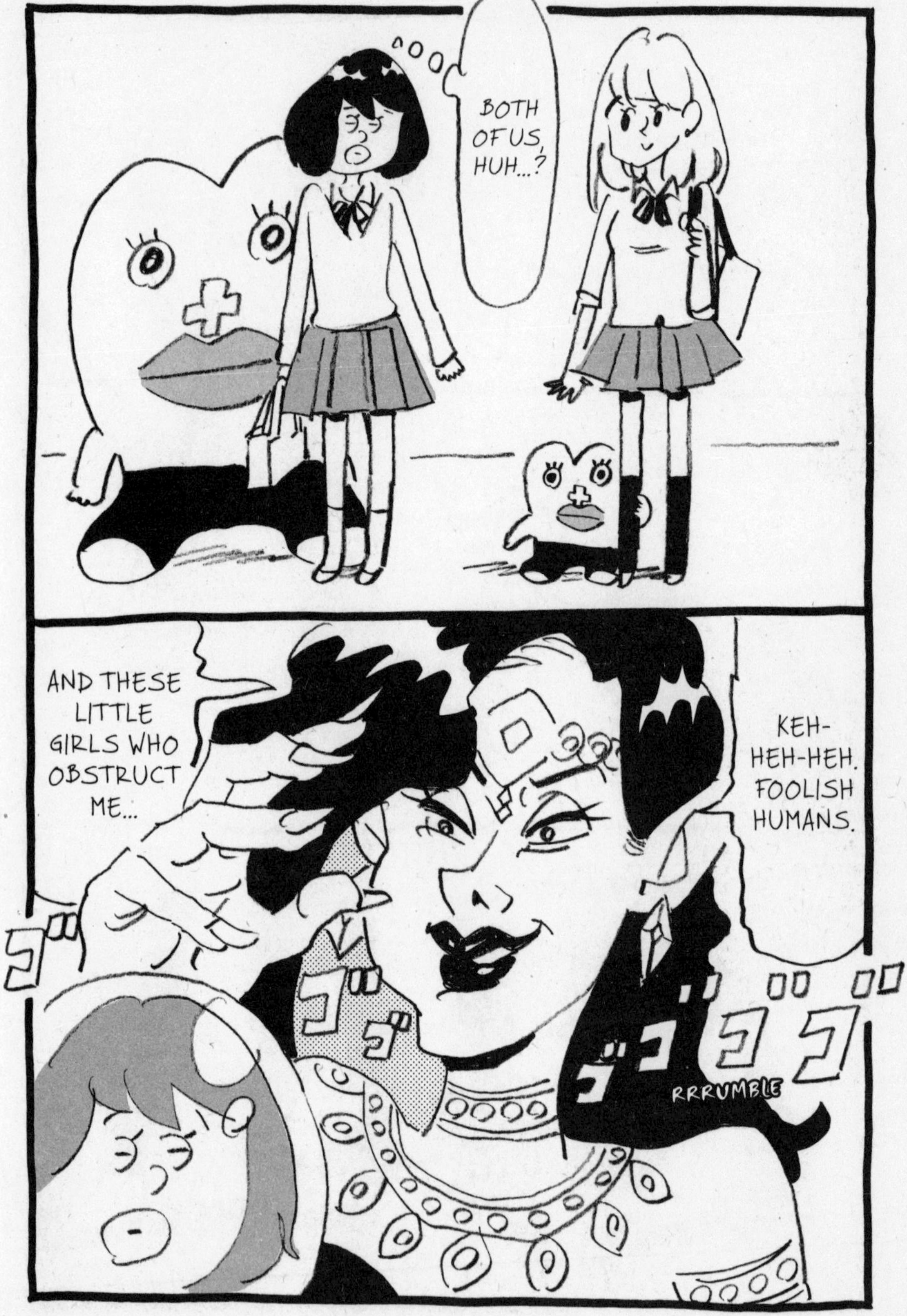
BOTH OF US, HUH...?
KEH-HEH-HEH. FOOLISH HUMANS.
AND THESE LITTLE GIRLS WHO OBSTRUCT ME...
RRRUMBLE

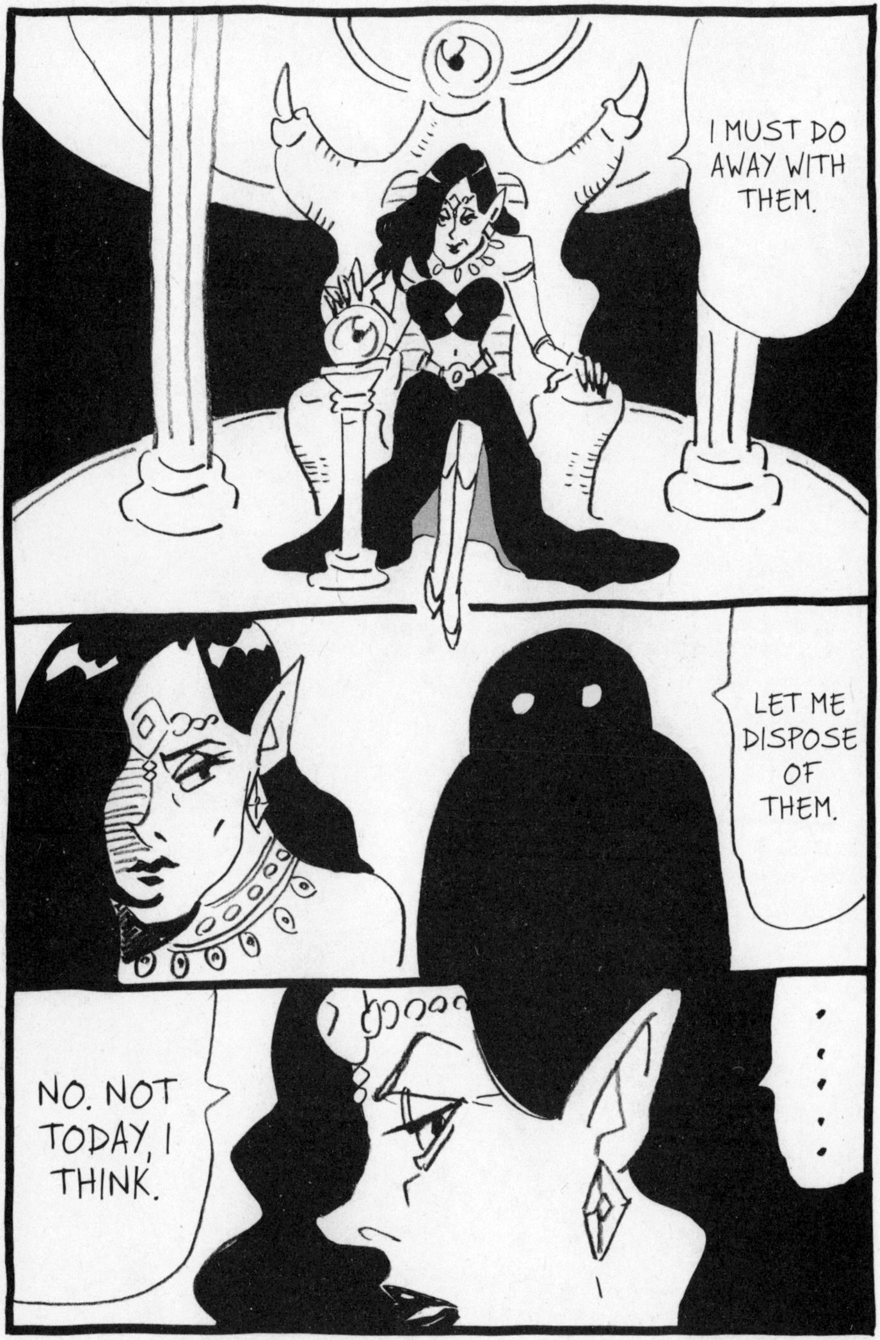
I MUST DO AWAY WITH THEM.
LET ME DISPOSE OF THEM.
.....
NO. NOT TODAY, I THINK.

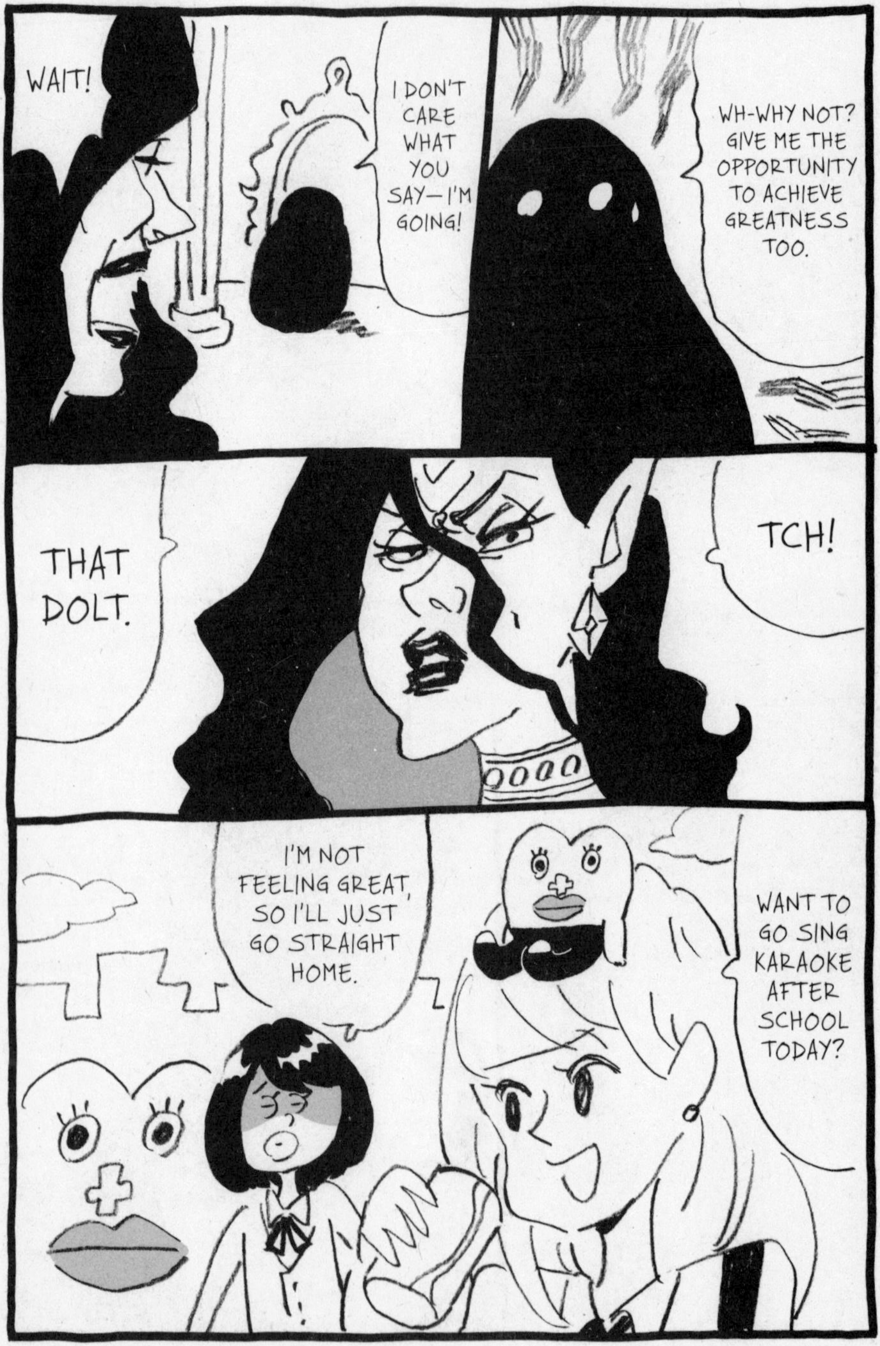
WH-WHY NOT? GIVE ME THE OPPORTUNITY TO ACHIEVE GREATNESS TOO.
I DON'T CARE WHAT YOU SAY—I'M GOING!
WAIT!
TCH!
THAT DOLT.
WANT TO GO SING KARAOKE AFTER SCHOOL TODAY?
I'M NOT FEELING GREAT, SO I'LL JUST GO STRAIGHT HOME.

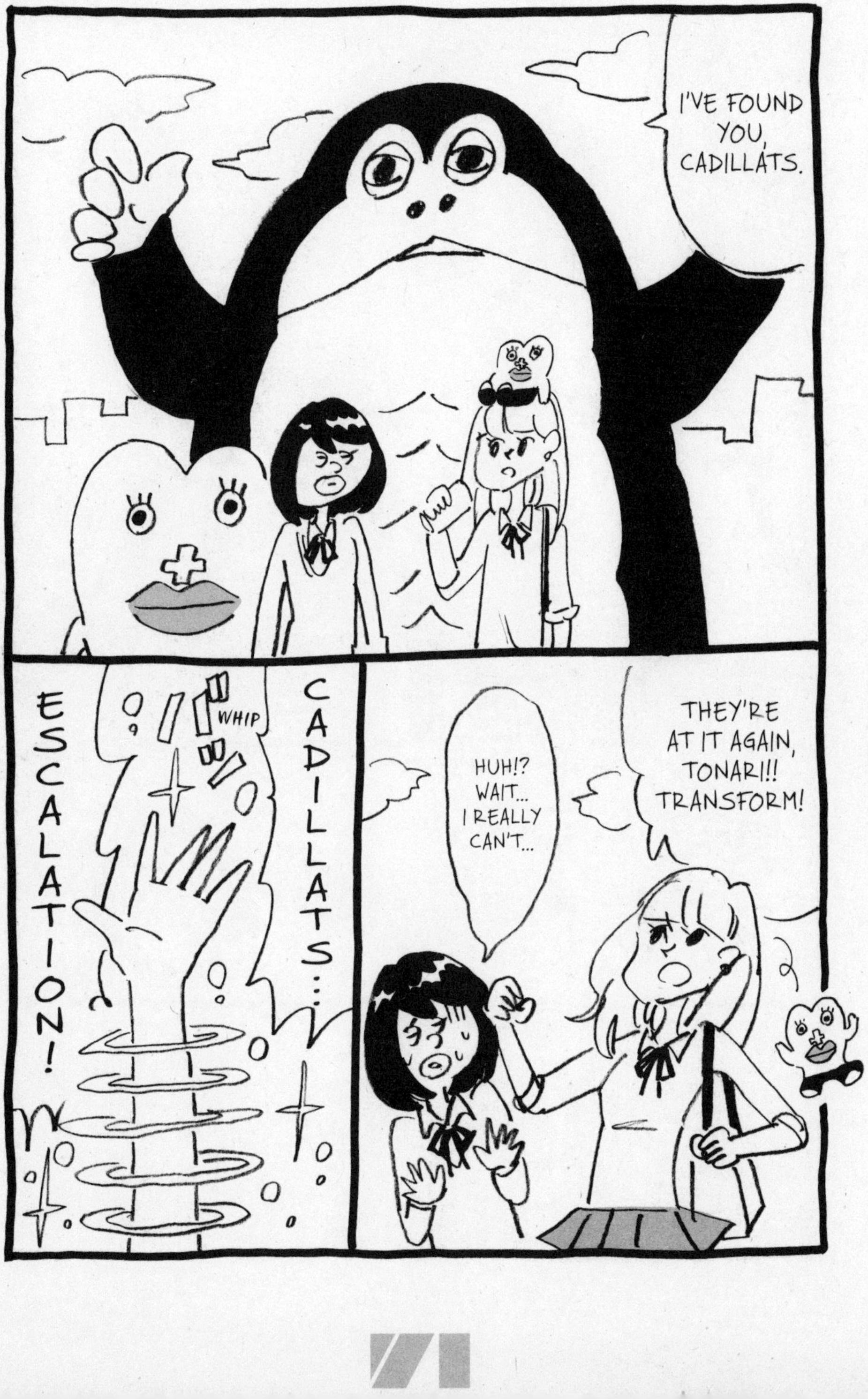
I'VE FOUND YOU, CADILLATS.
THEY'RE AT IT AGAIN, TONARI!! TRANSFORM!
HUH!? WAIT... I REALLY CAN'T...
CADILLATS...
WHIP
ESCALATION!

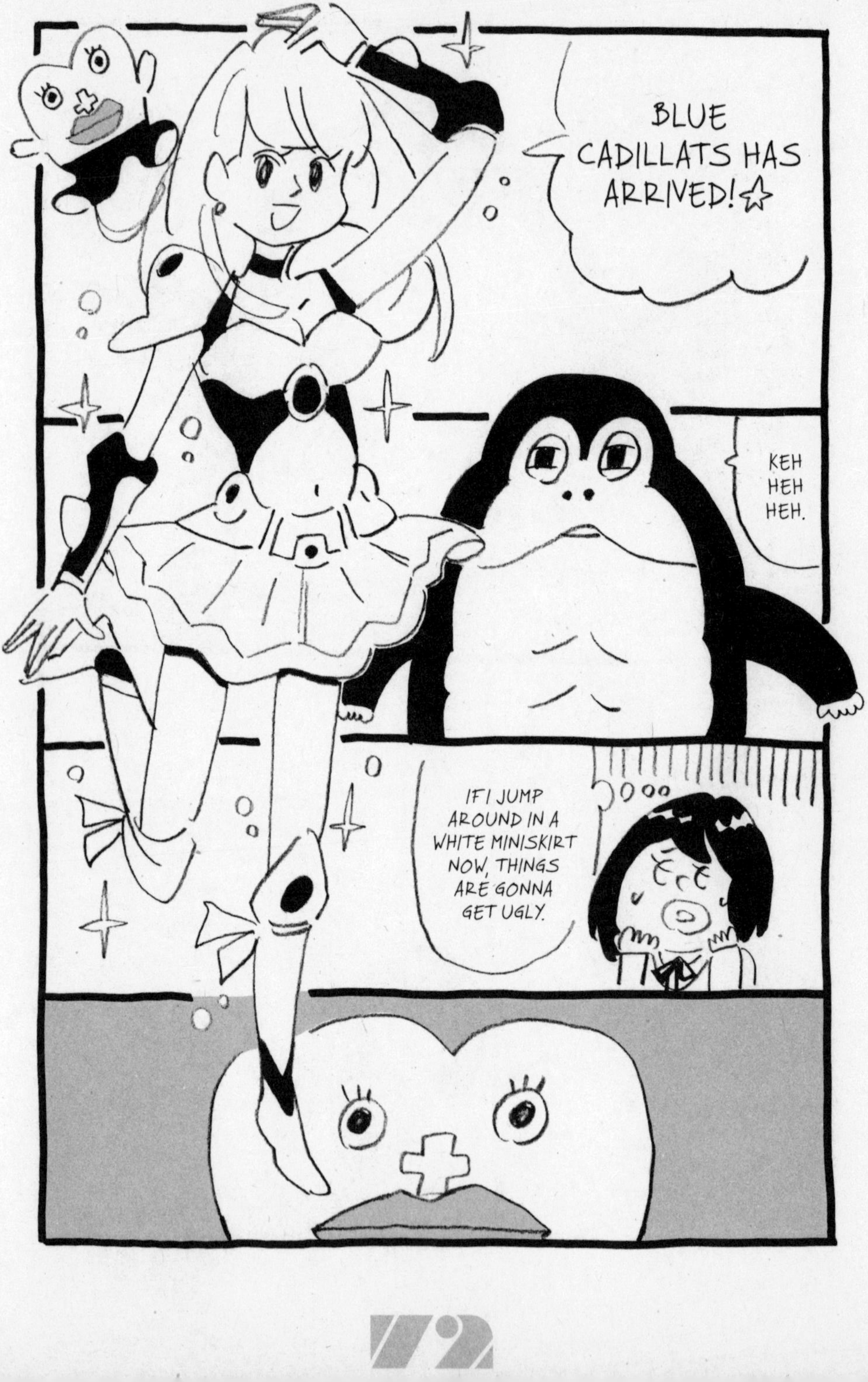
BLUE CADILLATS HAS ARRIVED!☆
KEH HEH HEH.
IF I JUMP AROUND IN A WHITE MINISKIRT NOW, THINGS ARE GONNA GET UGLY.

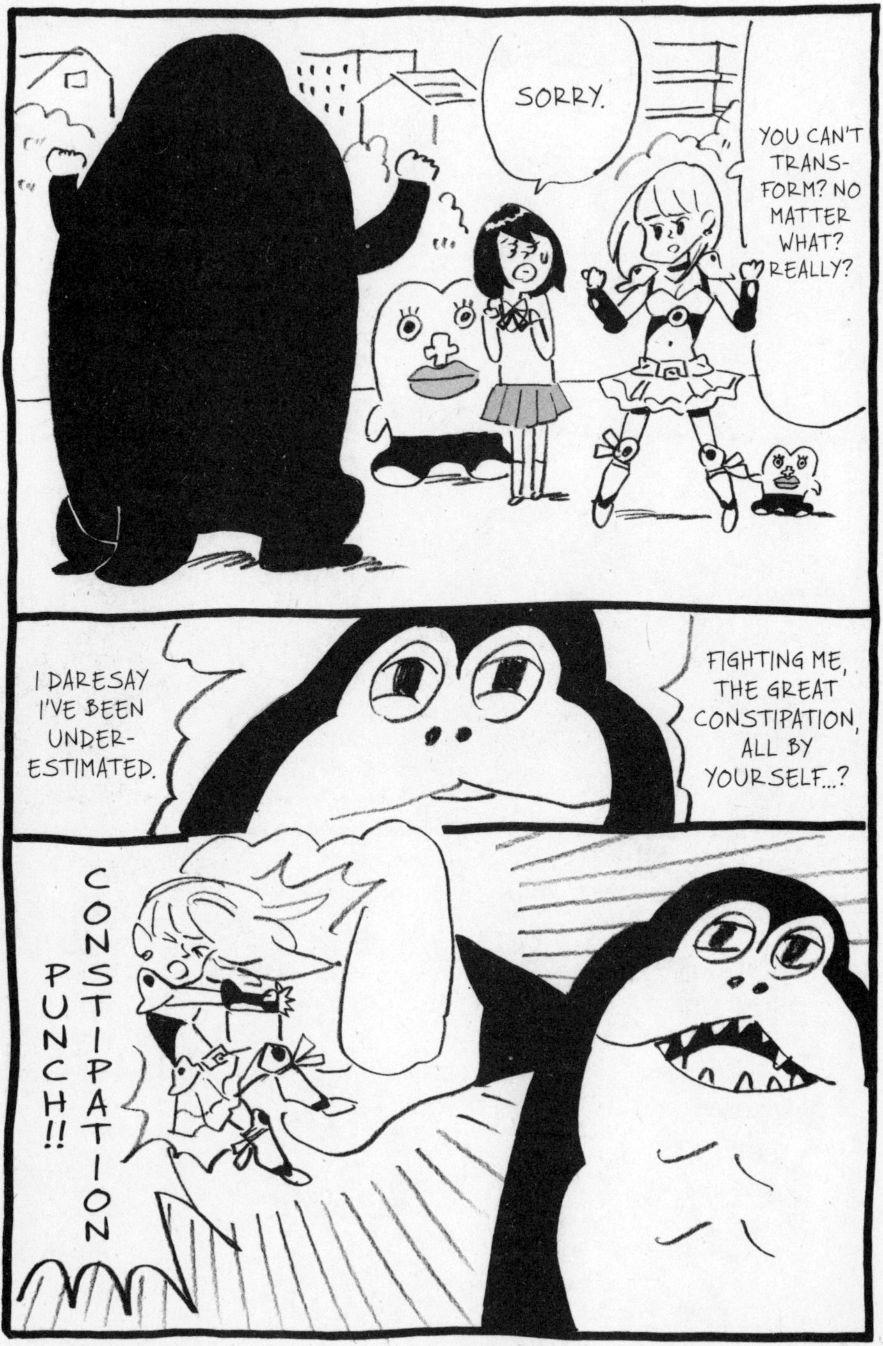
YOU CAN'T TRANS-FORM? NO MATTER WHAT? REALLY?
SORRY.
FIGHTING ME, THE GREAT CONSTIPATION, ALL BY YOURSELF...?
I DARESAY I'VE BEEN UNDER-ESTIMATED.
CONSTIPATION PUNCH!!

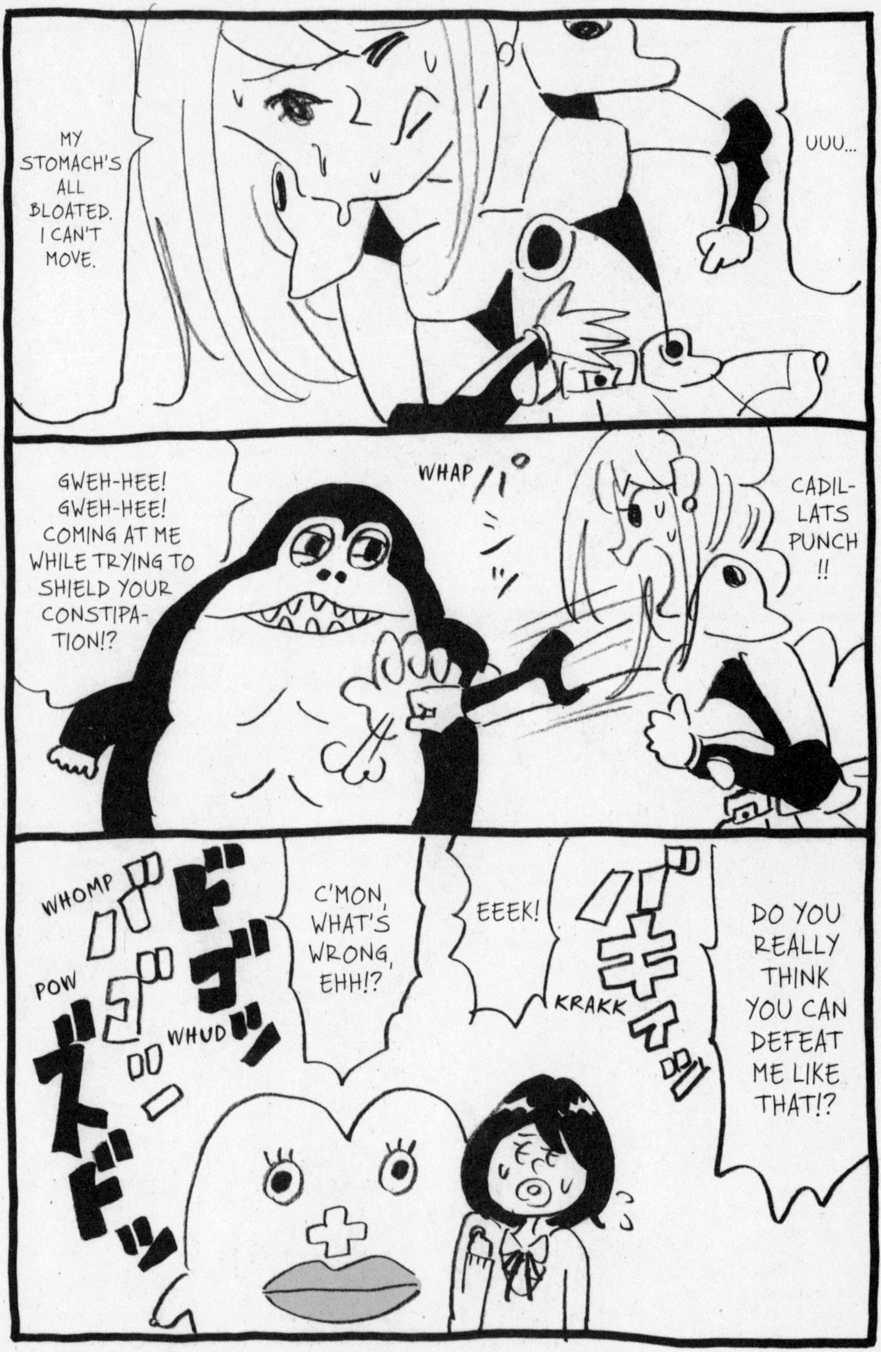
UUU...
MY STOMACH'S ALL BLOATED. I CAN'T MOVE.
CADIL-LATS PUNCH !!
WHAP
GWEH-HEE! GWEH-HEE! COMING AT ME WHILE TRYING TO SHIELD YOUR CONSTIPA-TION!?
DO YOU REALLY THINK YOU CAN DEFEAT ME LIKE THAT!?
KRAKK
EEEK!
C'MON, WHAT'S WRONG, EHH!?
WHUD
POW
WHOMP

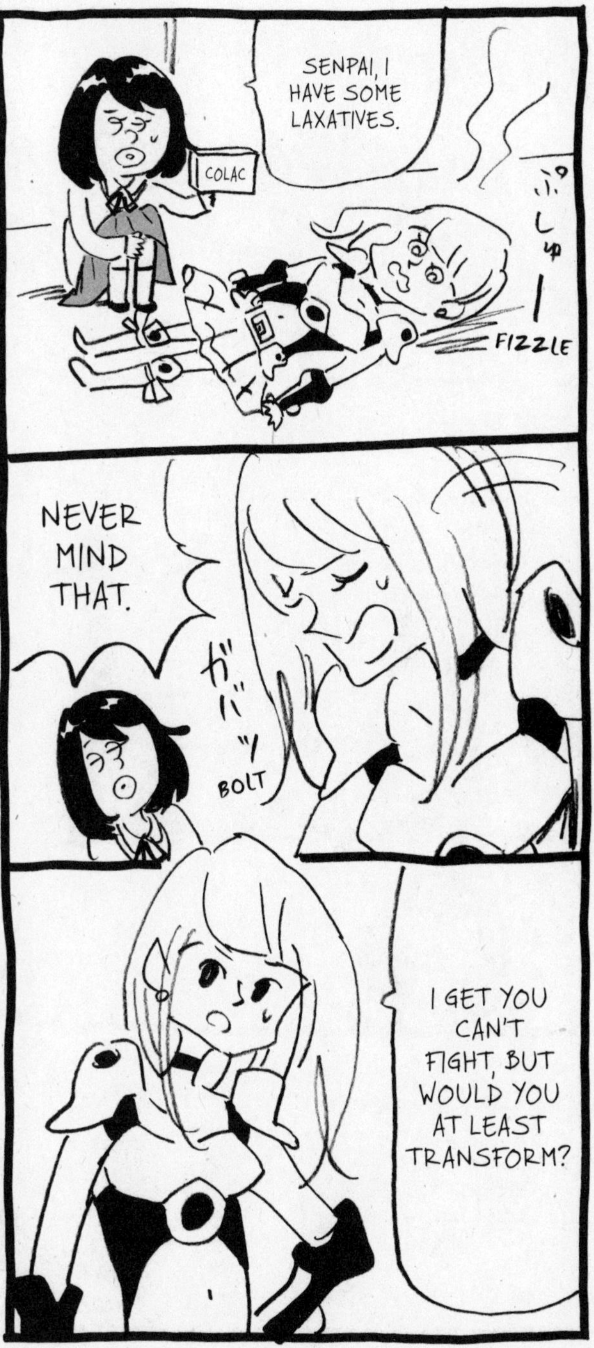
SENPAI, I HAVE SOME LAXATIVES.
COLAC
ぷしゅー
FIZZLE
NEVER MIND THAT.
ガバッ
BOLT
I GET YOU CAN'T FIGHT, BUT WOULD YOU AT LEAST TRANSFORM?

Hello! This is Koyama, the creator of Little Miss P! Thank you very much for buying my book. (ᵔᴗᵔ) I've been wanting to drive recently, so I've been studying up in an attempt to actually use my driver's license. The thing is, though, I had the idea that this symbol → ⦸ on road signs meant you couldn't go through there, so I thought, "Man, this place is lousy with roads you can't drive on...!" But it turns out I had the "No Parking" and "Do Not Enter" signs mixed up. Ha-ha-ha... At this rate, it's going to be a long time before I can drive up to a hot spring in Izu. ...But that has nothing to do with anything. Please continue to support Little Miss P! There are LINE stamps available too, so make sure to use 'em! They're also releasing merchandise! Okay, see you later!

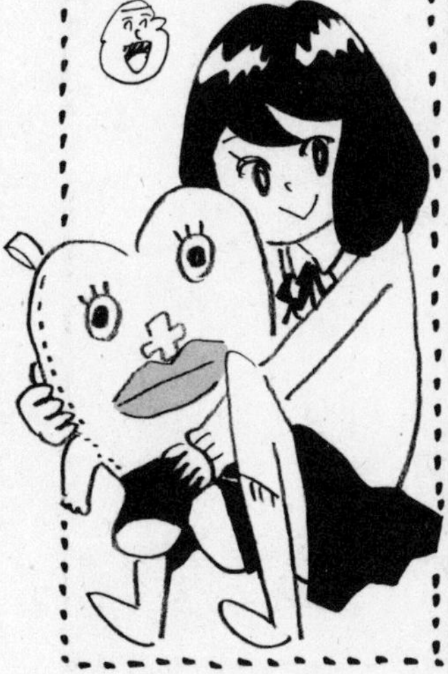

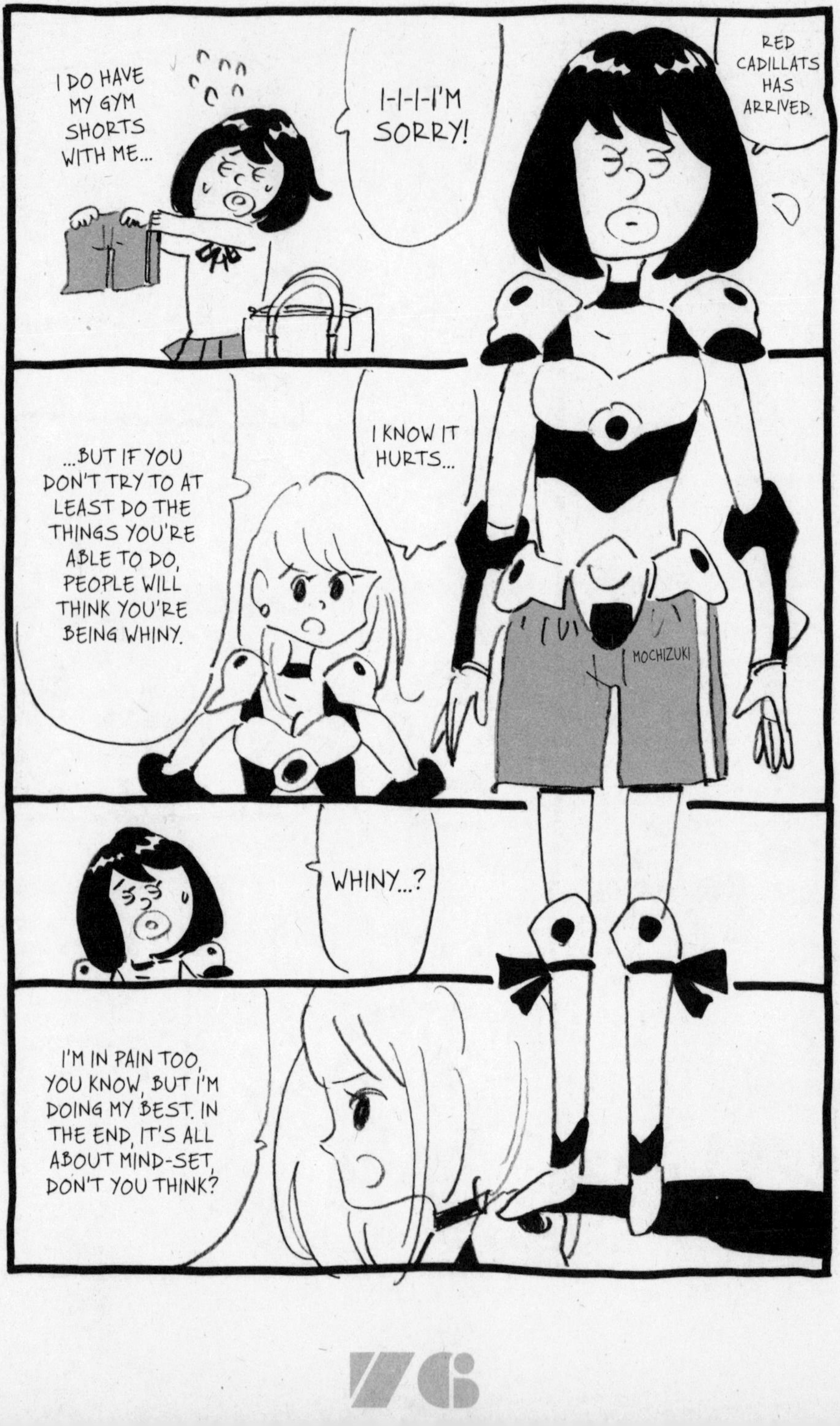
RED CADILLATS HAS ARRIVED.
I-I-I-I'M SORRY!
I DO HAVE MY GYM SHORTS WITH ME...
MOCHIZUKI
I KNOW IT HURTS...
...BUT IF YOU DON'T TRY TO AT LEAST DO THE THINGS YOU'RE ABLE TO DO, PEOPLE WILL THINK YOU'RE BEING WHINY.
WHINY...?
I'M IN PAIN TOO, YOU KNOW, BUT I'M DOING MY BEST. IN THE END, IT'S ALL ABOUT MIND-SET, DON'T YOU THINK?

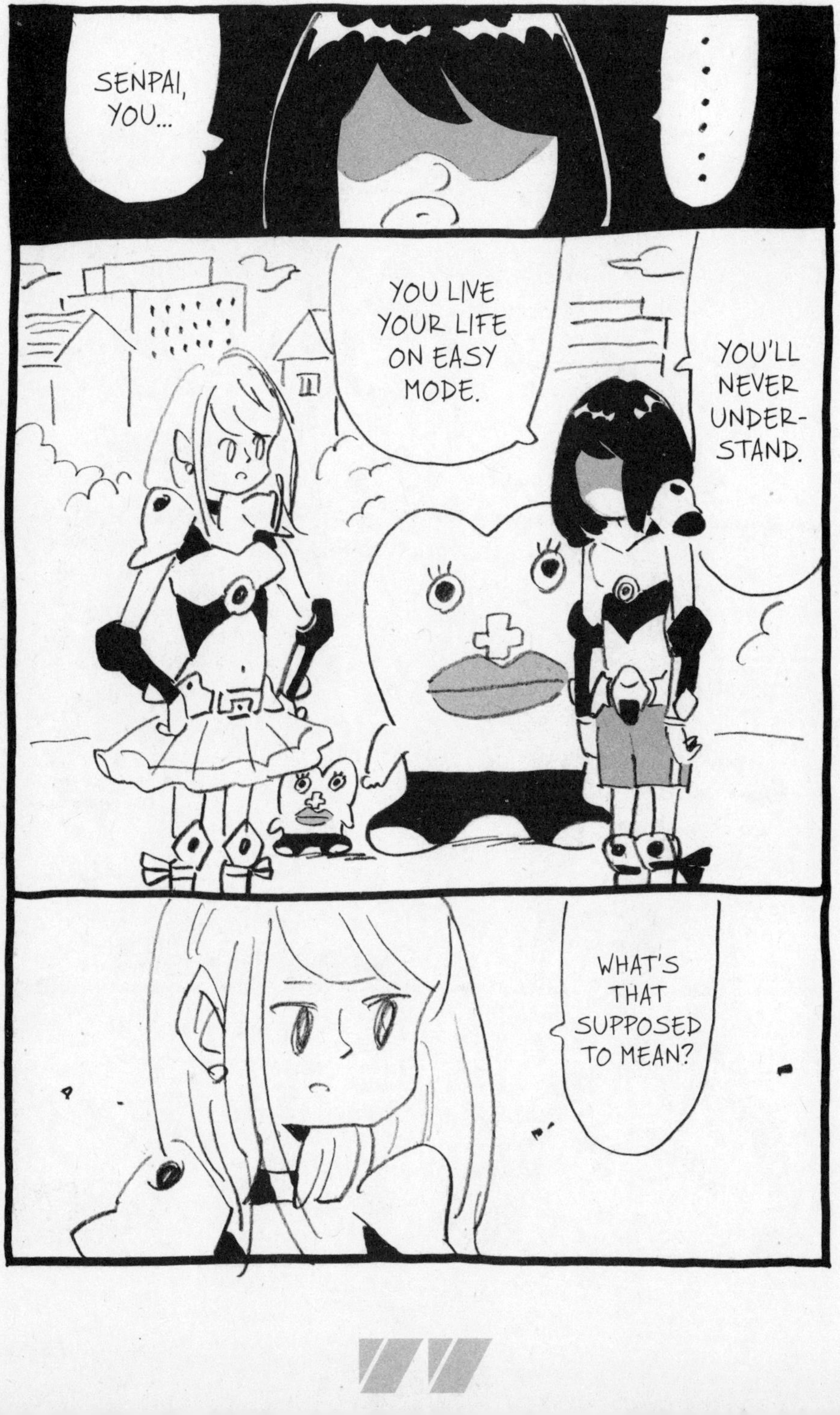
……
SENPAI, YOU...
YOU'LL NEVER UNDERSTAND.
YOU LIVE YOUR LIFE ON EASY MODE.
WHAT'S THAT SUPPOSED TO MEAN?

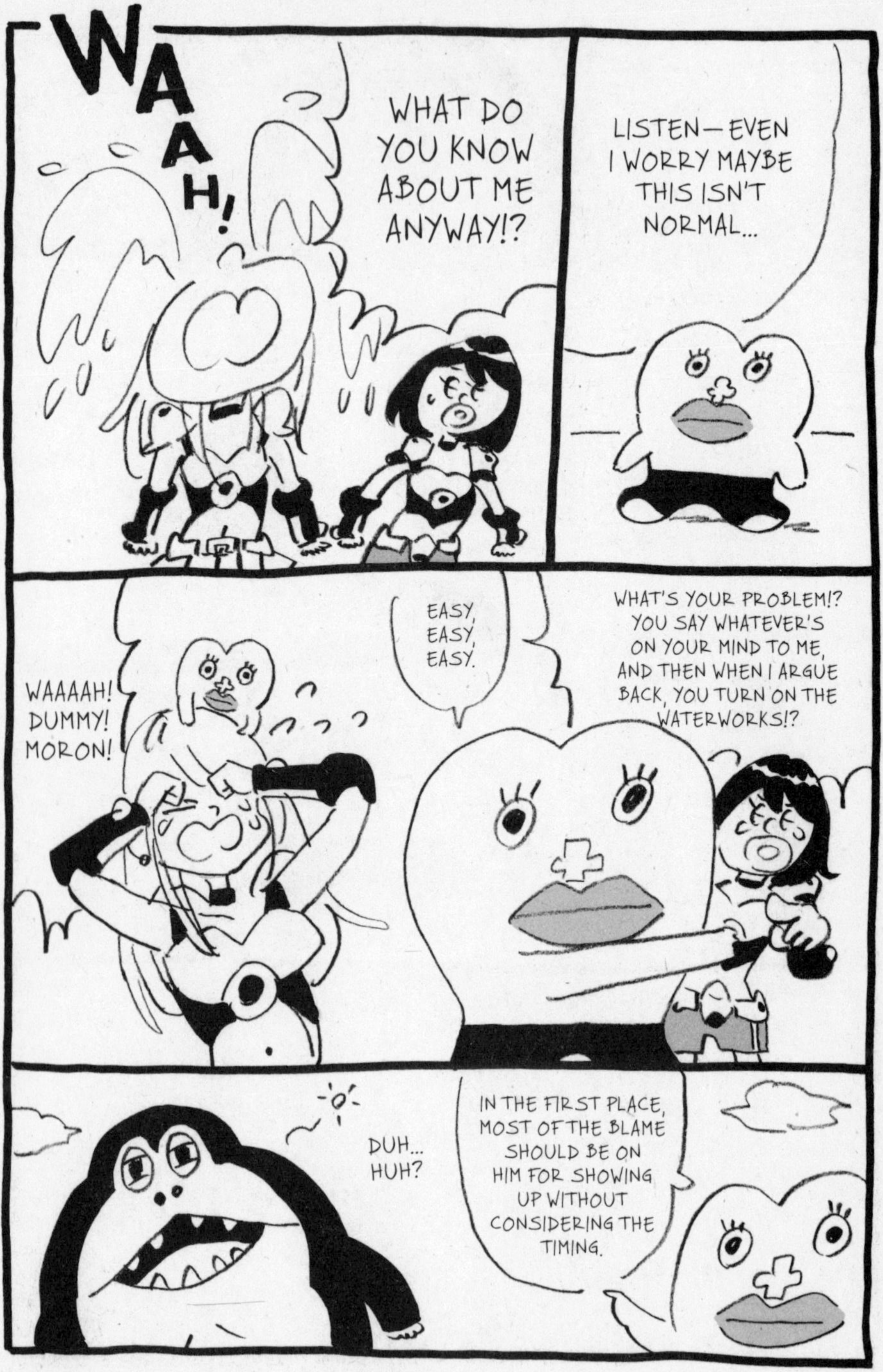
LISTEN—EVEN I WORRY MAYBE THIS ISN'T NORMAL...
WHAT DO YOU KNOW ABOUT ME ANYWAY!?
WAAAH!
WHAT'S YOUR PROBLEM!? YOU SAY WHATEVER'S ON YOUR MIND TO ME, AND THEN WHEN I ARGUE BACK, YOU TURN ON THE WATERWORKS!?
EASY, EASY, EASY.
WAAAAH! DUMMY! MORON!
IN THE FIRST PLACE, MOST OF THE BLAME SHOULD BE ON HIM FOR SHOWING UP WITHOUT CONSIDERING THE TIMING.
DUH... HUH?

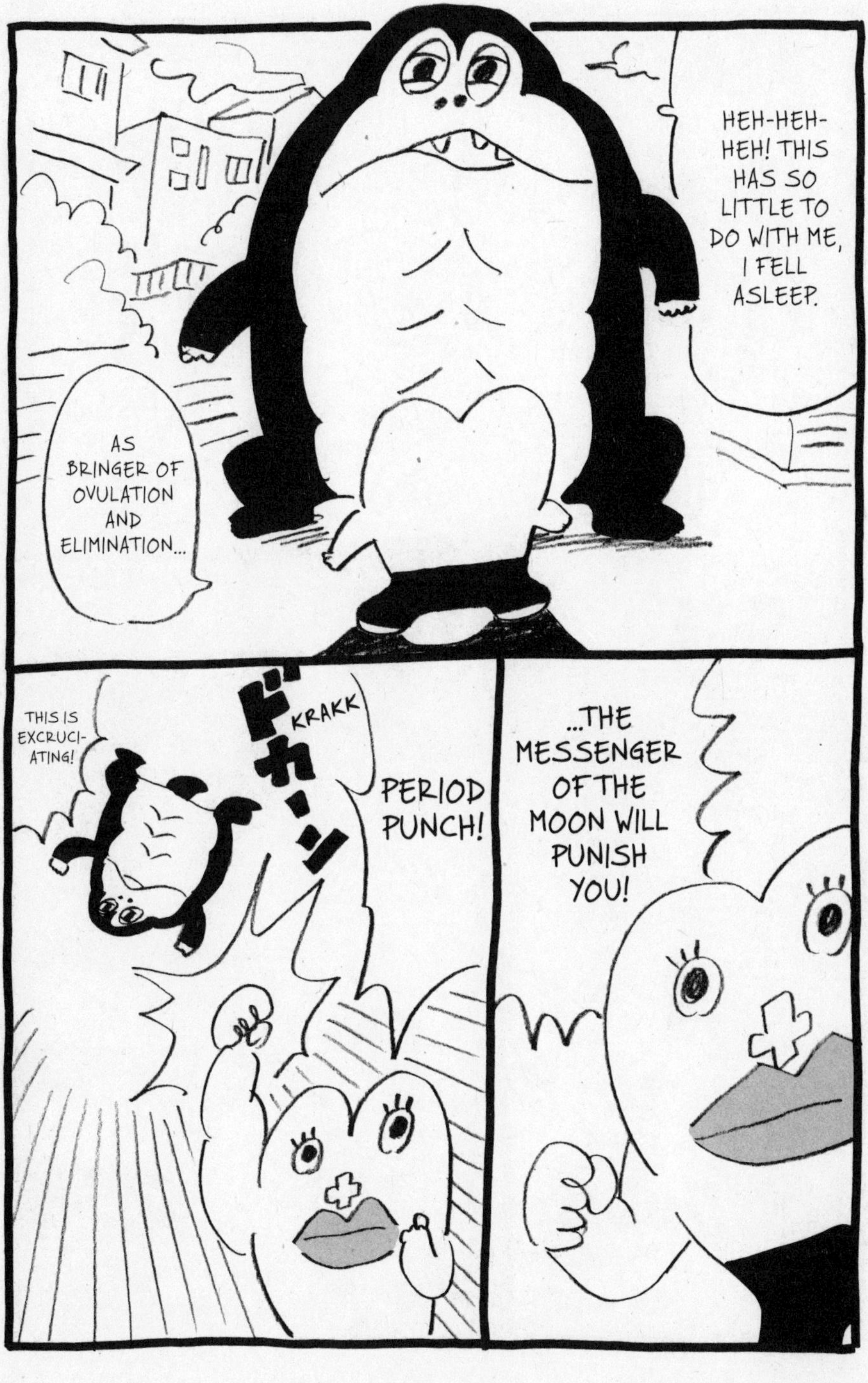
HEH-HEH-HEH! THIS HAS SO LITTLE TO DO WITH ME, I FELL ASLEEP.
AS BRINGER OF OVULATION AND ELIMINATION...
...THE MESSENGER OF THE MOON WILL PUNISH YOU!
PERIOD PUNCH!
ドカッ
KRAKK
THIS IS EXCRUCIATING!

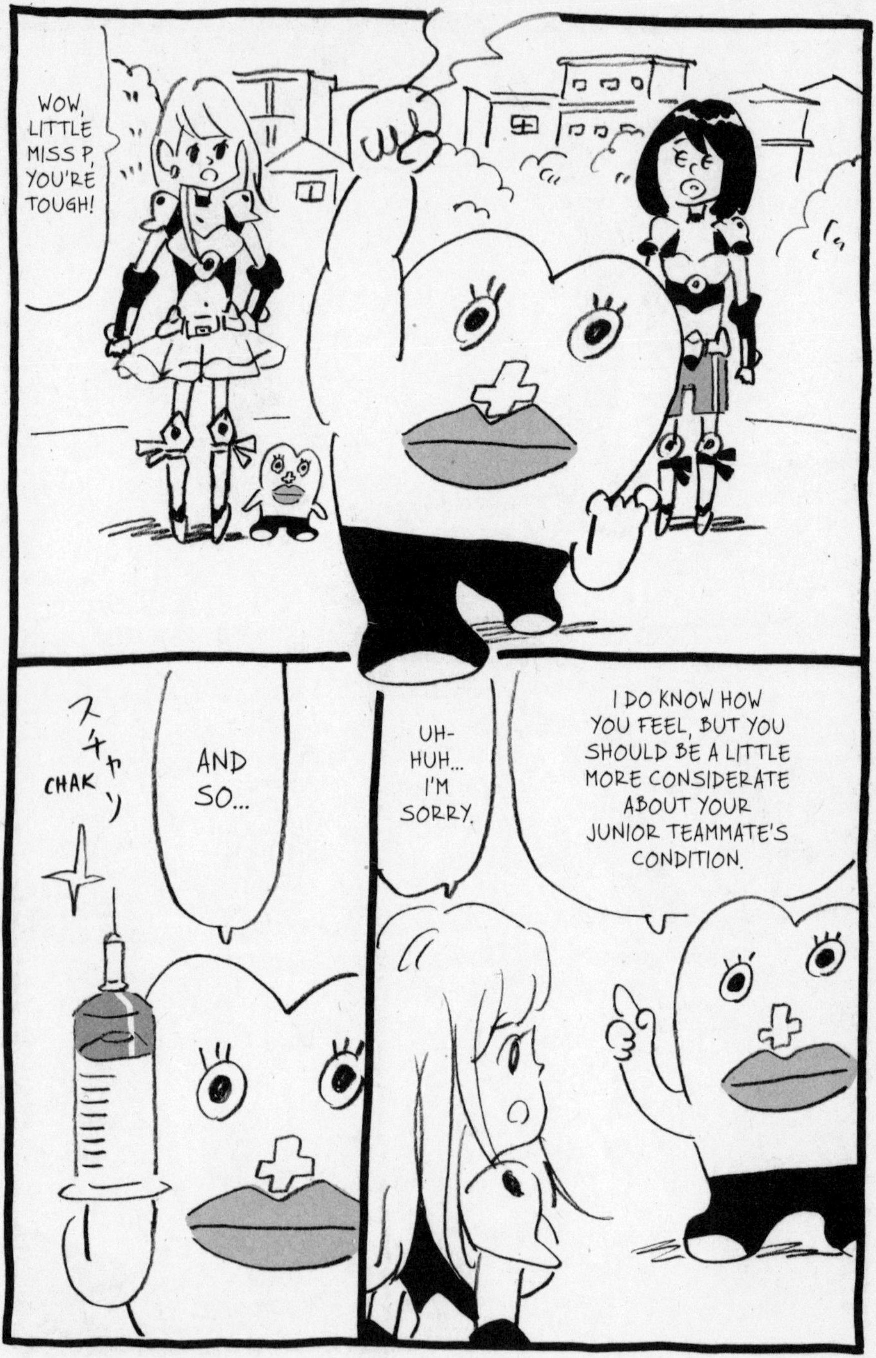
WOW, LITTLE MISS P, YOU'RE TOUGH!
I DO KNOW HOW YOU FEEL, BUT YOU SHOULD BE A LITTLE MORE CONSIDERATE ABOUT YOUR JUNIOR TEAMMATE'S CONDITION.
UH-HUH... I'M SORRY.
AND SO...
スチャッ
CHAK

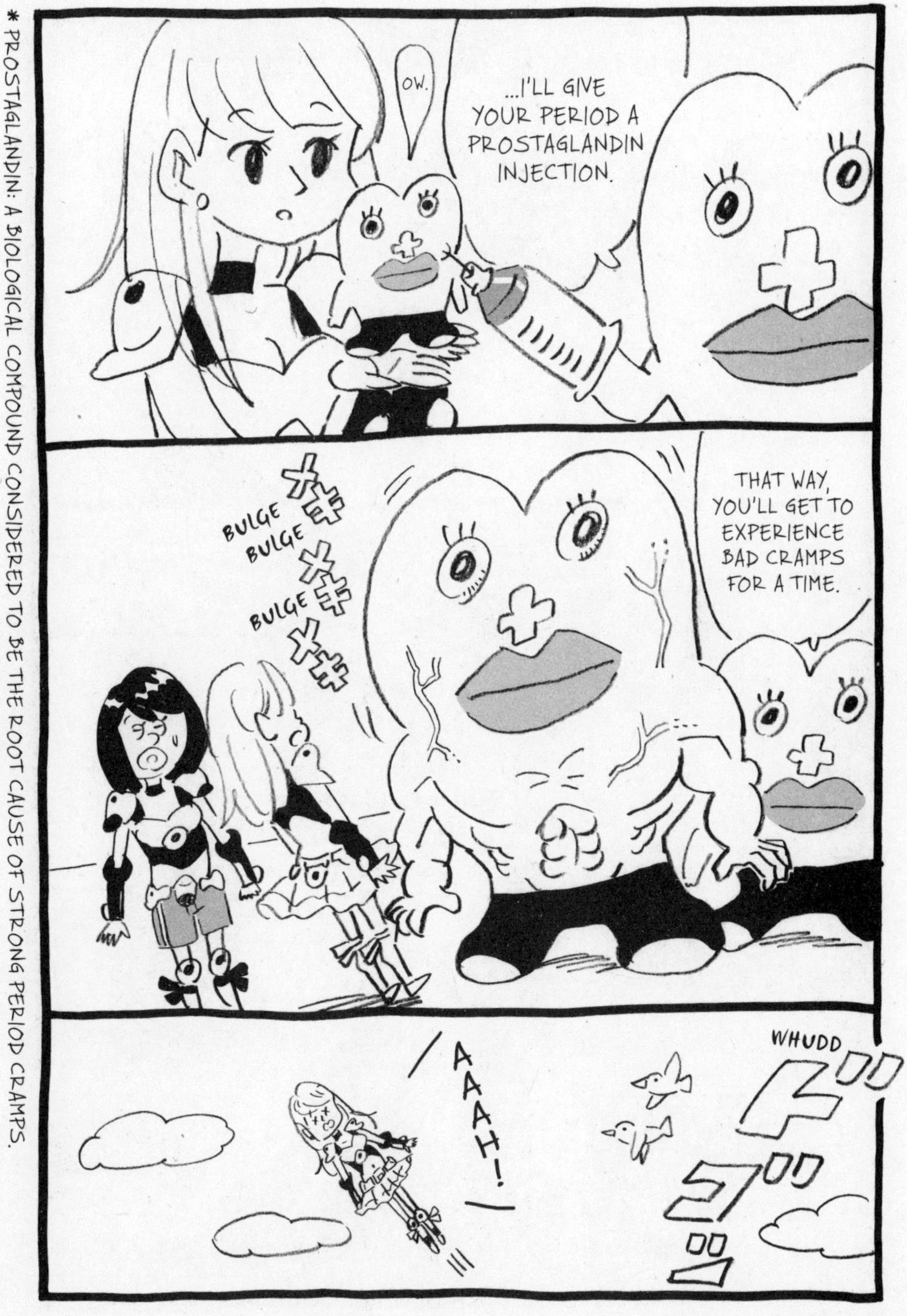
...I'LL GIVE YOUR PERIOD A PROSTAGLANDIN INJECTION.
OW.
THAT WAY, YOU'LL GET TO EXPERIENCE BAD CRAMPS FOR A TIME.
BULGE
BULGE
BULGE
WHUDD
AAAH!

* PROSTAGLANDIN: A BIOLOGICAL COMPOUND CONSIDERED TO BE THE ROOT CAUSE OF STRONG PERIOD CRAMPS.

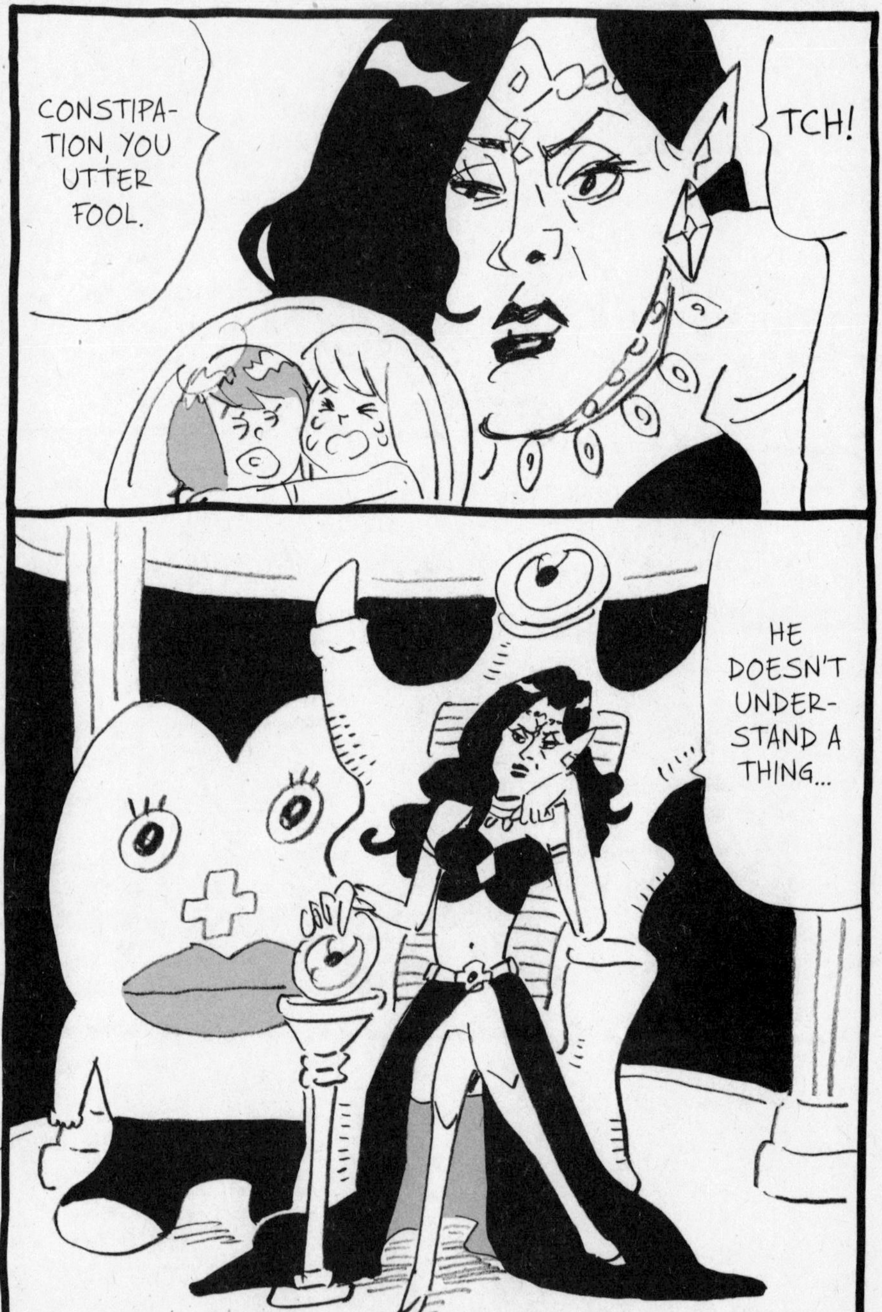
TCH!
CONSTIPATION, YOU UTTER FOOL.
HE DOESN'T UNDERSTAND A THING...

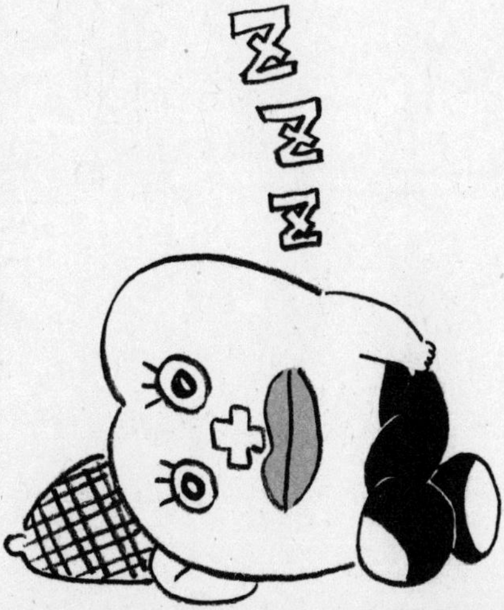
ZZZ

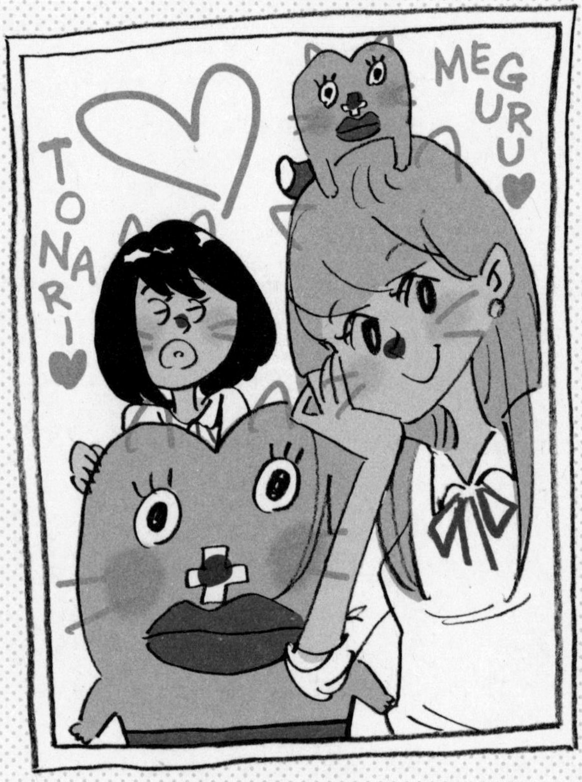
TONARI
MEGURU

TOWN GIRL AND LITTLE MISS P

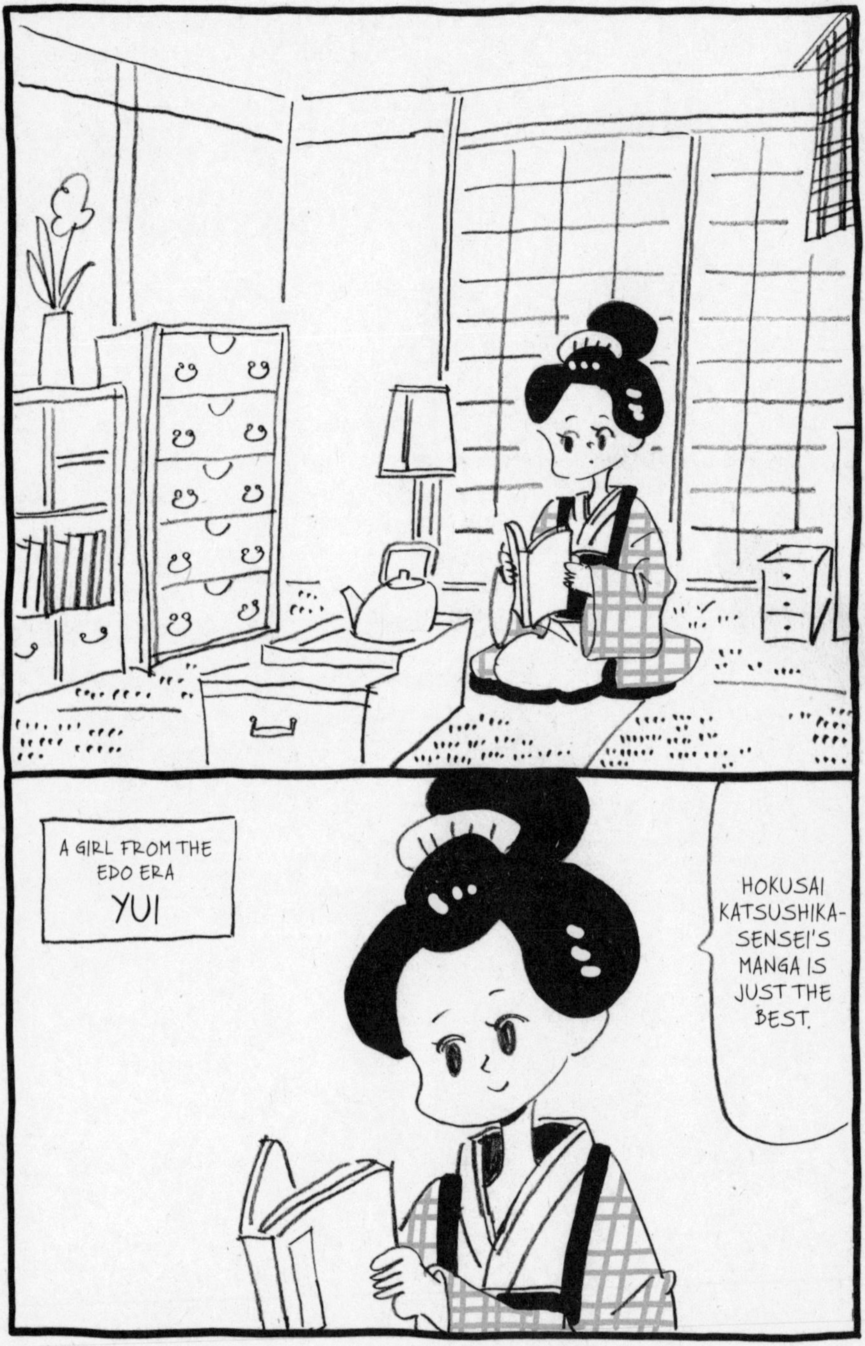
HOKUSAI KATSUSHIKA-SENSEI'S MANGA IS JUST THE BEST.
A GIRL FROM THE EDO ERA
YUI

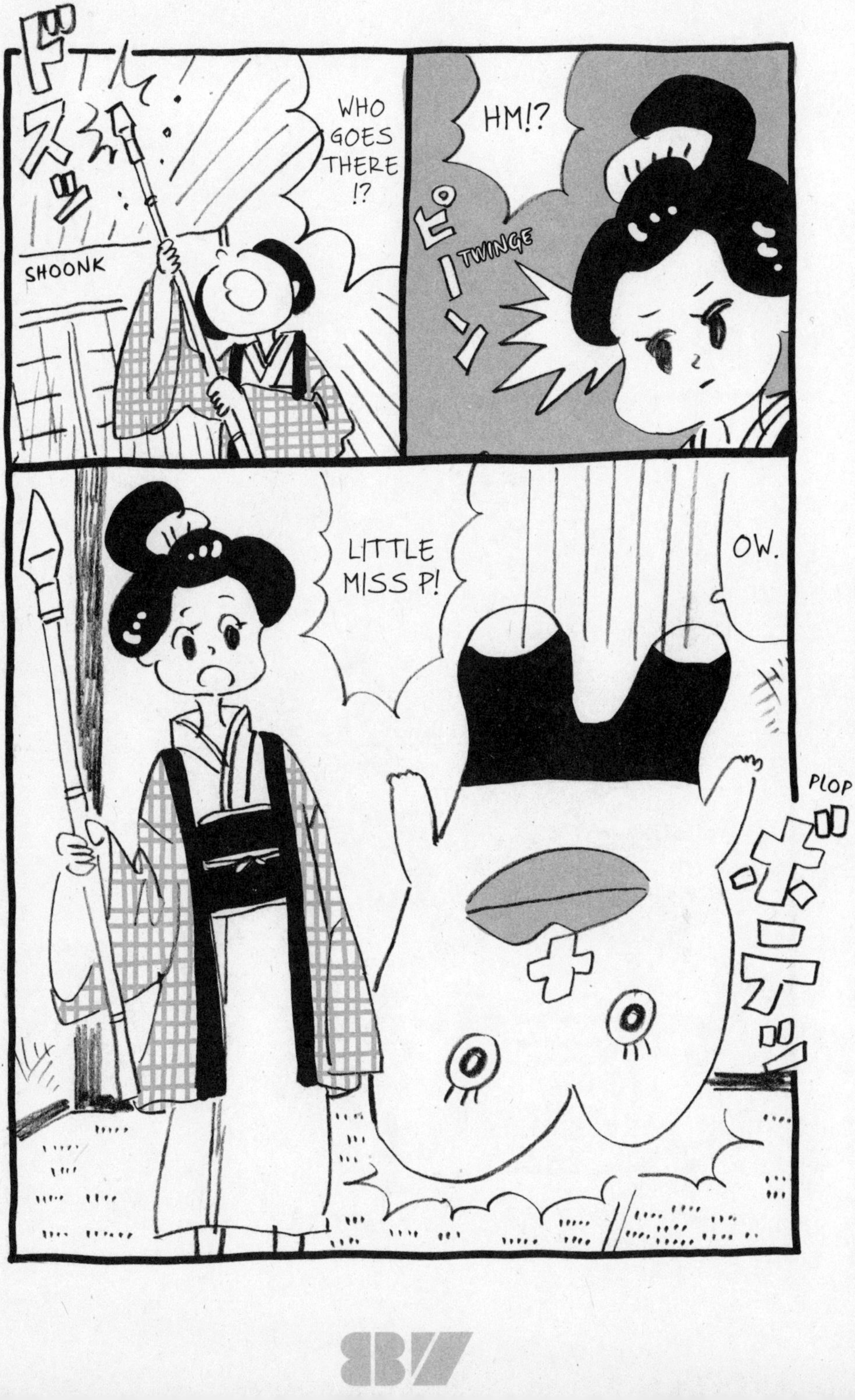
HM!?
ピーン
TWINGE
WHO GOES THERE !?
ドスッ
SHOONK
OW.
ボテッ
PLOP
LITTLE MISS P!

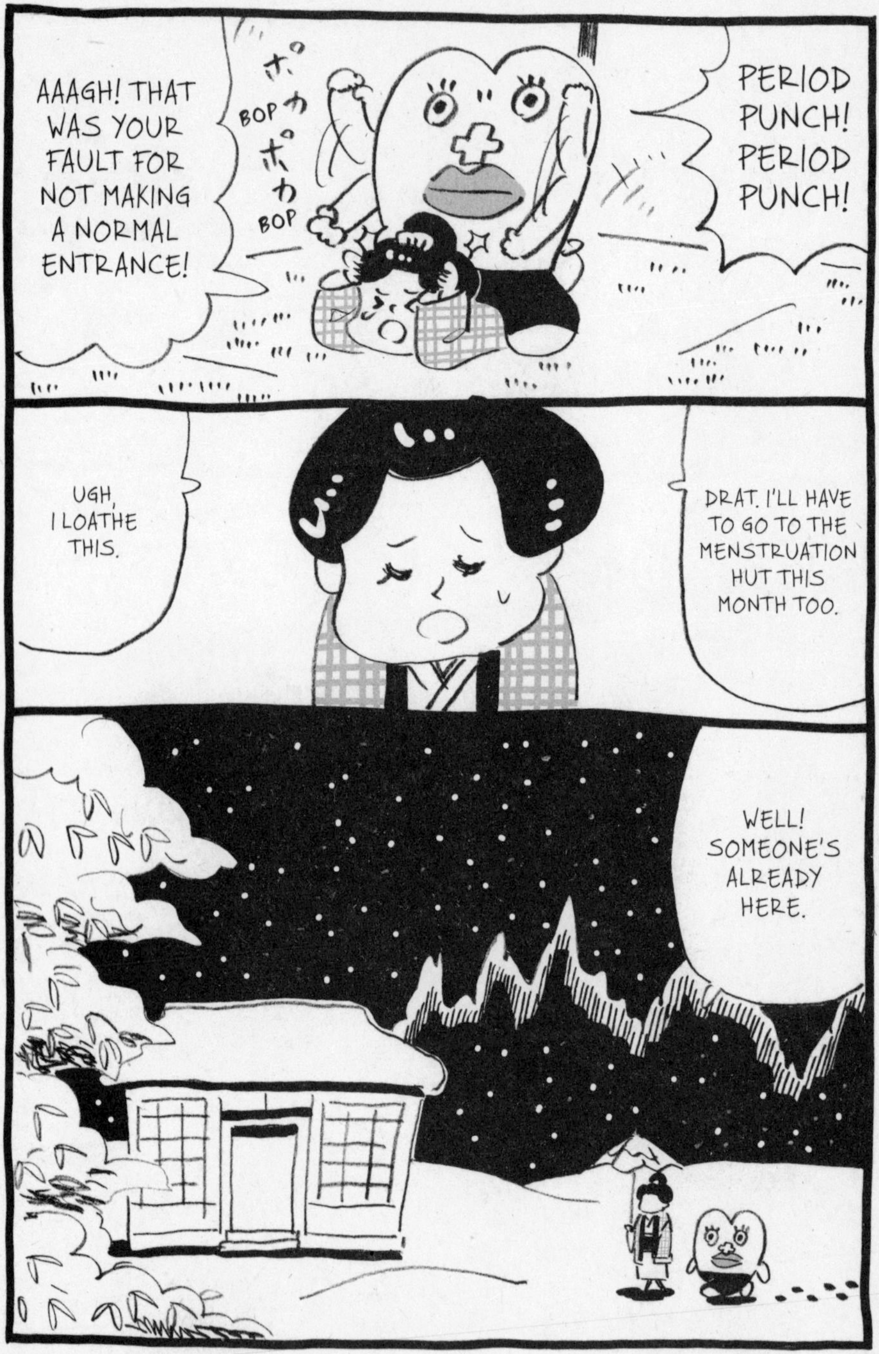
PERIOD PUNCH! PERIOD PUNCH!
ポカ BOP ポカ BOP
AAAGH! THAT WAS YOUR FAULT FOR NOT MAKING A NORMAL ENTRANCE!
DRAT. I'LL HAVE TO GO TO THE MENSTRUATION HUT THIS MONTH TOO.
UGH, I LOATHE THIS.
WELL! SOMEONE'S ALREADY HERE.

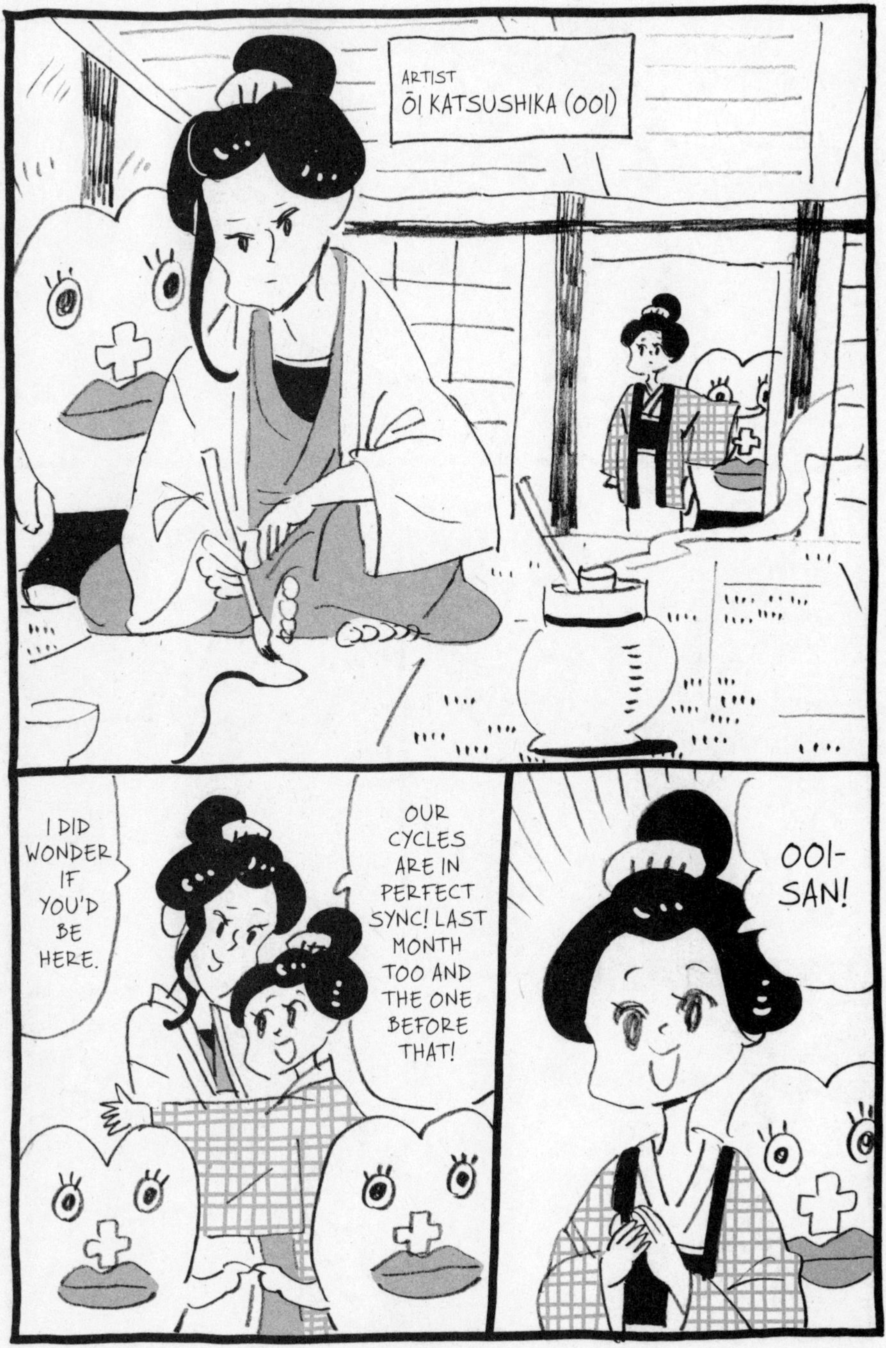
ARTIST
ŌI KATSUSHIKA (OOI)
OOI-SAN!
OUR CYCLES ARE IN PERFECT SYNC! LAST MONTH TOO AND THE ONE BEFORE THAT!
I DID WONDER IF YOU'D BE HERE.

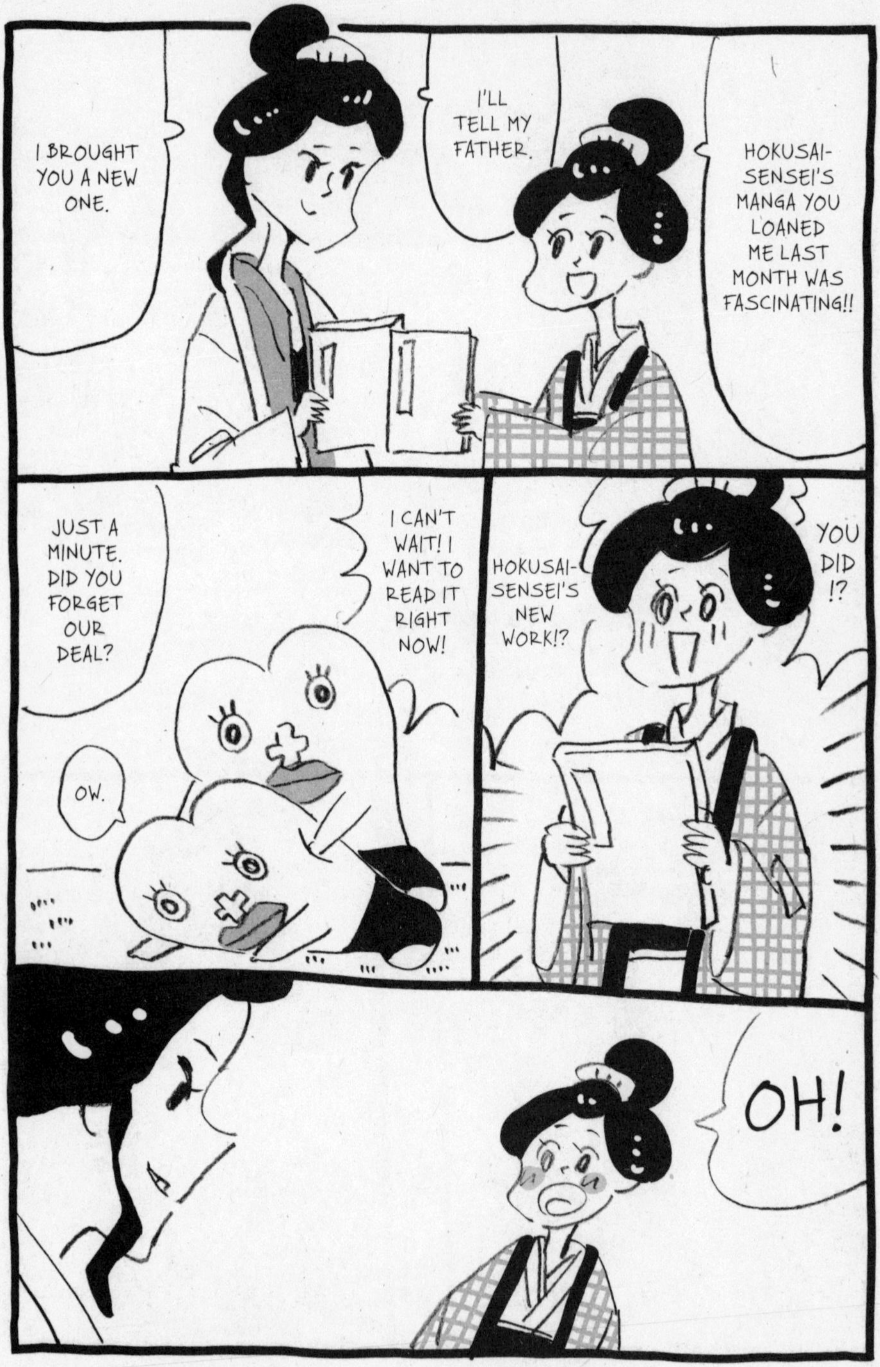
HOKUSAI-SENSEI'S MANGA YOU LOANED ME LAST MONTH WAS FASCINATING!!
I'LL TELL MY FATHER.
I BROUGHT YOU A NEW ONE.
YOU DID!?
HOKUSAI-SENSEI'S NEW WORK!?
I CAN'T WAIT! I WANT TO READ IT RIGHT NOW!
JUST A MINUTE. DID YOU FORGET OUR DEAL?
OW.
OH!

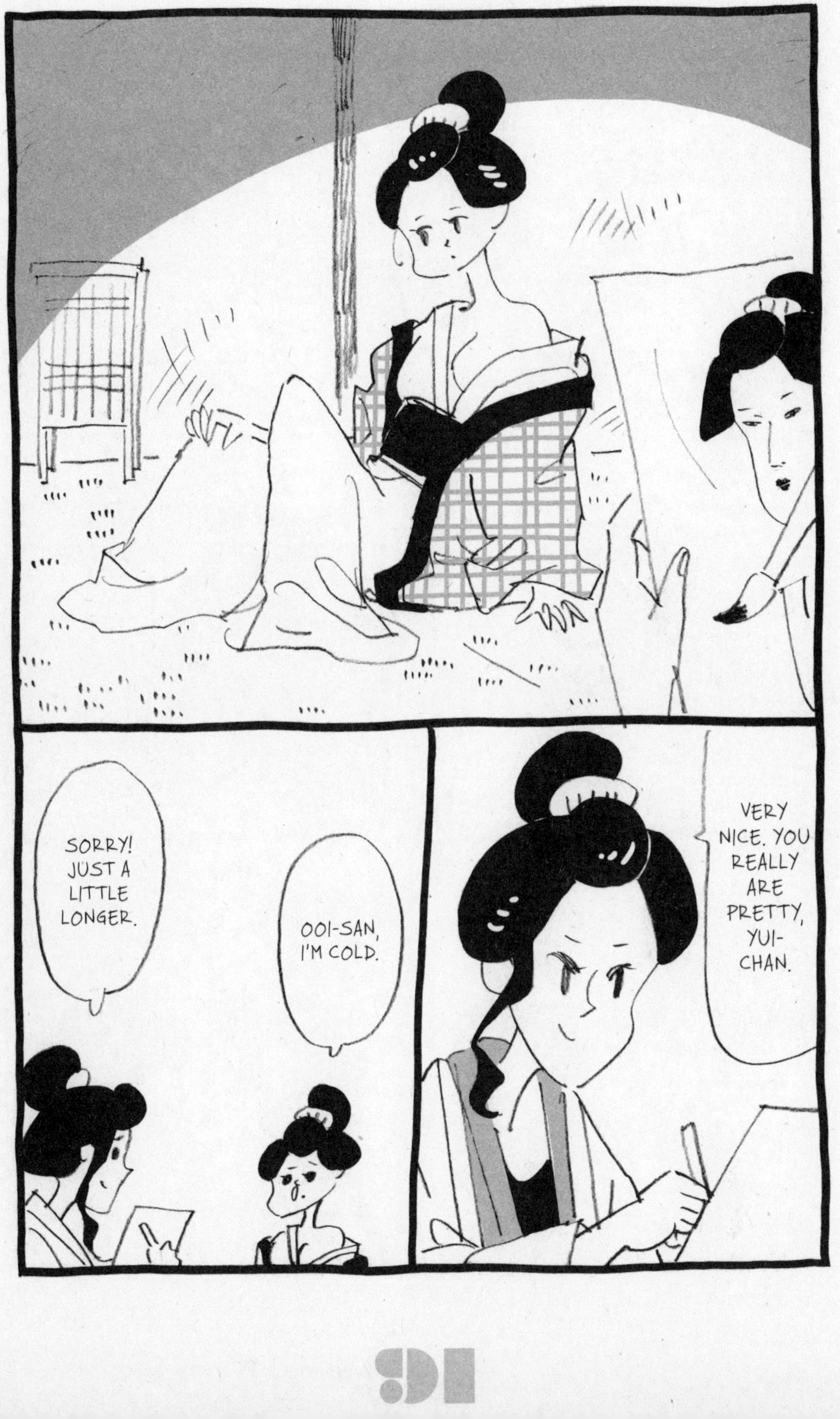
VERY NICE. YOU REALLY ARE PRETTY, YUI-CHAN.
OOI-SAN, I'M COLD.
SORRY! JUST A LITTLE LONGER.

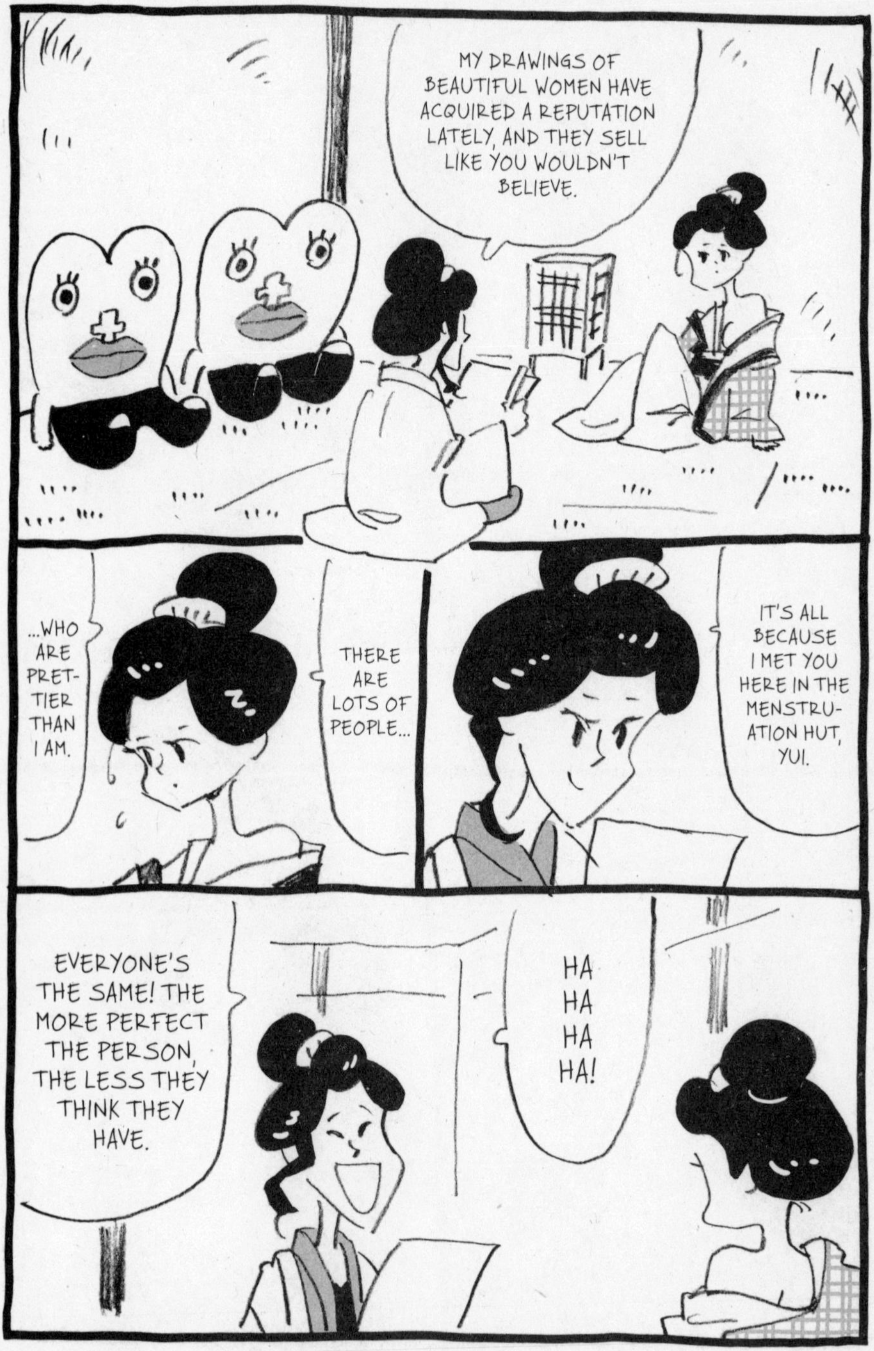
MY DRAWINGS OF BEAUTIFUL WOMEN HAVE ACQUIRED A REPUTATION LATELY, AND THEY SELL LIKE YOU WOULDN'T BELIEVE.
IT'S ALL BECAUSE I MET YOU HERE IN THE MENSTRUATION HUT, YUI.
THERE ARE LOTS OF PEOPLE...
...WHO ARE PRETTIER THAN I AM.
HA HA HA HA!
EVERYONE'S THE SAME! THE MORE PERFECT THE PERSON, THE LESS THEY THINK THEY HAVE.

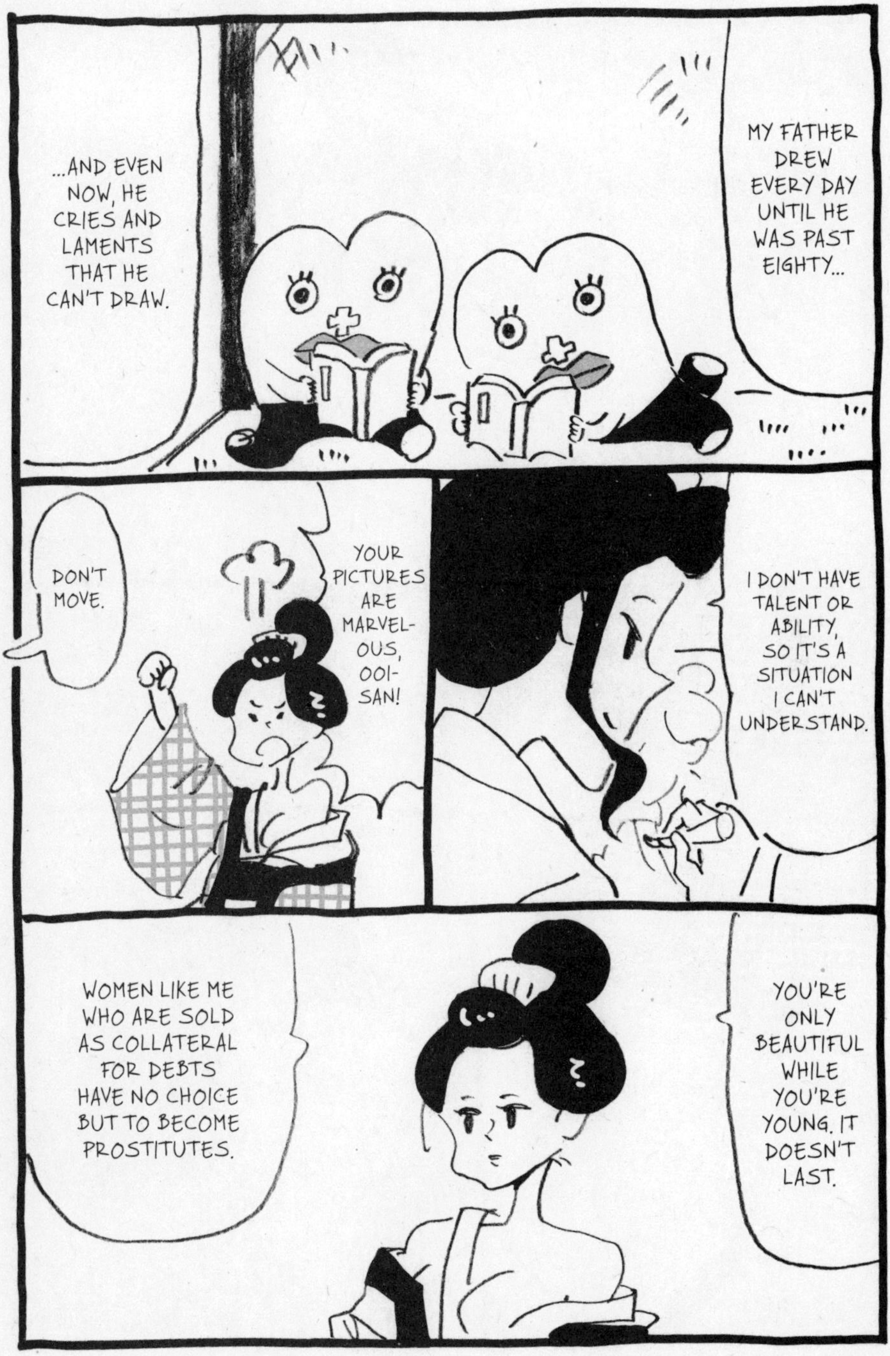
MY FATHER DREW EVERY DAY UNTIL HE WAS PAST EIGHTY...
...AND EVEN NOW, HE CRIES AND LAMENTS THAT HE CAN'T DRAW.
I DON'T HAVE TALENT OR ABILITY, SO IT'S A SITUATION I CAN'T UNDERSTAND.
YOUR PICTURES ARE MARVEL-OUS, OOI-SAN!
DON'T MOVE.
YOU'RE ONLY BEAUTIFUL WHILE YOU'RE YOUNG. IT DOESN'T LAST.
WOMEN LIKE ME WHO ARE SOLD AS COLLATERAL FOR DEBTS HAVE NO CHOICE BUT TO BECOME PROSTITUTES.

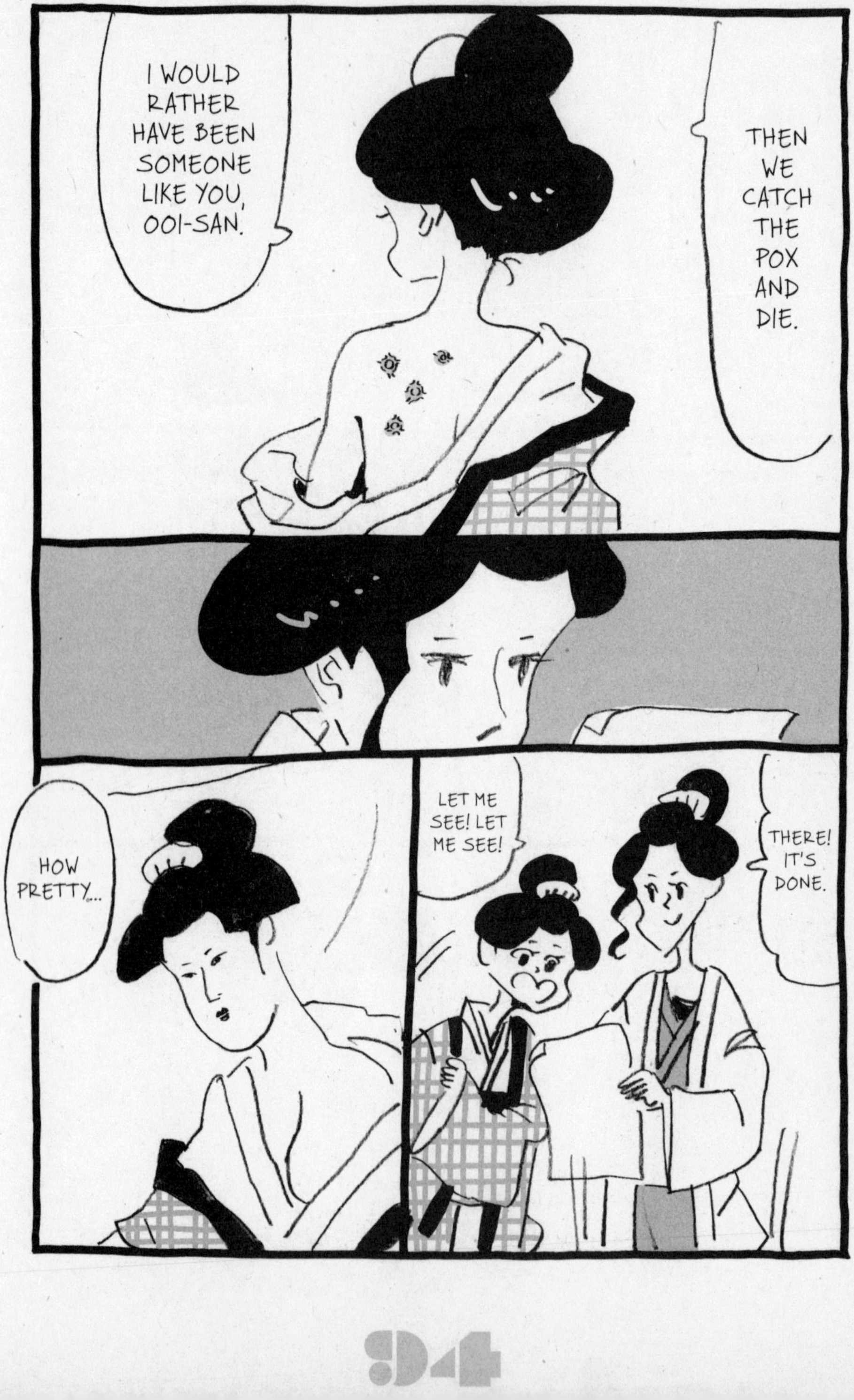
THEN WE CATCH THE POX AND DIE.
I WOULD RATHER HAVE BEEN SOMEONE LIKE YOU, OOI-SAN.
THERE! IT'S DONE.
LET ME SEE! LET ME SEE!
HOW PRETTY...

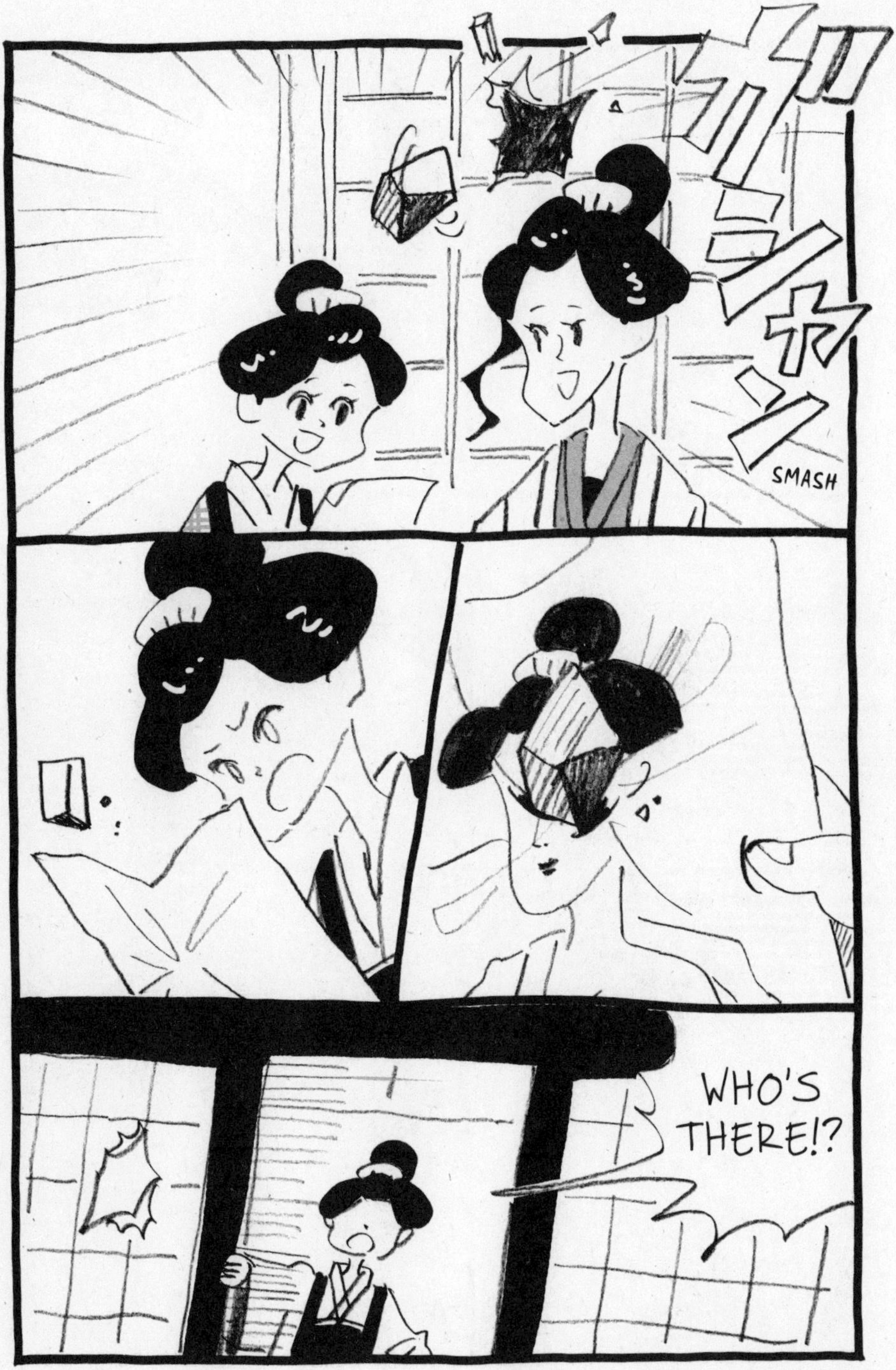
ガシャン
SMASH
WHO'S THERE!?

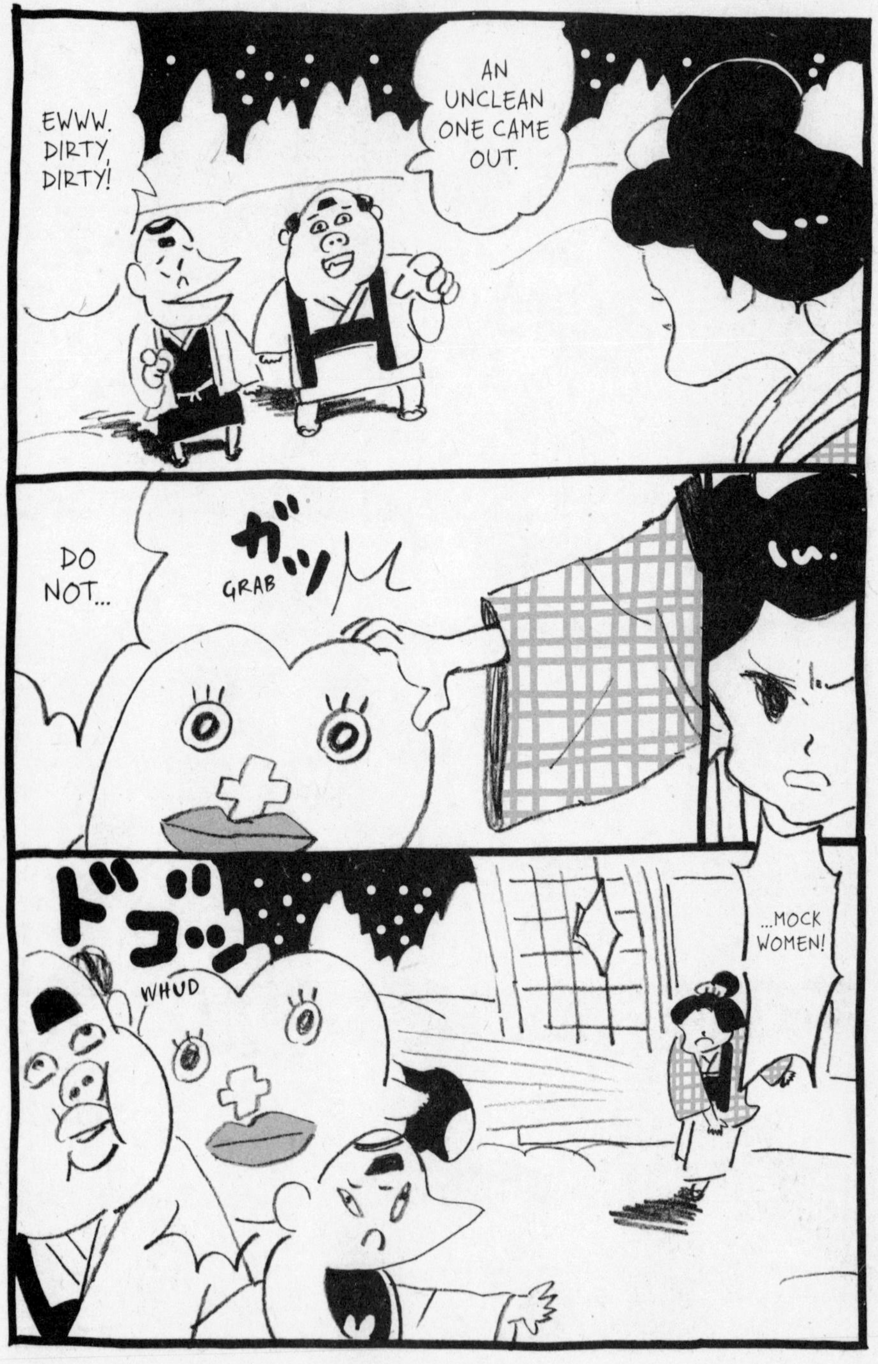
AN UNCLEAN ONE CAME OUT.
EWWW. DIRTY, DIRTY!
ガッ
GRAB
DO NOT...
...MOCK WOMEN!
ドゴッ
WHUD

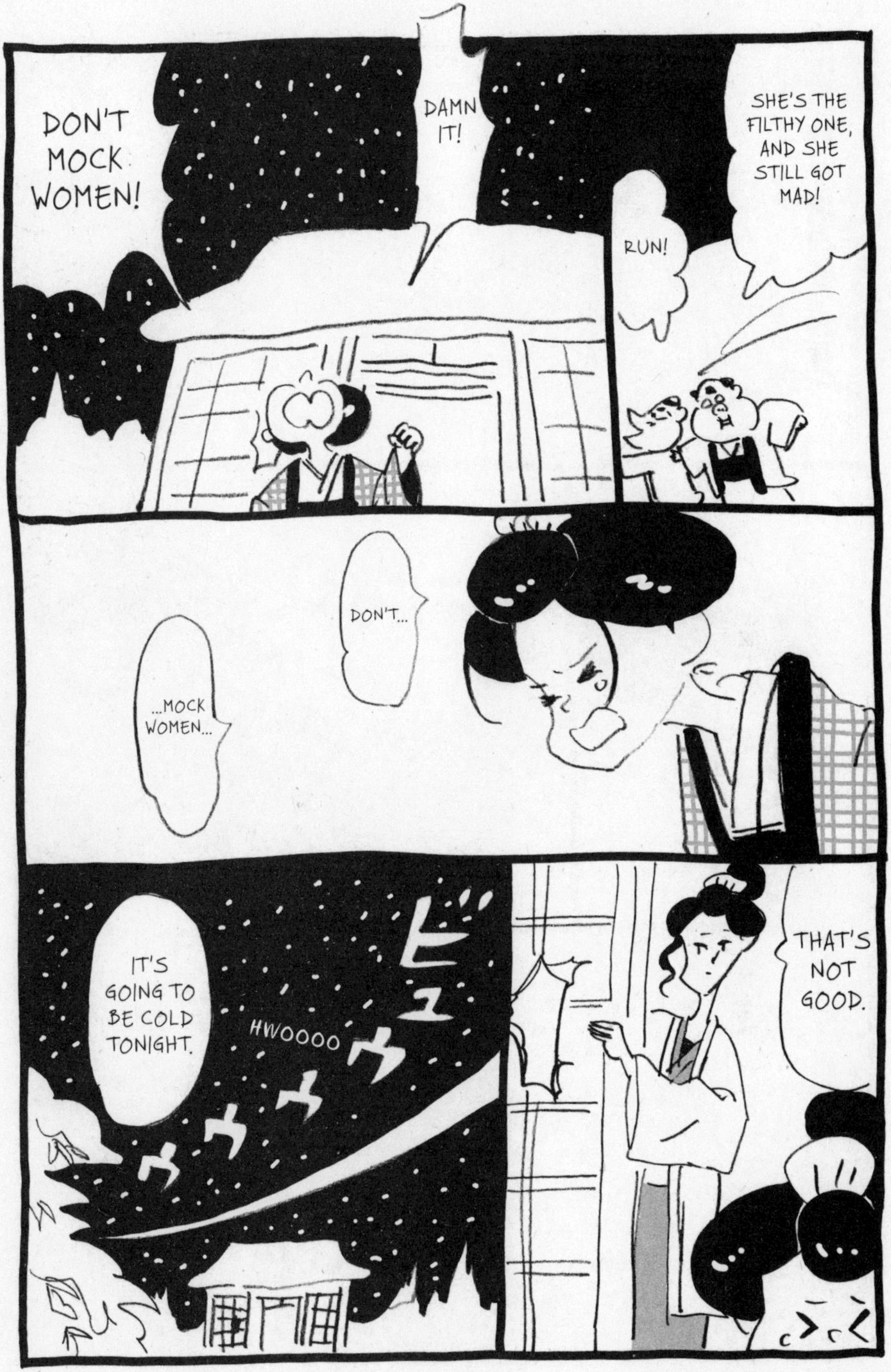
SHE'S THE FILTHY ONE, AND SHE STILL GOT MAD!
RUN!
DAMN IT!
DON'T MOCK WOMEN!
DON'T...
...MOCK WOMEN...
THAT'S NOT GOOD.
ビュウウウウ
HWOOOO
IT'S GOING TO BE COLD TONIGHT.

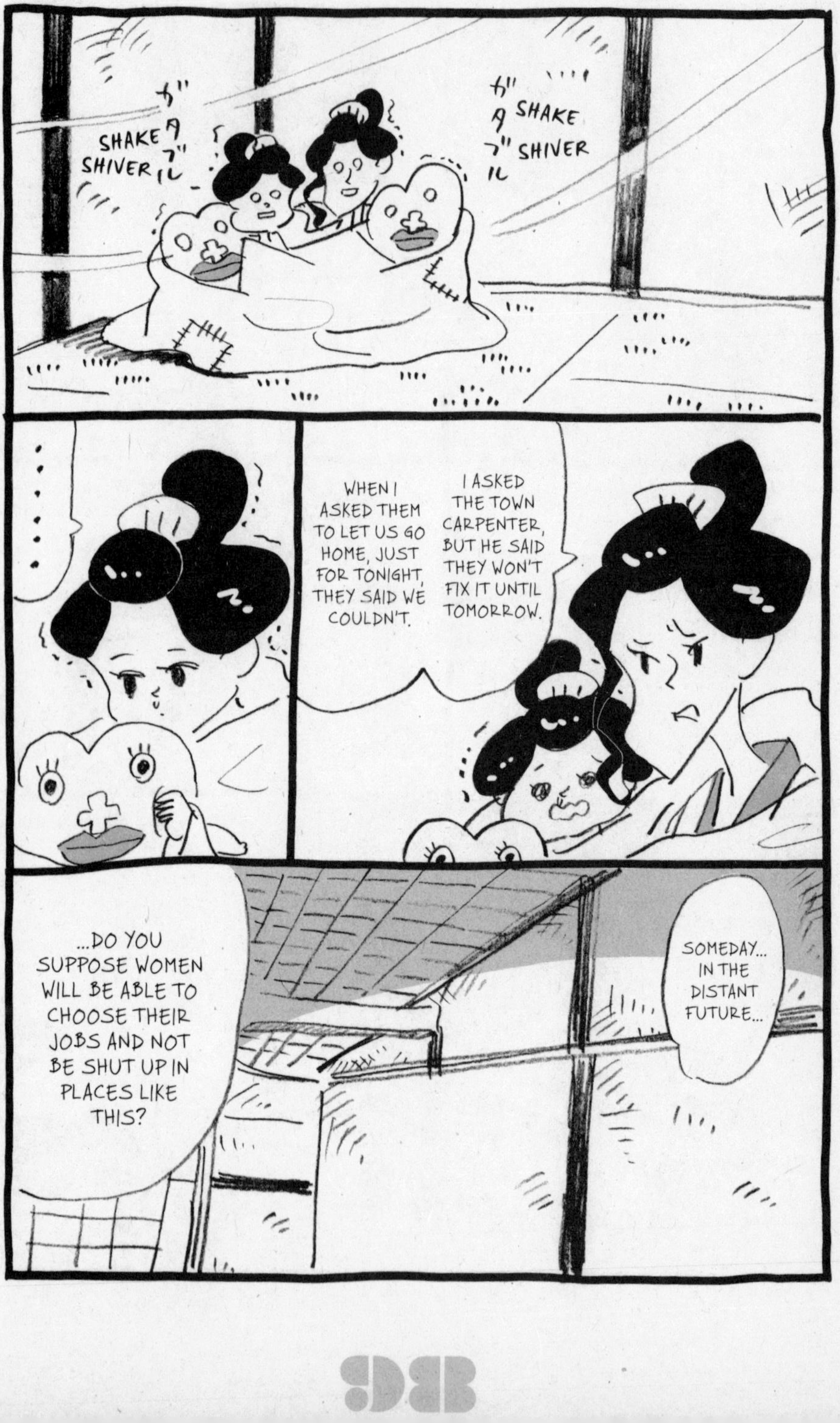
ガタ SHAKE
ブル SHIVER
ガタ SHAKE
ブル SHIVER
I ASKED THE TOWN CARPENTER, BUT HE SAID THEY WON'T FIX IT UNTIL TOMORROW.
WHEN I ASKED THEM TO LET US GO HOME, JUST FOR TONIGHT, THEY SAID WE COULDN'T.
......
SOMEDAY... IN THE DISTANT FUTURE...
...DO YOU SUPPOSE WOMEN WILL BE ABLE TO CHOOSE THEIR JOBS AND NOT BE SHUT UP IN PLACES LIKE THIS?

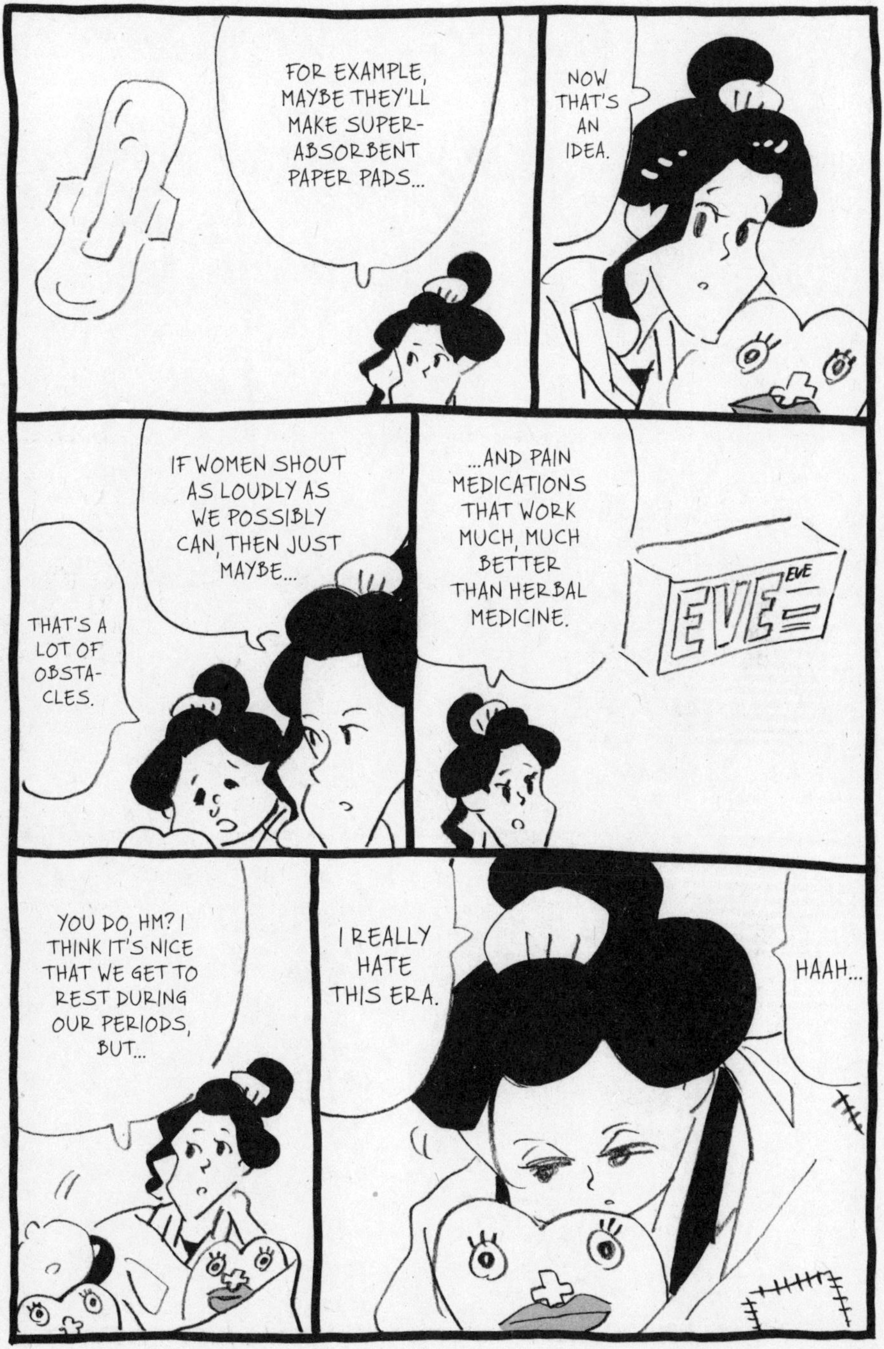
NOW THAT'S AN IDEA.
FOR EXAMPLE, MAYBE THEY'LL MAKE SUPER-ABSORBENT PAPER PADS...
...AND PAIN MEDICATIONS THAT WORK MUCH, MUCH BETTER THAN HERBAL MEDICINE.
EVE
EVE
IF WOMEN SHOUT AS LOUDLY AS WE POSSIBLY CAN, THEN JUST MAYBE...
THAT'S A LOT OF OBSTA-CLES.
HAAH...
I REALLY HATE THIS ERA.
YOU DO, HM? I THINK IT'S NICE THAT WE GET TO REST DURING OUR PERIODS, BUT...

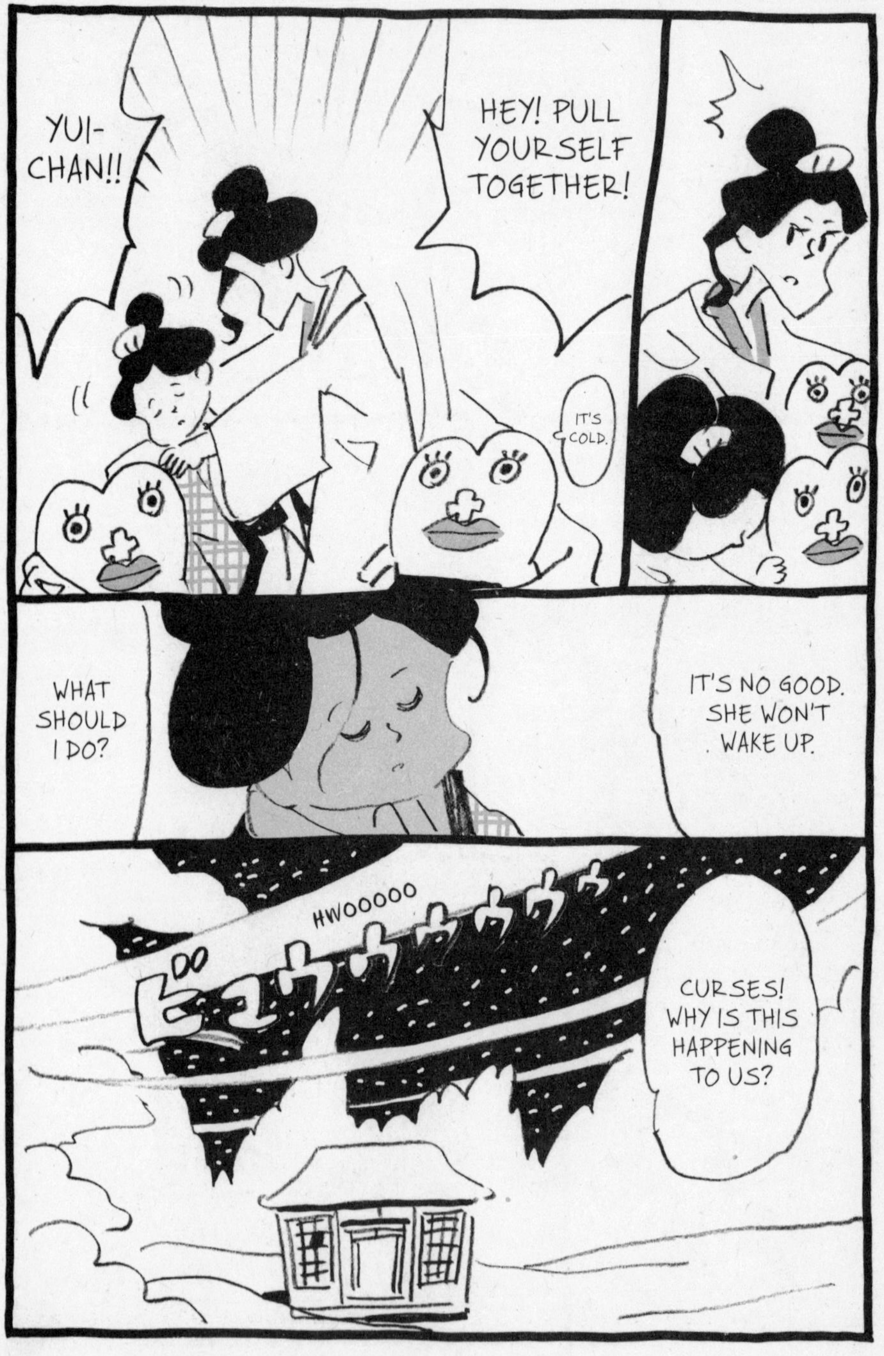
HEY! PULL YOURSELF TOGETHER!
YUI-CHAN!!
IT'S COLD.
IT'S NO GOOD. SHE WON'T WAKE UP.
WHAT SHOULD I DO?
CURSES! WHY IS THIS HAPPENING TO US?
HWOOOOO
DO

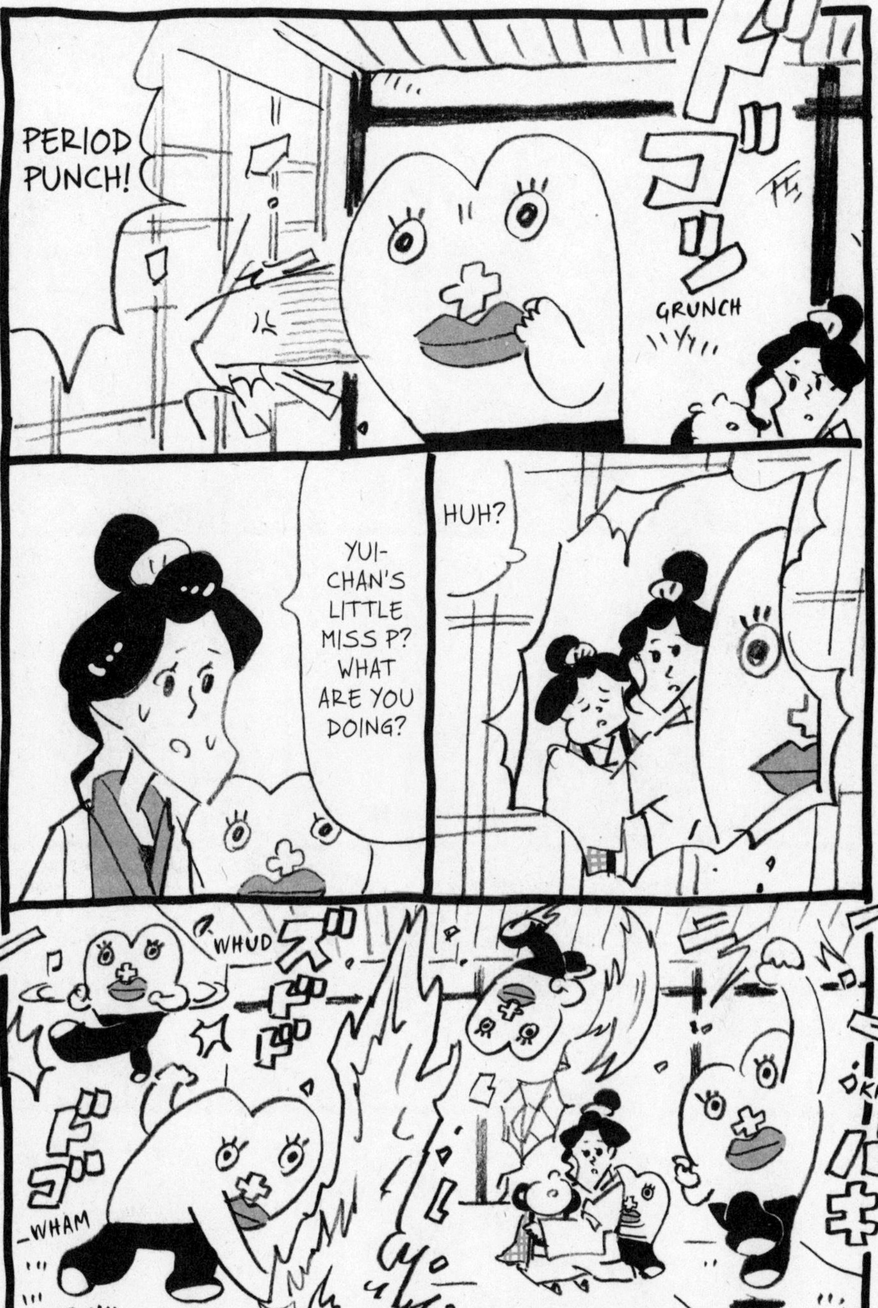
GRUNCH
PERIOD PUNCH!
HUH?
YUI-CHAN'S LITTLE MISS P? WHAT ARE YOU DOING?
KRAKK
WHUD
WHAM

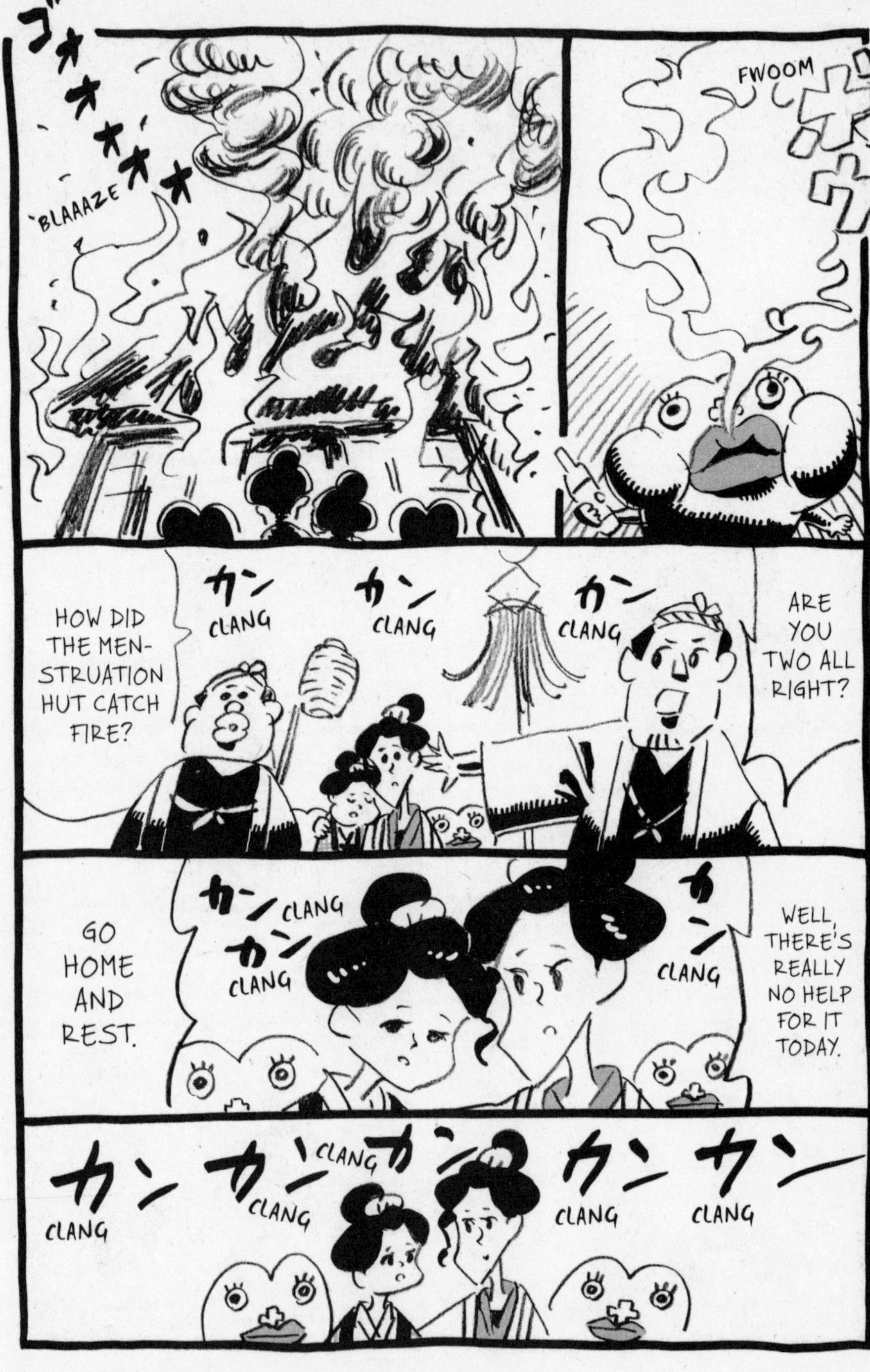
FWOOM
ボオウ
ゴオオオオオ
BLAAAZE
ARE YOU TWO ALL RIGHT?
カン CLANG
カン CLANG
カン CLANG
HOW DID THE MEN-STRUATION HUT CATCH FIRE?
WELL, THERE'S REALLY NO HELP FOR IT TODAY.
カン CLANG
カン CLANG
カン CLANG
GO HOME AND REST.
カン CLANG
カン CLANG
カン CLANG
カン CLANG
カン CLANG

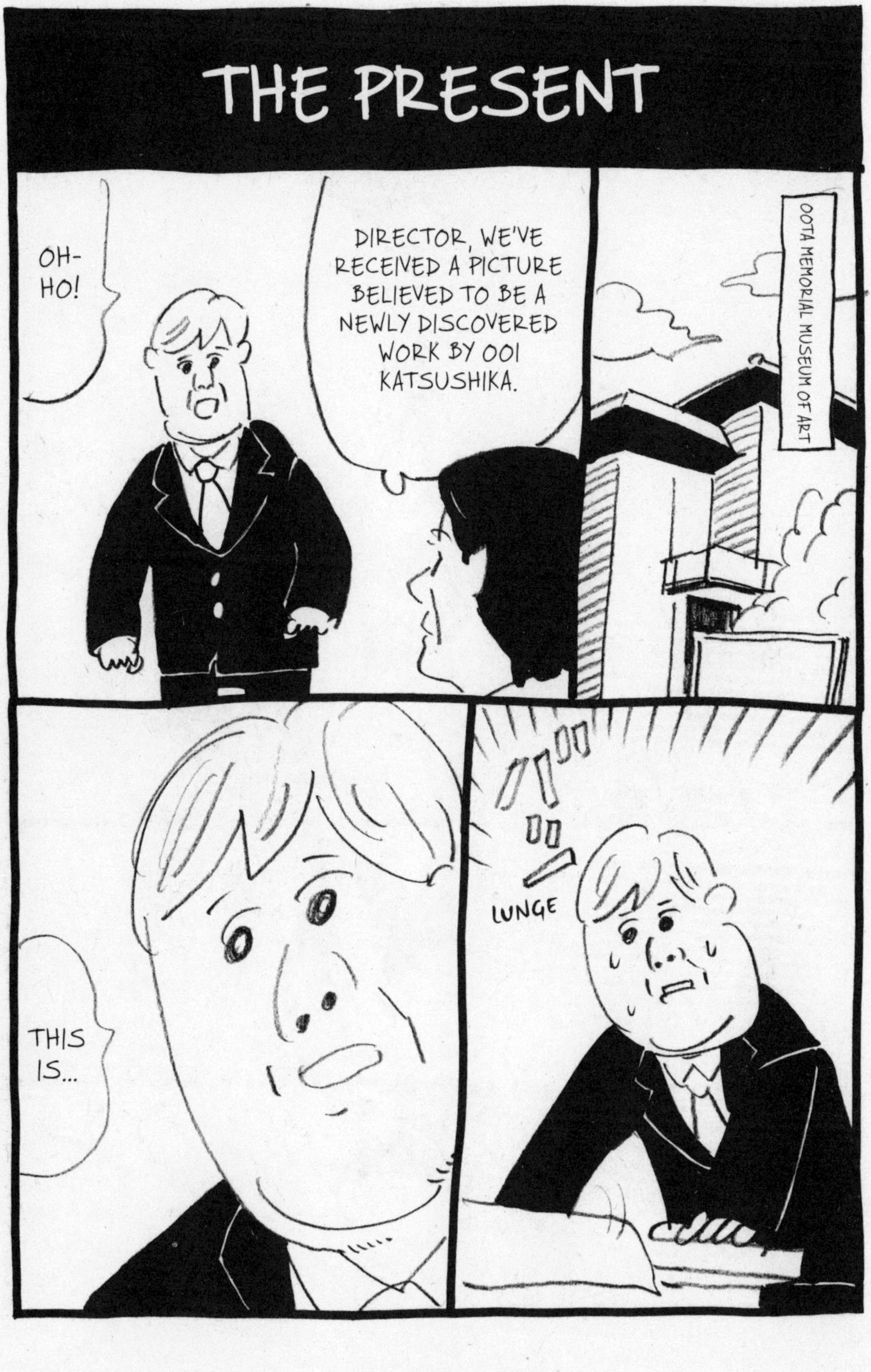
THE PRESENT
OOTA MEMORIAL MUSEUM OF ART
DIRECTOR, WE'VE RECEIVED A PICTURE BELIEVED TO BE A NEWLY DISCOVERED WORK BY OOI KATSUSHIKA.
OH-HO!
LUNGE
THIS IS...

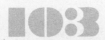

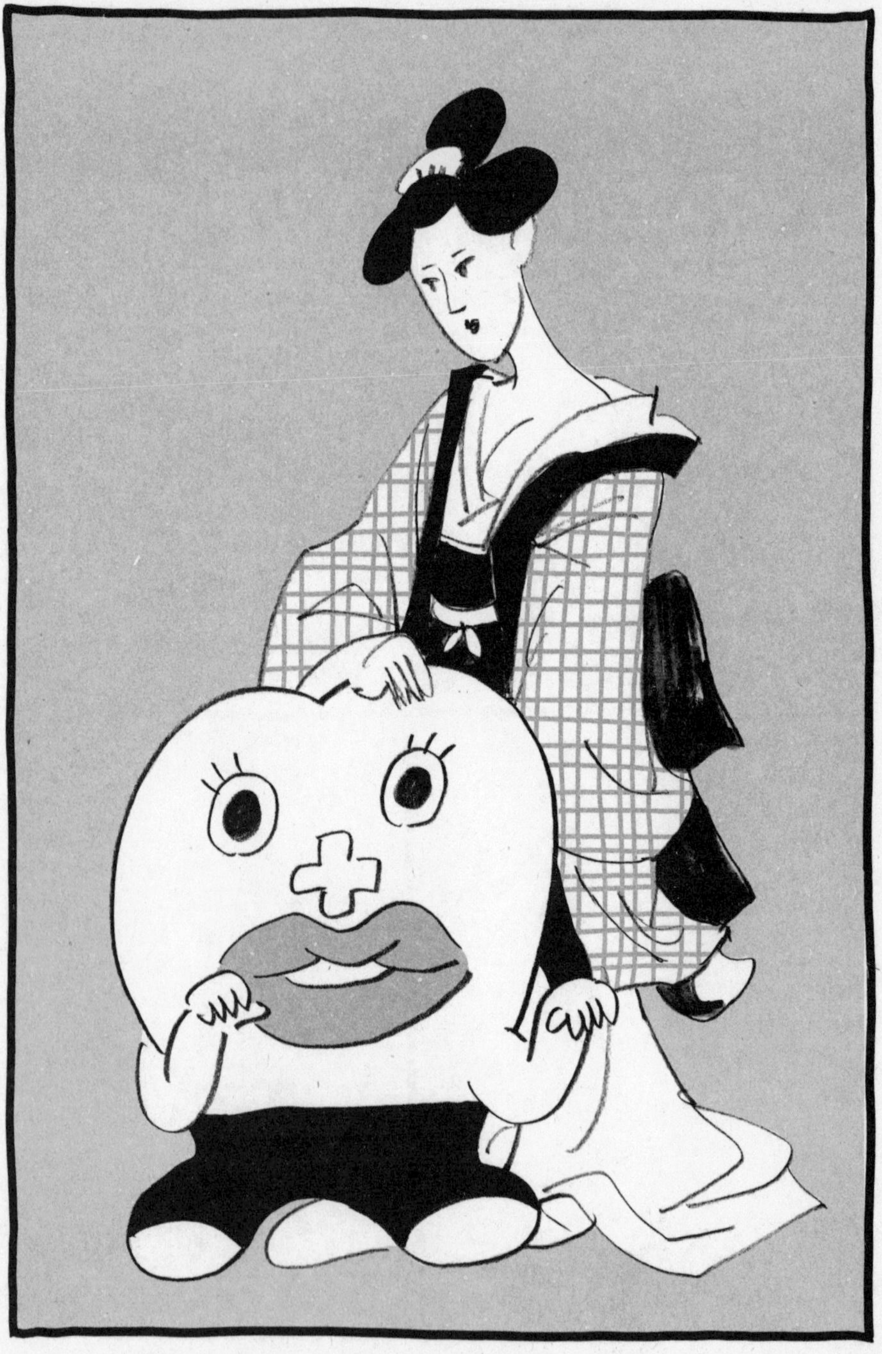

HIGH SCHOOL GIRL
AND LITTLE MISS P

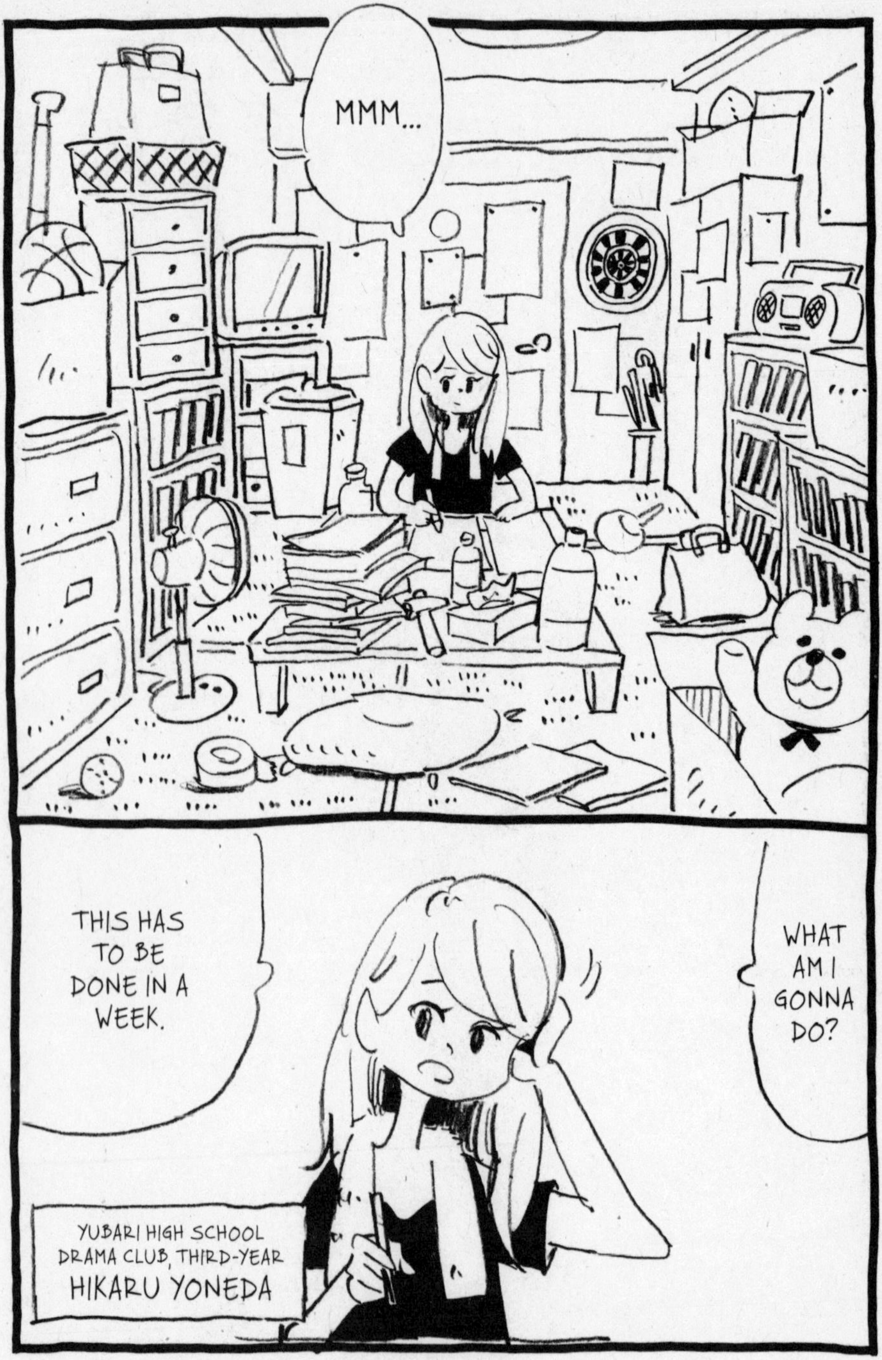
MMM...
WHAT AM I GONNA DO?
THIS HAS TO BE DONE IN A WEEK.
YUBARI HIGH SCHOOL DRAMA CLUB, THIRD-YEAR
HIKARU YONEDA

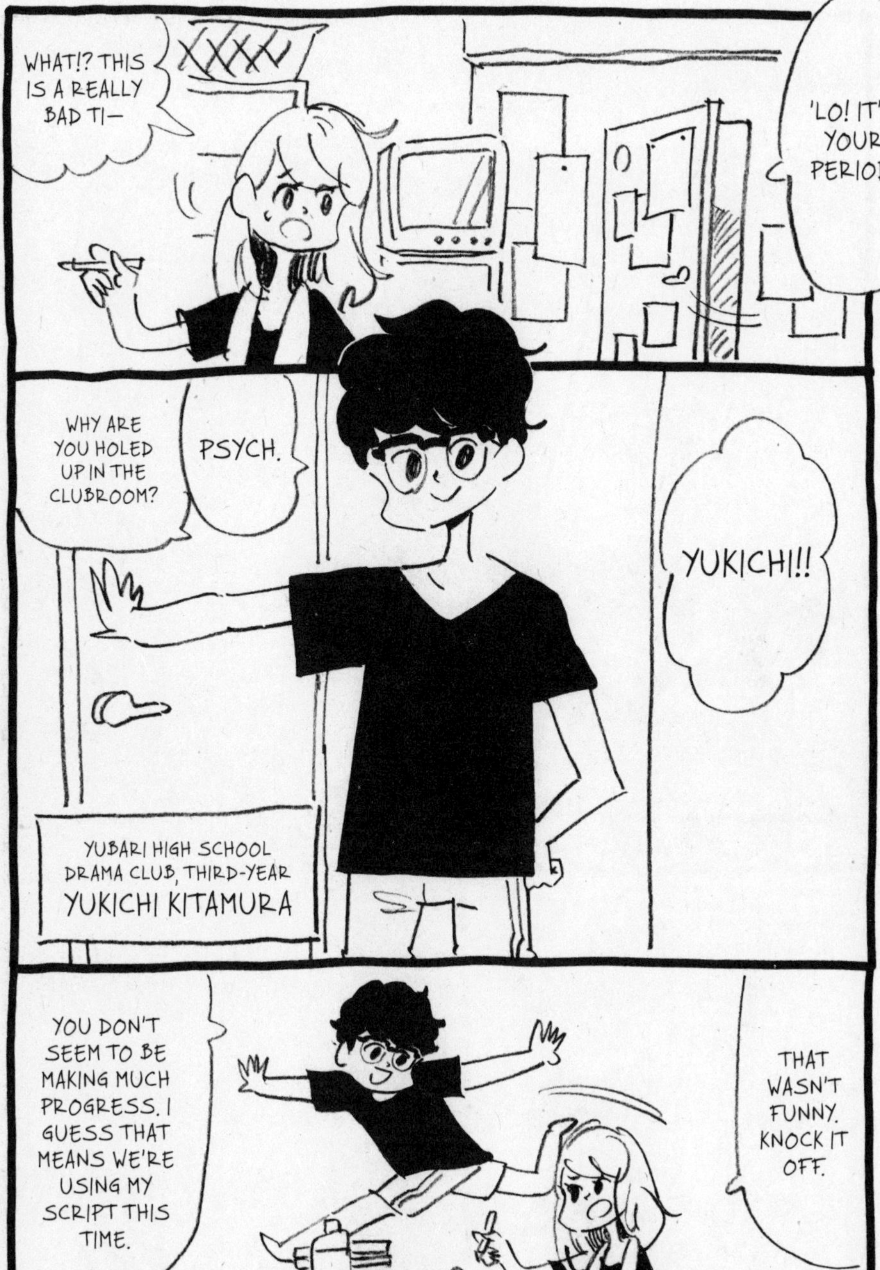
'LO! IT'S YOUR PERIOD!
WHAT!? THIS IS A REALLY BAD TI—
YUKICHI!!!
PSYCH.
WHY ARE YOU HOLED UP IN THE CLUBROOM?
YUBARI HIGH SCHOOL DRAMA CLUB, THIRD-YEAR YUKICHI KITAMURA
THAT WASN'T FUNNY. KNOCK IT OFF.
YOU DON'T SEEM TO BE MAKING MUCH PROGRESS. I GUESS THAT MEANS WE'RE USING MY SCRIPT THIS TIME.

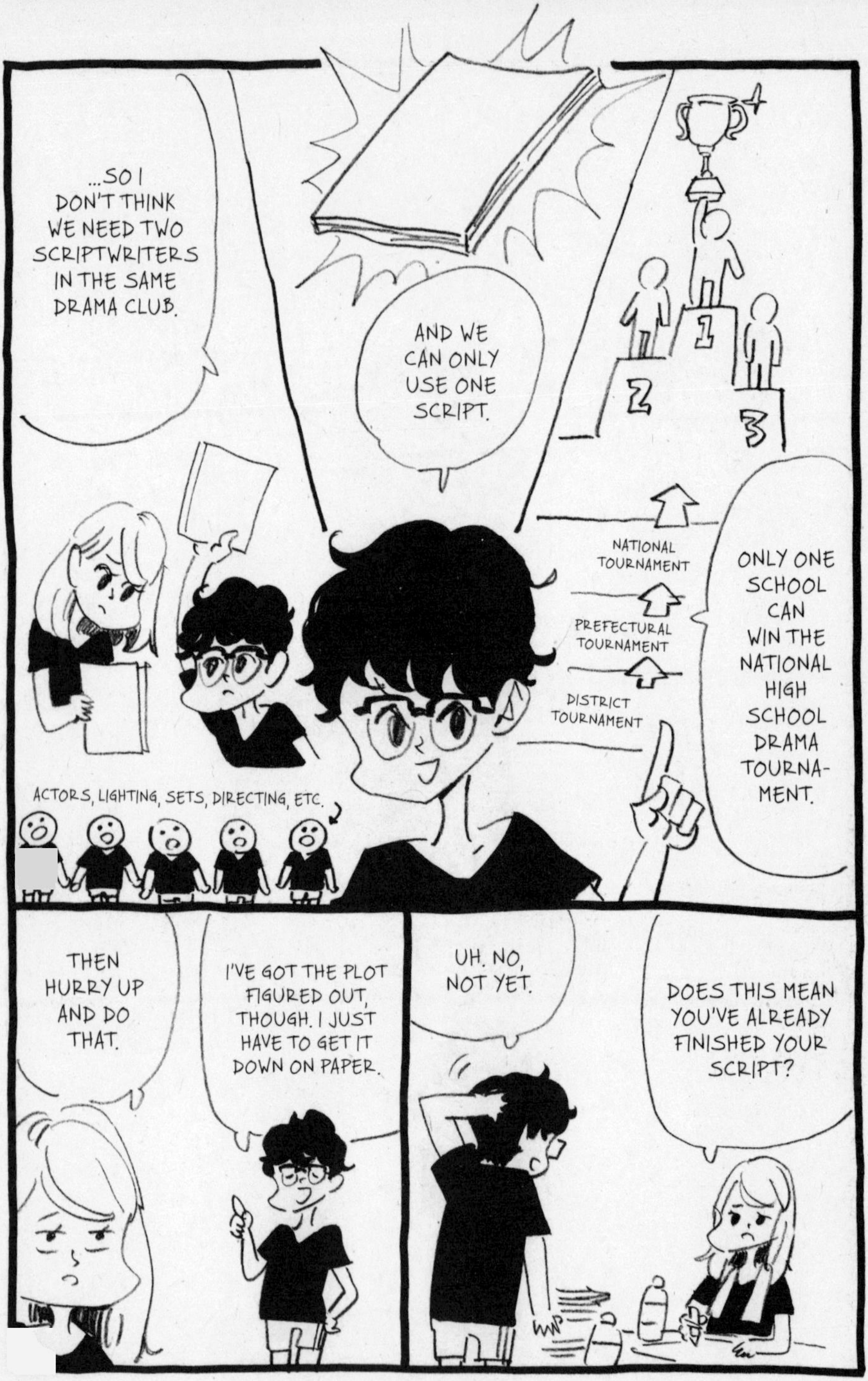
ONLY ONE SCHOOL CAN WIN THE NATIONAL HIGH SCHOOL DRAMA TOURNA-MENT.
NATIONAL TOURNAMENT
PREFECTURAL TOURNAMENT
DISTRICT TOURNAMENT
1
2
3
AND WE CAN ONLY USE ONE SCRIPT.
...SO I DON'T THINK WE NEED TWO SCRIPTWRITERS IN THE SAME DRAMA CLUB.
ACTORS, LIGHTING, SETS, DIRECTING, ETC.
DOES THIS MEAN YOU'VE ALREADY FINISHED YOUR SCRIPT?
UH. NO, NOT YET.
I'VE GOT THE PLOT FIGURED OUT, THOUGH. I JUST HAVE TO GET IT DOWN ON PAPER.
THEN HURRY UP AND DO THAT.

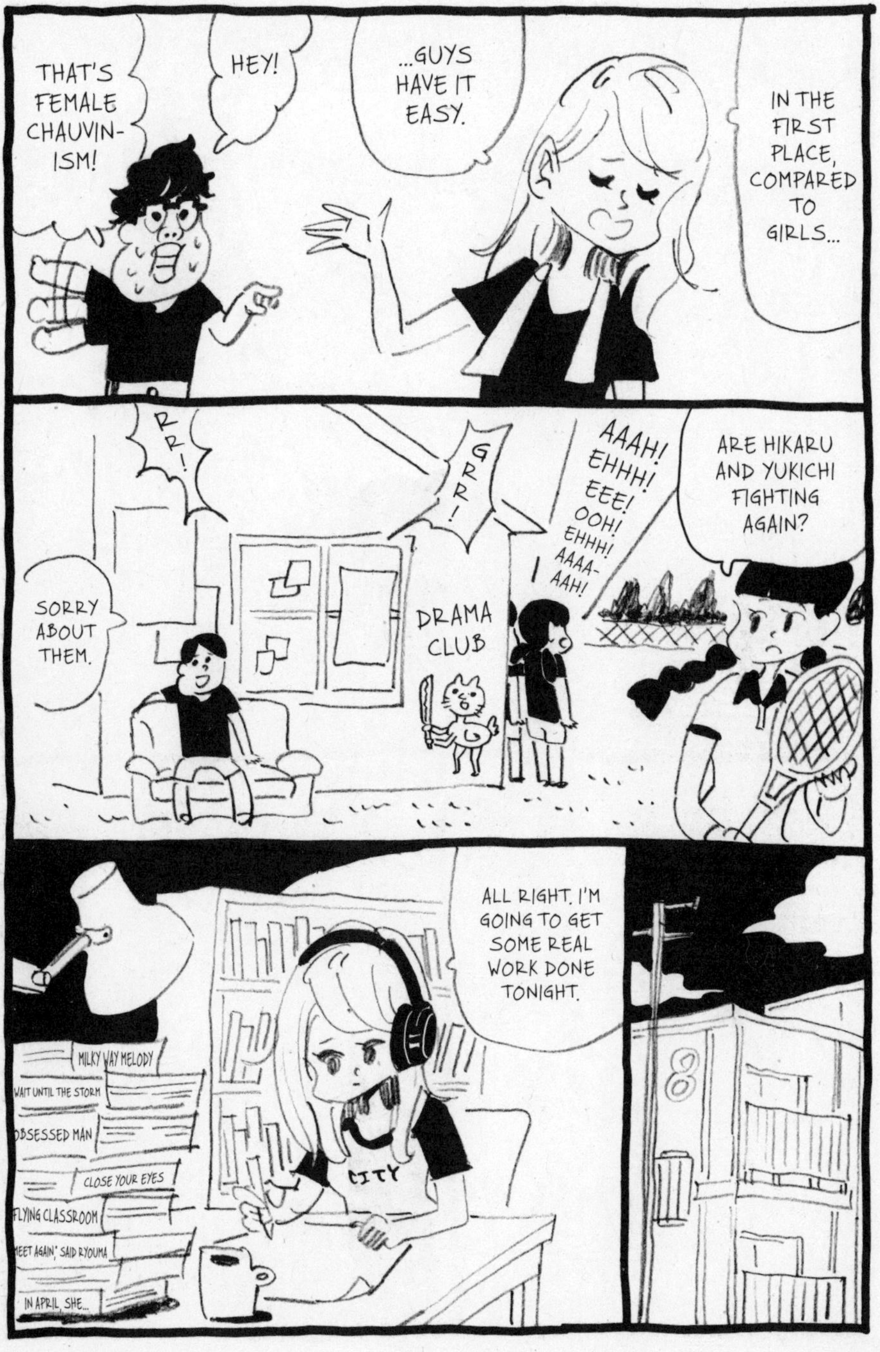
IN THE FIRST PLACE, COMPARED TO GIRLS...
...GUYS HAVE IT EASY.
HEY!
THAT'S FEMALE CHAUVIN-ISM!
ARE HIKARU AND YUKICHI FIGHTING AGAIN?
AAAH! EHHH! EEE! OOH! EHHH! AAAA-AAH!
GRR!
RR!
DRAMA CLUB
SORRY ABOUT THEM.
8
ALL RIGHT. I'M GOING TO GET SOME REAL WORK DONE TONIGHT.
CITY
MILKY WAY MELODY
WAIT UNTIL THE STORM
OBSESSED MAN
CLOSE YOUR EYES
FLYING CLASSROOM
MEET AGAIN," SAID RYOUMA
IN APRIL, SHE...

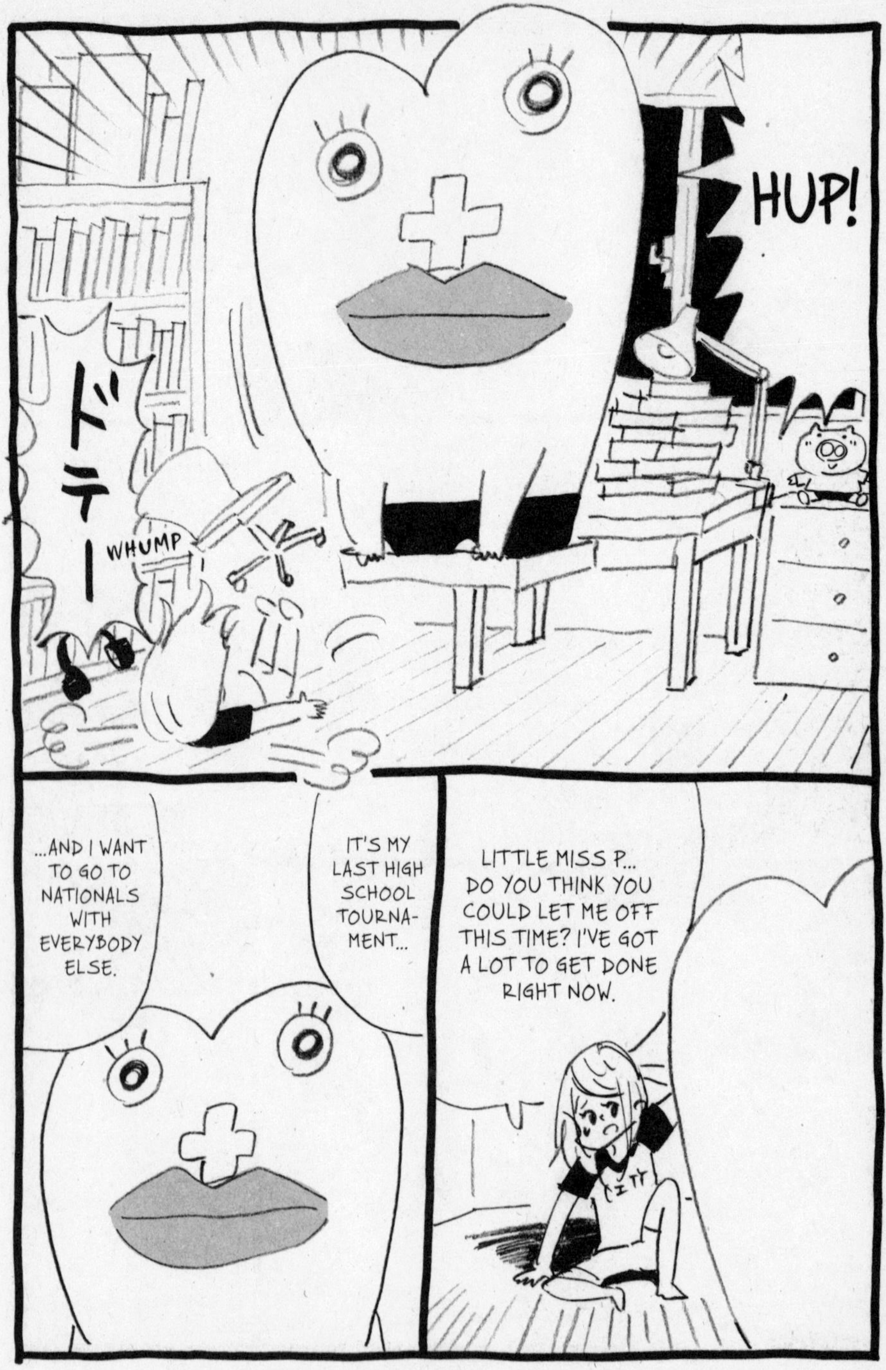
HUP!
ドテー
WHUMP
LITTLE MISS P... DO YOU THINK YOU COULD LET ME OFF THIS TIME? I'VE GOT A LOT TO GET DONE RIGHT NOW.
IT'S MY LAST HIGH SCHOOL TOURNA-MENT...
...AND I WANT TO GO TO NATIONALS WITH EVERYBODY ELSE.

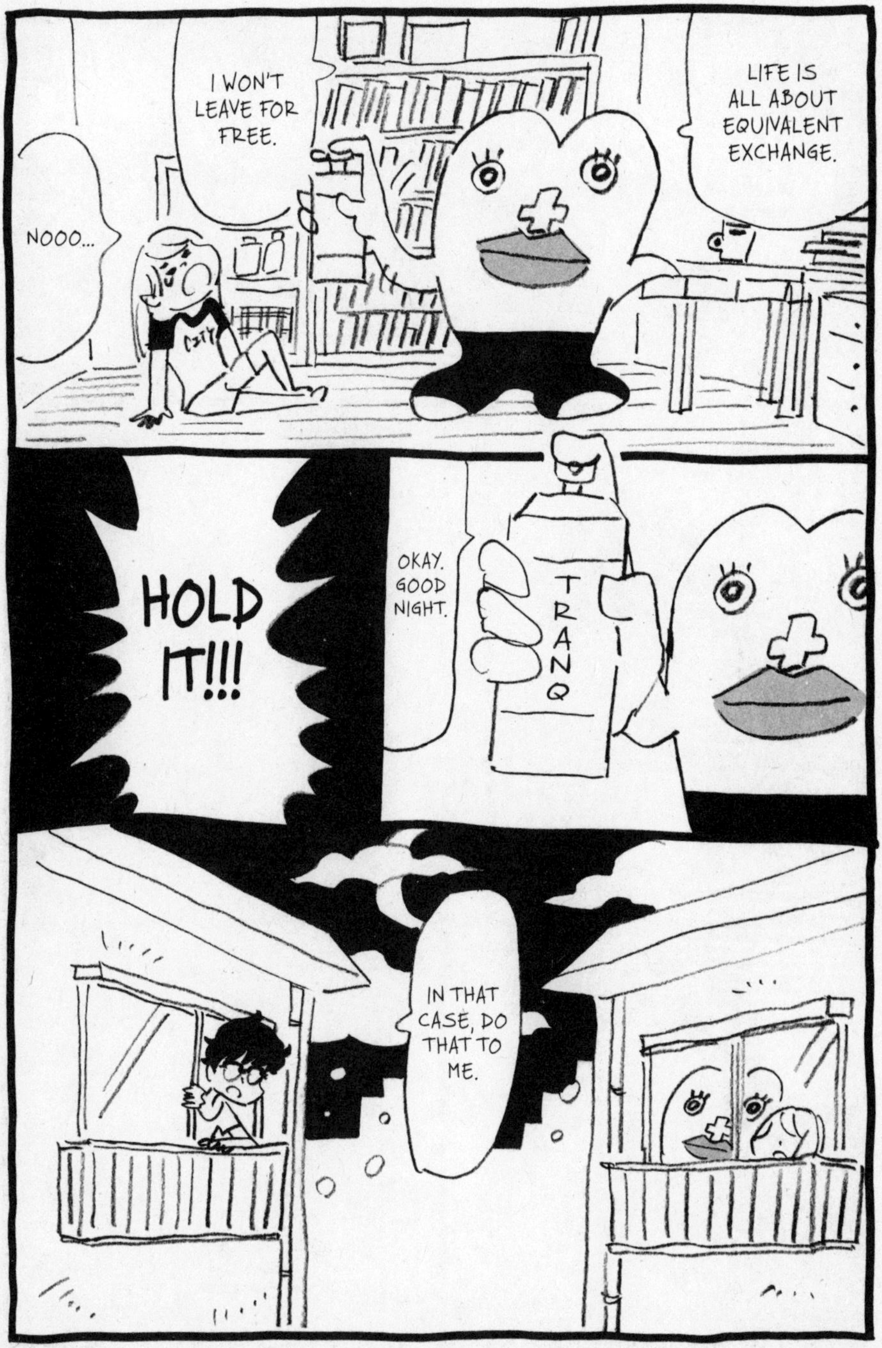
LIFE IS ALL ABOUT EQUIVALENT EXCHANGE.
I WON'T LEAVE FOR FREE.
NOOO...
OKAY. GOOD NIGHT.
TRANQ
HOLD IT!!!
IN THAT CASE, DO THAT TO ME.

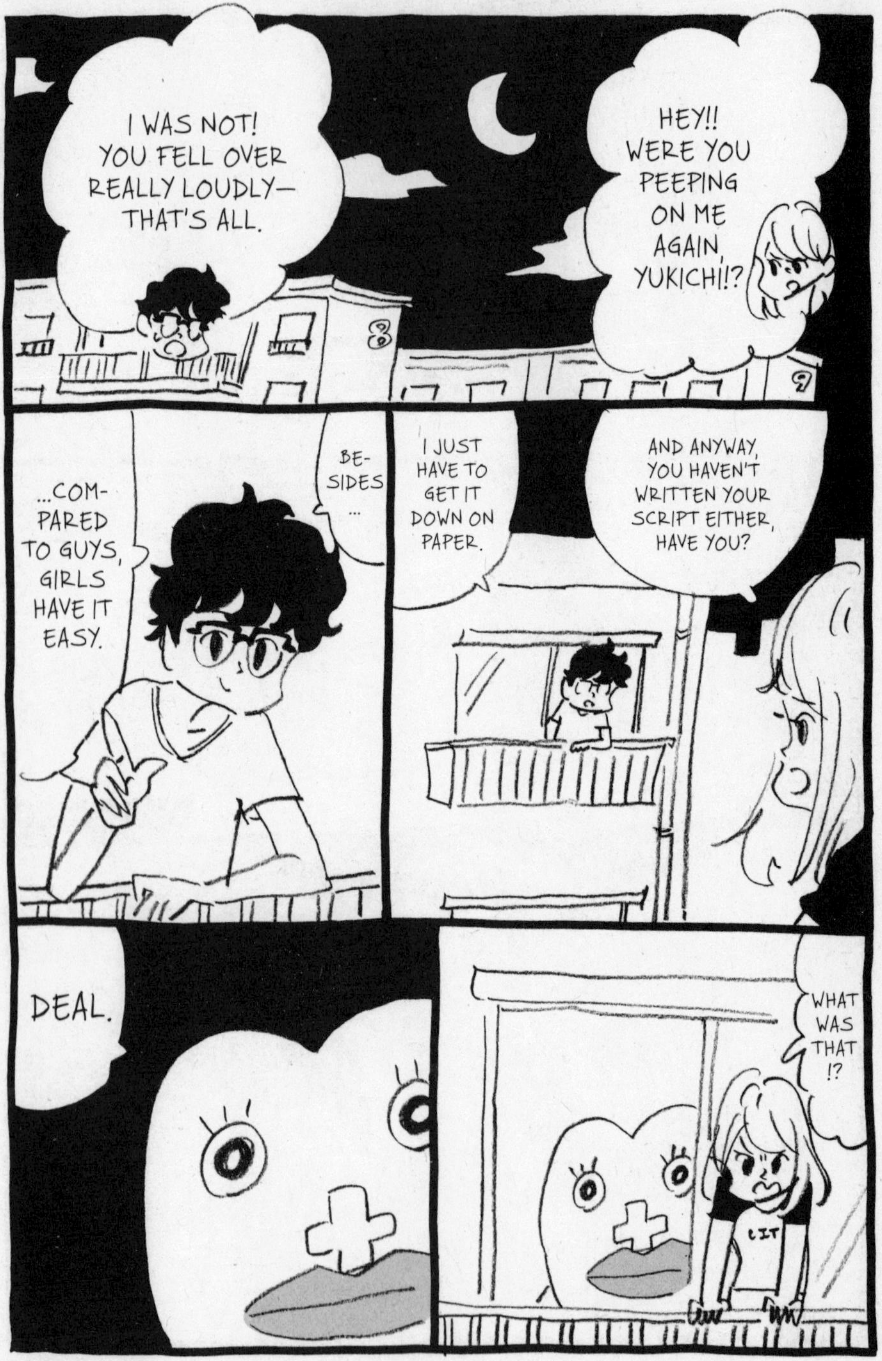
HEY!! WERE YOU PEEPING ON ME AGAIN, YUKICHI!?
I WAS NOT! YOU FELL OVER REALLY LOUDLY— THAT'S ALL.
AND ANYWAY, YOU HAVEN'T WRITTEN YOUR SCRIPT EITHER, HAVE YOU?
I JUST HAVE TO GET IT DOWN ON PAPER.
BE-SIDES...
...COM-PARED TO GUYS, GIRLS HAVE IT EASY.
WHAT WAS THAT!?
DEAL.

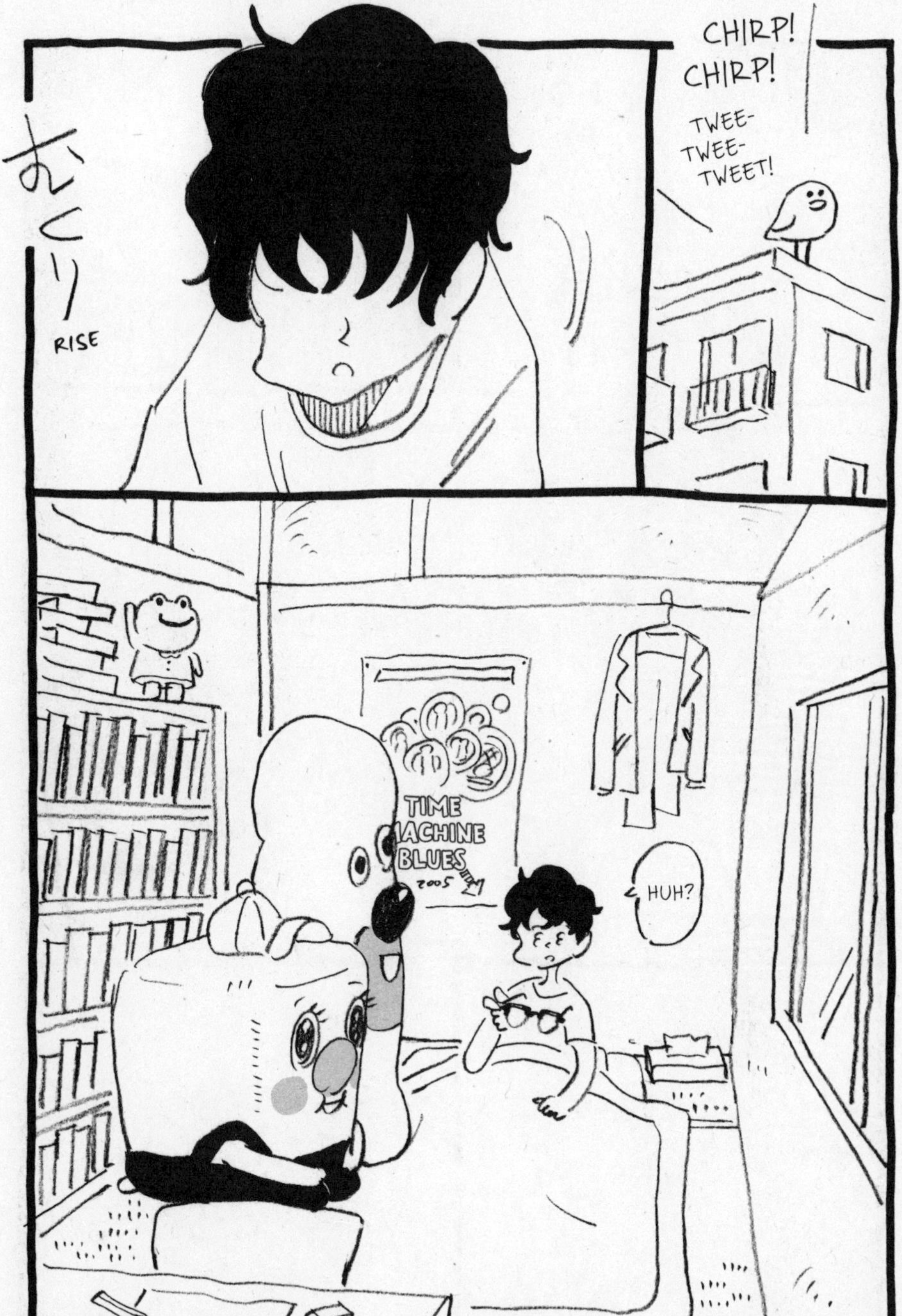
CHIRP!
CHIRP!
TWEE-
TWEE-
TWEET!
むくり
RISE
TIME
MACHINE
BLUES
2005
HUH?

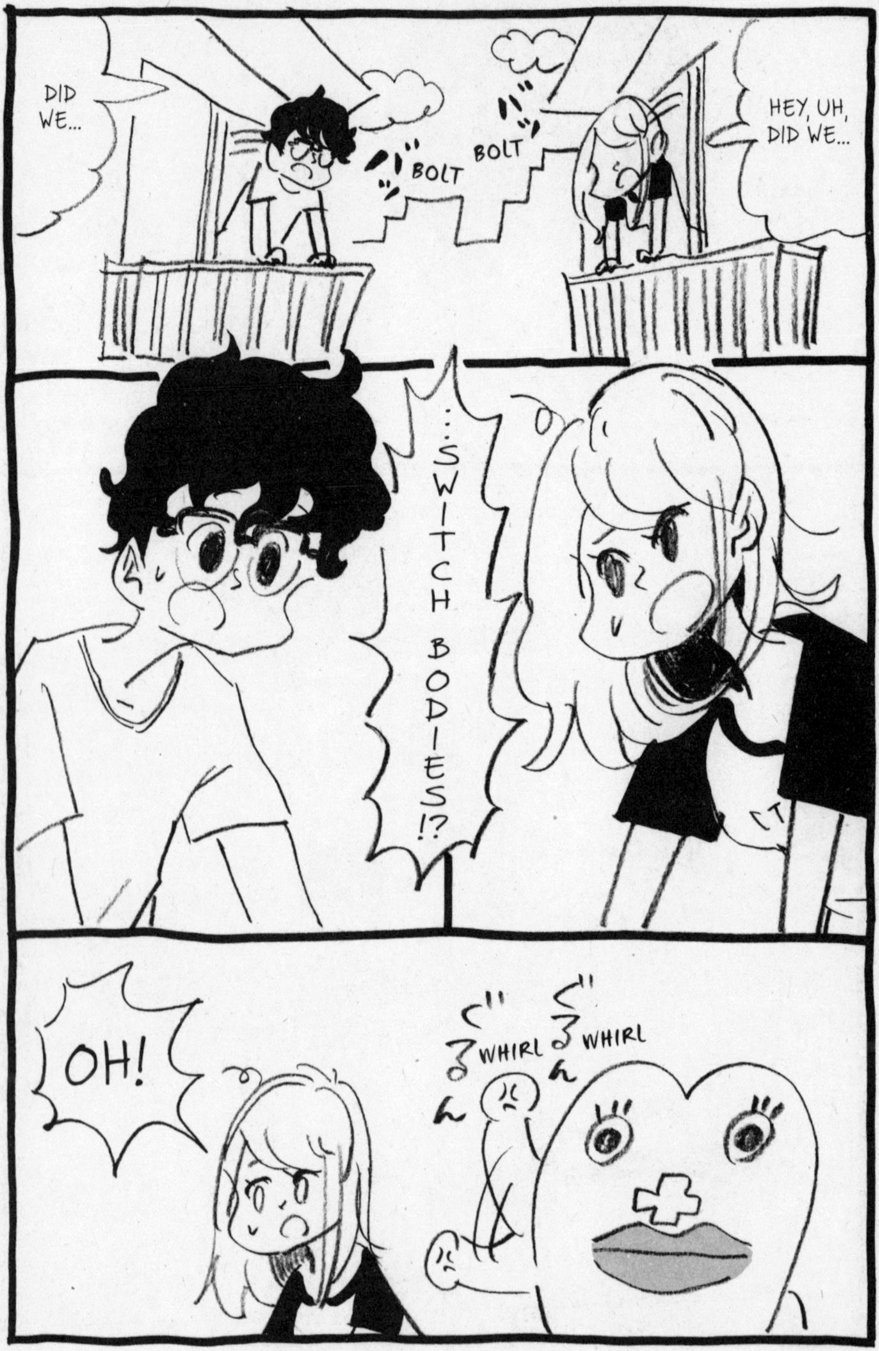
HEY, UH, DID WE...
BOLT
BOLT
DID WE...
...SWITCH BODIES!?
WHIRL
WHIRL
OH!

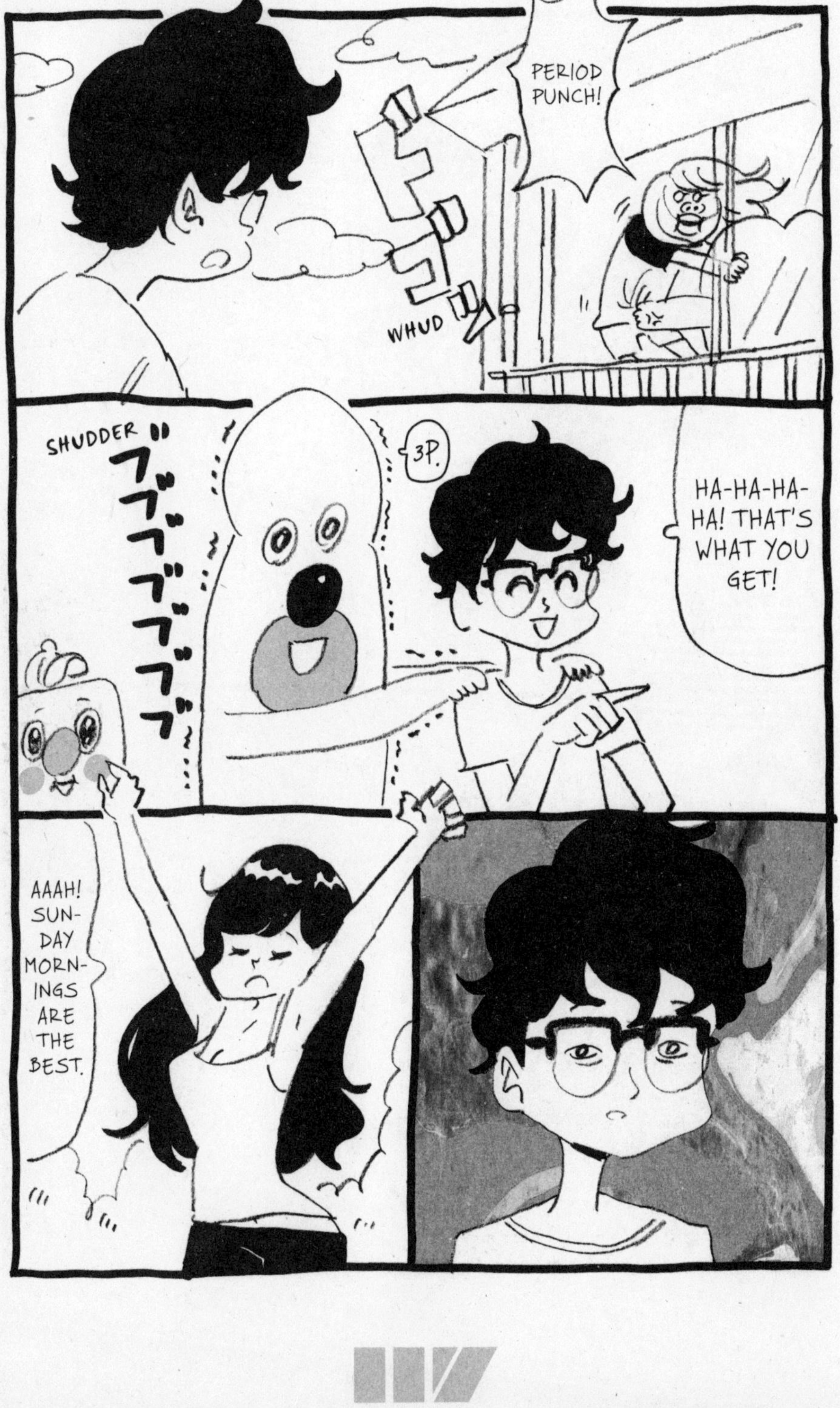
PERIOD PUNCH!
WHUD
HA-HA-HA-HA! THAT'S WHAT YOU GET!
3P.
SHUDDER
ブブブブブブ
AAAH! SUN-DAY MORN-INGS ARE THE BEST.

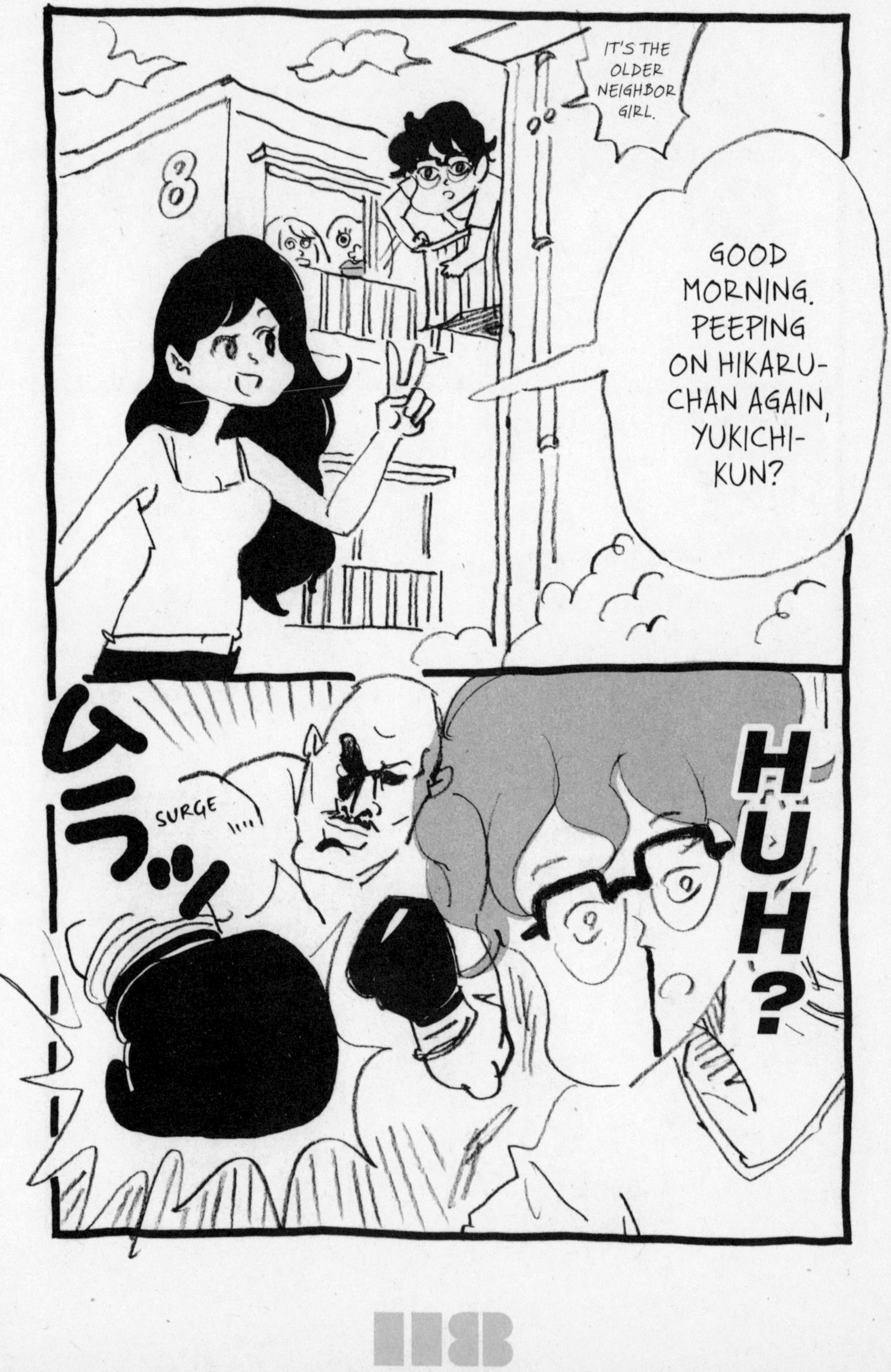
IT'S THE OLDER NEIGHBOR GIRL.
GOOD MORNING. PEEPING ON HIKARU-CHAN AGAIN, YUKICHI-KUN?
HUH?
ムラッ
SURGE

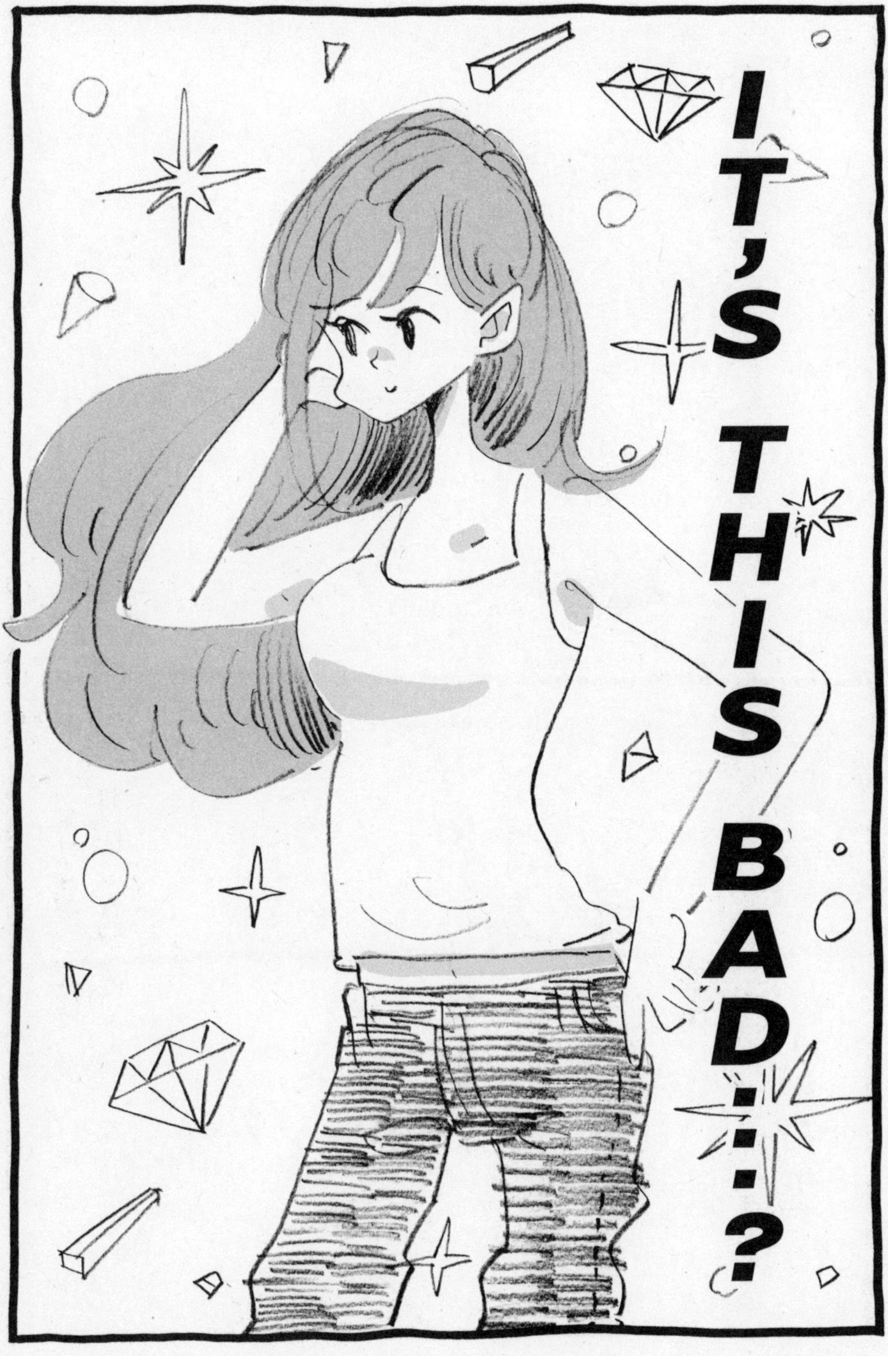
IT'S THIS BAD...?

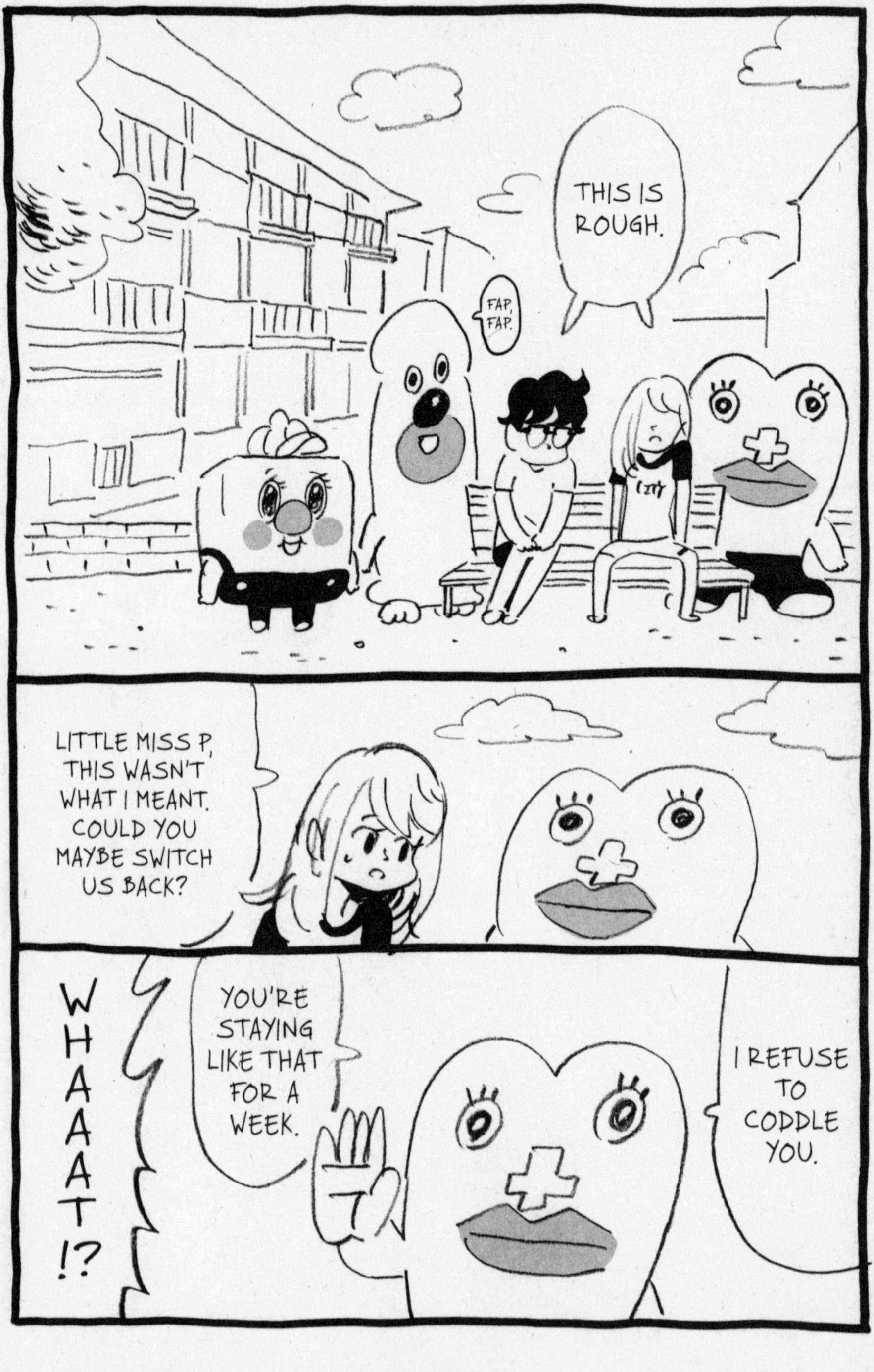
THIS IS ROUGH.
FAP, FAP.
LITTLE MISS P, THIS WASN'T WHAT I MEANT. COULD YOU MAYBE SWITCH US BACK?
I REFUSE TO CODDLE YOU.
YOU'RE STAYING LIKE THAT FOR A WEEK.
WHAAAT!?

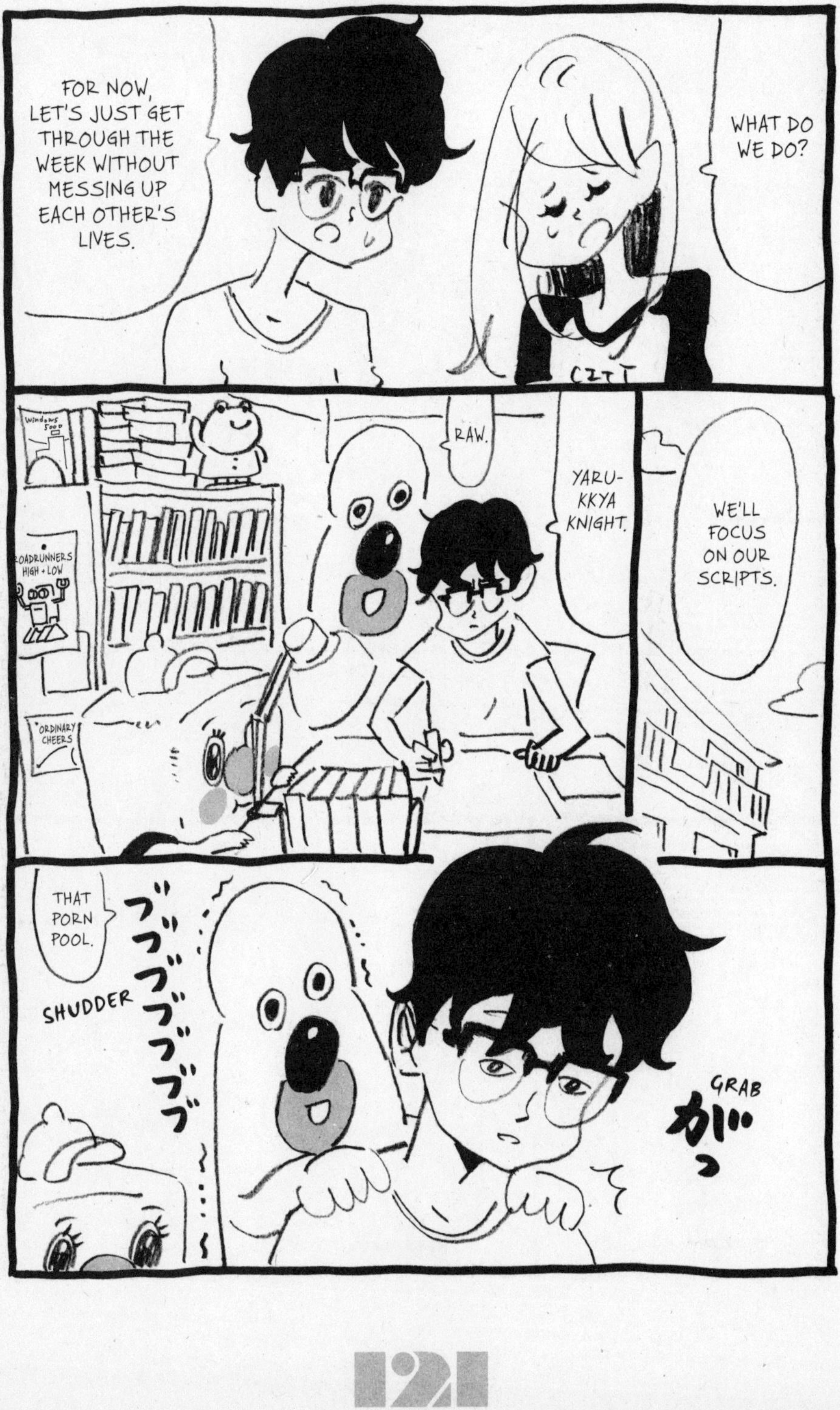
WHAT DO WE DO?
FOR NOW, LET'S JUST GET THROUGH THE WEEK WITHOUT MESSING UP EACH OTHER'S LIVES.
WE'LL FOCUS ON OUR SCRIPTS.
YARU-KKYA KNIGHT.
RAW.
Windows 5000
ROADRUNNERS HIGH + LOW
ORDINARY CHEERS
GRAB
ガッ
THAT PORN POOL.
ブブブブブブブ
SHUDDER

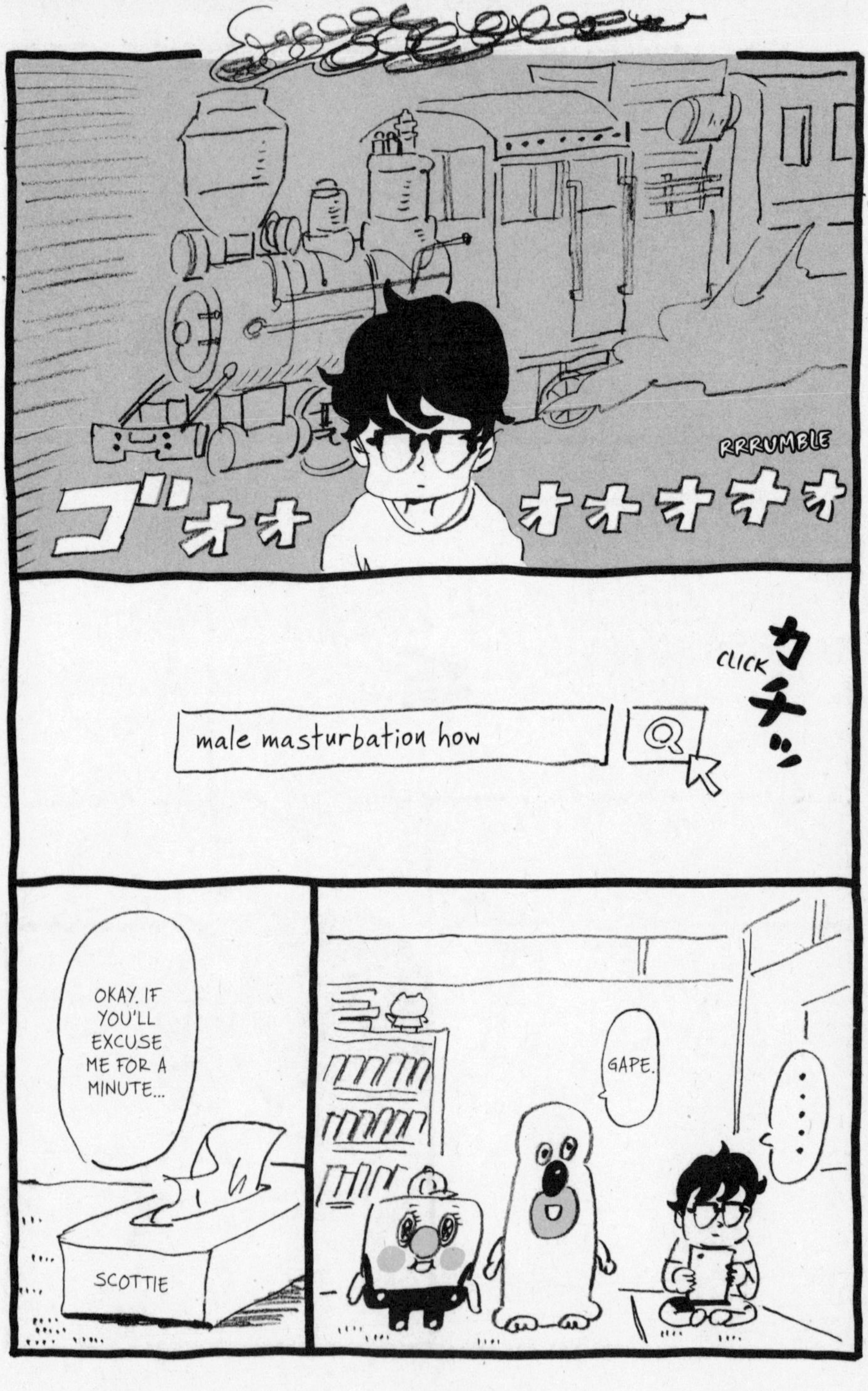
RRRUMBLE
ゴオオオオオオオ
CLICK
カチッ
male masturbation how
GAPE.
.....
OKAY. IF YOU'LL EXCUSE ME FOR A MINUTE...
SCOTTIE

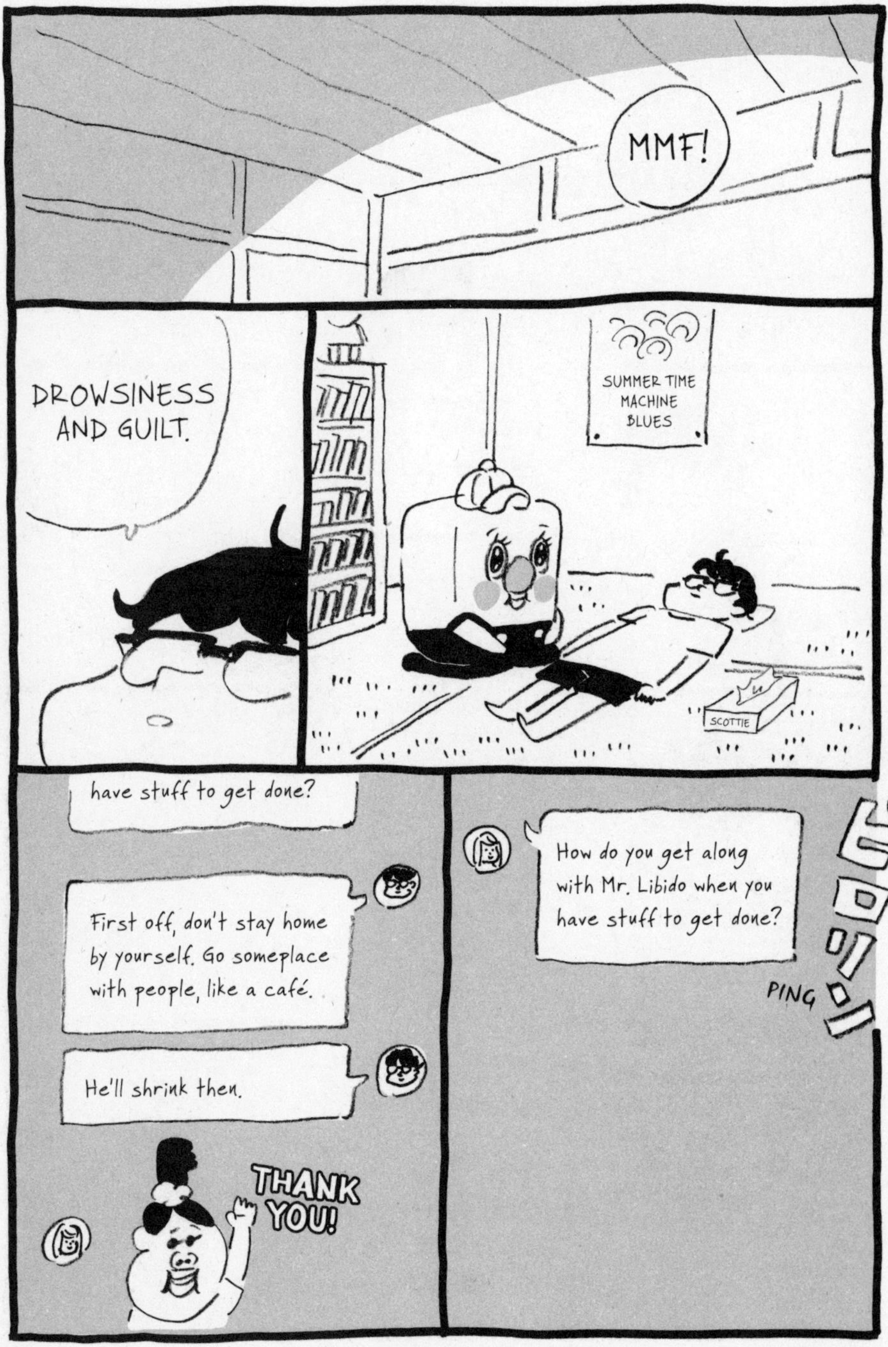
MMF!
SUMMER TIME MACHINE BLUES
SCOTTIE
DROWSINESS AND GUILT.
How do you get along with Mr. Libido when you have stuff to get done?
ピロリン
PING
have stuff to get done?
First off, don't stay home by yourself. Go someplace with people, like a café.
He'll shrink then.
THANK YOU!

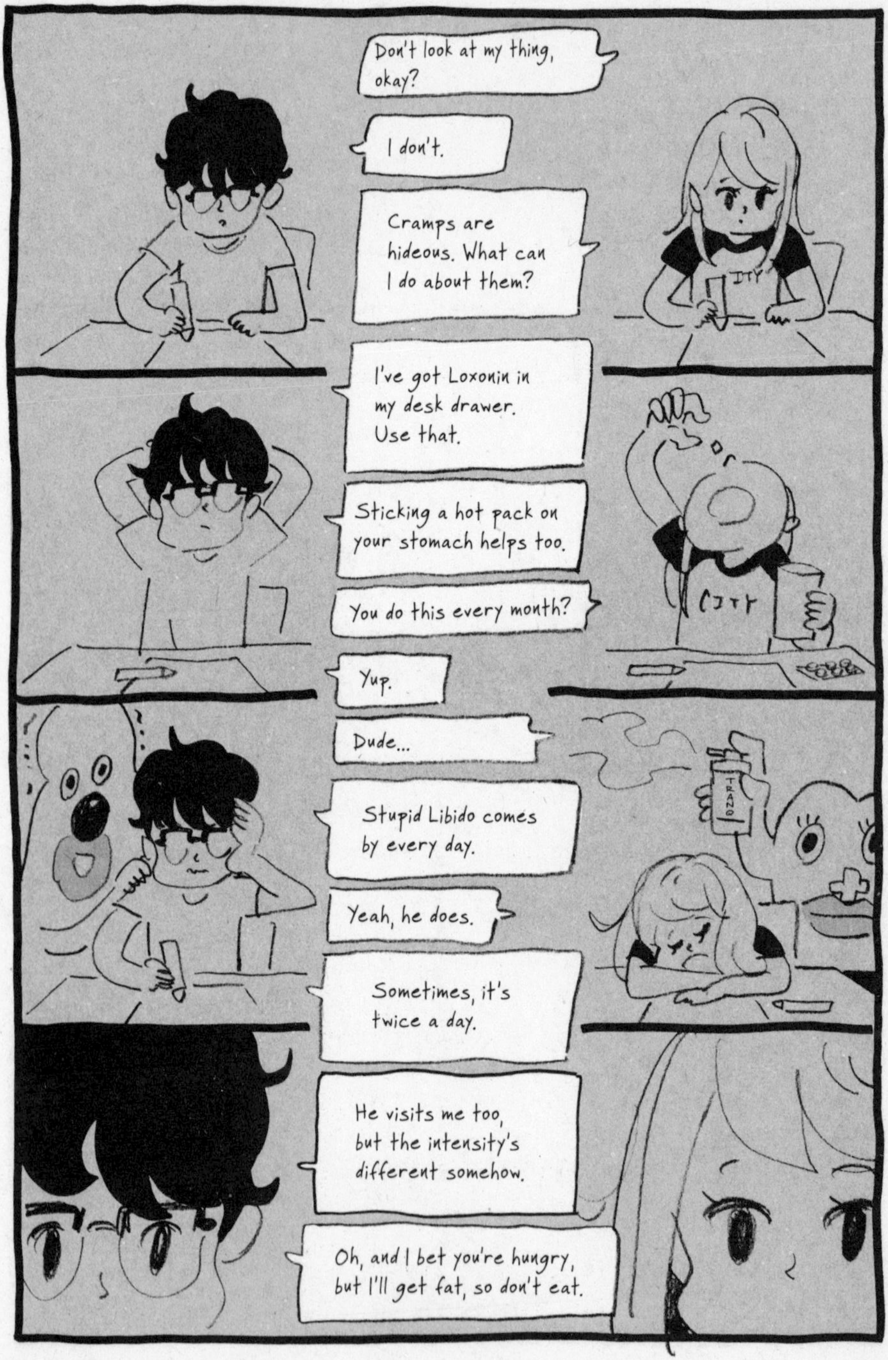
Don't look at my thing, okay?
I don't.
Cramps are hideous. What can I do about them?
I've got Loxonin in my desk drawer. Use that.
Sticking a hot pack on your stomach helps too.
You do this every month?
Yup.
Dude...
Stupid Libido comes by every day.
Yeah, he does.
Sometimes, it's twice a day.
He visits me too, but the intensity's different somehow.
Oh, and I bet you're hungry, but I'll get fat, so don't eat.

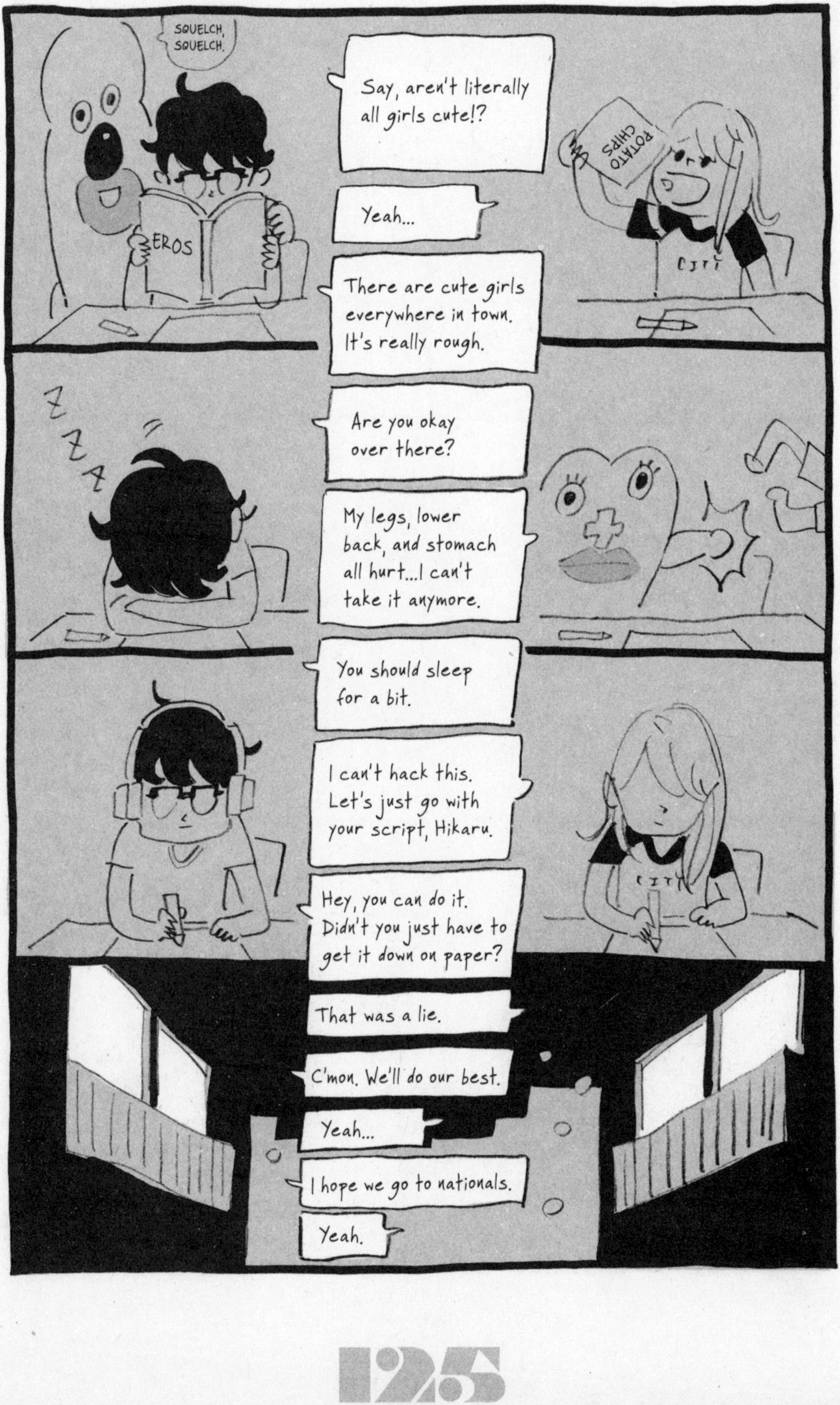
POTATO CHIPS
Say, aren't literally all girls cute!?
SQUELCH, SQUELCH.
EROS
Yeah...
There are cute girls everywhere in town. It's really rough.
Are you okay over there?
My legs, lower back, and stomach all hurt...I can't take it anymore.
ZZZ
You should sleep for a bit.
I can't hack this. Let's just go with your script, Hikaru.
Hey, you can do it. Didn't you just have to get it down on paper?
That was a lie.
C'mon. We'll do our best.
Yeah...
I hope we go to nationals.
Yeah.

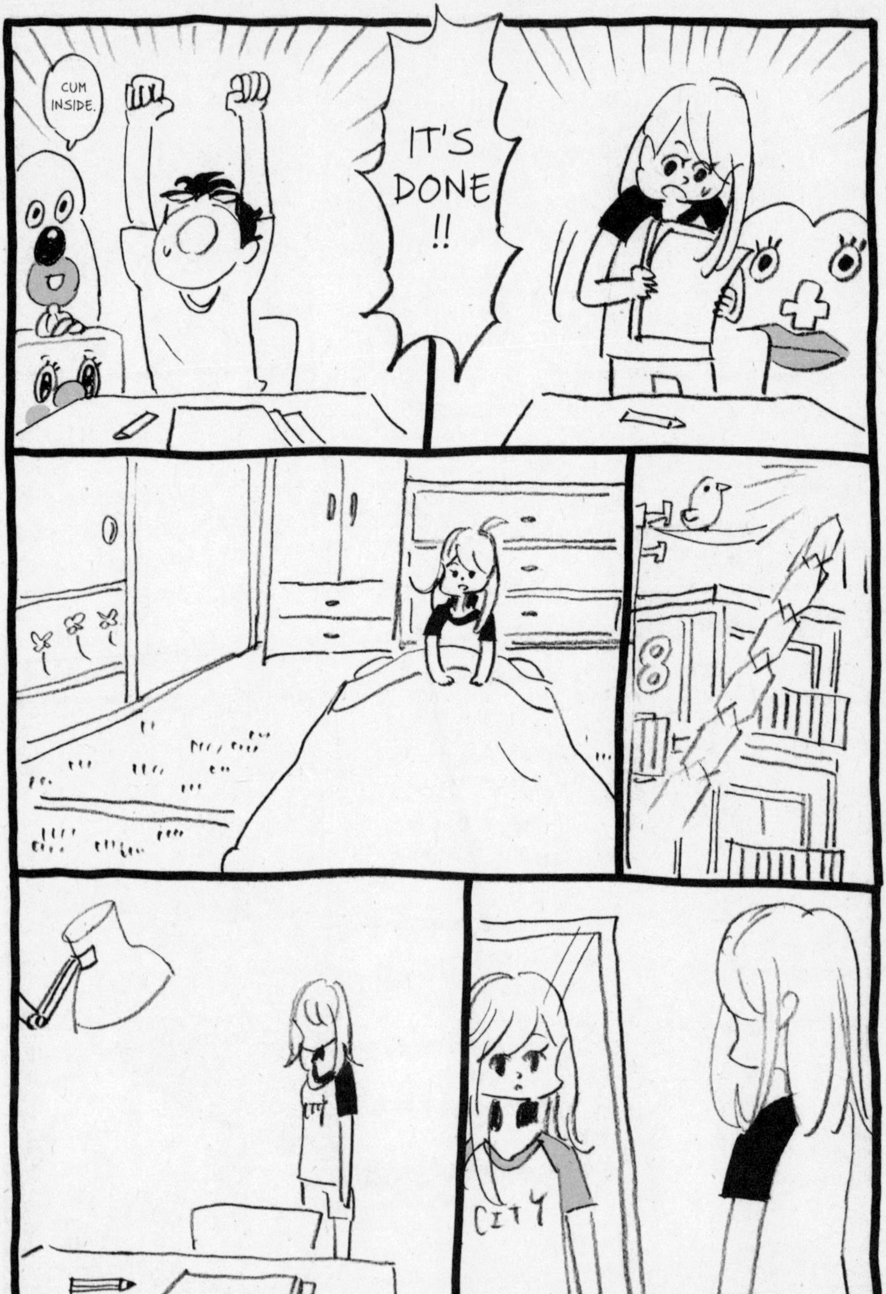
IT'S DONE !!
CUM INSIDE.
CITY

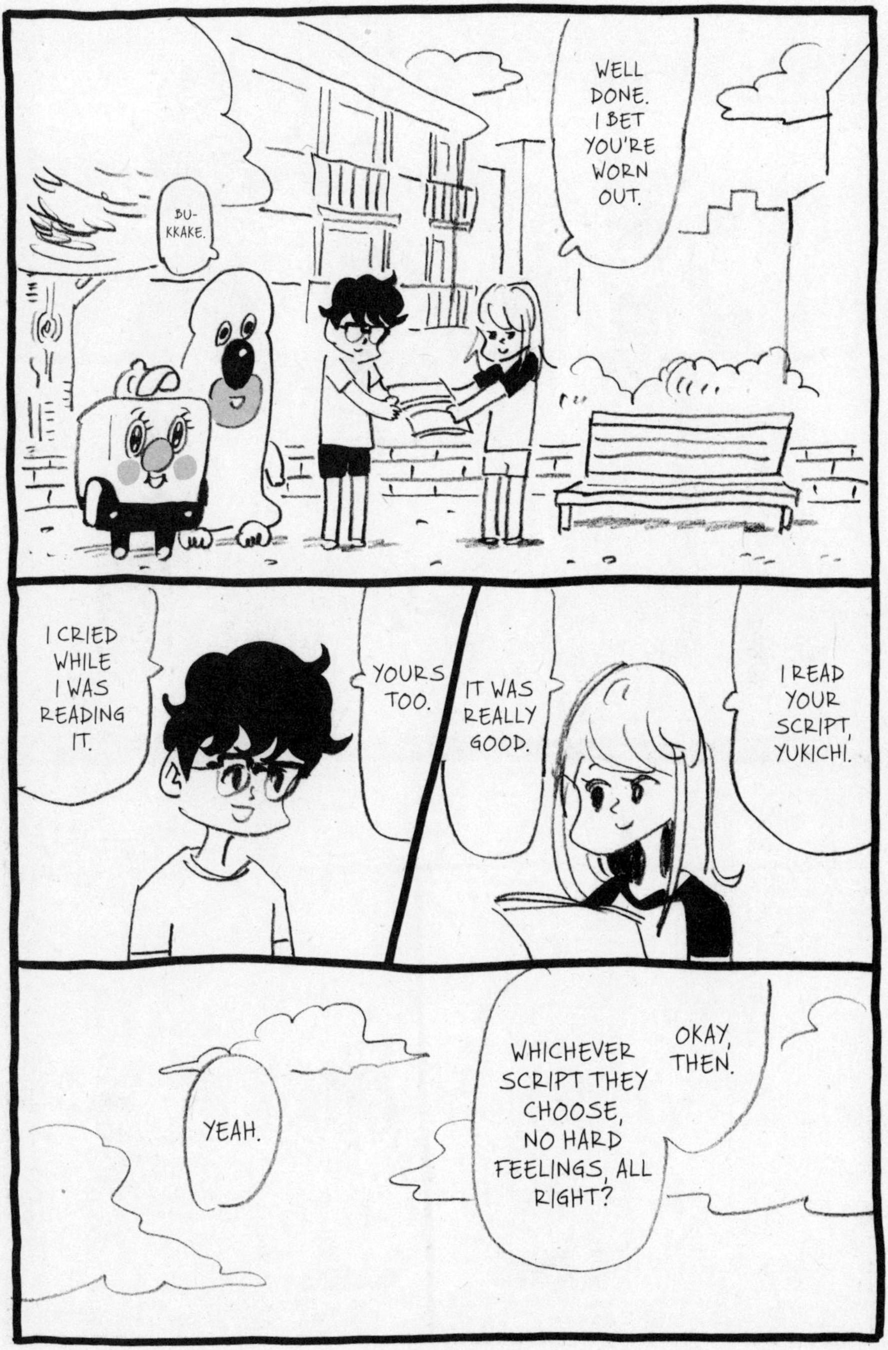
WELL DONE. I BET YOU'RE WORN OUT.
BU-KKAKE.
I READ YOUR SCRIPT, YUKICHI.
IT WAS REALLY GOOD.
YOURS TOO.
I CRIED WHILE I WAS READING IT.
OKAY, THEN.
WHICHEVER SCRIPT THEY CHOOSE, NO HARD FEELINGS, ALL RIGHT?
YEAH.

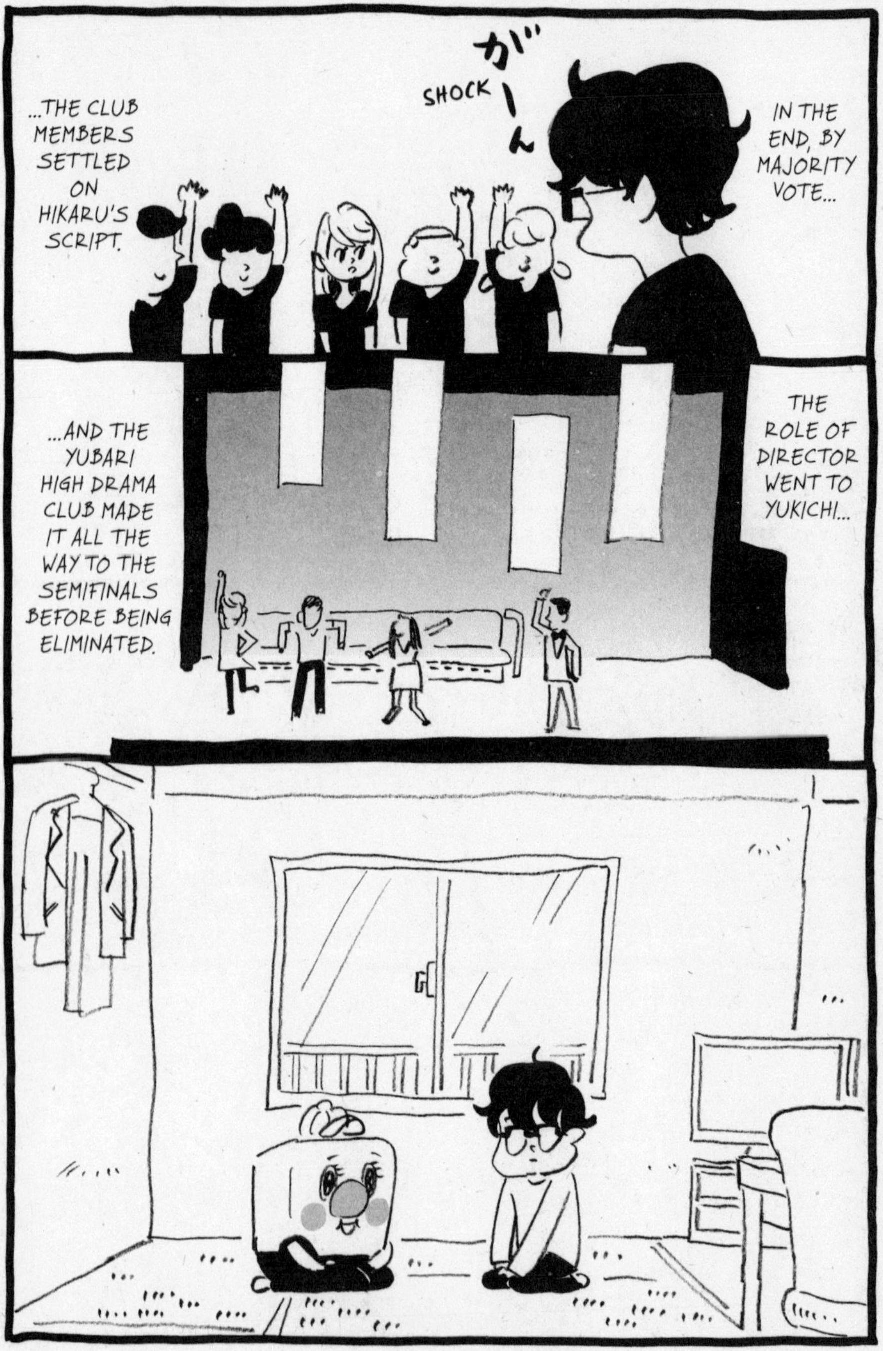
IN THE END, BY MAJORITY VOTE...
がーん
SHOCK
...THE CLUB MEMBERS SETTLED ON HIKARU'S SCRIPT.
THE ROLE OF DIRECTOR WENT TO YUKICHI...
...AND THE YUBARI HIGH DRAMA CLUB MADE IT ALL THE WAY TO THE SEMIFINALS BEFORE BEING ELIMINATED.

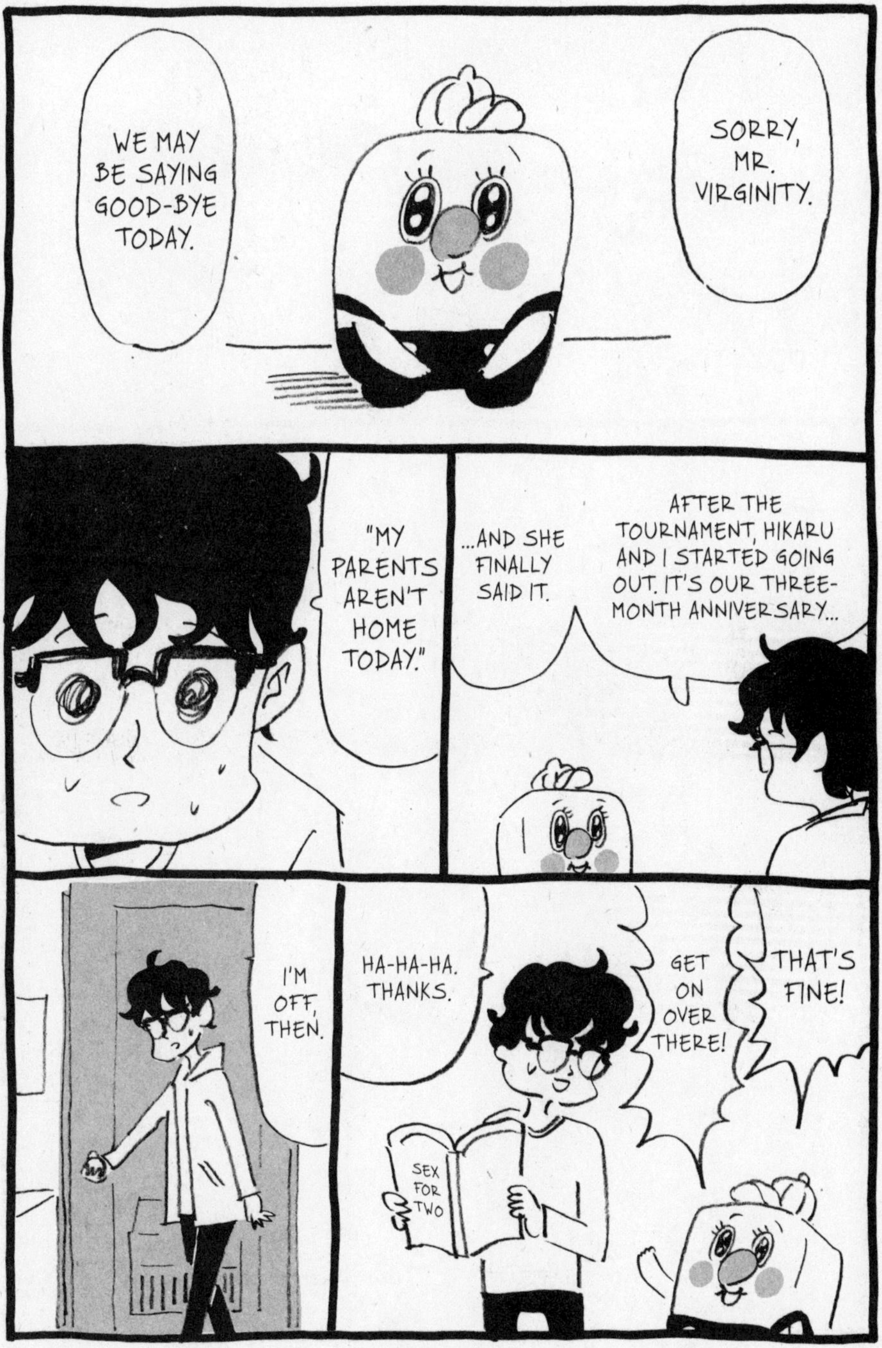
SORRY, MR. VIRGINITY.
WE MAY BE SAYING GOOD-BYE TODAY.
AFTER THE TOURNAMENT, HIKARU AND I STARTED GOING OUT. IT'S OUR THREE-MONTH ANNIVERSARY...
...AND SHE FINALLY SAID IT.
"MY PARENTS AREN'T HOME TODAY."
THAT'S FINE!
GET ON OVER THERE!
HA-HA-HA. THANKS.
SEX FOR TWO
I'M OFF, THEN.

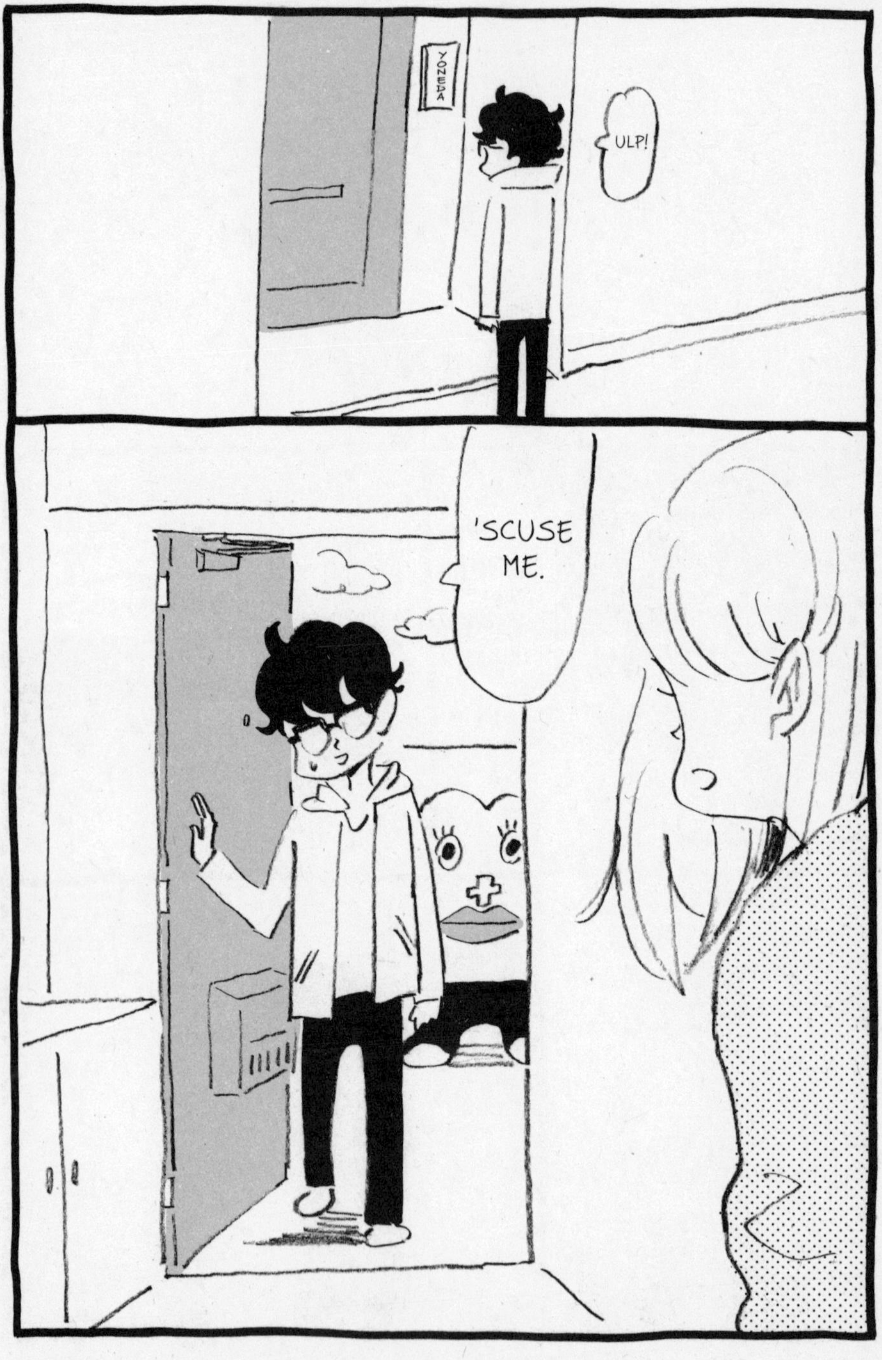
YONEDA
ULP!
'SCUSE ME.

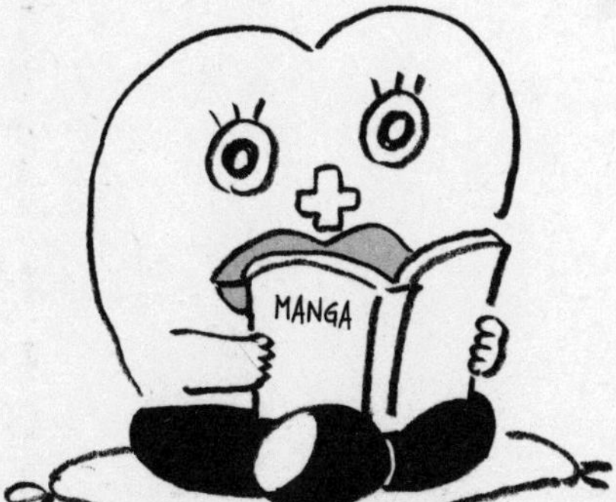
MANGA

A WOMAN OF A CERTAIN AGE AND LITTLE MISS P

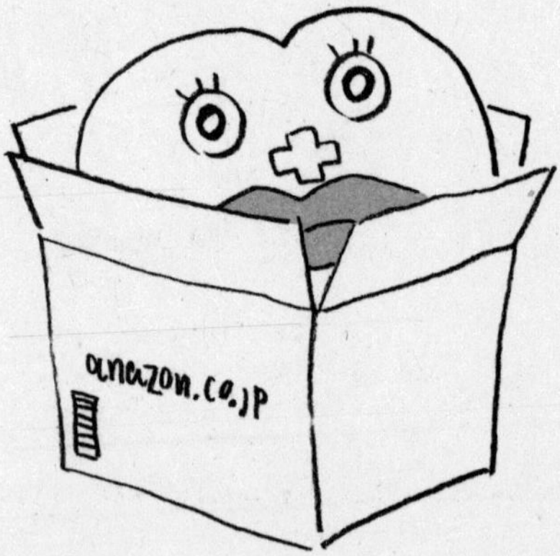
amazon.co.jp

WOULD YOU MARRY ME?

I WAS PROPOSED TO...

CERTIFIED CARE WORKER
AOKO UMINO (28)

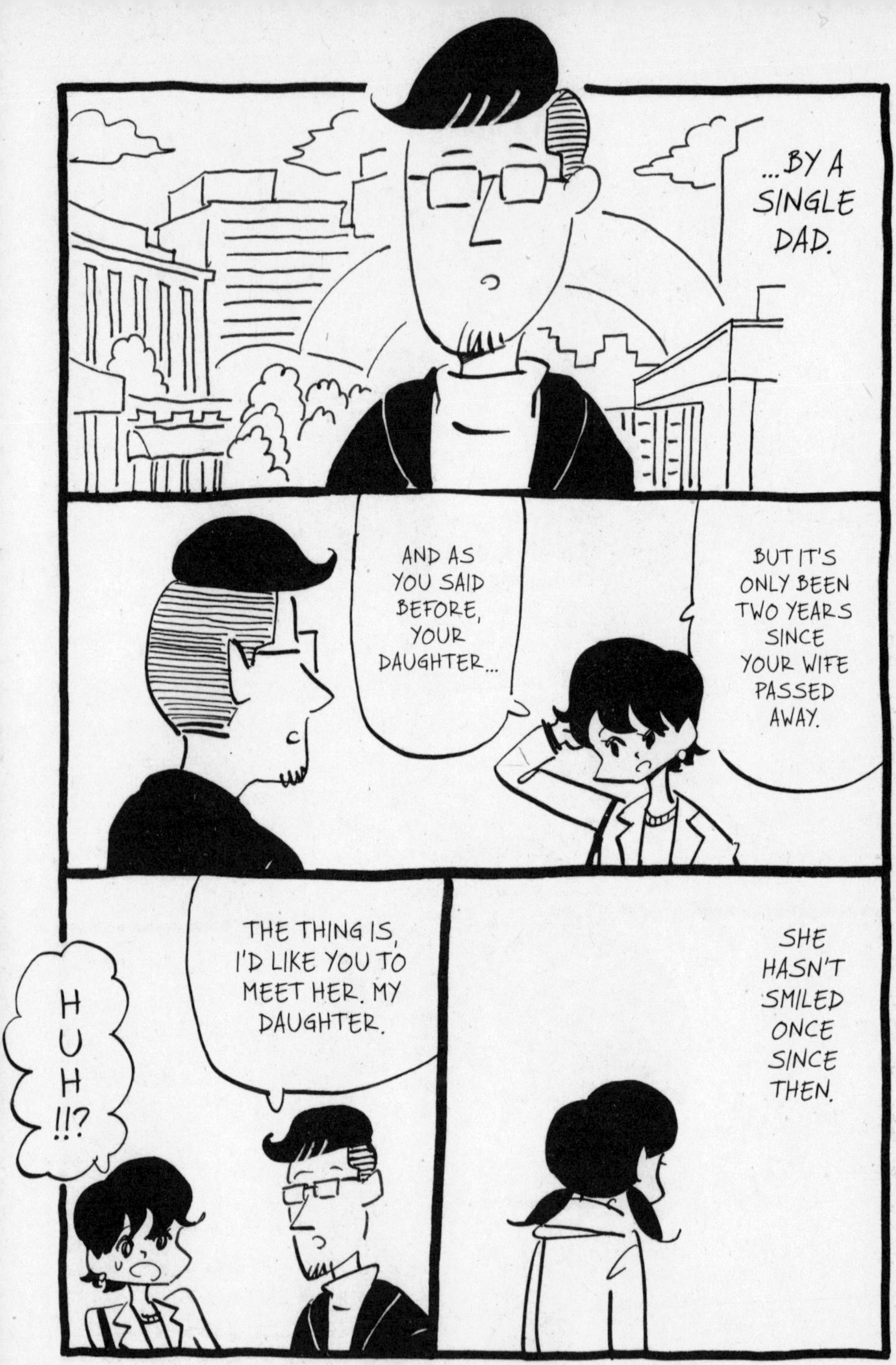
...BY A SINGLE DAD.
BUT IT'S ONLY BEEN TWO YEARS SINCE YOUR WIFE PASSED AWAY.
AND AS YOU SAID BEFORE, YOUR DAUGHTER...
SHE HASN'T SMILED ONCE SINCE THEN.
THE THING IS, I'D LIKE YOU TO MEET HER. MY DAUGHTER.
HUH!!?

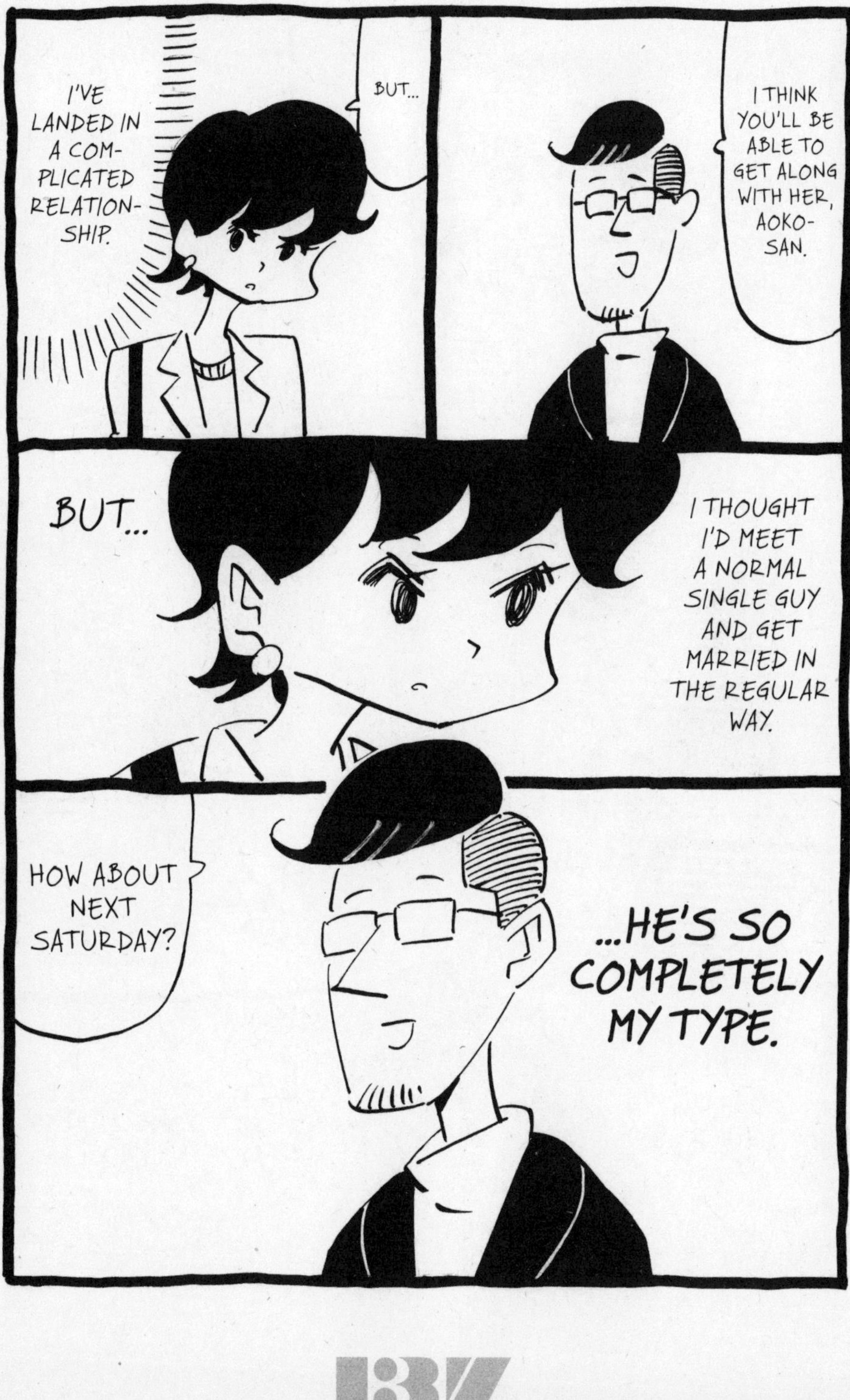
I THINK YOU'LL BE ABLE TO GET ALONG WITH HER, AOKO-SAN.
BUT...
I'VE LANDED IN A COMPLICATED RELATIONSHIP.
I THOUGHT I'D MEET A NORMAL SINGLE GUY AND GET MARRIED IN THE REGULAR WAY.
BUT...
HOW ABOUT NEXT SATURDAY?
...HE'S SO COMPLETELY MY TYPE.

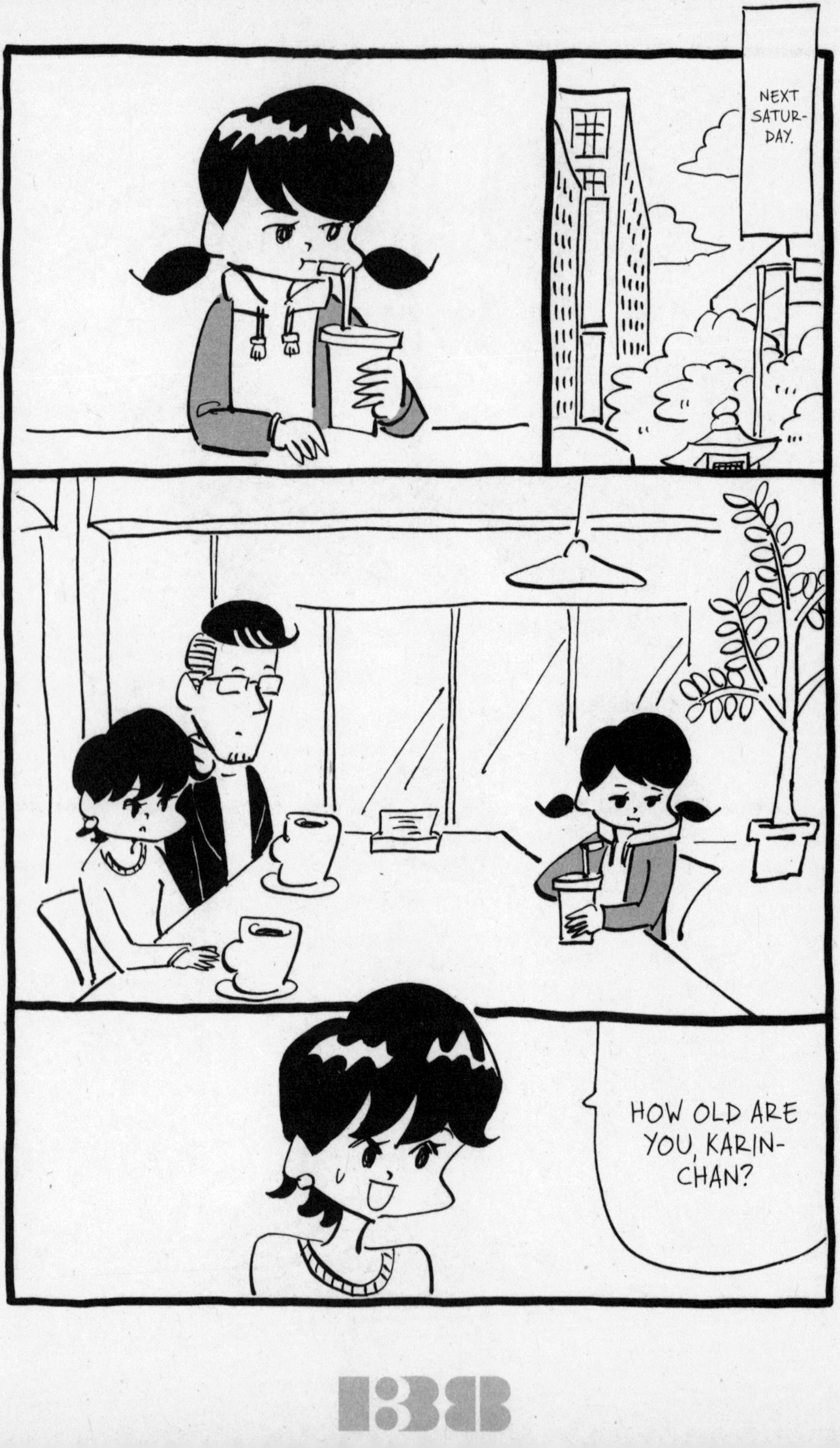
NEXT SATUR-DAY.
HOW OLD ARE YOU, KARIN-CHAN?

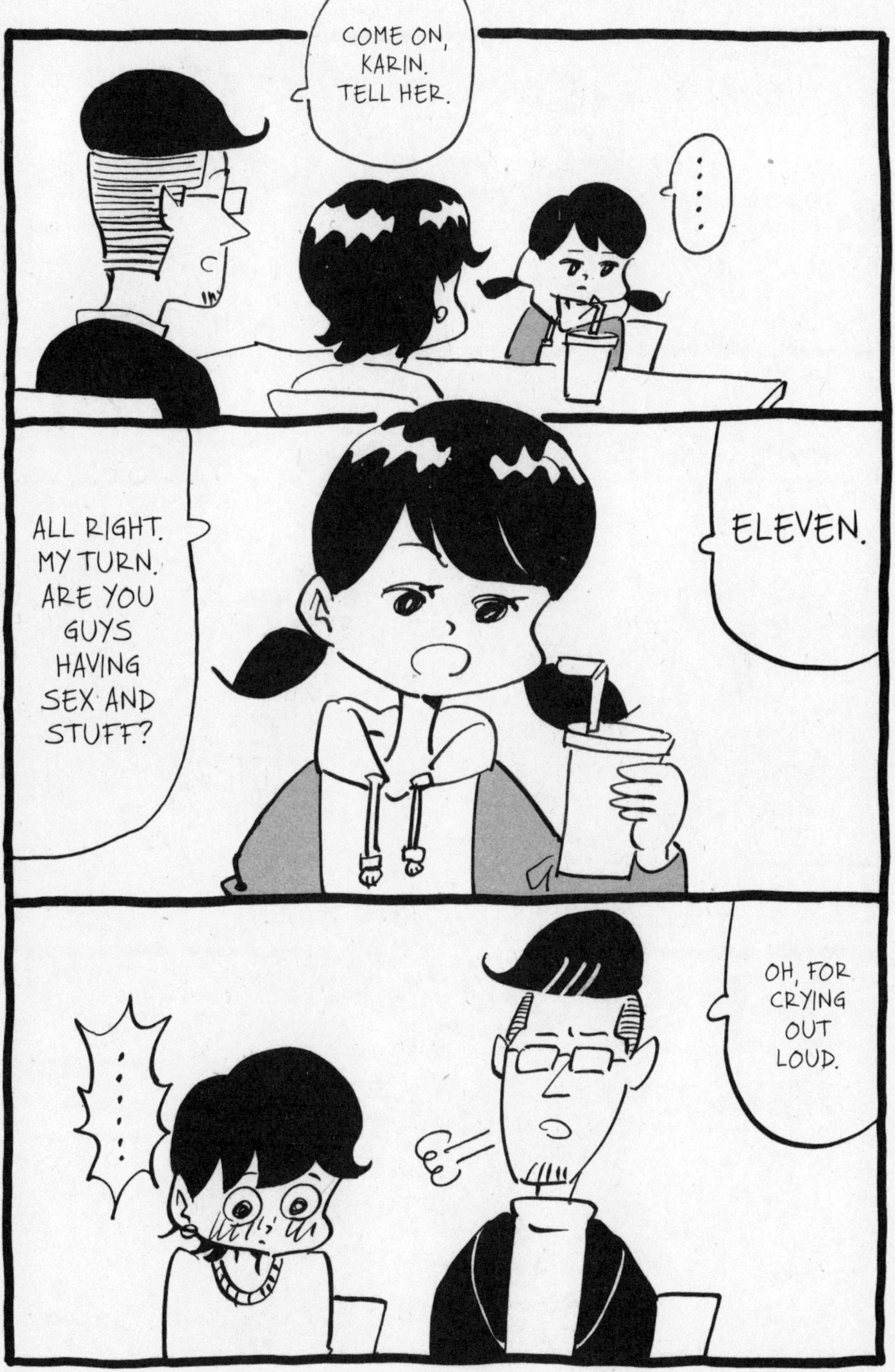
COME ON, KARIN. TELL HER.
.....
ELEVEN.
ALL RIGHT. MY TURN. ARE YOU GUYS HAVING SEX AND STUFF?
OH, FOR CRYING OUT LOUD.
......

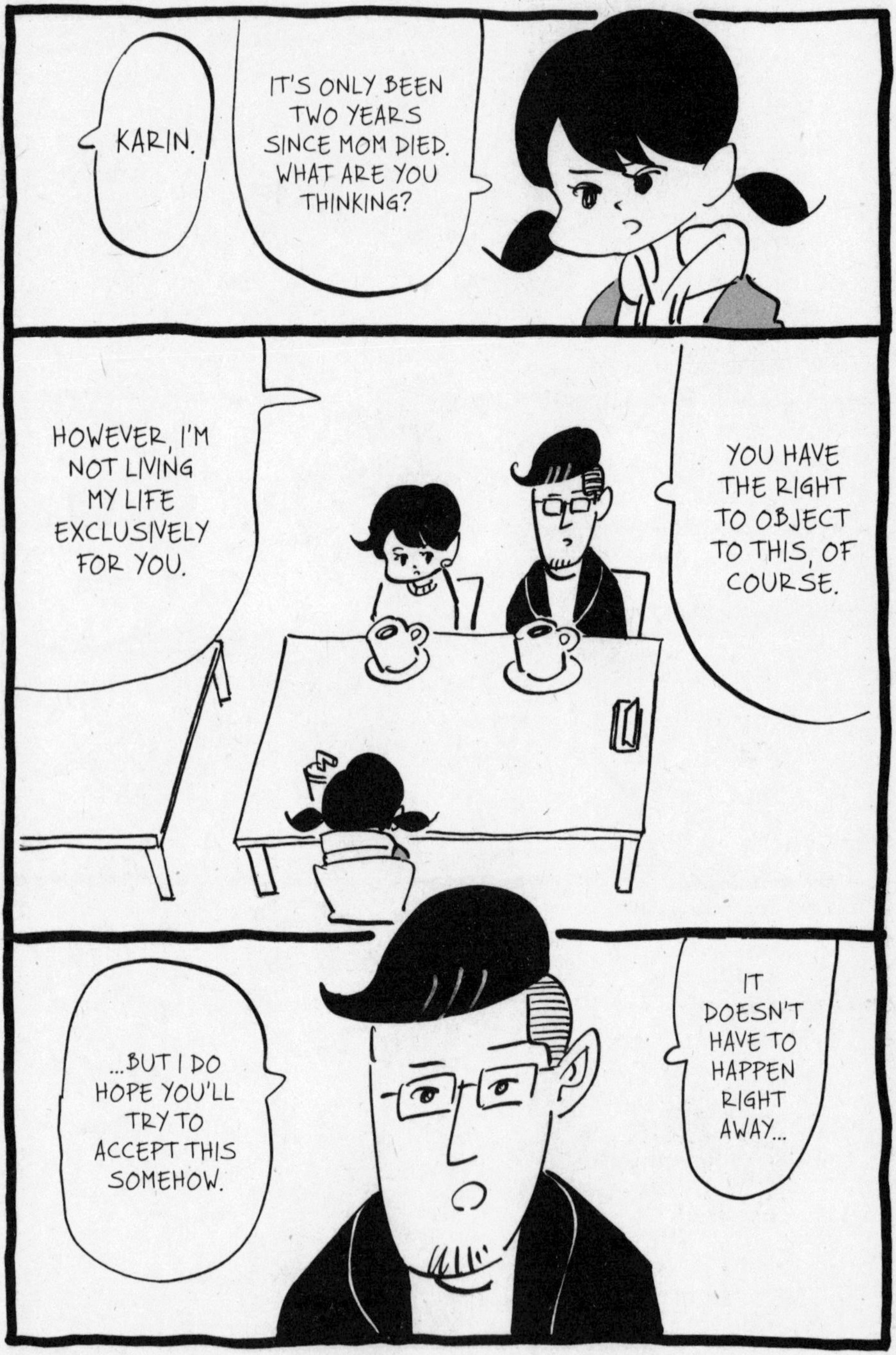
IT'S ONLY BEEN TWO YEARS SINCE MOM DIED. WHAT ARE YOU THINKING?
KARIN.
YOU HAVE THE RIGHT TO OBJECT TO THIS, OF COURSE.
HOWEVER, I'M NOT LIVING MY LIFE EXCLUSIVELY FOR YOU.
IT DOESN'T HAVE TO HAPPEN RIGHT AWAY...
...BUT I DO HOPE YOU'LL TRY TO ACCEPT THIS SOMEHOW.

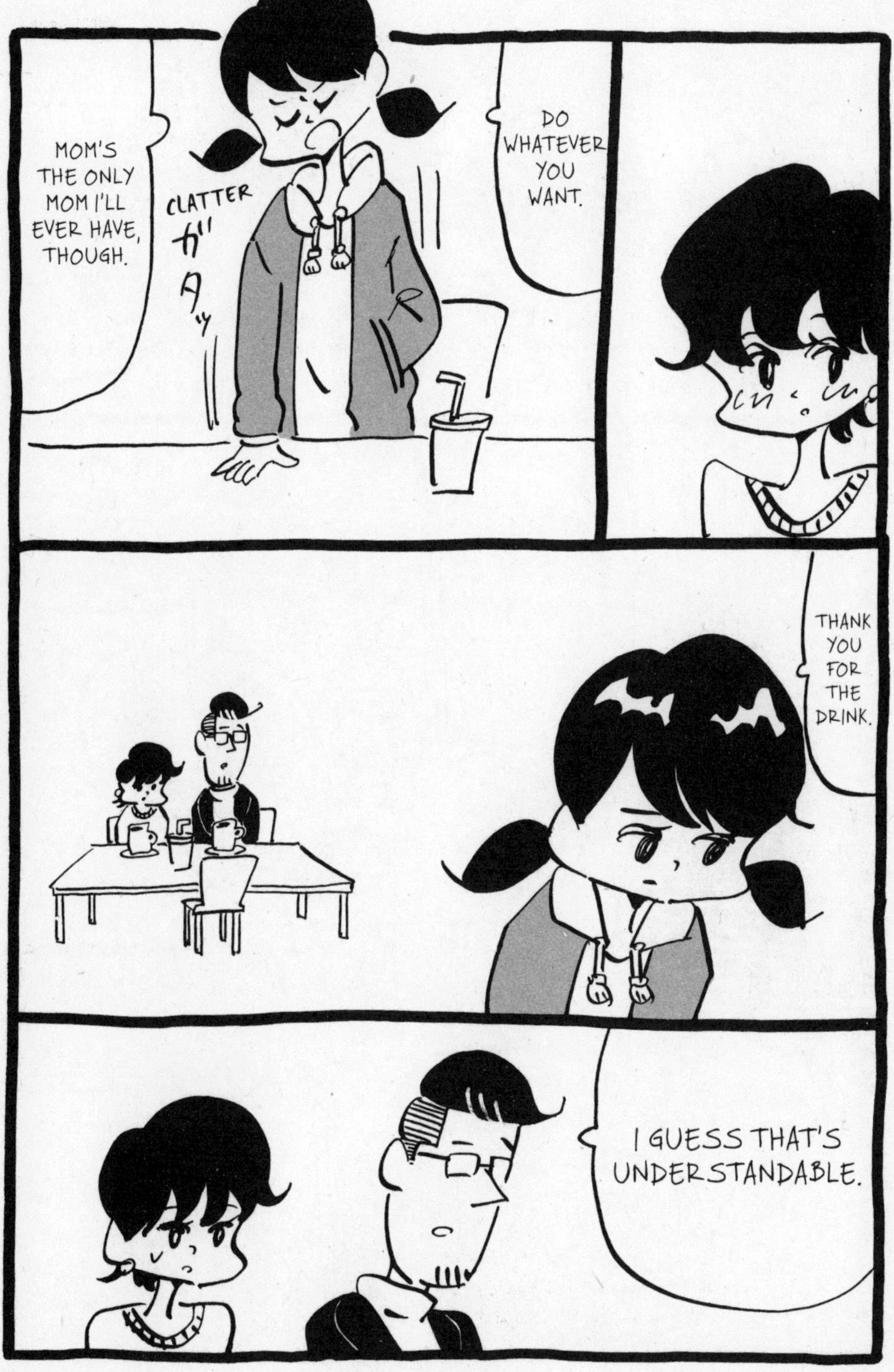
DO WHATEVER YOU WANT.
CLATTER
ガタッ
MOM'S THE ONLY MOM I'LL EVER HAVE, THOUGH.
THANK YOU FOR THE DRINK.
I GUESS THAT'S UNDERSTANDABLE.

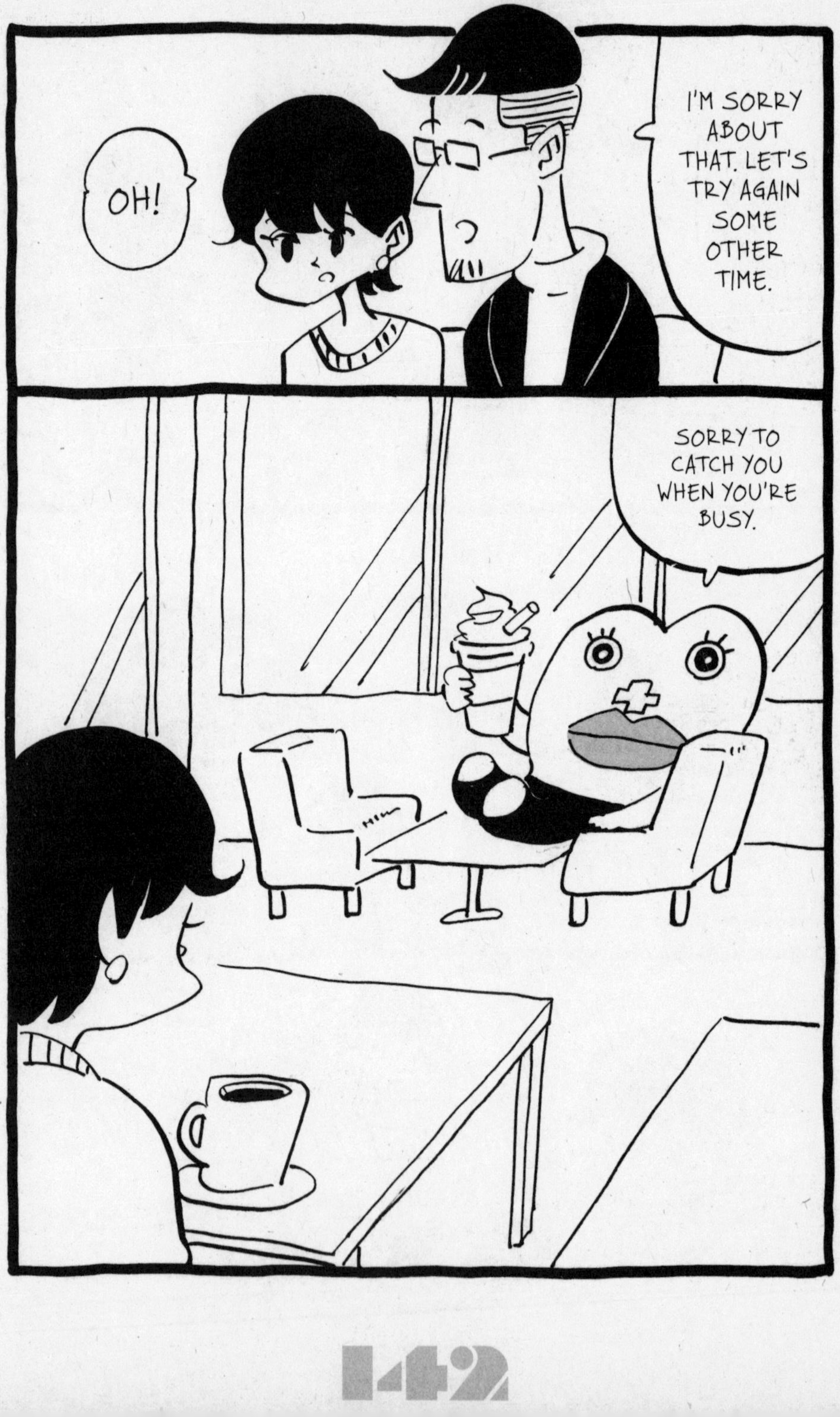
I'M SORRY ABOUT THAT. LET'S TRY AGAIN SOME OTHER TIME.
OH!
SORRY TO CATCH YOU WHEN YOU'RE BUSY.

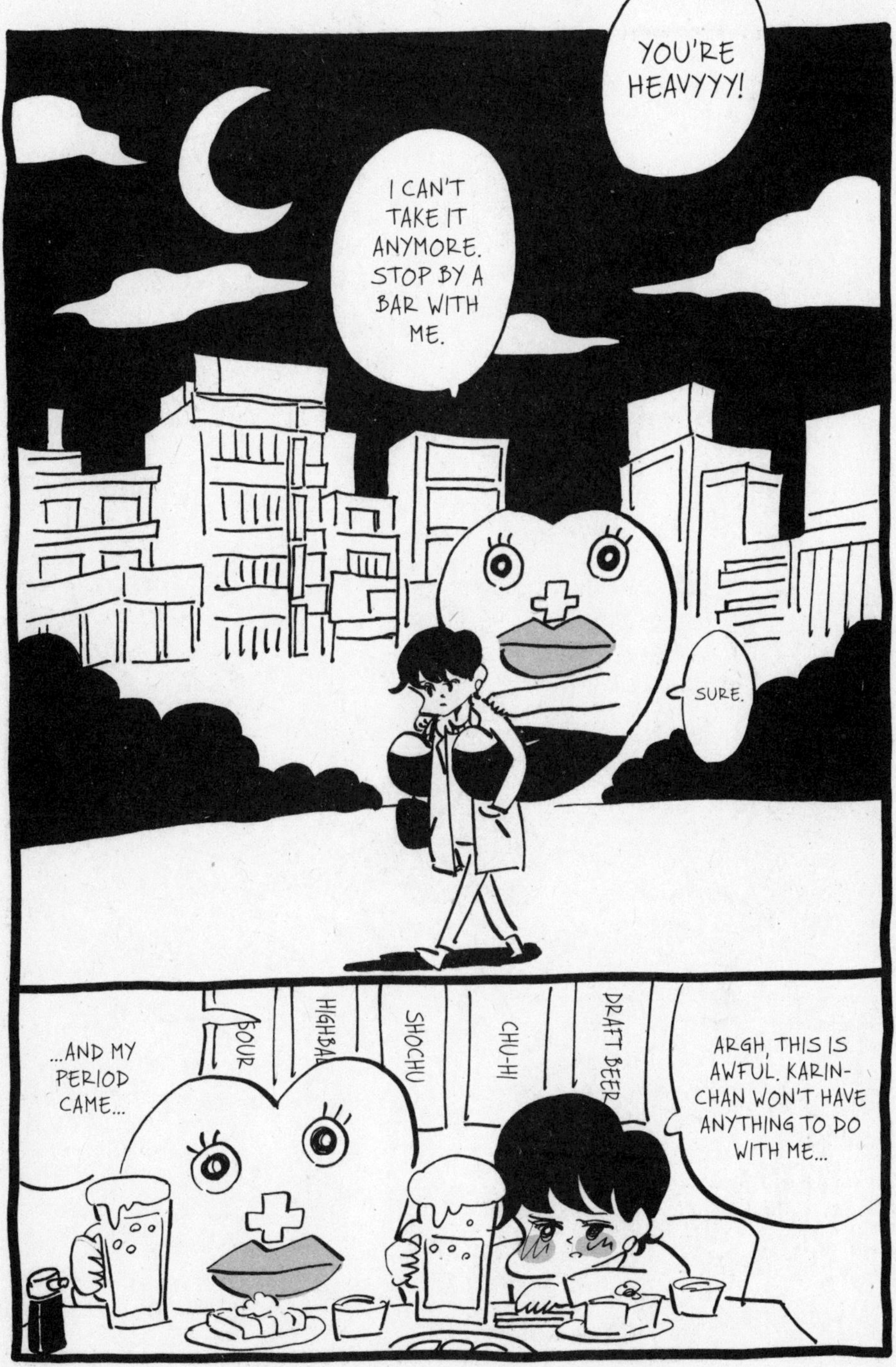
YOU'RE HEAVYYY!
I CAN'T TAKE IT ANYMORE. STOP BY A BAR WITH ME.
SURE.
ARGH, THIS IS AWFUL. KARIN-CHAN WON'T HAVE ANYTHING TO DO WITH ME...
DRAFT BEER
CHU-HI
SHOCHU
SOUR
...AND MY PERIOD CAME...

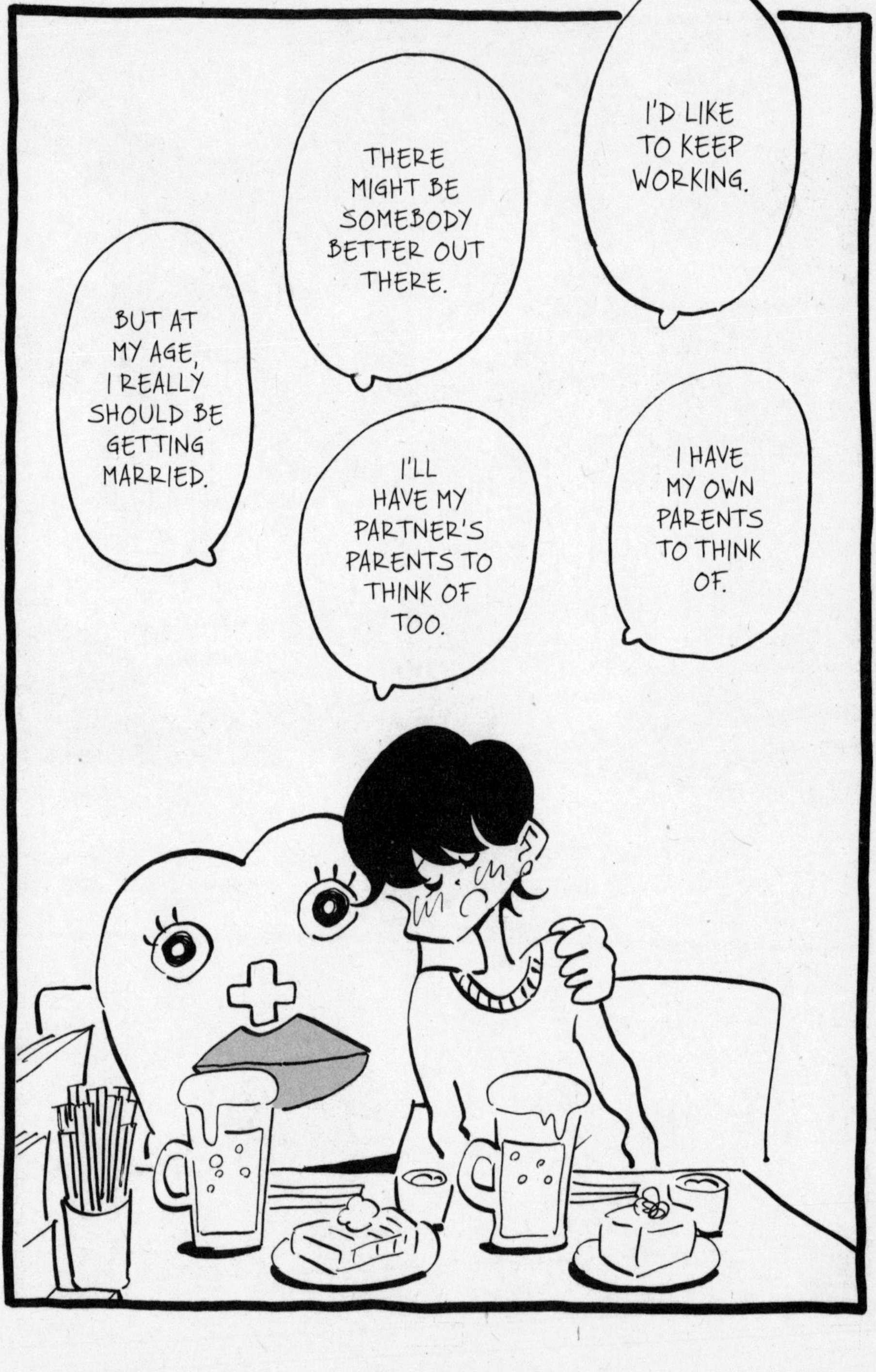
I'D LIKE TO KEEP WORKING.
THERE MIGHT BE SOMEBODY BETTER OUT THERE.
I HAVE MY OWN PARENTS TO THINK OF.
I'LL HAVE MY PARTNER'S PARENTS TO THINK OF TOO.
BUT AT MY AGE, I REALLY SHOULD BE GETTING MARRIED.

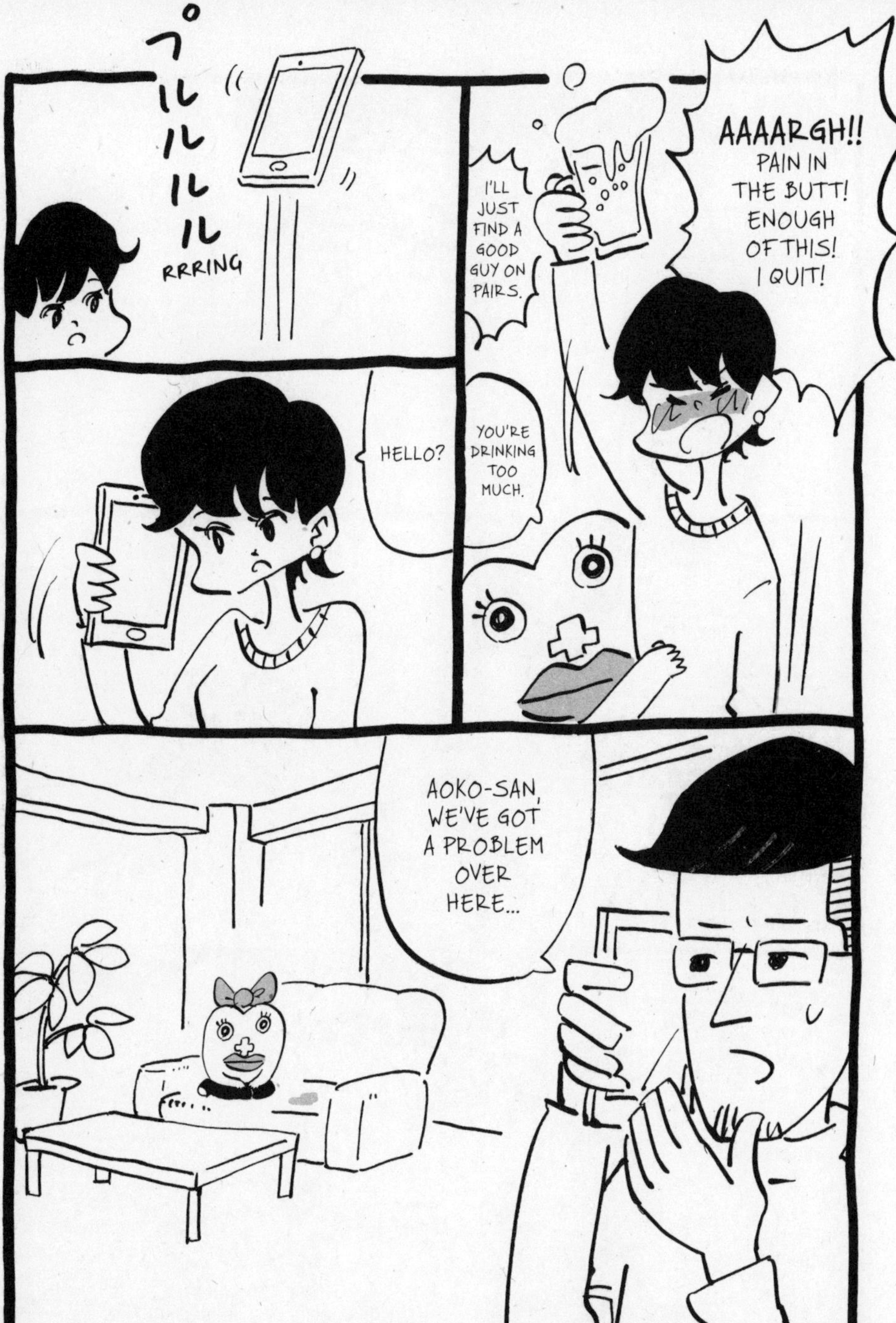
AAAARGH!! PAIN IN THE BUTT! ENOUGH OF THIS! I QUIT!
I'LL JUST FIND A GOOD GUY ON PAIRS.
YOU'RE DRINKING TOO MUCH.
プルルルル
RRRING
HELLO?
AOKO-SAN, WE'VE GOT A PROBLEM OVER HERE...

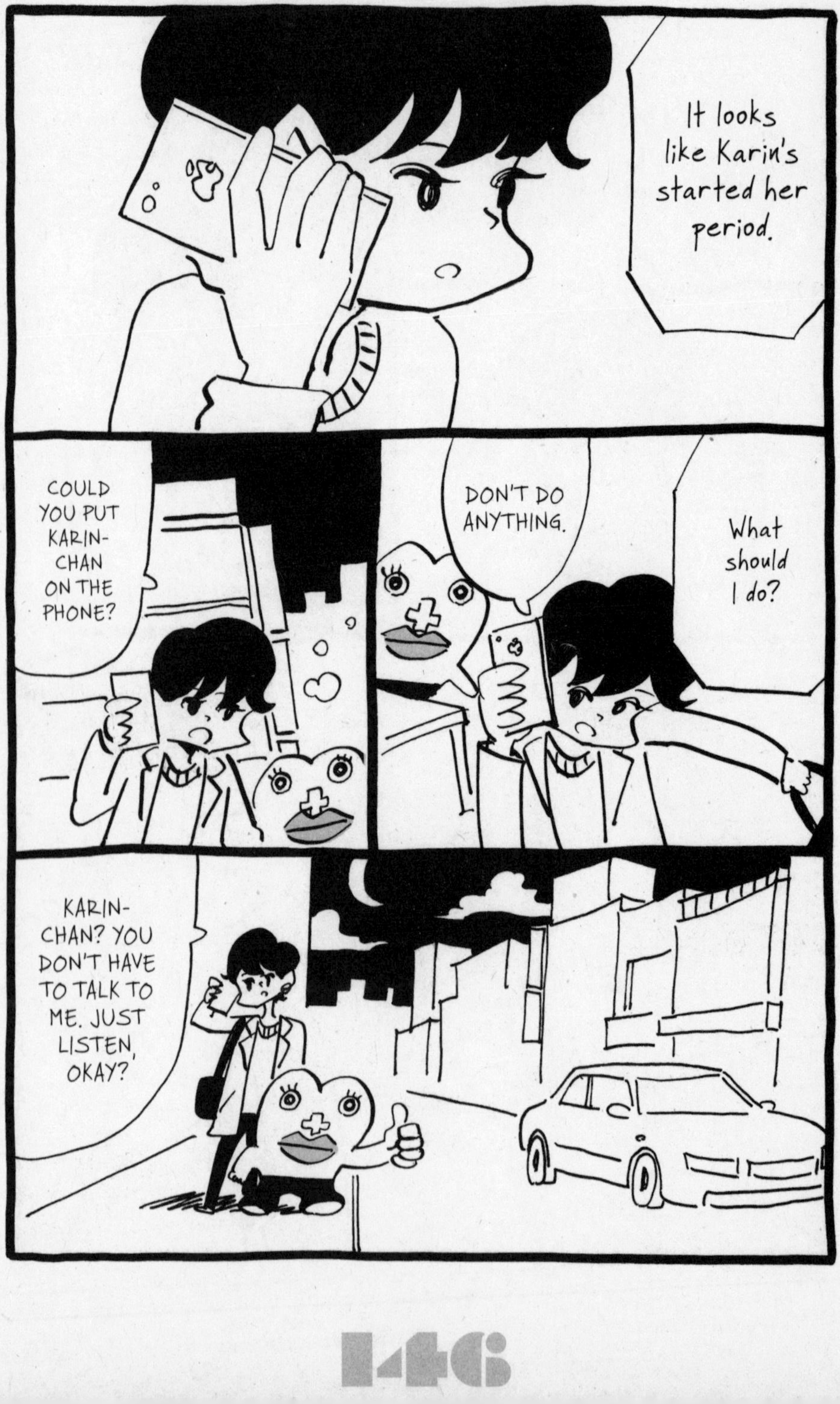
It looks like Karin's started her period.
What should I do?
DON'T DO ANYTHING.
COULD YOU PUT KARIN-CHAN ON THE PHONE?
KARIN-CHAN? YOU DON'T HAVE TO TALK TO ME. JUST LISTEN, OKAY?

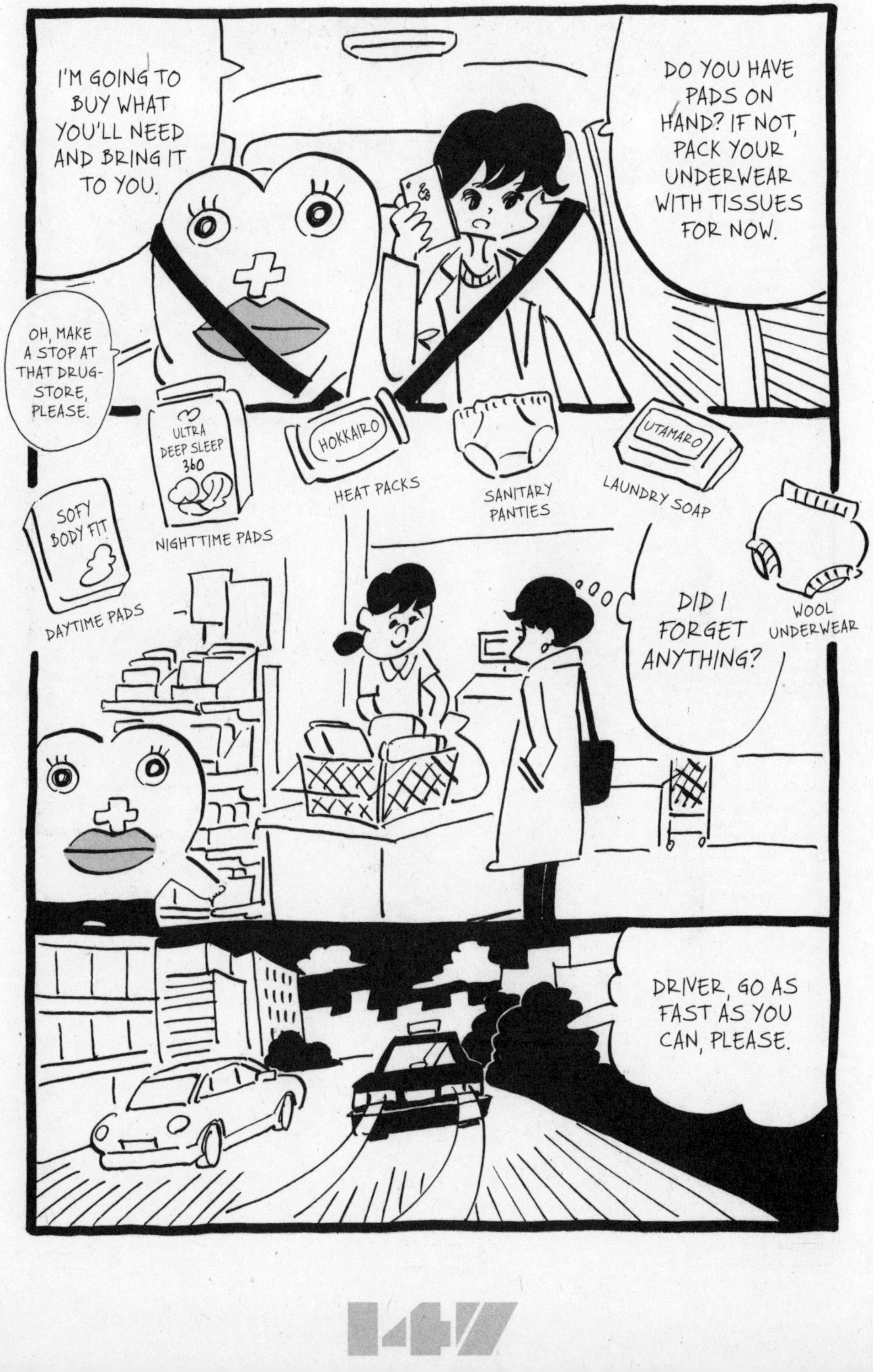
DO YOU HAVE PADS ON HAND? IF NOT, PACK YOUR UNDERWEAR WITH TISSUES FOR NOW.
I'M GOING TO BUY WHAT YOU'LL NEED AND BRING IT TO YOU.
OH, MAKE A STOP AT THAT DRUG-STORE, PLEASE.
WOOL UNDERWEAR
UTAMARO
LAUNDRY SOAP
SANITARY PANTIES
HOKKAIRO
HEAT PACKS
ULTRA DEEP SLEEP 360
NIGHTTIME PADS
SOFY BODY FIT
DAYTIME PADS
DID I FORGET ANYTHING?
DRIVER, GO AS FAST AS YOU CAN, PLEASE.

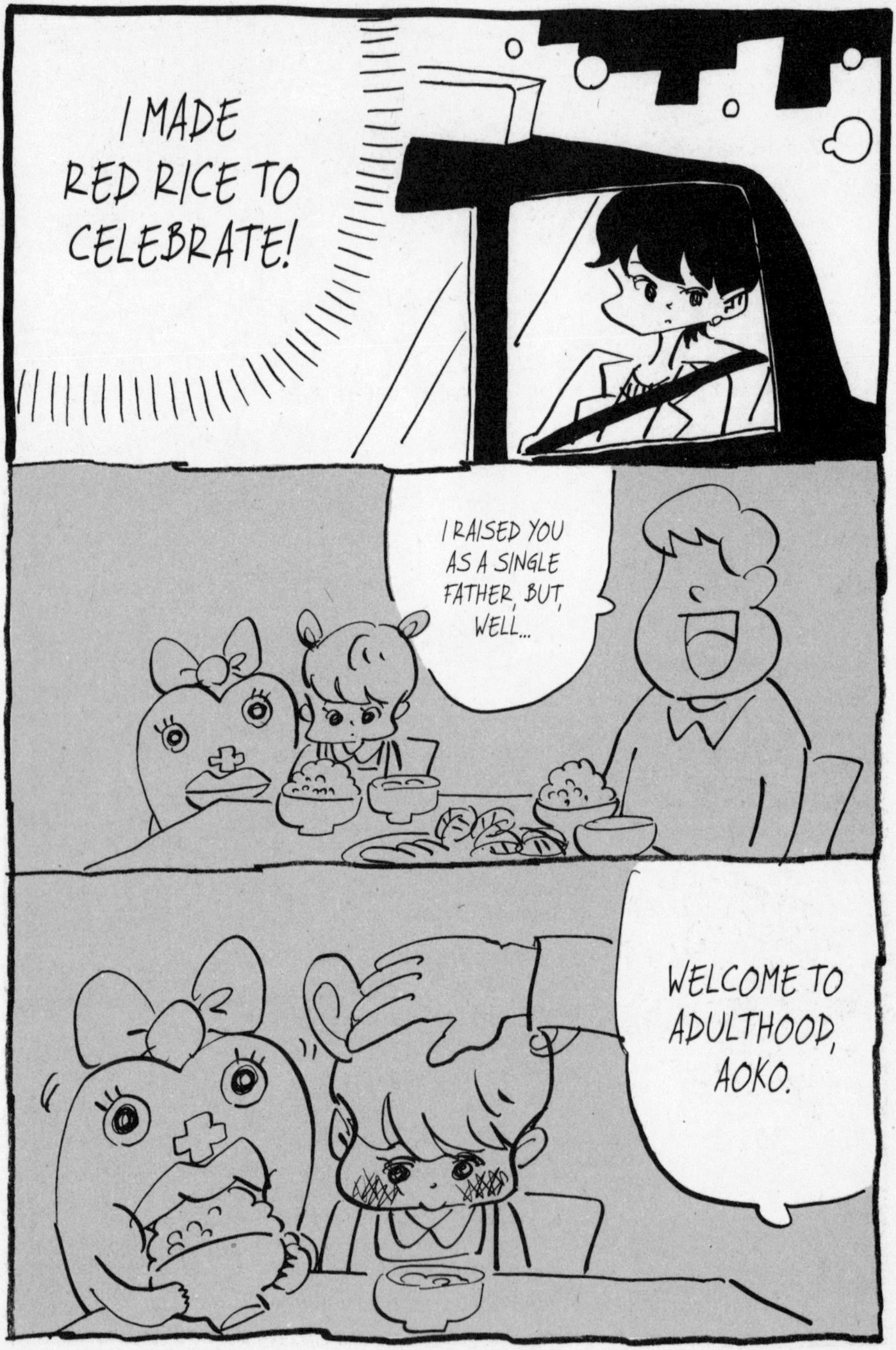
I MADE RED RICE TO CELEBRATE!
I RAISED YOU AS A SINGLE FATHER, BUT, WELL...
WELCOME TO ADULTHOOD, AOKO.

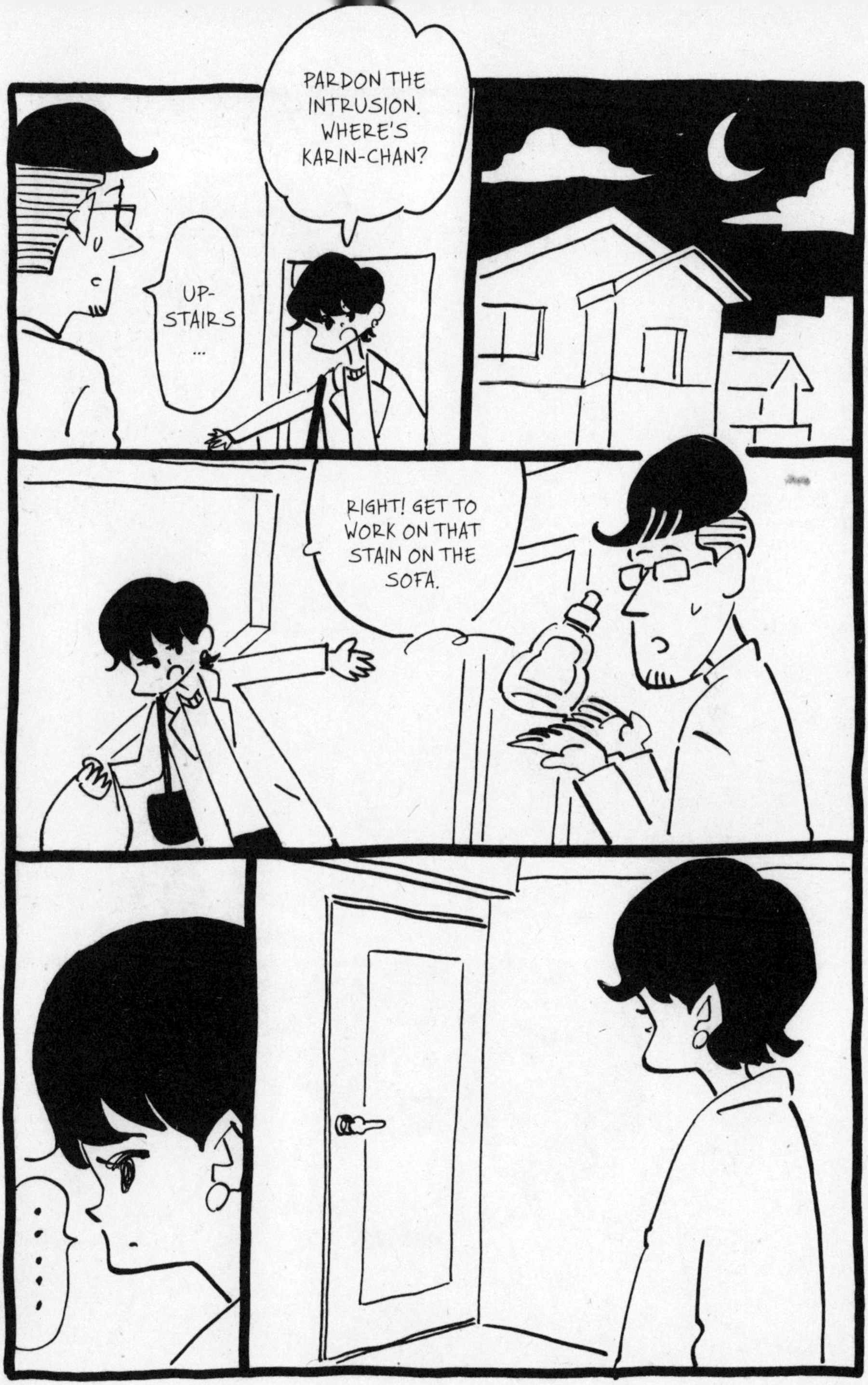
PARDON THE INTRUSION. WHERE'S KARIN-CHAN?
UP-STAIRS ...
RIGHT! GET TO WORK ON THAT STAIN ON THE SOFA.
......

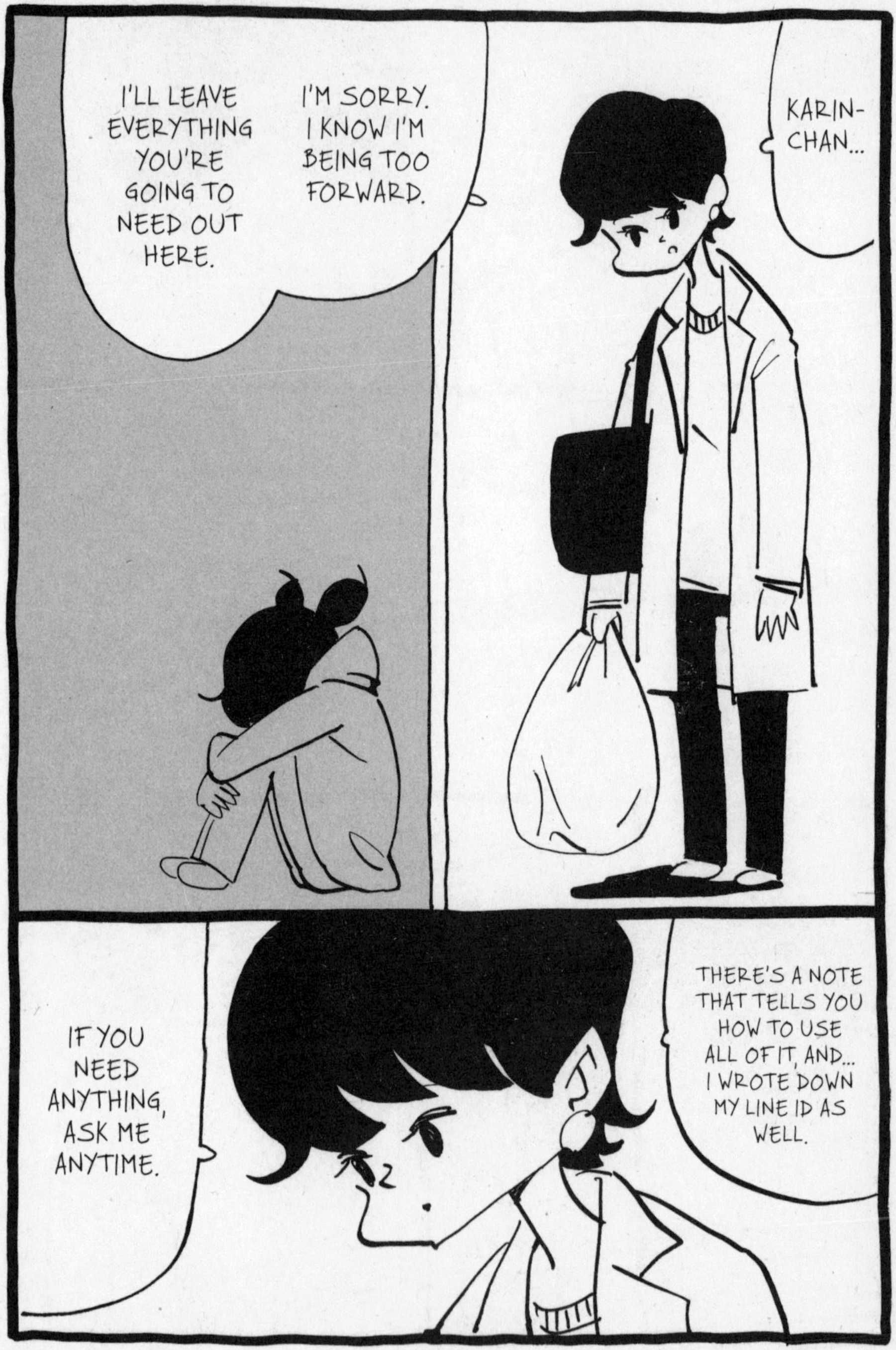
KARIN-CHAN...
I'M SORRY. I KNOW I'M BEING TOO FORWARD.
I'LL LEAVE EVERYTHING YOU'RE GOING TO NEED OUT HERE.
THERE'S A NOTE THAT TELLS YOU HOW TO USE ALL OF IT, AND... I WROTE DOWN MY LINE ID AS WELL.
IF YOU NEED ANYTHING, ASK ME ANYTIME.

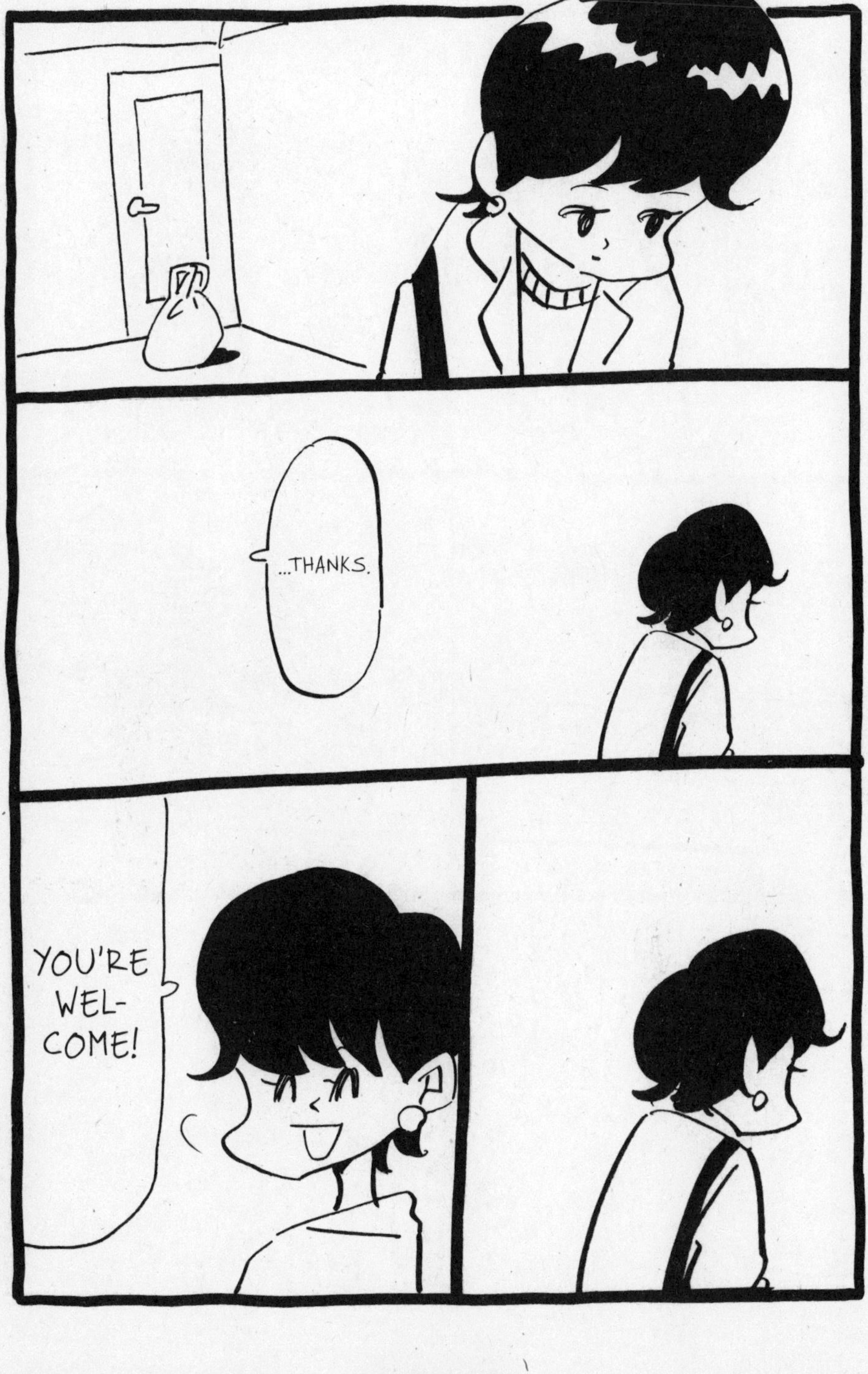
...THANKS.
YOU'RE WEL- COME!

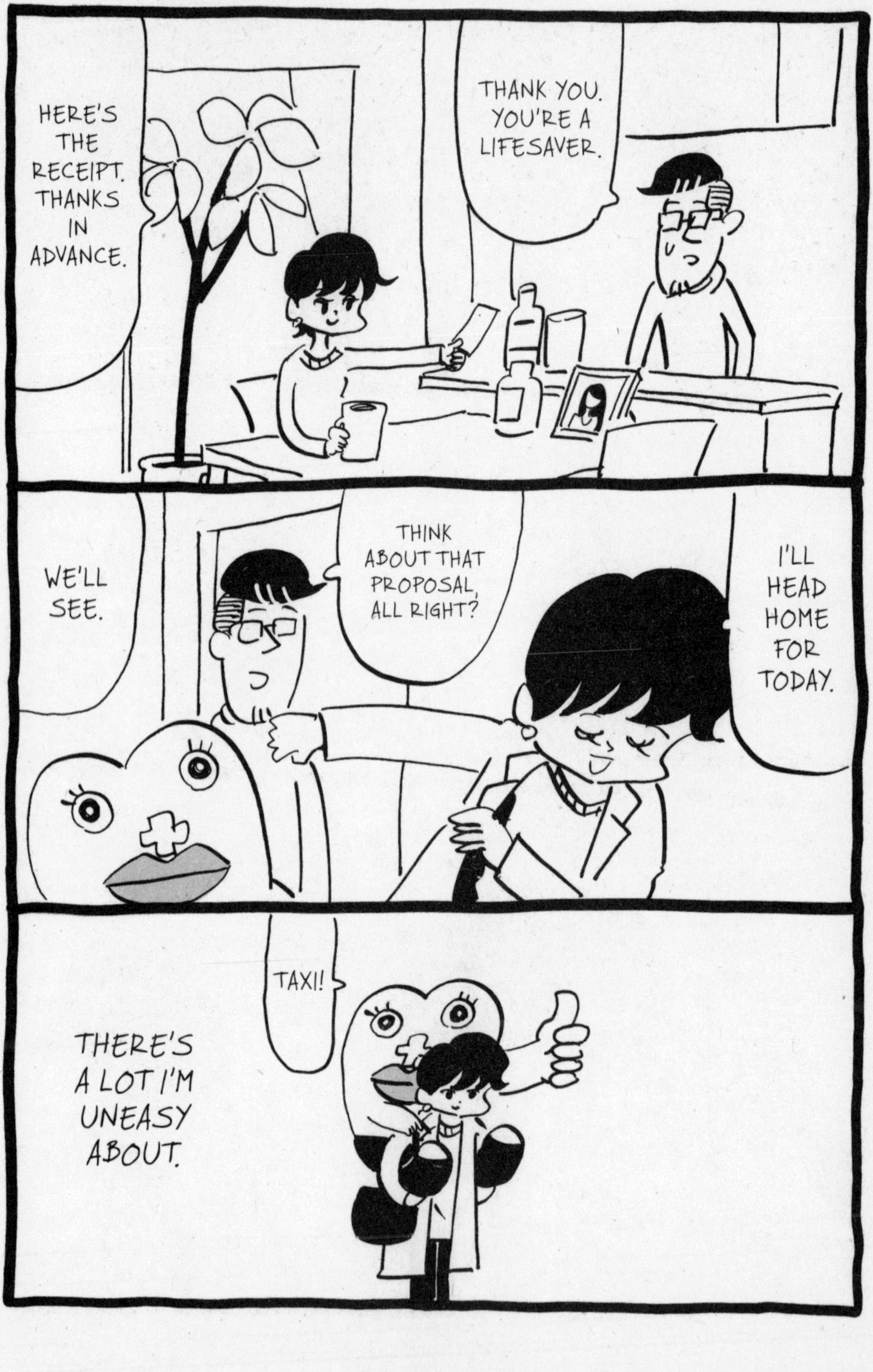
THANK YOU. YOU'RE A LIFESAVER.
HERE'S THE RECEIPT. THANKS IN ADVANCE.
I'LL HEAD HOME FOR TODAY.
THINK ABOUT THAT PROPOSAL, ALL RIGHT?
WE'LL SEE.
TAXI!
THERE'S A LOT I'M UNEASY ABOUT.

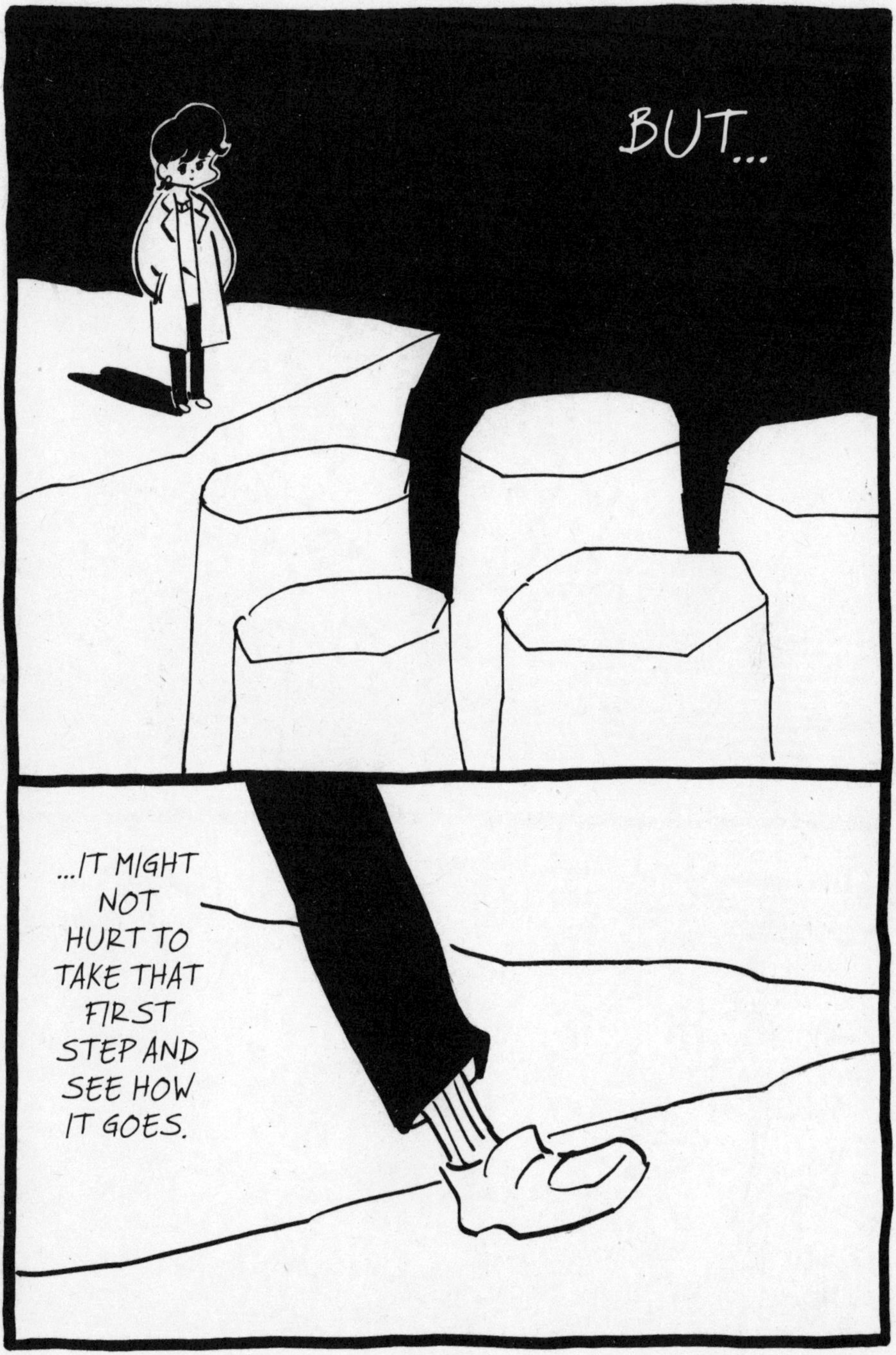
BUT...
...IT MIGHT NOT HURT TO TAKE THAT FIRST STEP AND SEE HOW IT GOES.

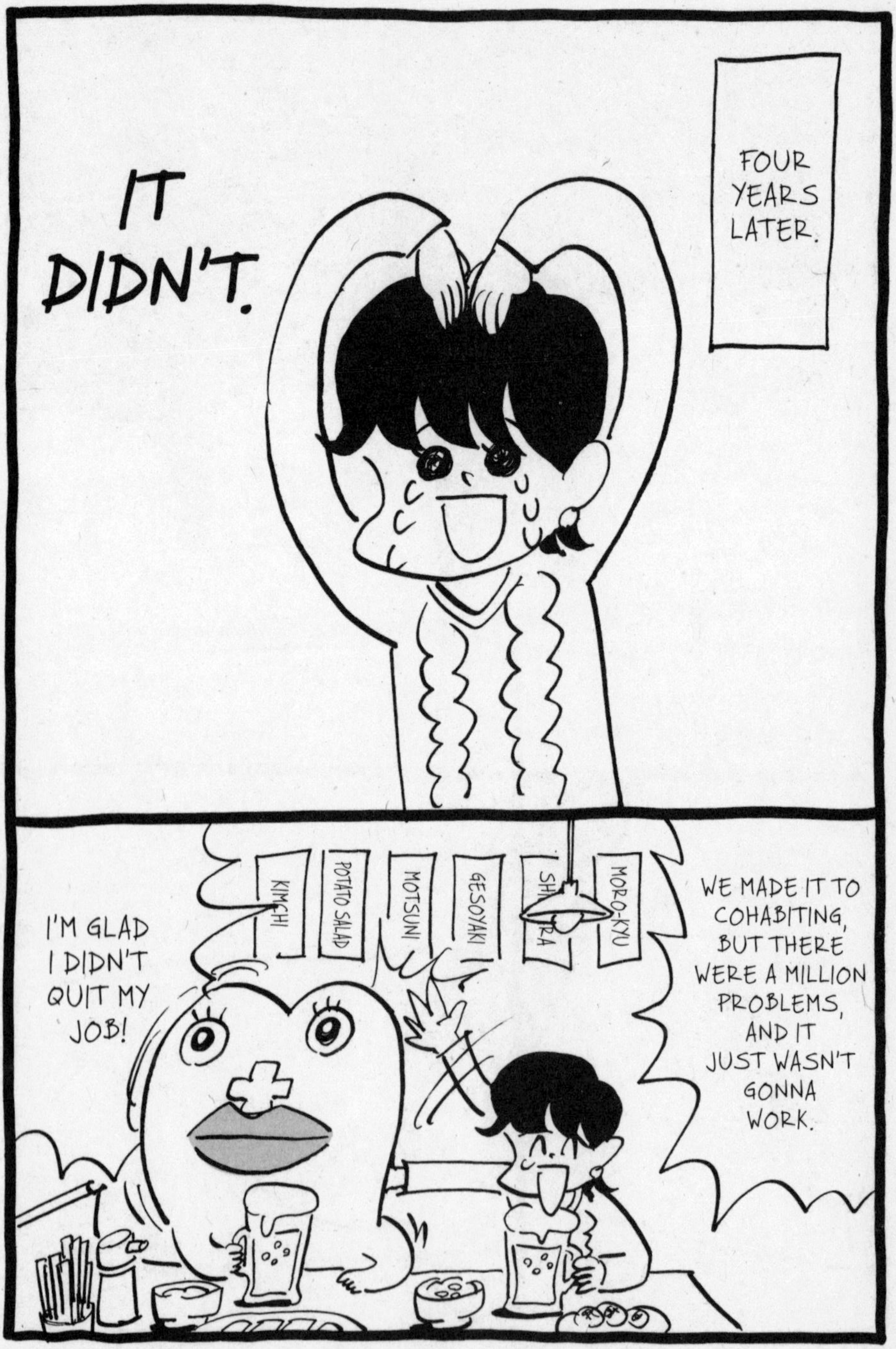
FOUR YEARS LATER.
IT DIDN'T.
WE MADE IT TO COHABITING, BUT THERE WERE A MILLION PROBLEMS, AND IT JUST WASN'T GONNA WORK.
MORO-KYU
GESOYAKI
MOTSUNI
POTATO SALAD
KIMCHI
I'M GLAD I DIDN'T QUIT MY JOB!

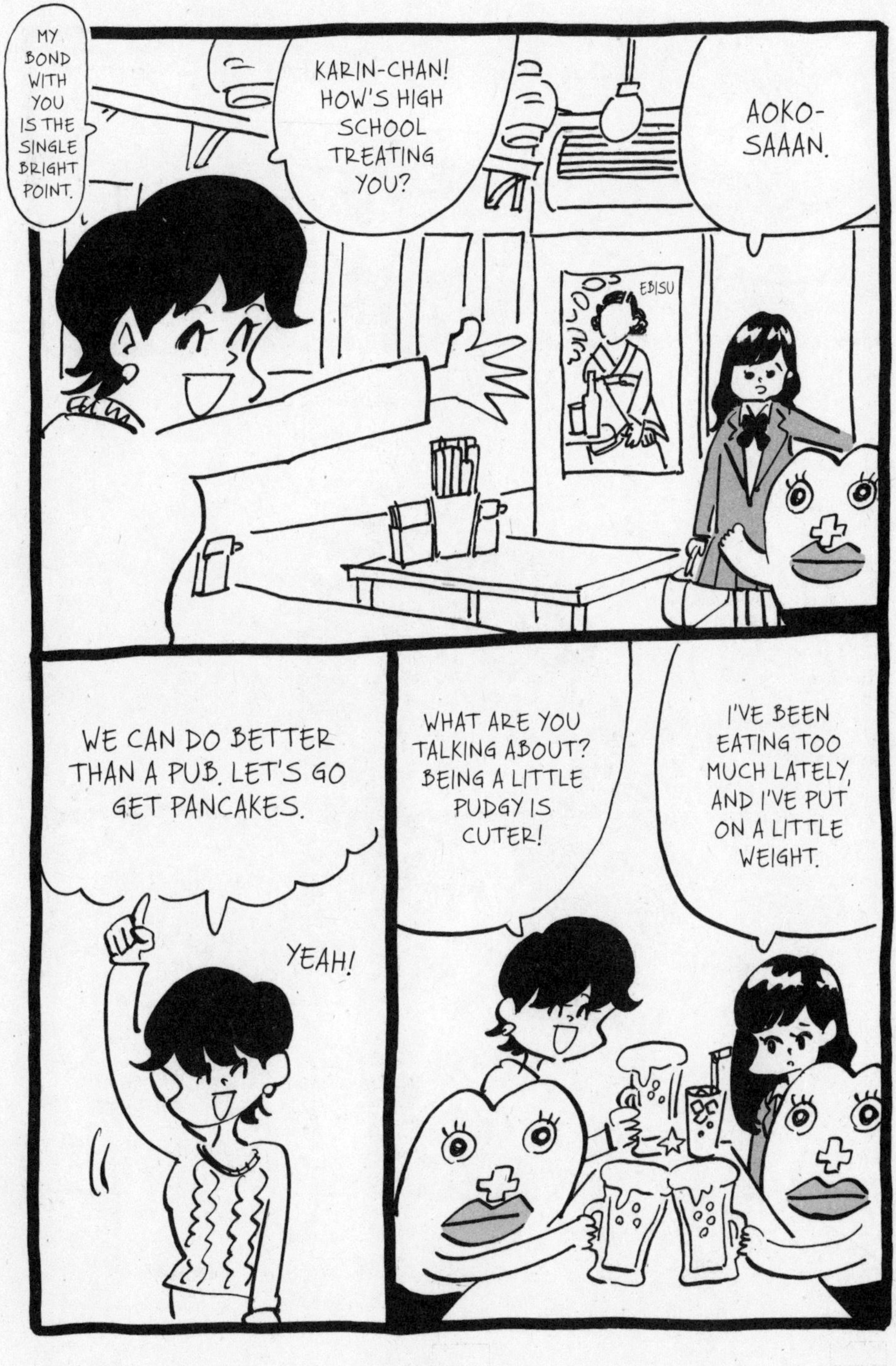
AOKO-SAAAN.
KARIN-CHAN! HOW'S HIGH SCHOOL TREATING YOU?
MY BOND WITH YOU IS THE SINGLE BRIGHT POINT.
EBISU
I'VE BEEN EATING TOO MUCH LATELY, AND I'VE PUT ON A LITTLE WEIGHT.
WHAT ARE YOU TALKING ABOUT? BEING A LITTLE PUDGY IS CUTER!
WE CAN DO BETTER THAN A PUB. LET'S GO GET PANCAKES.
YEAH!

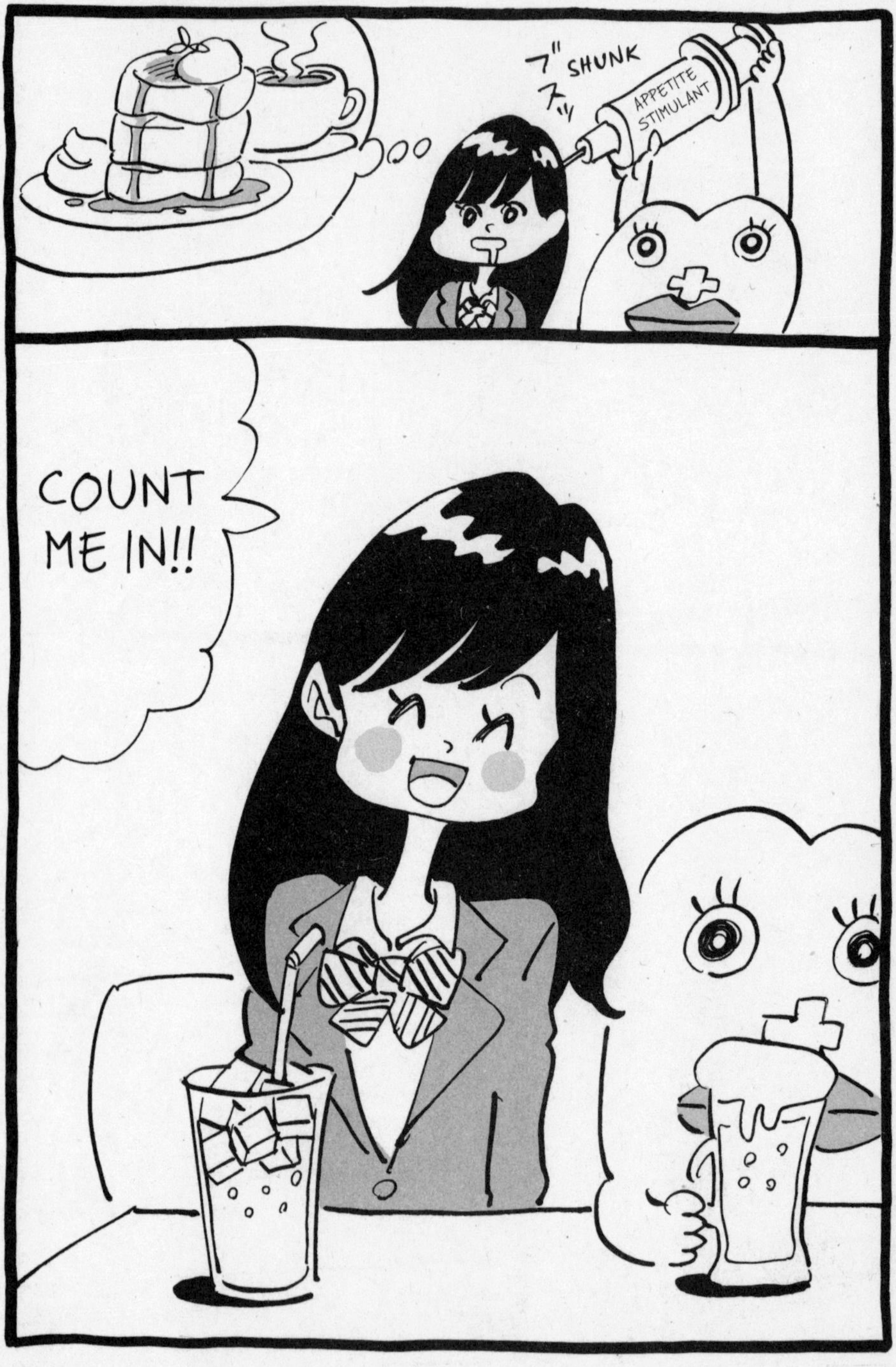
ブスッ
SHUNK
APPETITE STIMULANT
COUNT ME IN!!

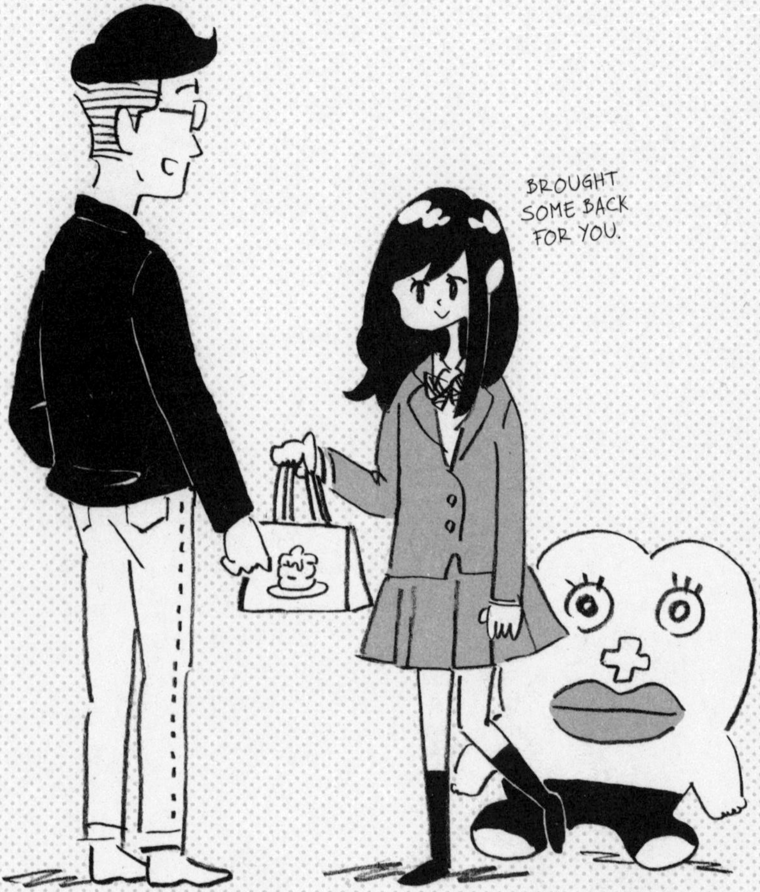
BROUGHT SOME BACK FOR YOU.

CAFÉ WORKER AND LITTLE MISS P

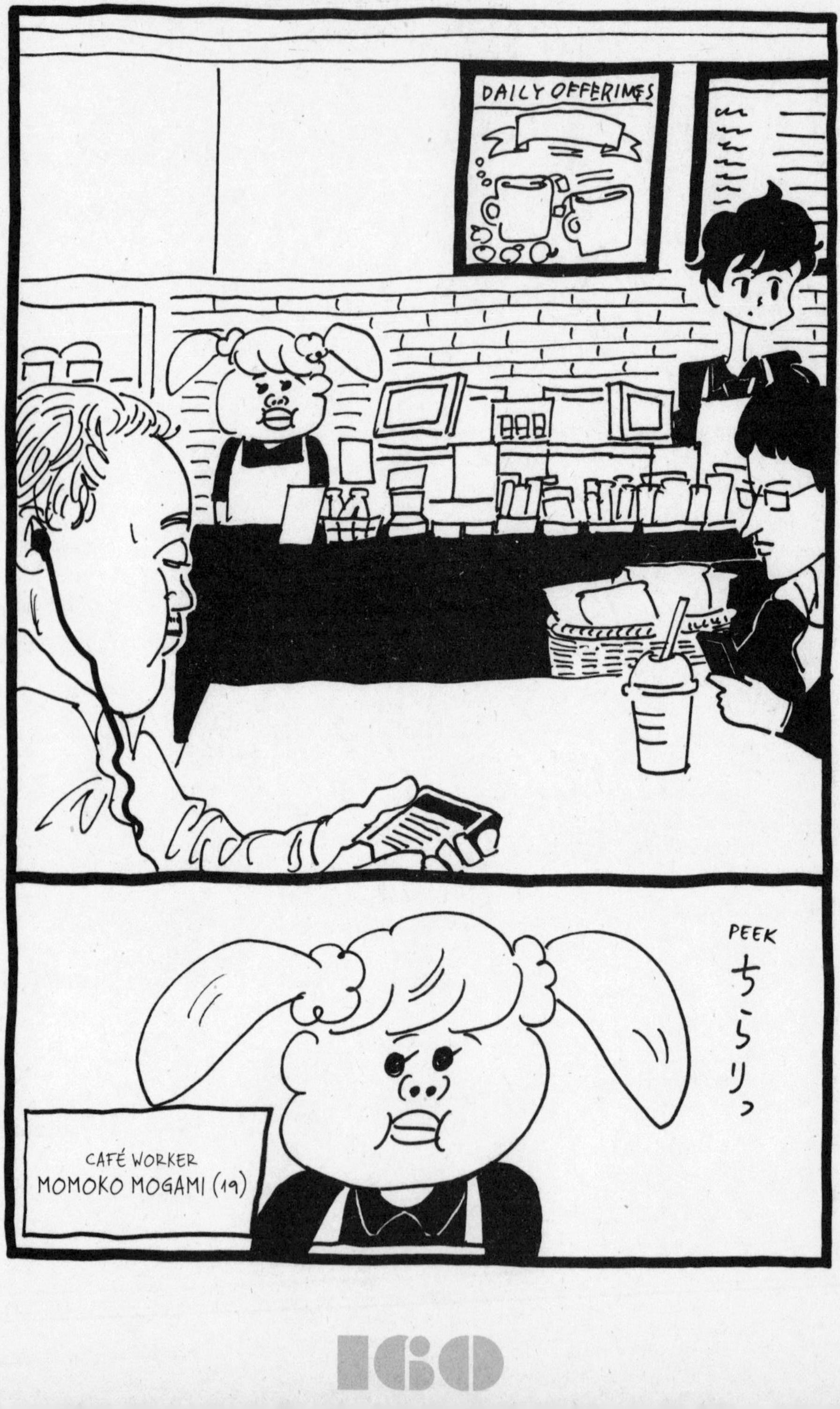
DAILY OFFERINGS
PEEK
ちらりっ
CAFÉ WORKER
MOMOKO MOGAMI (19)

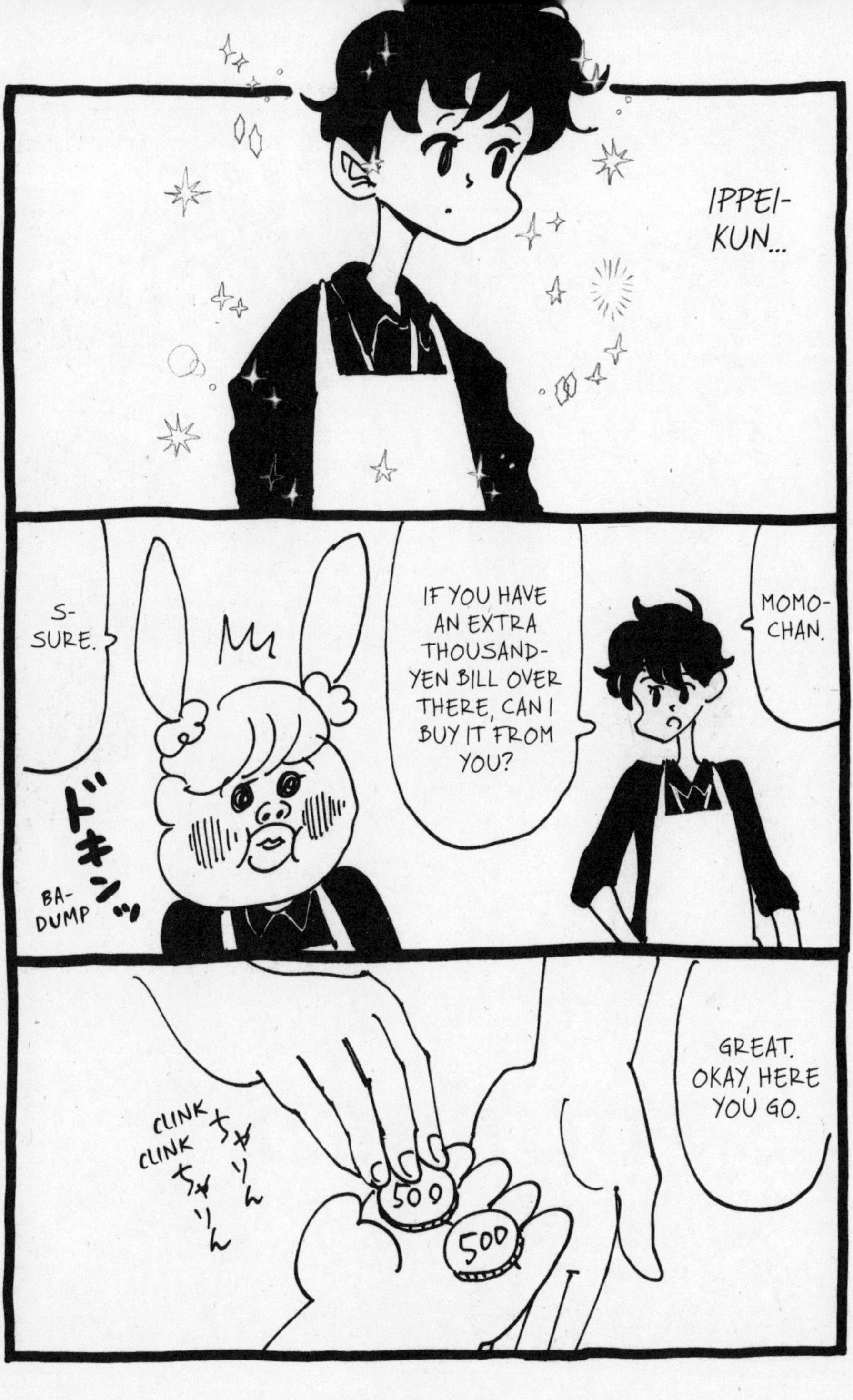
IPPEI-KUN...
MOMO-CHAN.
IF YOU HAVE AN EXTRA THOUSAND-YEN BILL OVER THERE, CAN I BUY IT FROM YOU?
S-SURE.
ドキンッ
BA-DUMP
GREAT. OKAY, HERE YOU GO.
ちゃりん
ちゃりん
CLINK CLINK
500
500

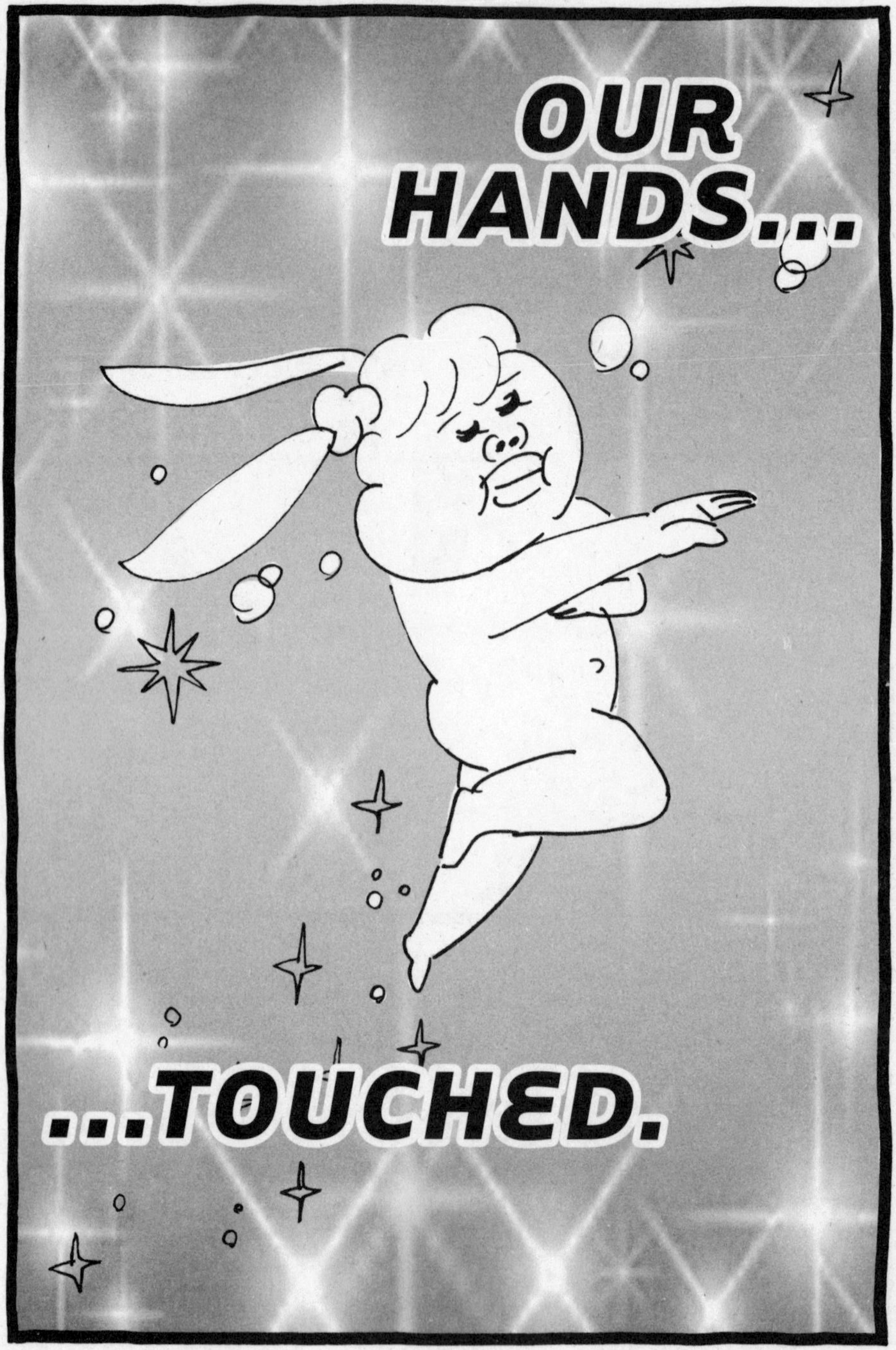
OUR HANDS...
...TOUCHED.

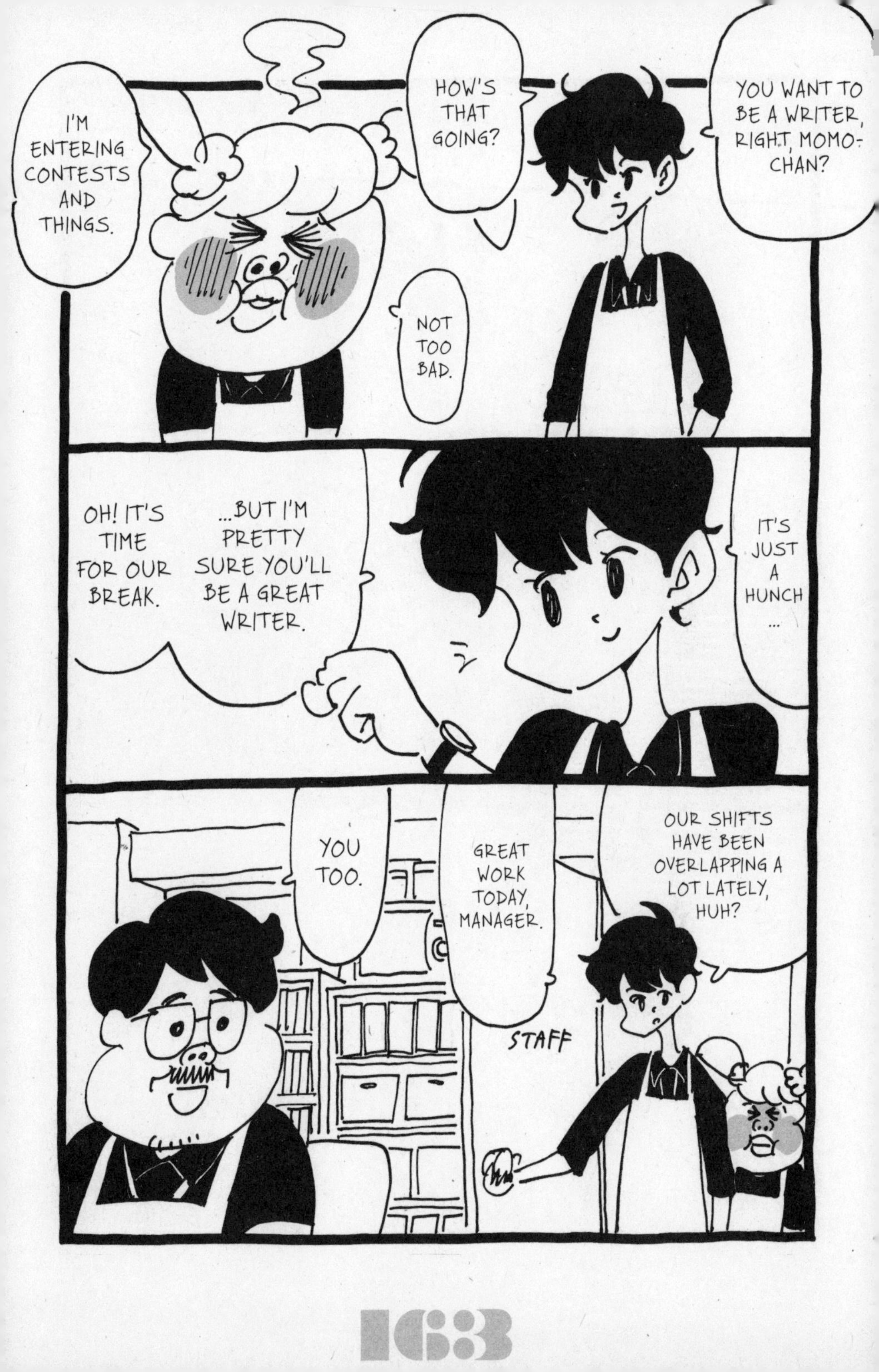
YOU WANT TO BE A WRITER, RIGHT, MOMO-CHAN?
HOW'S THAT GOING?
I'M ENTERING CONTESTS AND THINGS.
NOT TOO BAD.
IT'S JUST A HUNCH...
...BUT I'M PRETTY SURE YOU'LL BE A GREAT WRITER.
OH! IT'S TIME FOR OUR BREAK.
OUR SHIFTS HAVE BEEN OVERLAPPING A LOT LATELY, HUH?
GREAT WORK TODAY, MANAGER.
YOU TOO.
STAFF

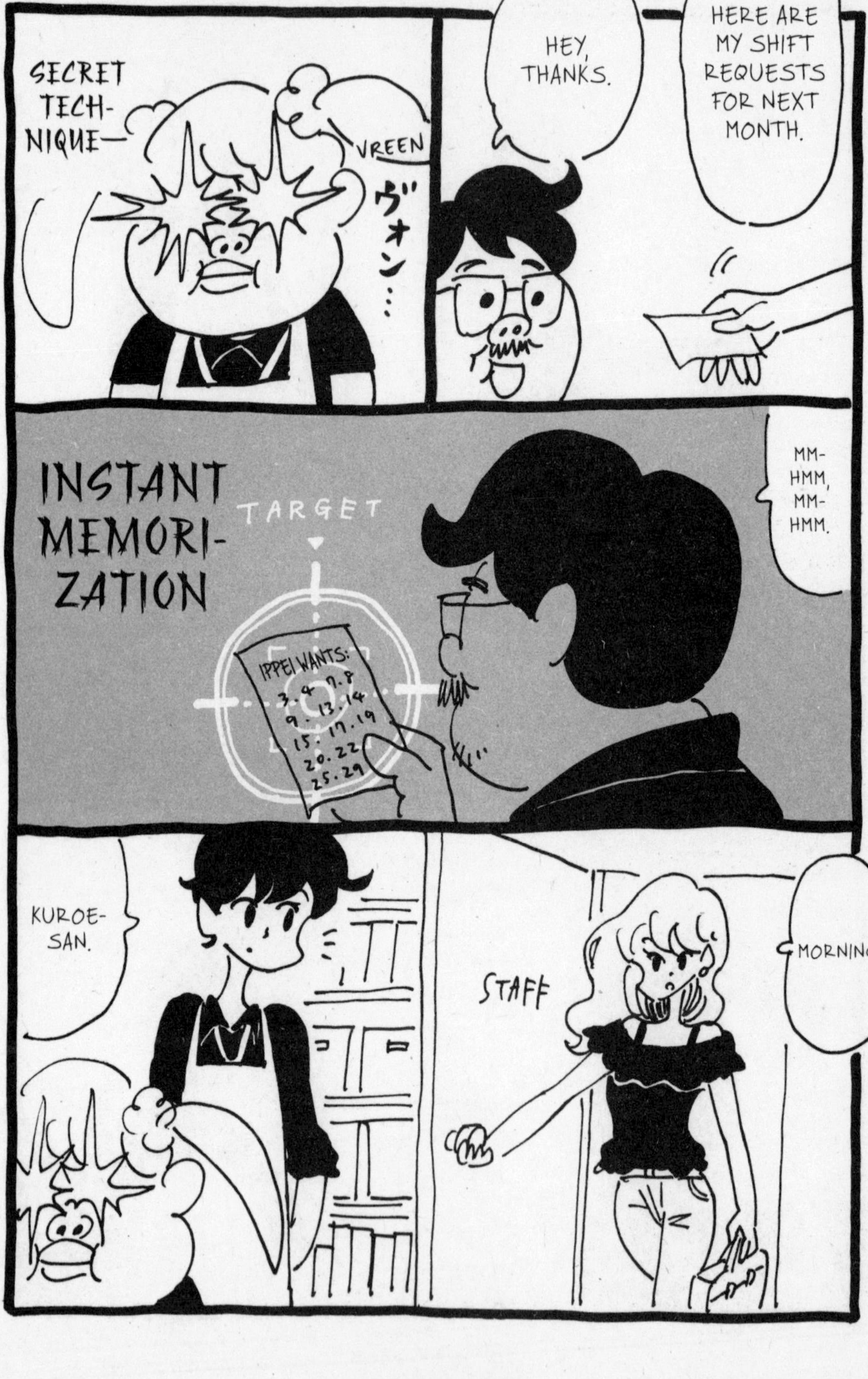
HERE ARE MY SHIFT REQUESTS FOR NEXT MONTH.
HEY, THANKS.
SECRET TECHNIQUE—
VREEN
ヴォン…
MM-HMM, MM-HMM.
INSTANT MEMORIZATION
TARGET
IPPEI WANTS:
3.4 7.8
9. 13.14
15. 17.19
20.22
25.29
MORNING.
STAFF
KUROE-SAN.

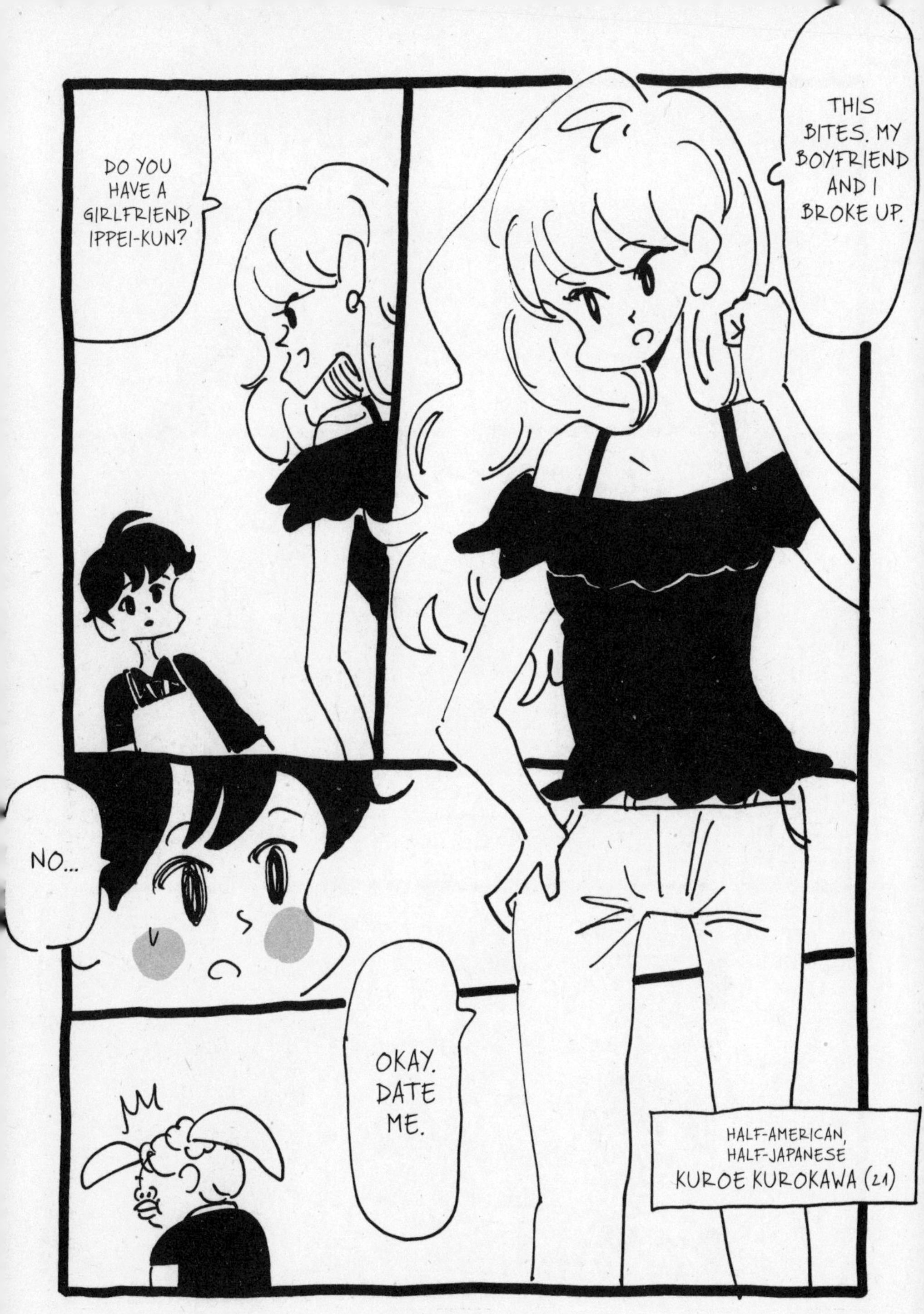
THIS BITES. MY BOYFRIEND AND I BROKE UP.
HALF-AMERICAN, HALF-JAPANESE KUROE KUROKAWA (21)
DO YOU HAVE A GIRLFRIEND, IPPEI-KUN?
NO...
OKAY. DATE ME.

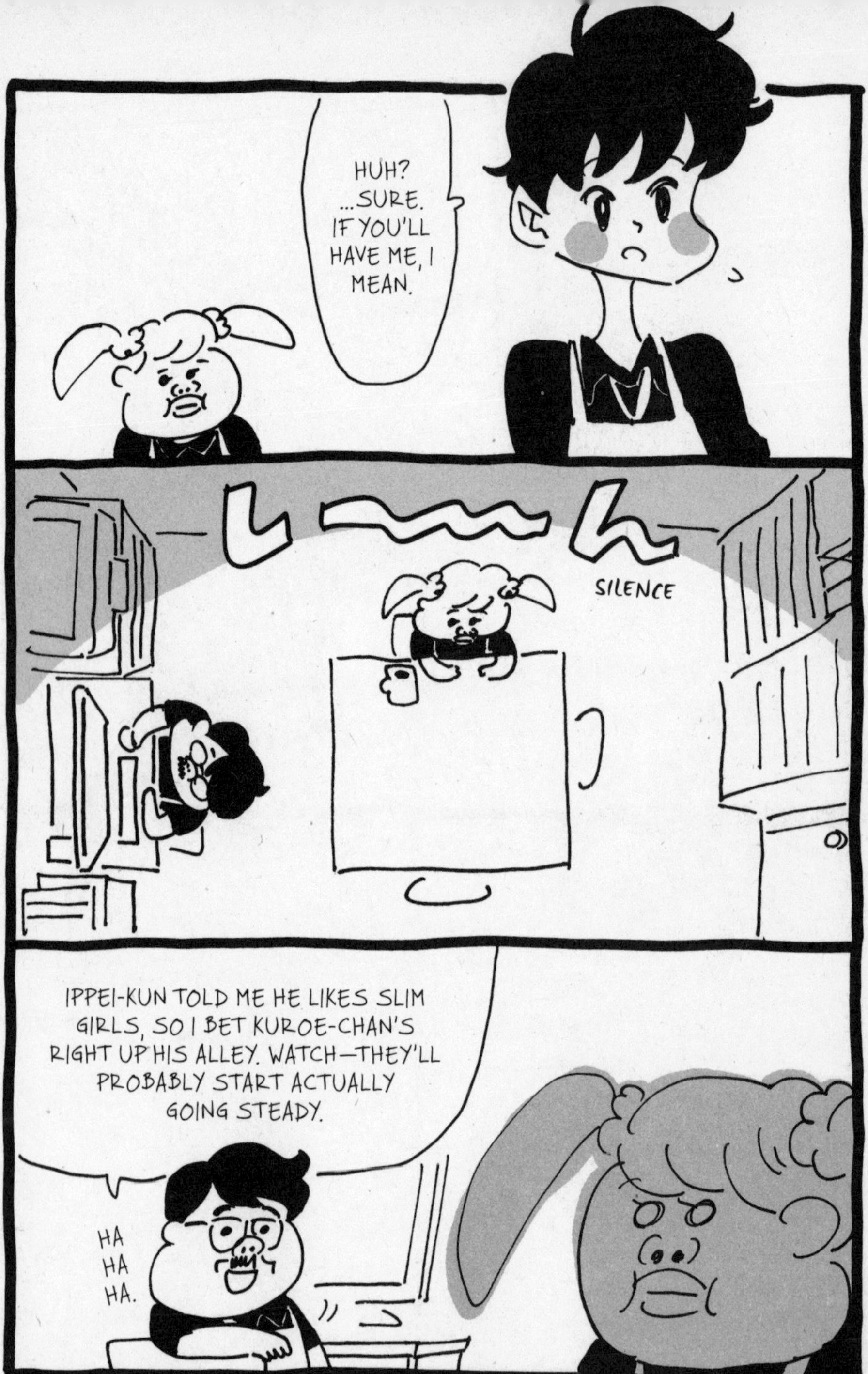
HUH? ...SURE. IF YOU'LL HAVE ME, I MEAN.
し〜ん
SILENCE
IPPEI-KUN TOLD ME HE LIKES SLIM GIRLS, SO I BET KUROE-CHAN'S RIGHT UP HIS ALLEY. WATCH—THEY'LL PROBABLY START ACTUALLY GOING STEADY.
HA HA HA.

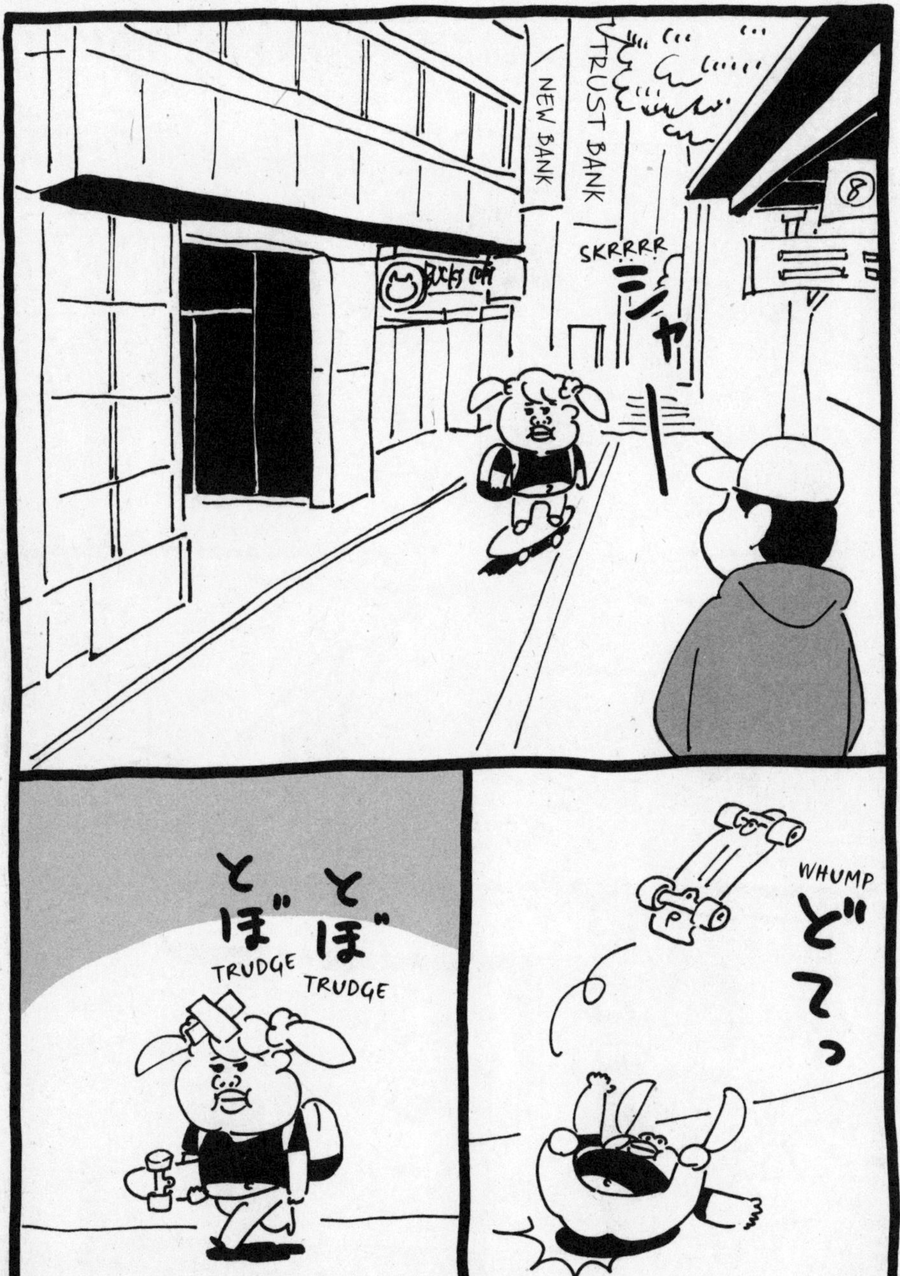
8
TRUST BANK
NEW BANK
SKRRRR
シャ
WHUMP
どてっ
とぼとぼ
TRUDGE
とぼとぼ
TRUDGE

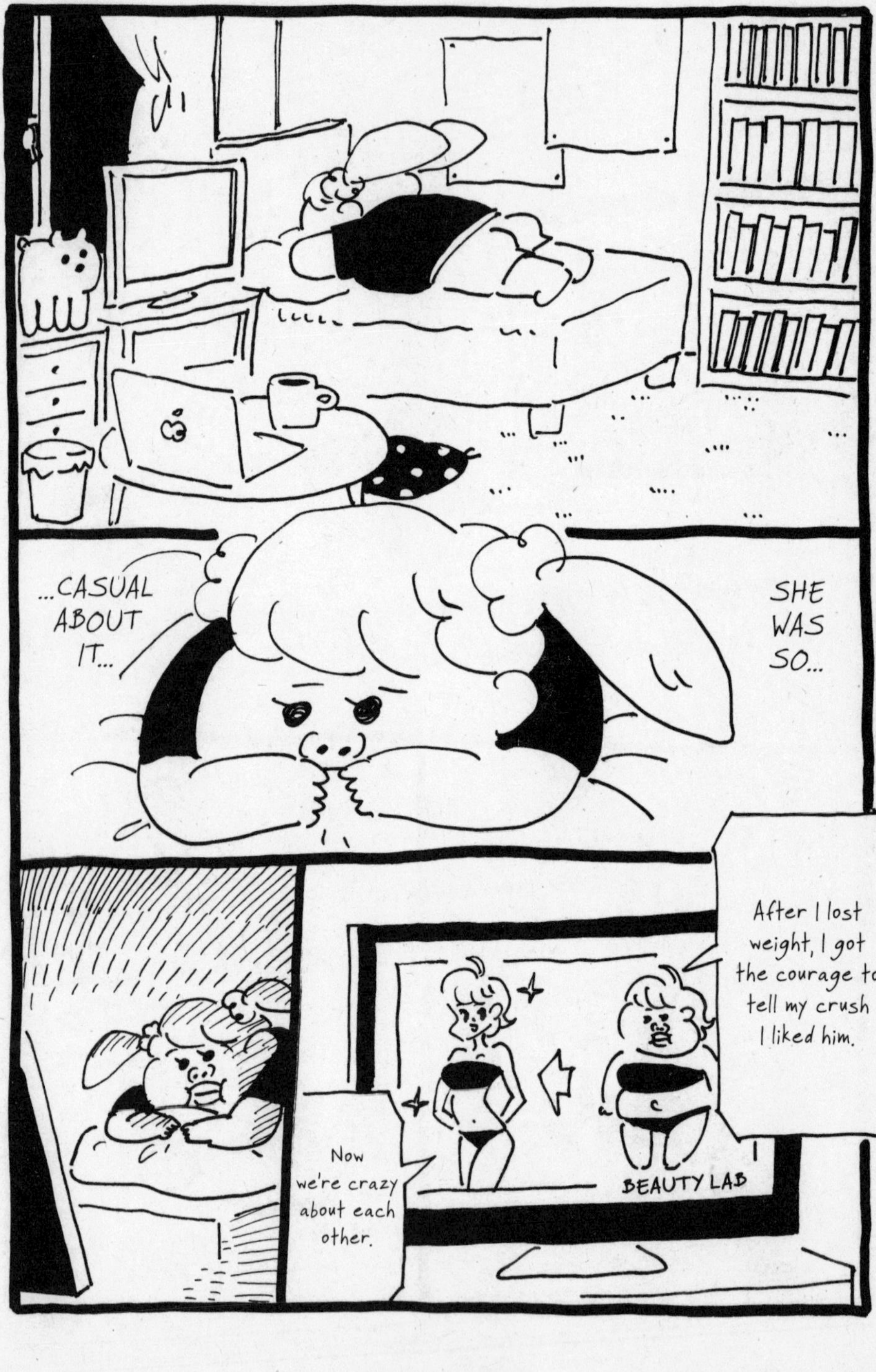
SHE WAS SO...
...CASUAL ABOUT IT...
After I lost weight, I got the courage to tell my crush I liked him.
BEAUTY LAB
Now we're crazy about each other.

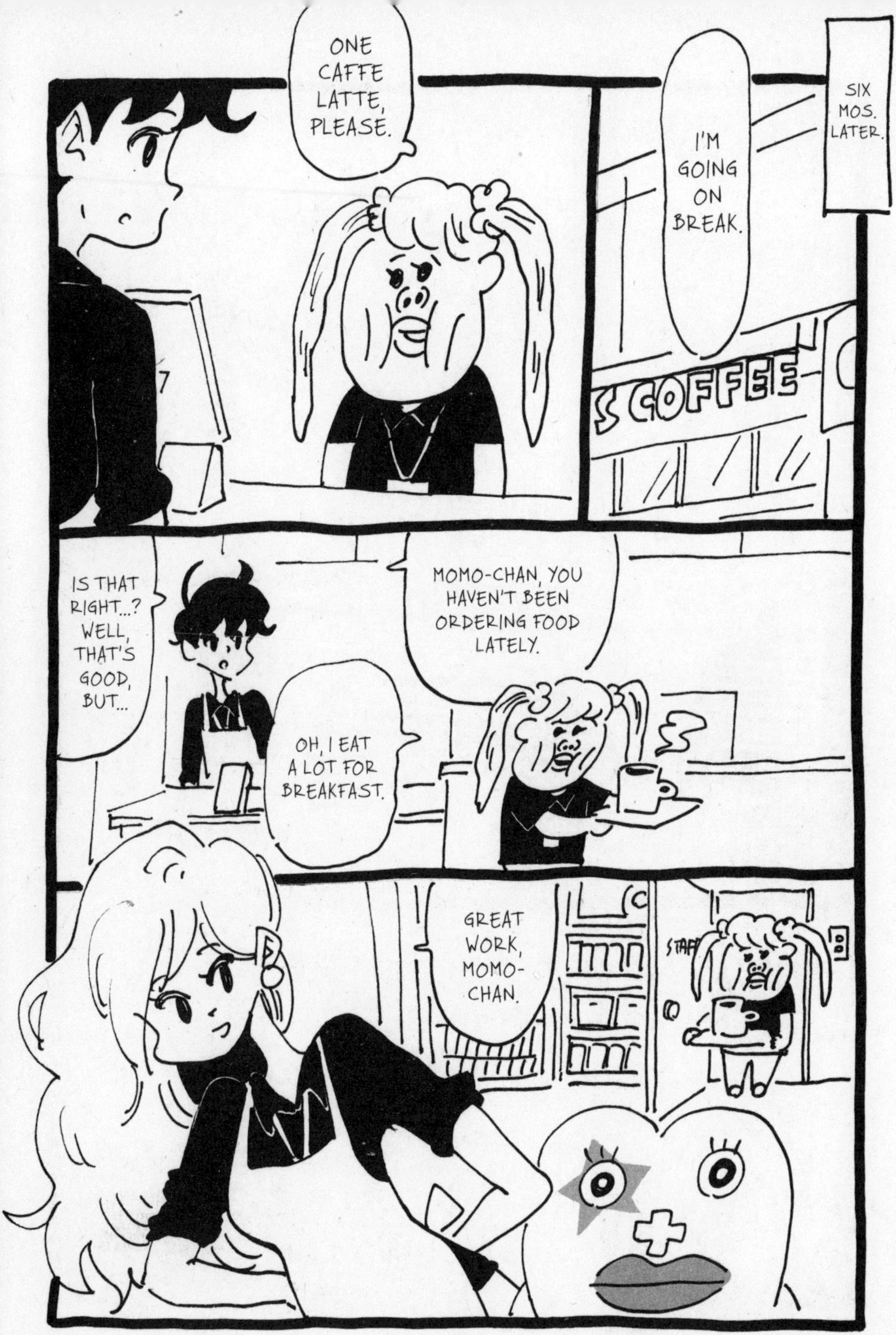

SIX MOS. LATER.
I'M GOING ON BREAK.
S COFFEE
ONE CAFFE LATTE, PLEASE.
MOMO-CHAN, YOU HAVEN'T BEEN ORDERING FOOD LATELY.
OH, I EAT A LOT FOR BREAKFAST.
IS THAT RIGHT...? WELL, THAT'S GOOD, BUT...
STAFF
GREAT WORK, MOMO-CHAN.

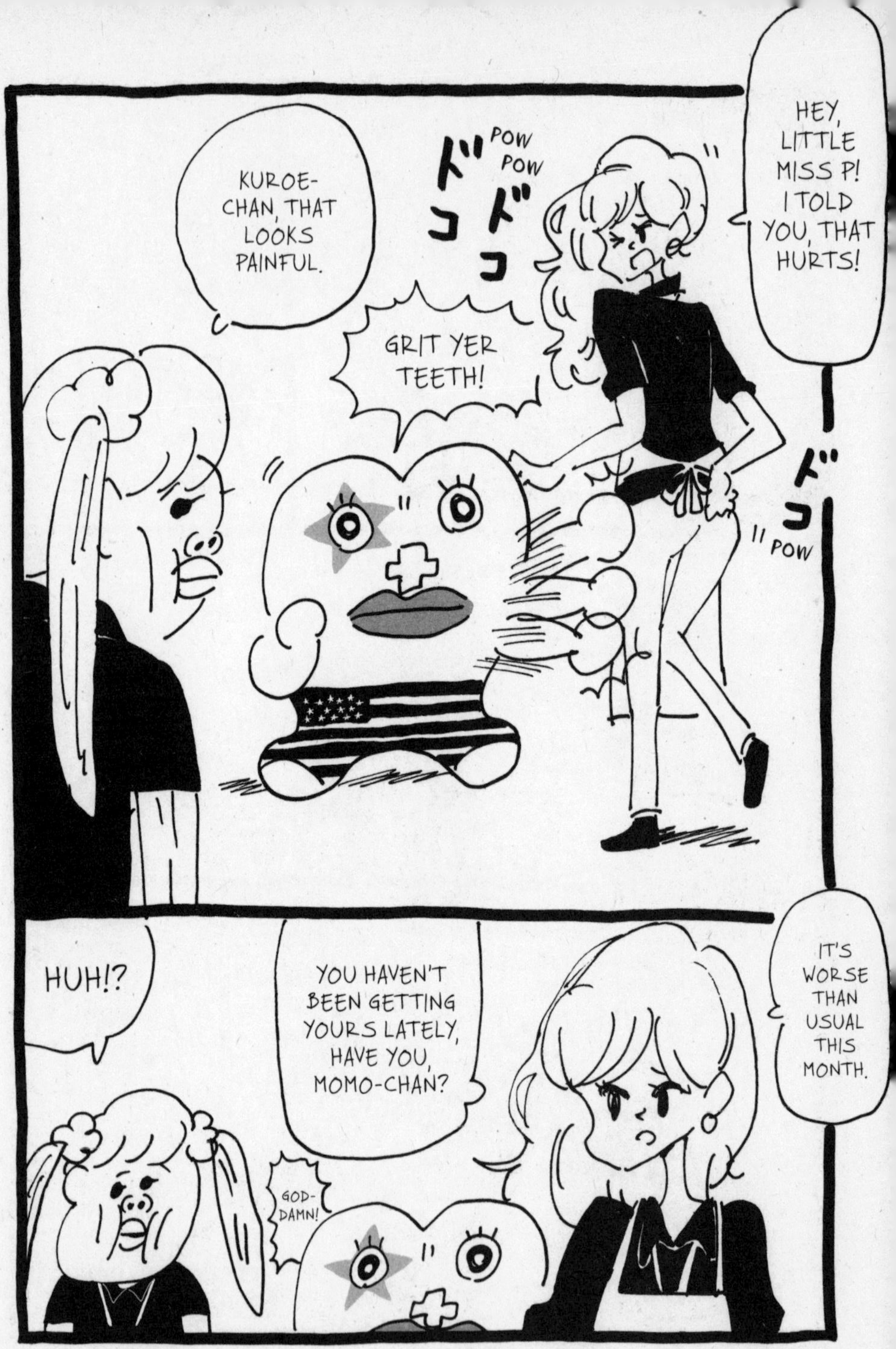
HEY, LITTLE MISS P! I TOLD YOU, THAT HURTS!
ドコ
POW POW
ドコ
KUROE-CHAN, THAT LOOKS PAINFUL.
GRIT YER TEETH!
ドコ
POW
IT'S WORSE THAN USUAL THIS MONTH.
YOU HAVEN'T BEEN GETTING YOURS LATELY, HAVE YOU, MOMO-CHAN?
HUH!?
GOD-DAMN!

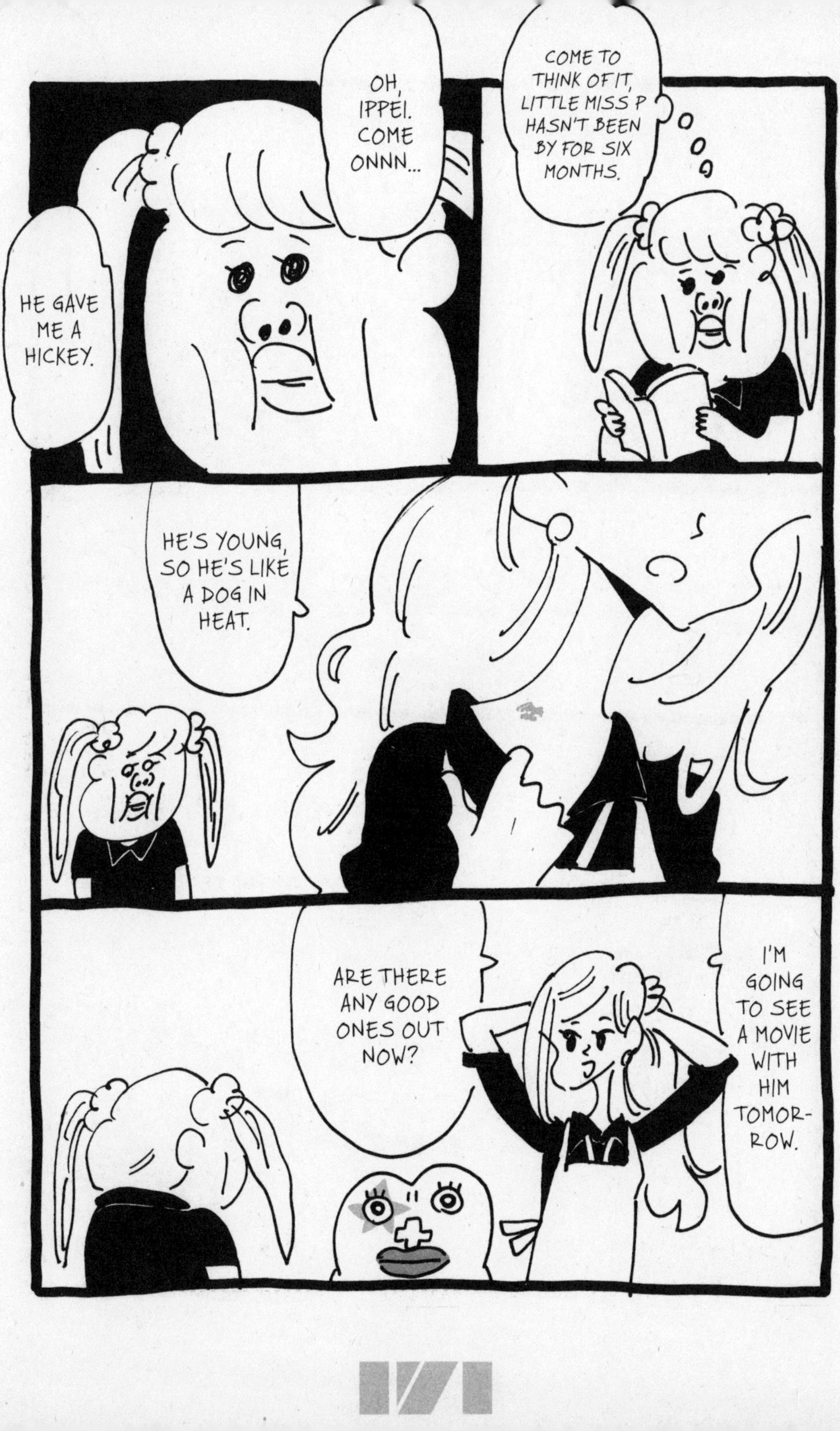
COME TO THINK OF IT, LITTLE MISS P HASN'T BEEN BY FOR SIX MONTHS.
OH, IPPEI. COME ONNN...
HE GAVE ME A HICKEY.
HE'S YOUNG, SO HE'S LIKE A DOG IN HEAT.
I'M GOING TO SEE A MOVIE WITH HIM TOMOR-ROW.
ARE THERE ANY GOOD ONES OUT NOW?

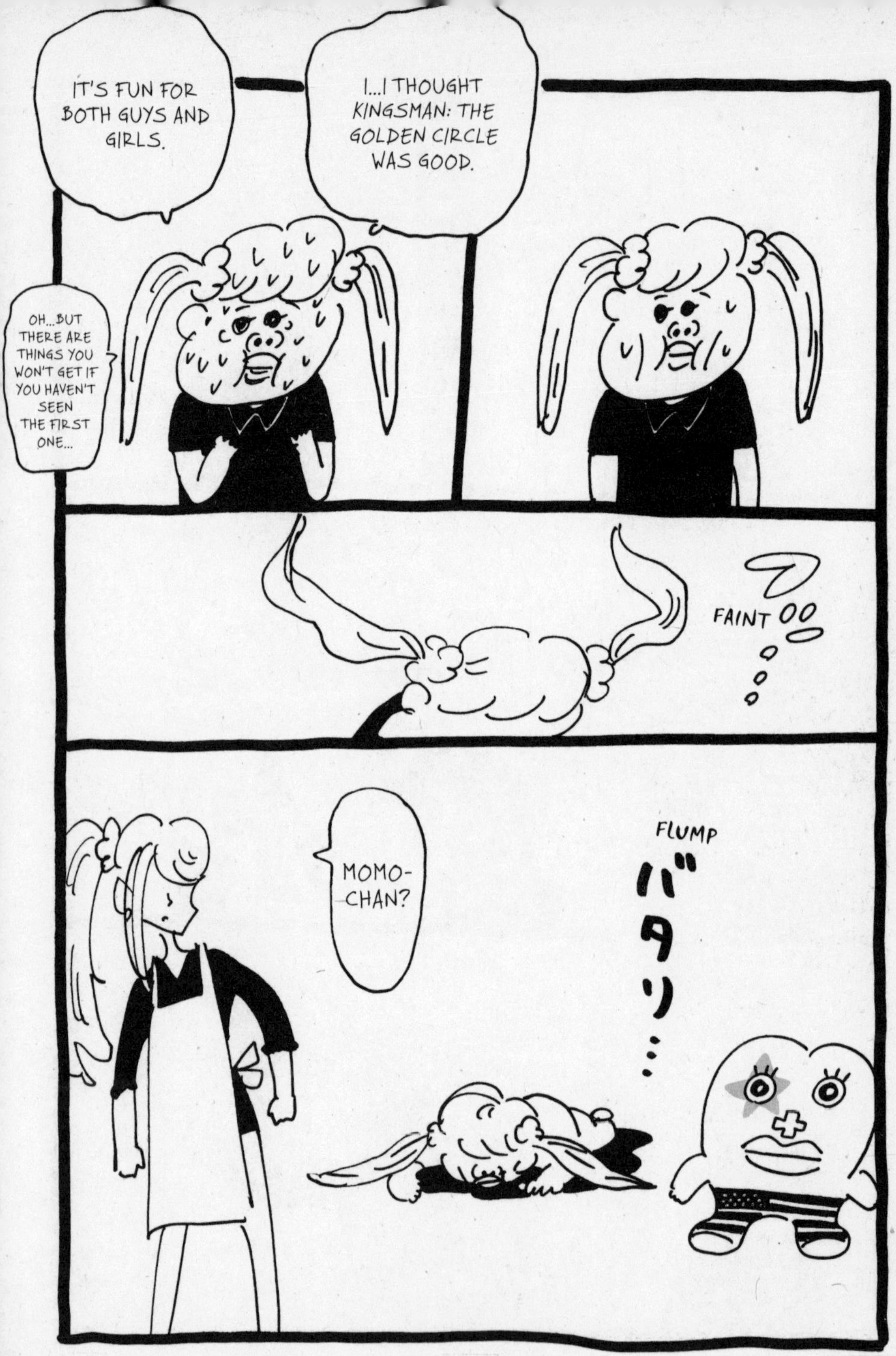
I...I THOUGHT KINGSMAN: THE GOLDEN CIRCLE WAS GOOD.
IT'S FUN FOR BOTH GUYS AND GIRLS.
OH...BUT THERE ARE THINGS YOU WON'T GET IF YOU HAVEN'T SEEN THE FIRST ONE...
FAINT
FLUMP
バタリ…
MOMO-CHAN?

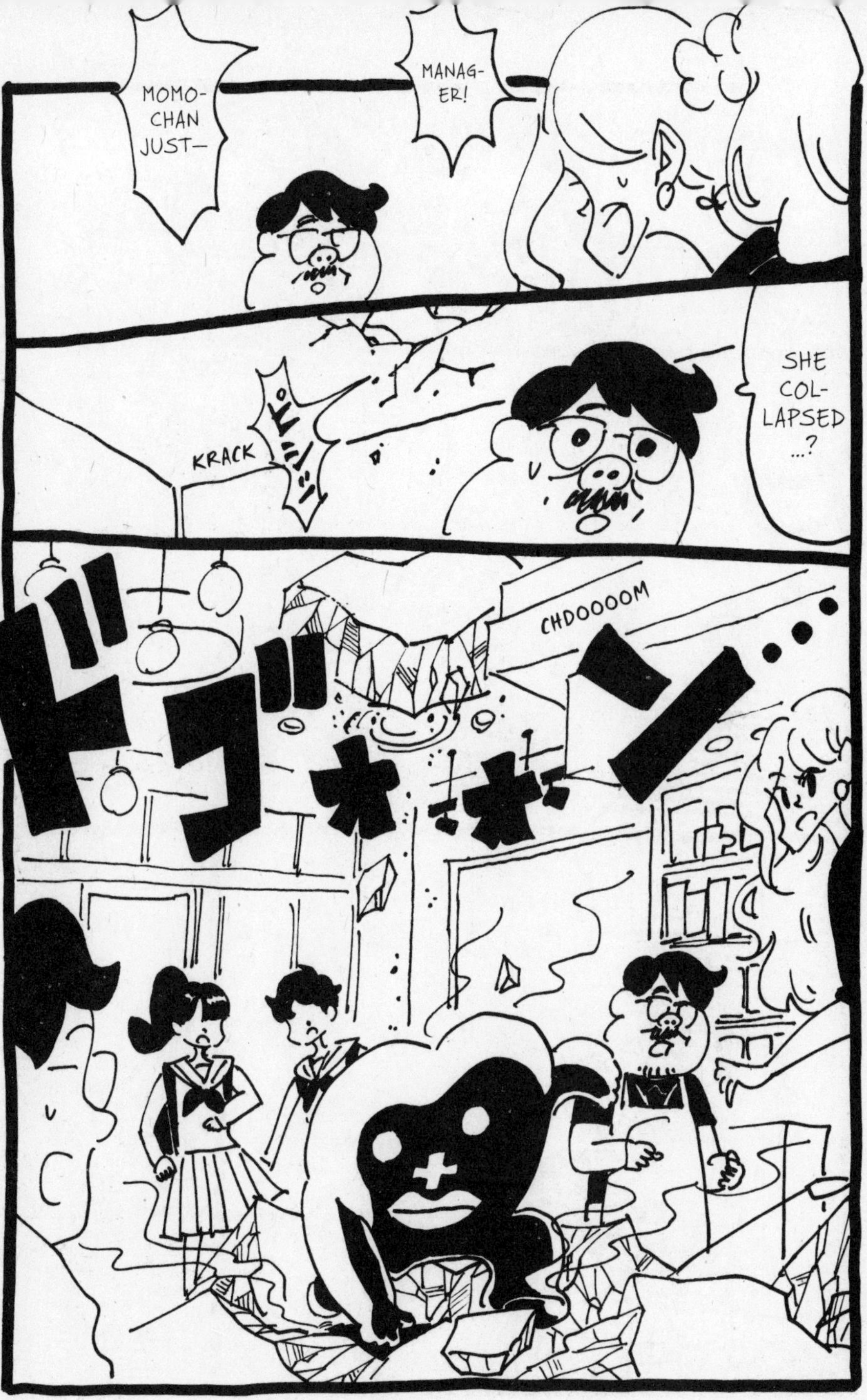
MANAG-ER!
MOMO-CHAN JUST—
SHE COL-LAPSED ...?
KRACK
CHDOOOOM

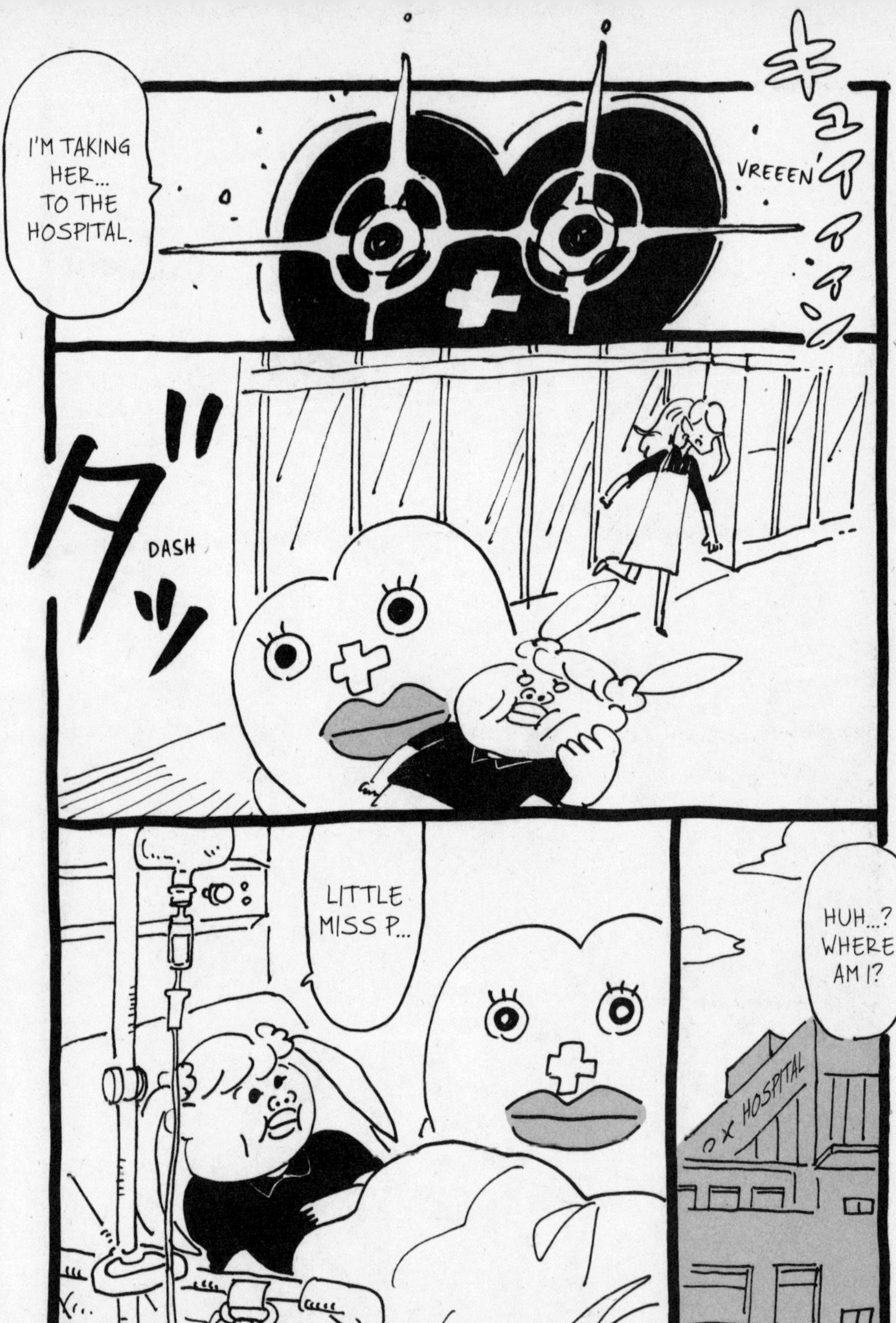
キュイイイイン
VREEEN
I'M TAKING HER... TO THE HOSPITAL.
ダッ
DASH
HUH...? WHERE AM I?
○× HOSPITAL
LITTLE MISS P...

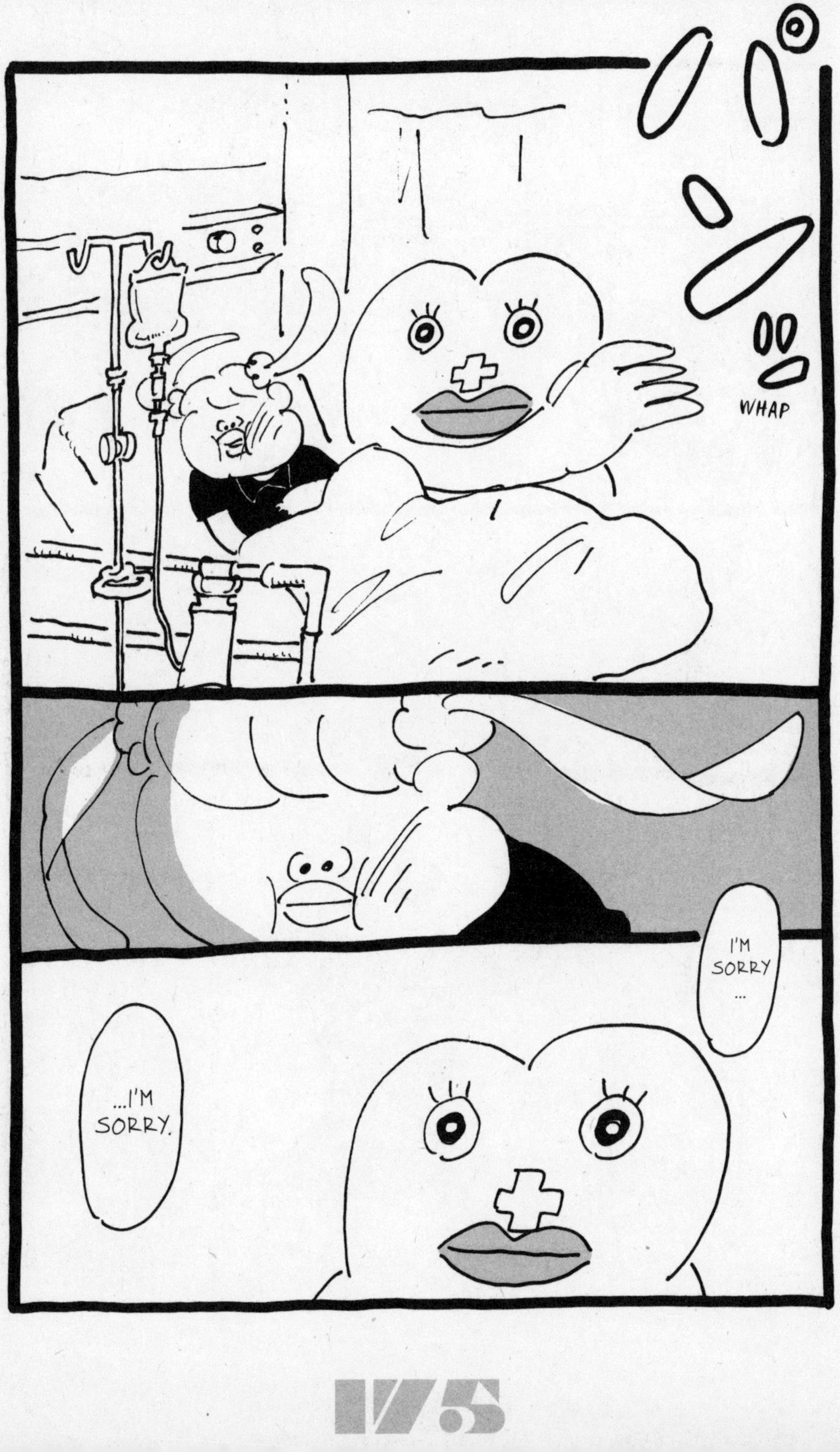
WHAP
I'M SORRY ...
...I'M SORRY.

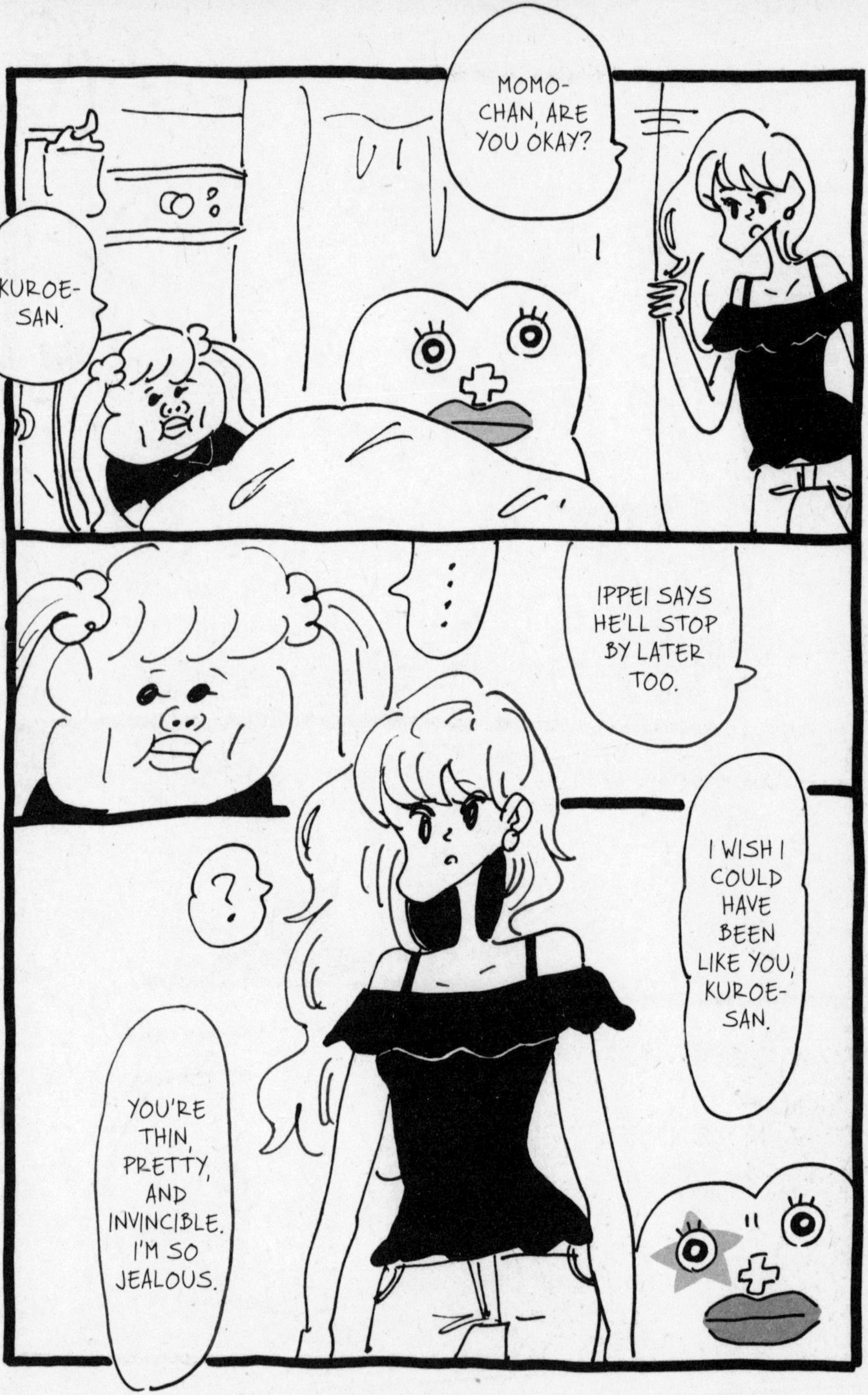
MOMO-CHAN, ARE YOU OKAY?
KUROE-SAN.
IPPEI SAYS HE'LL STOP BY LATER TOO.
...
I WISH I COULD HAVE BEEN LIKE YOU, KUROE-SAN.
?
YOU'RE THIN, PRETTY, AND INVINCIBLE. I'M SO JEALOUS.

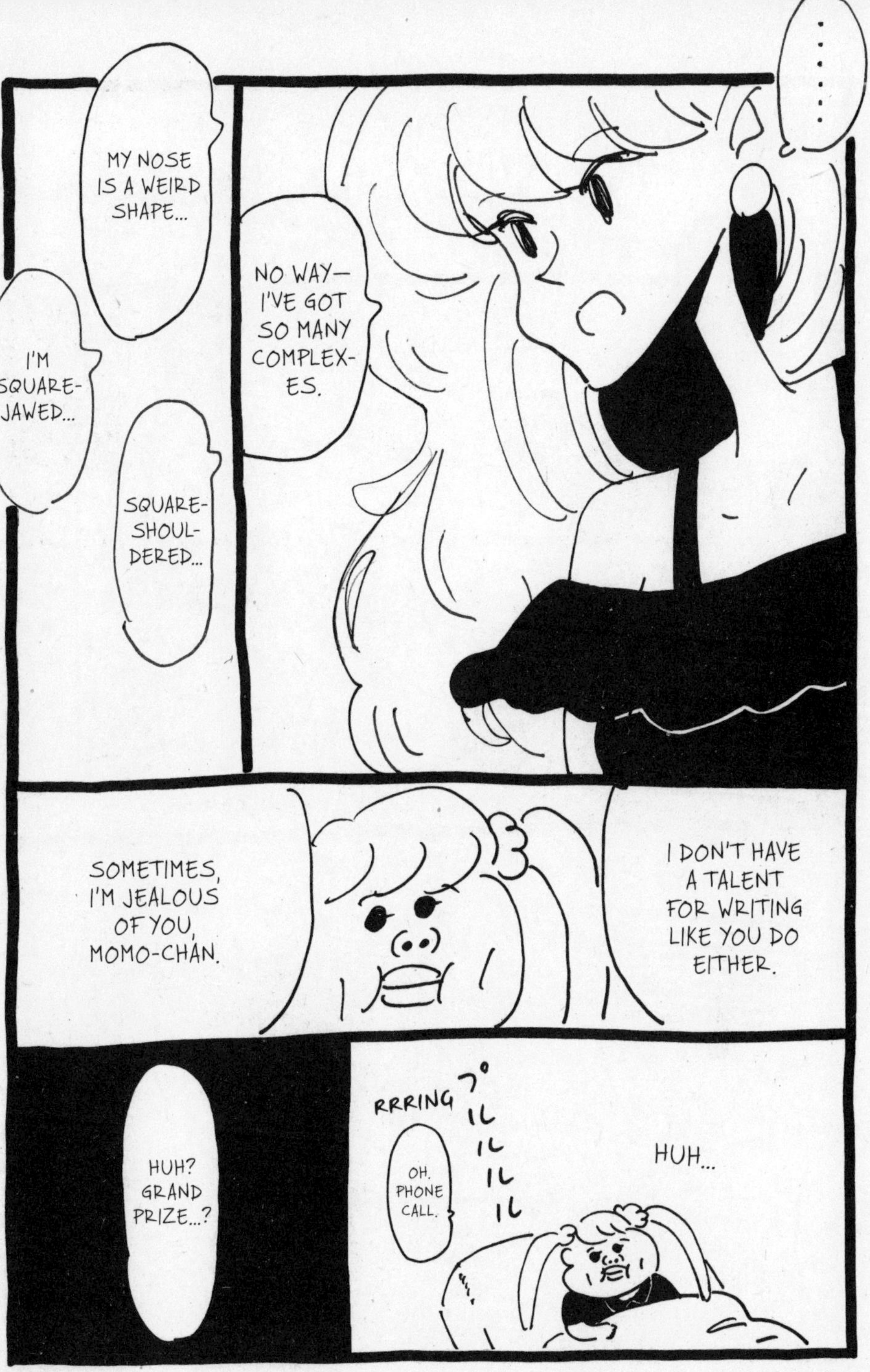
......
NO WAY— I'VE GOT SO MANY COMPLEX-ES.
MY NOSE IS A WEIRD SHAPE...
I'M SQUARE-JAWED...
SQUARE-SHOULDERED...
I DON'T HAVE A TALENT FOR WRITING LIKE YOU DO EITHER.
SOMETIMES, I'M JEALOUS OF YOU, MOMO-CHAN.
HUH...
RRRING
プルルルル
OH. PHONE CALL.
HUH? GRAND PRIZE...?

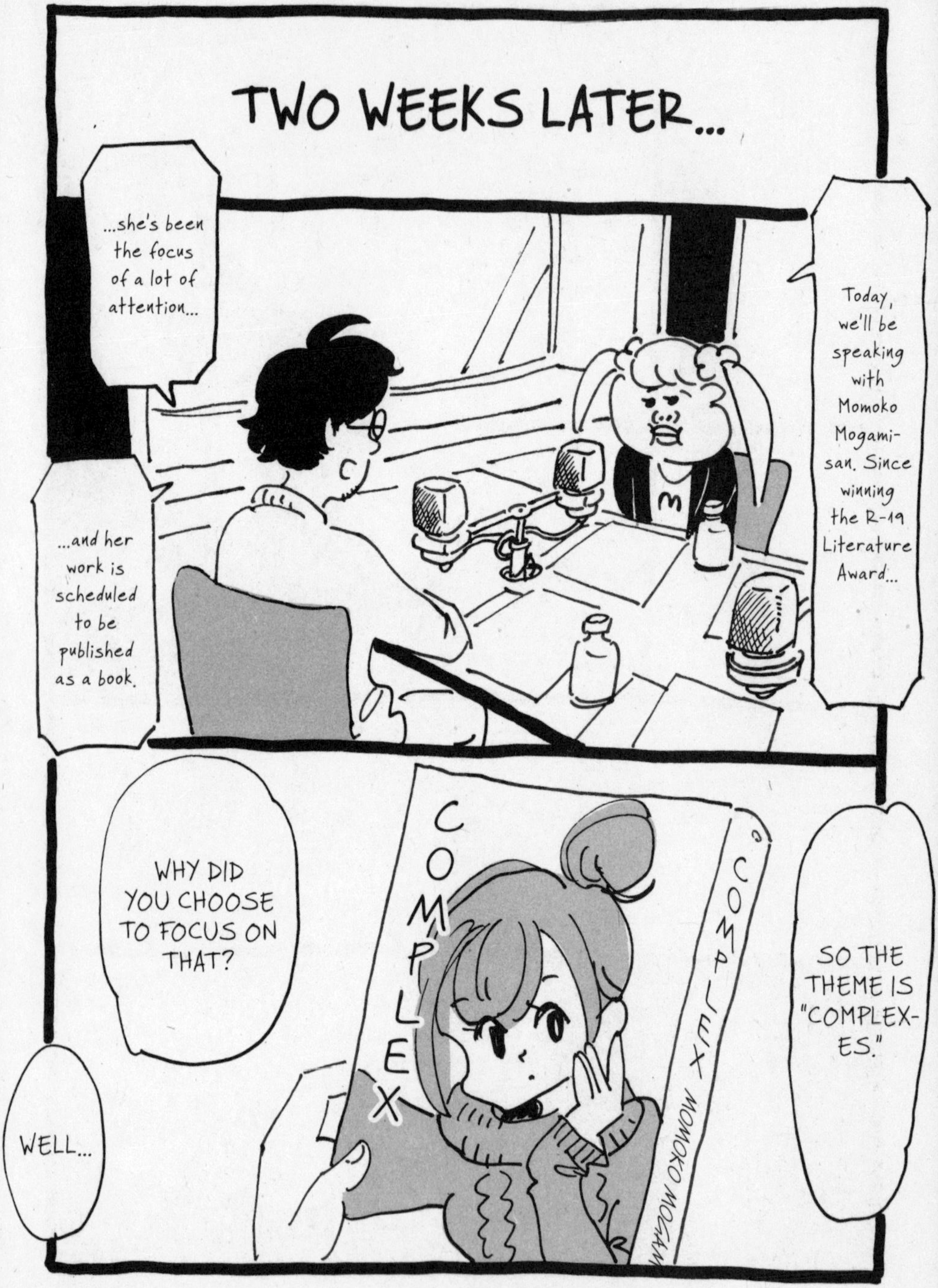
TWO WEEKS LATER...
Today, we'll be speaking with Momoko Mogami-san. Since winning the R-19 Literature Award...
...she's been the focus of a lot of attention...
...and her work is scheduled to be published as a book.
SO THE THEME IS "COMPLEXES."
COMPLEX
COMPLEX
WHY DID YOU CHOOSE TO FOCUS ON THAT?
WELL...

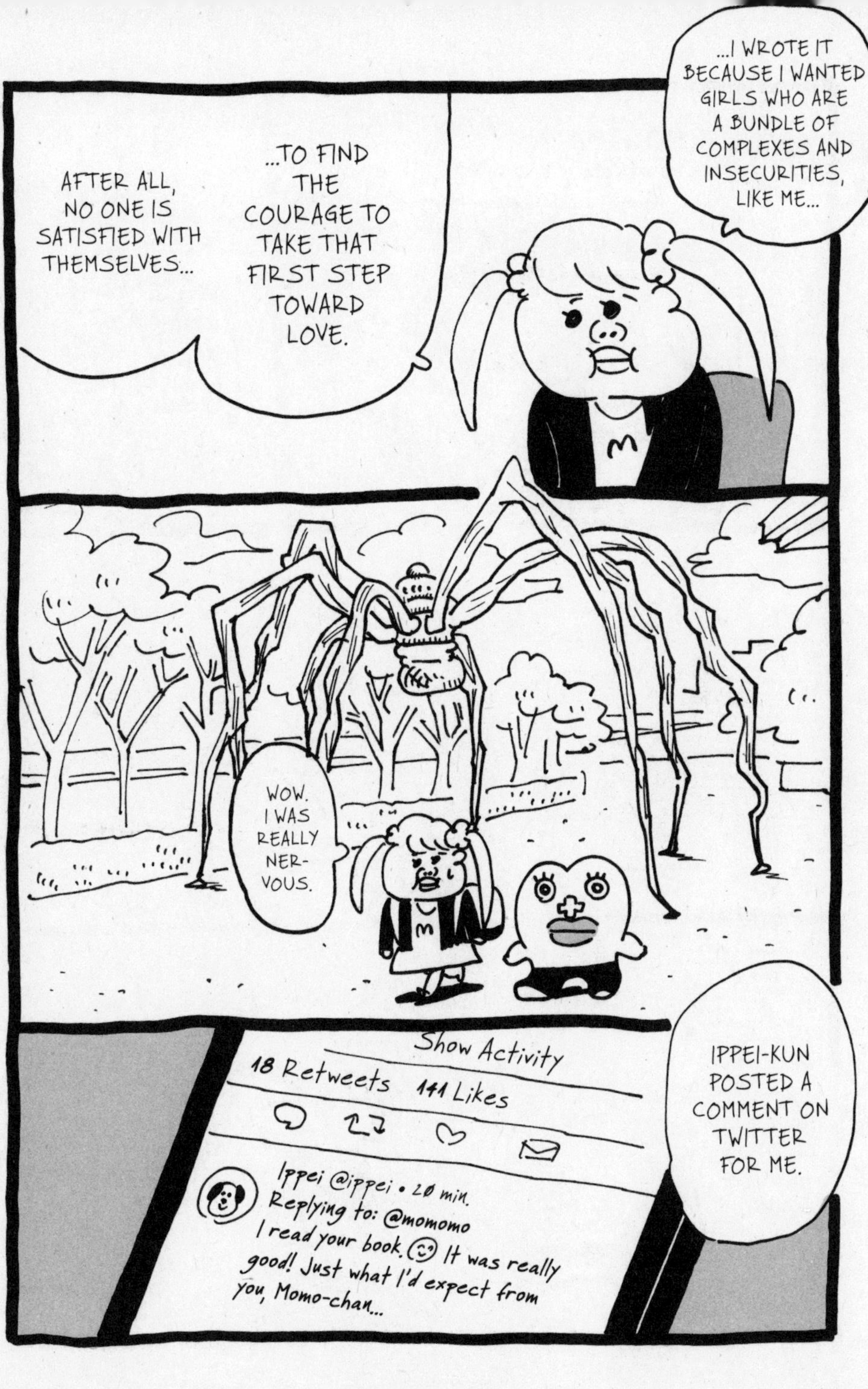

...I WROTE IT BECAUSE I WANTED GIRLS WHO ARE A BUNDLE OF COMPLEXES AND INSECURITIES, LIKE ME...
...TO FIND THE COURAGE TO TAKE THAT FIRST STEP TOWARD LOVE.
AFTER ALL, NO ONE IS SATISFIED WITH THEMSELVES...
WOW. I WAS REALLY NER-VOUS.
IPPEI-KUN POSTED A COMMENT ON TWITTER FOR ME.
Show Activity
18 Retweets 141 Likes
Ippei @ippei • 20 min.
Replying to: @momomo
I read your book. It was really good! Just what I'd expect from you, Momo-chan...

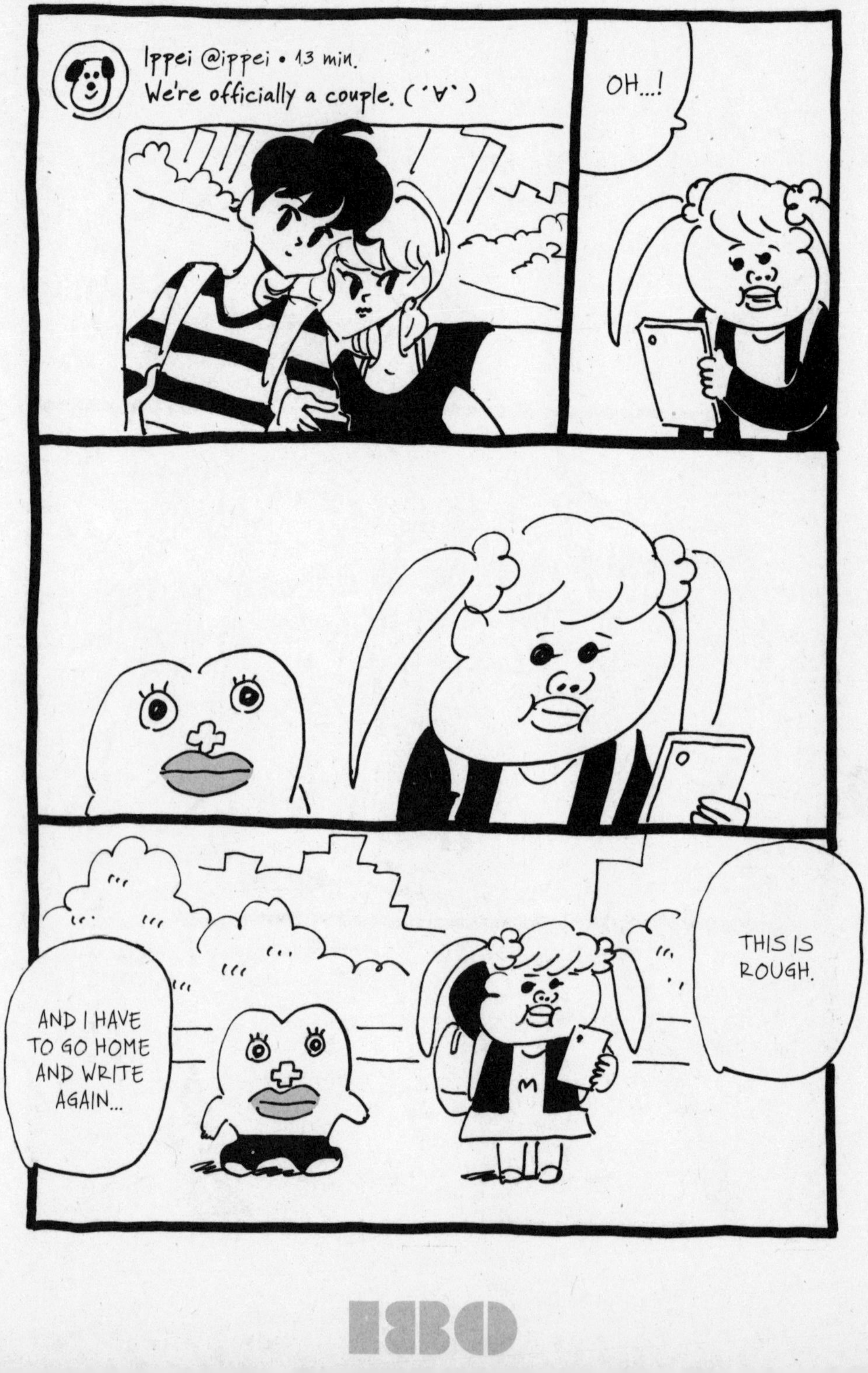
OH...!
Ippei @ippei • 13 min.
We're officially a couple. (´∀`)
THIS IS ROUGH.
AND I HAVE TO GO HOME AND WRITE AGAIN...

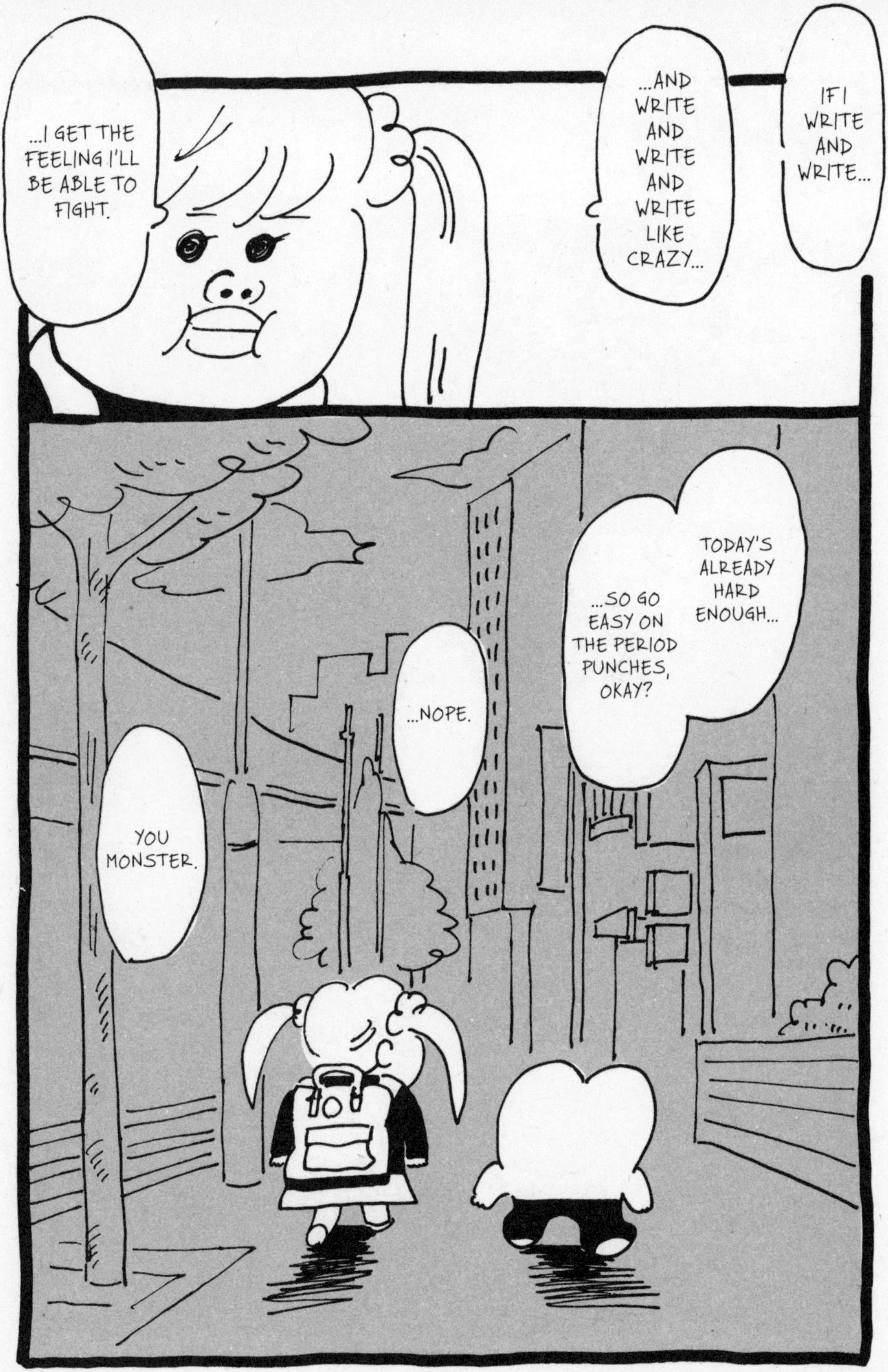
IF I WRITE AND WRITE...
...AND WRITE AND WRITE AND WRITE LIKE CRAZY...
...I GET THE FEELING I'LL BE ABLE TO FIGHT.
TODAY'S ALREADY HARD ENOUGH...
...SO GO EASY ON THE PERIOD PUNCHES, OKAY?
...NOPE.
YOU MONSTER.

I WAS
SUPPOSED
TO TURN
OUT LIKE
THIS.

GRANDMA AND LITTLE MISS P

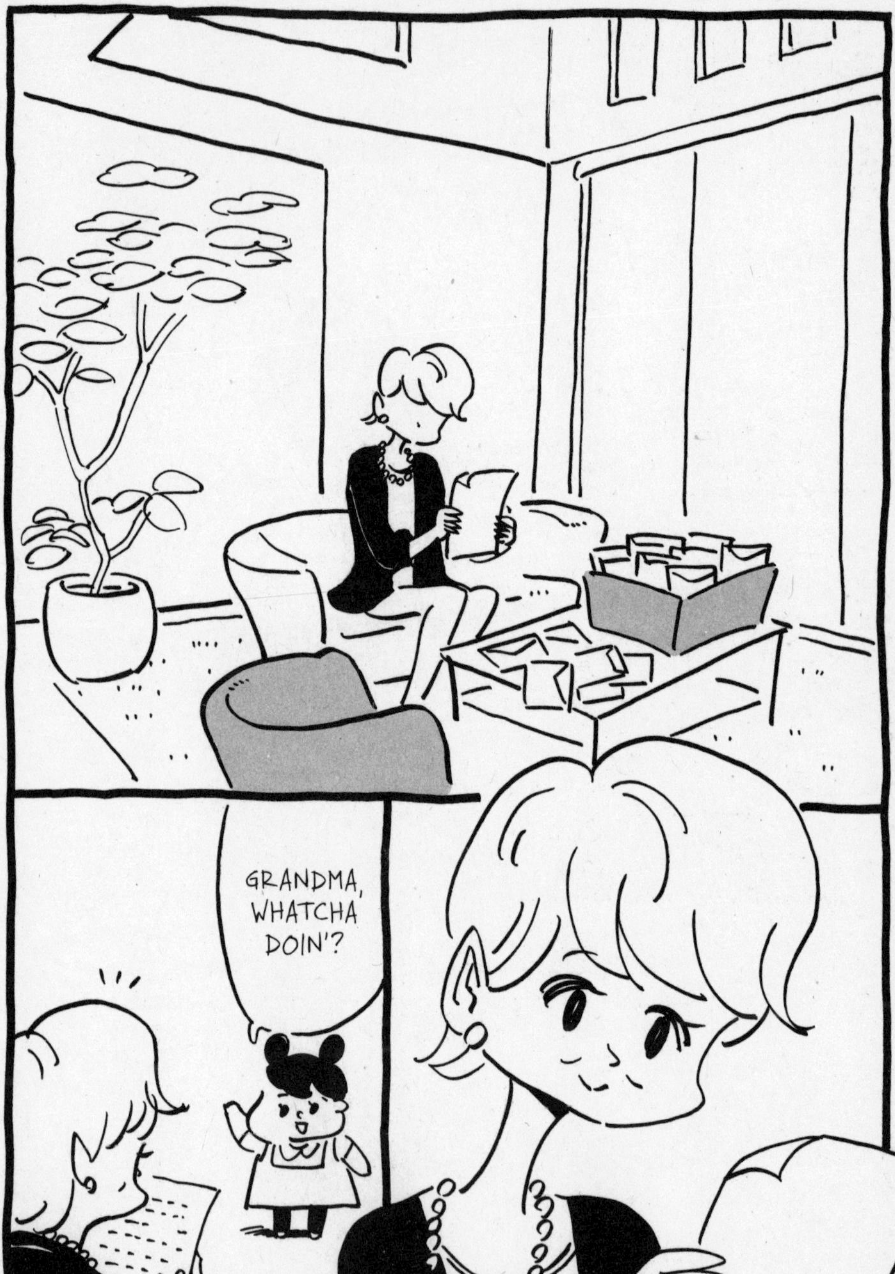
GRANDMA, WHATCHA DOIN'?

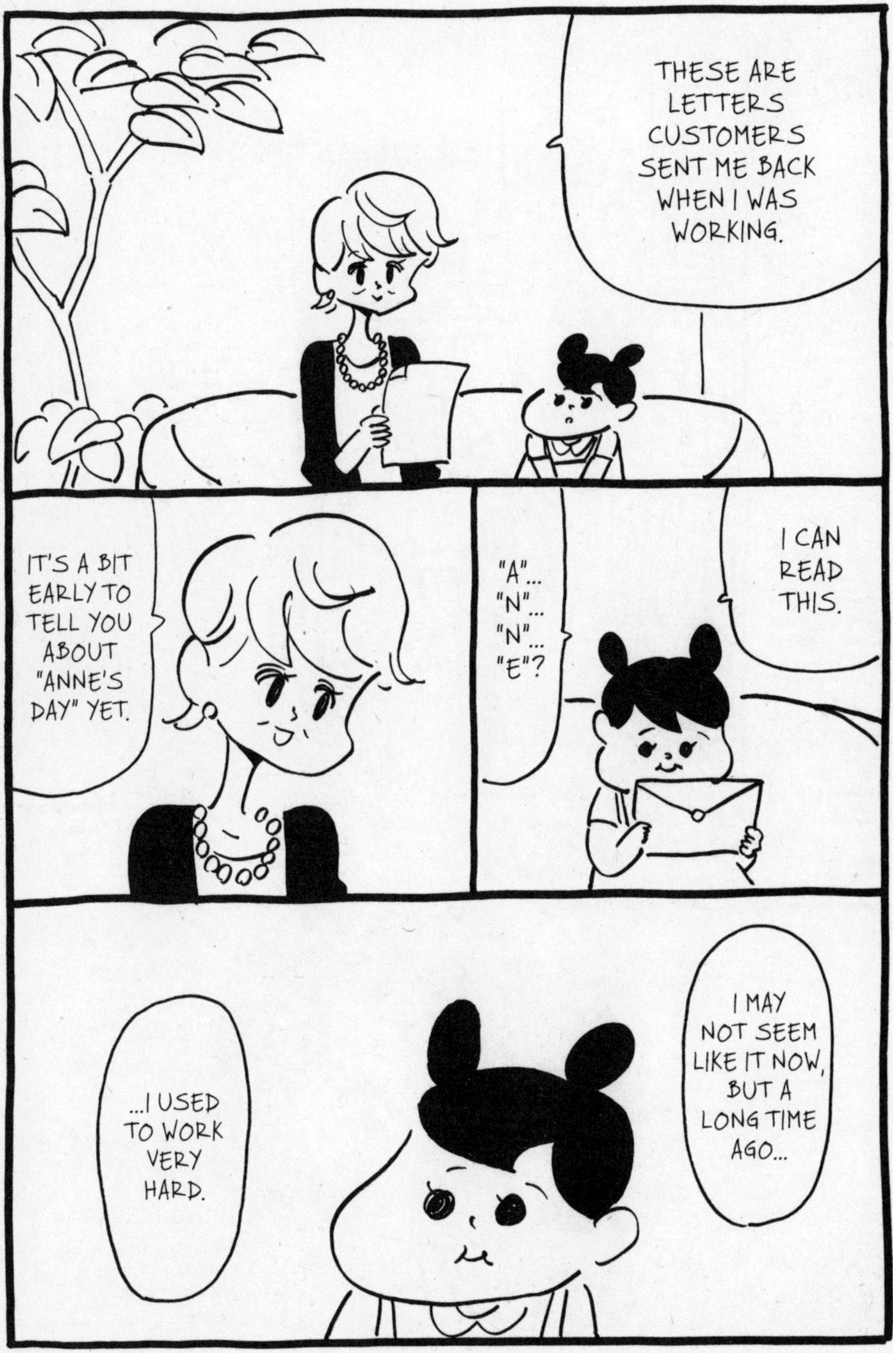
THESE ARE LETTERS CUSTOMERS SENT ME BACK WHEN I WAS WORKING.
I CAN READ THIS.
"A"... "N"... "N"... "E"?
IT'S A BIT EARLY TO TELL YOU ABOUT "ANNE'S DAY" YET.
I MAY NOT SEEM LIKE IT NOW, BUT A LONG TIME AGO...
...I USED TO WORK VERY HARD.

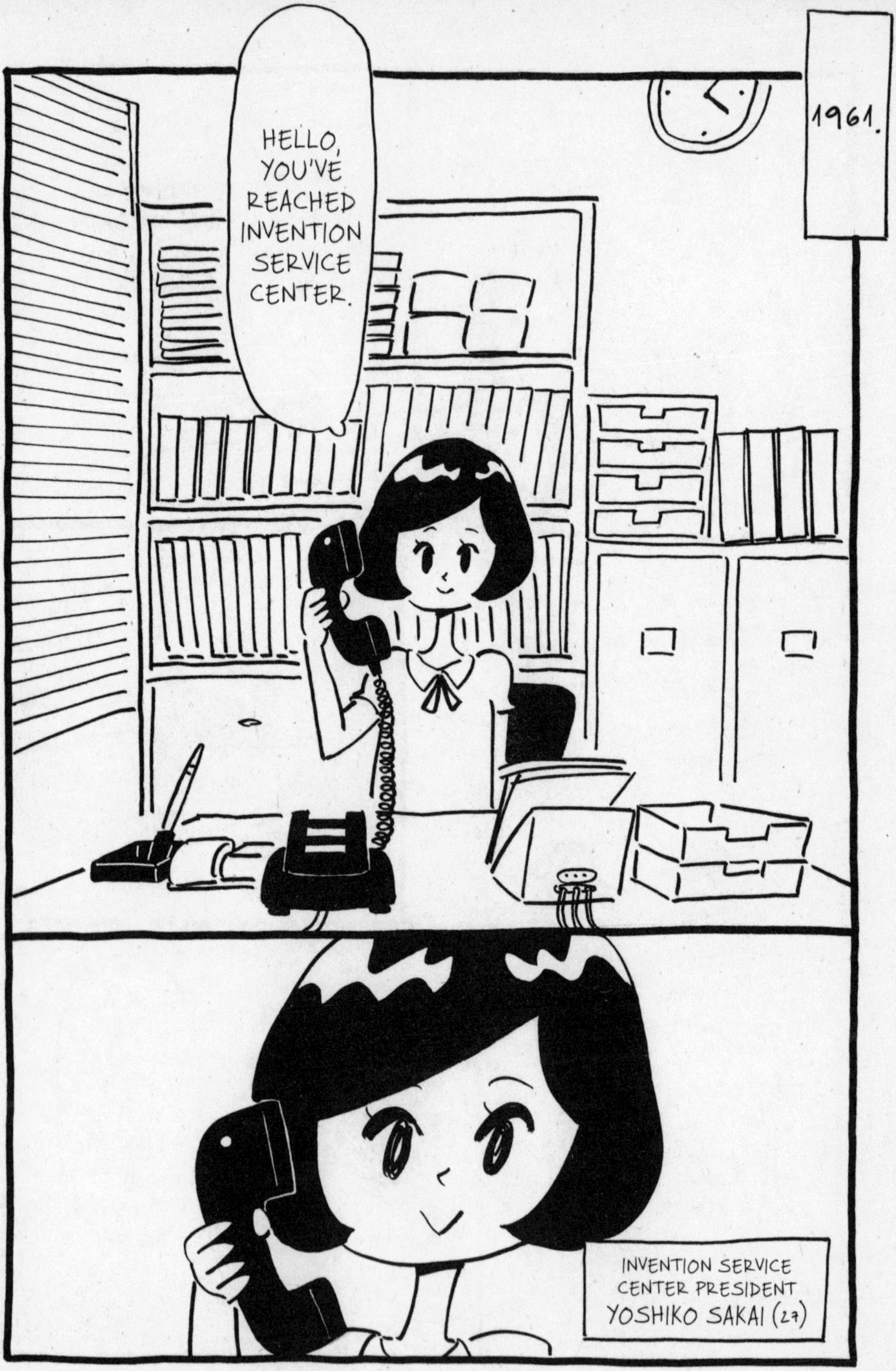
1961.
HELLO, YOU'VE REACHED INVENTION SERVICE CENTER.
INVENTION SERVICE CENTER PRESIDENT YOSHIKO SAKAI (27)

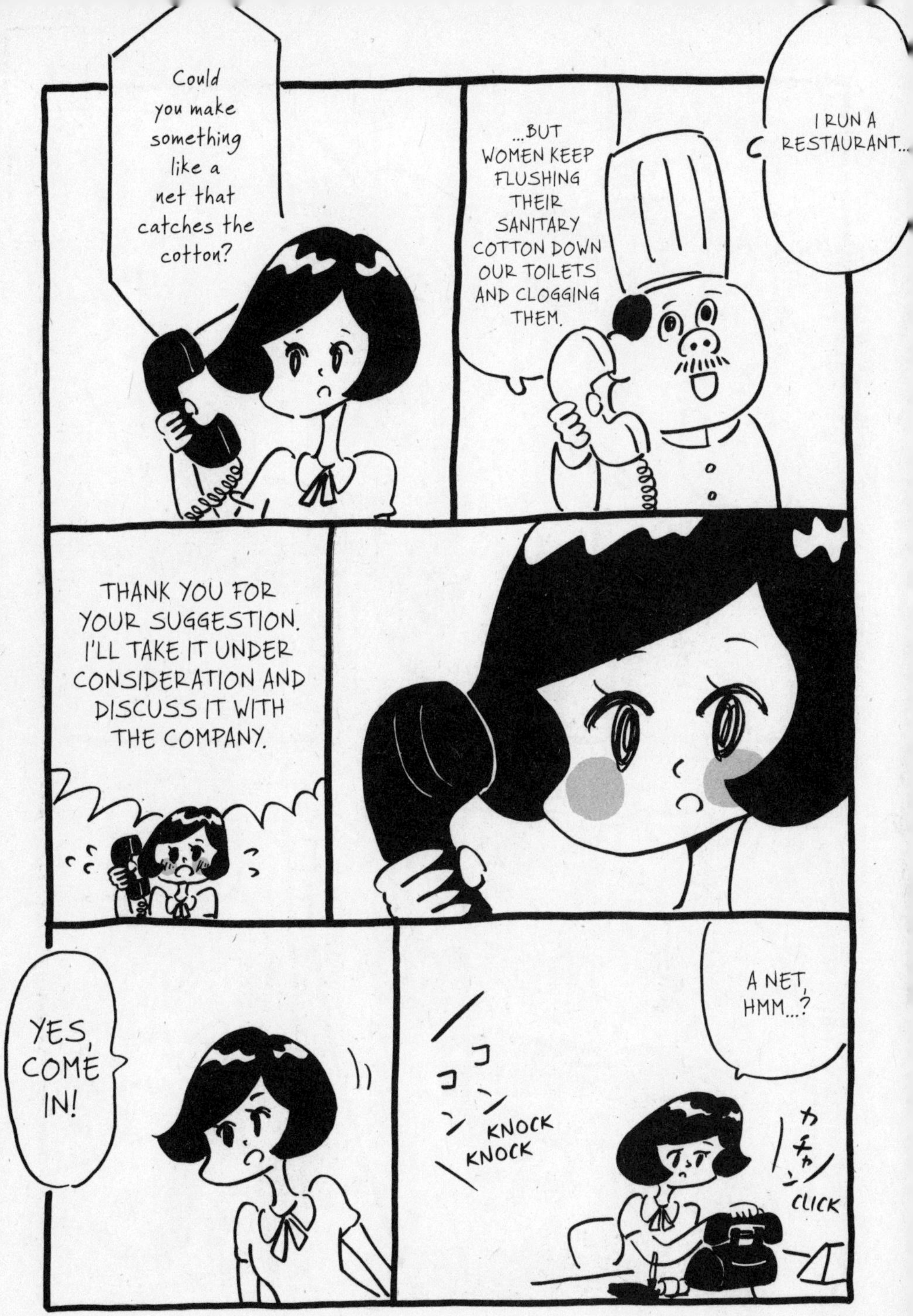
I RUN A RESTAURANT...
...BUT WOMEN KEEP FLUSHING THEIR SANITARY COTTON DOWN OUR TOILETS AND CLOGGING THEM.
Could you make something like a net that catches the cotton?
THANK YOU FOR YOUR SUGGESTION. I'LL TAKE IT UNDER CONSIDERATION AND DISCUSS IT WITH THE COMPANY.
A NET, HMM...?
カチャン CLICK
コンコン KNOCK KNOCK
YES, COME IN!

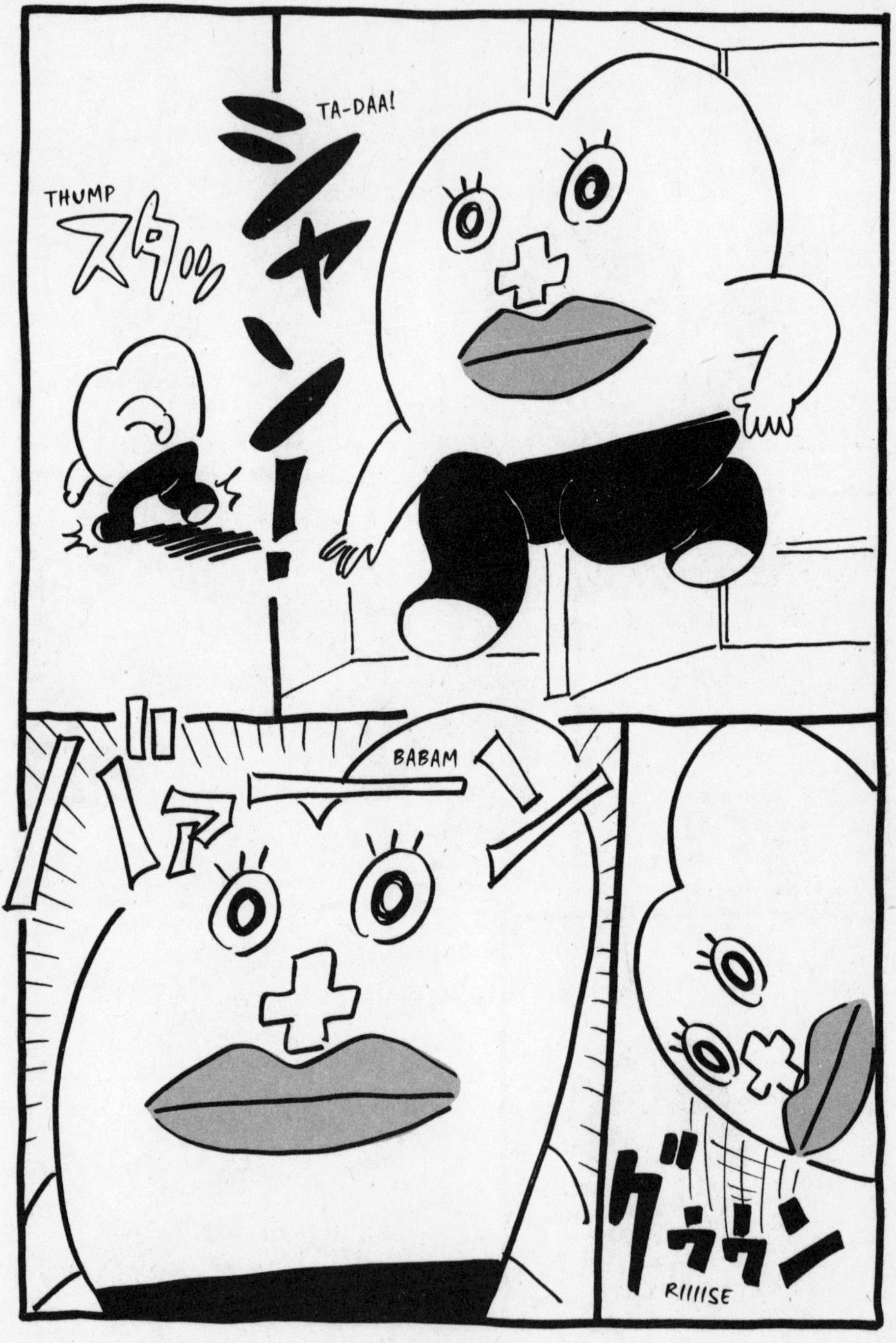
TA-DAA!
THUMP
RIIIISE
BABAM

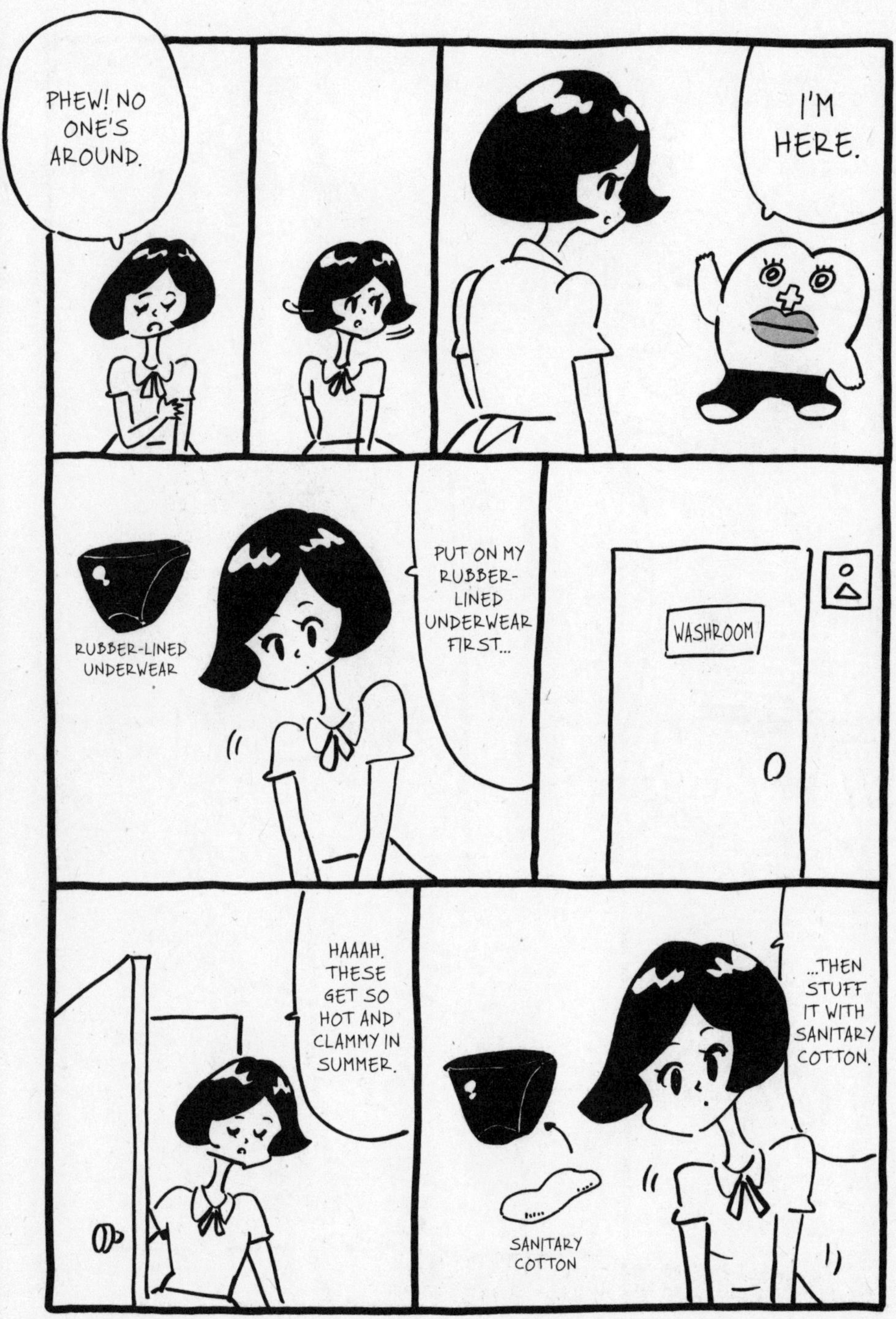
PHEW! NO ONE'S AROUND.
I'M HERE.
RUBBER-LINED UNDERWEAR
PUT ON MY RUBBER-LINED UNDERWEAR FIRST...
WASHROOM
HAAAH. THESE GET SO HOT AND CLAMMY IN SUMMER.
SANITARY COTTON
...THEN STUFF IT WITH SANITARY COTTON.

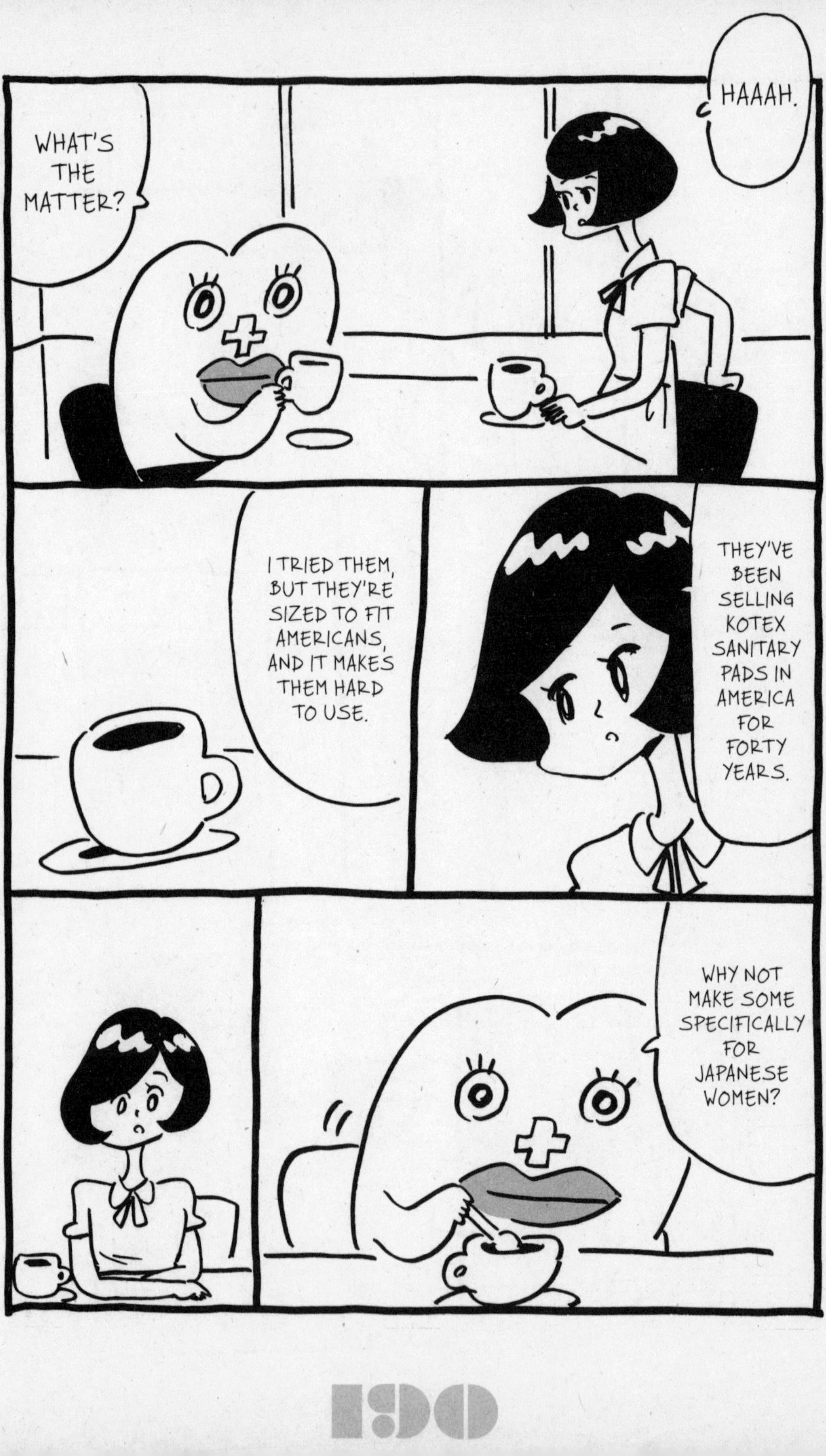
HAAAH.
WHAT'S THE MATTER?
THEY'VE BEEN SELLING KOTEX SANITARY PADS IN AMERICA FOR FORTY YEARS.
I TRIED THEM, BUT THEY'RE SIZED TO FIT AMERICANS, AND IT MAKES THEM HARD TO USE.
WHY NOT MAKE SOME SPECIFICALLY FOR JAPANESE WOMEN?

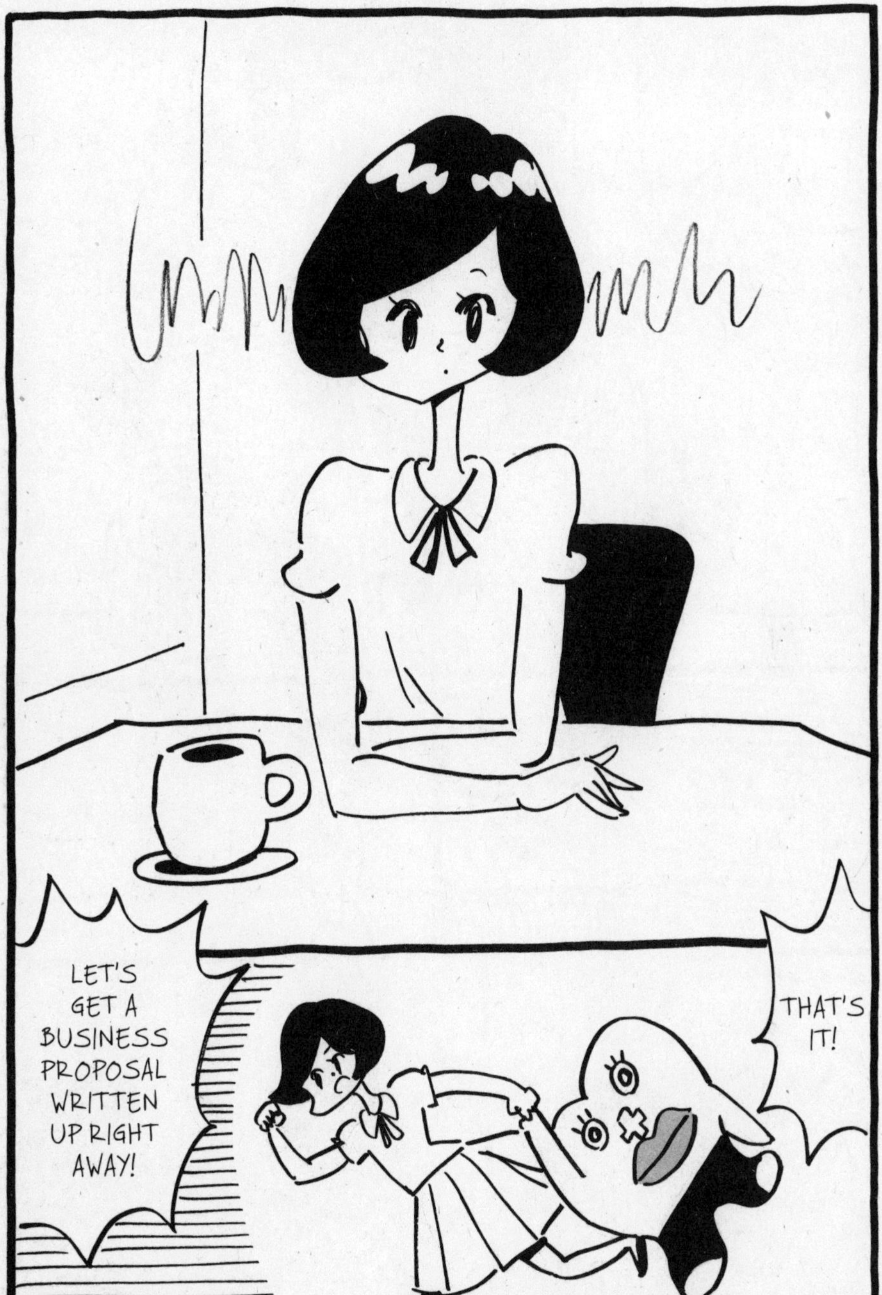
THAT'S IT!
LET'S GET A BUSINESS PROPOSAL WRITTEN UP RIGHT AWAY!

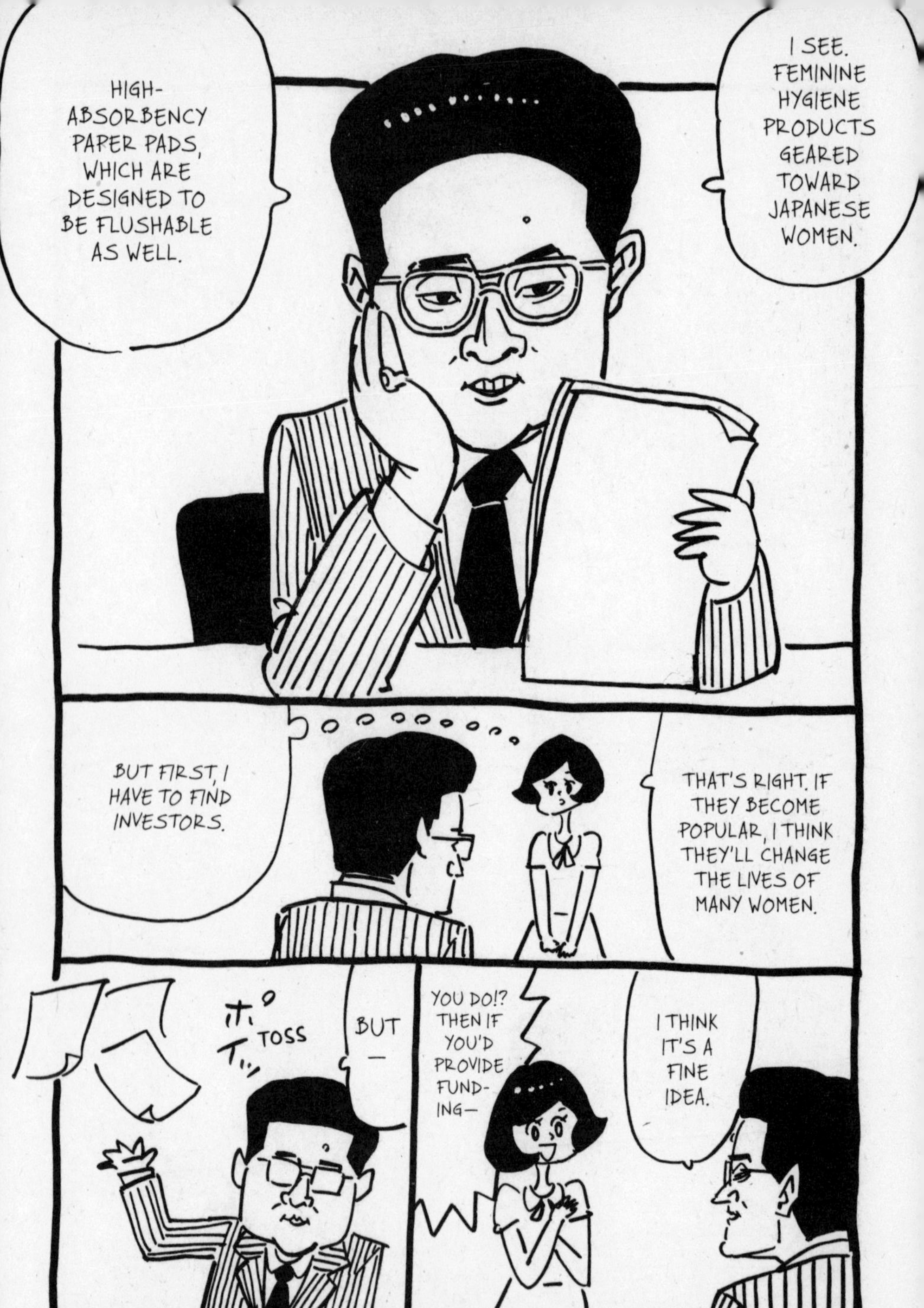
I SEE. FEMININE HYGIENE PRODUCTS GEARED TOWARD JAPANESE WOMEN.
HIGH-ABSORBENCY PAPER PADS, WHICH ARE DESIGNED TO BE FLUSHABLE AS WELL.
THAT'S RIGHT. IF THEY BECOME POPULAR, I THINK THEY'LL CHANGE THE LIVES OF MANY WOMEN.
BUT FIRST, I HAVE TO FIND INVESTORS.
I THINK IT'S A FINE IDEA.
YOU DO!? THEN IF YOU'D PROVIDE FUND-ING—
BUT —
ポイッ
TOSS

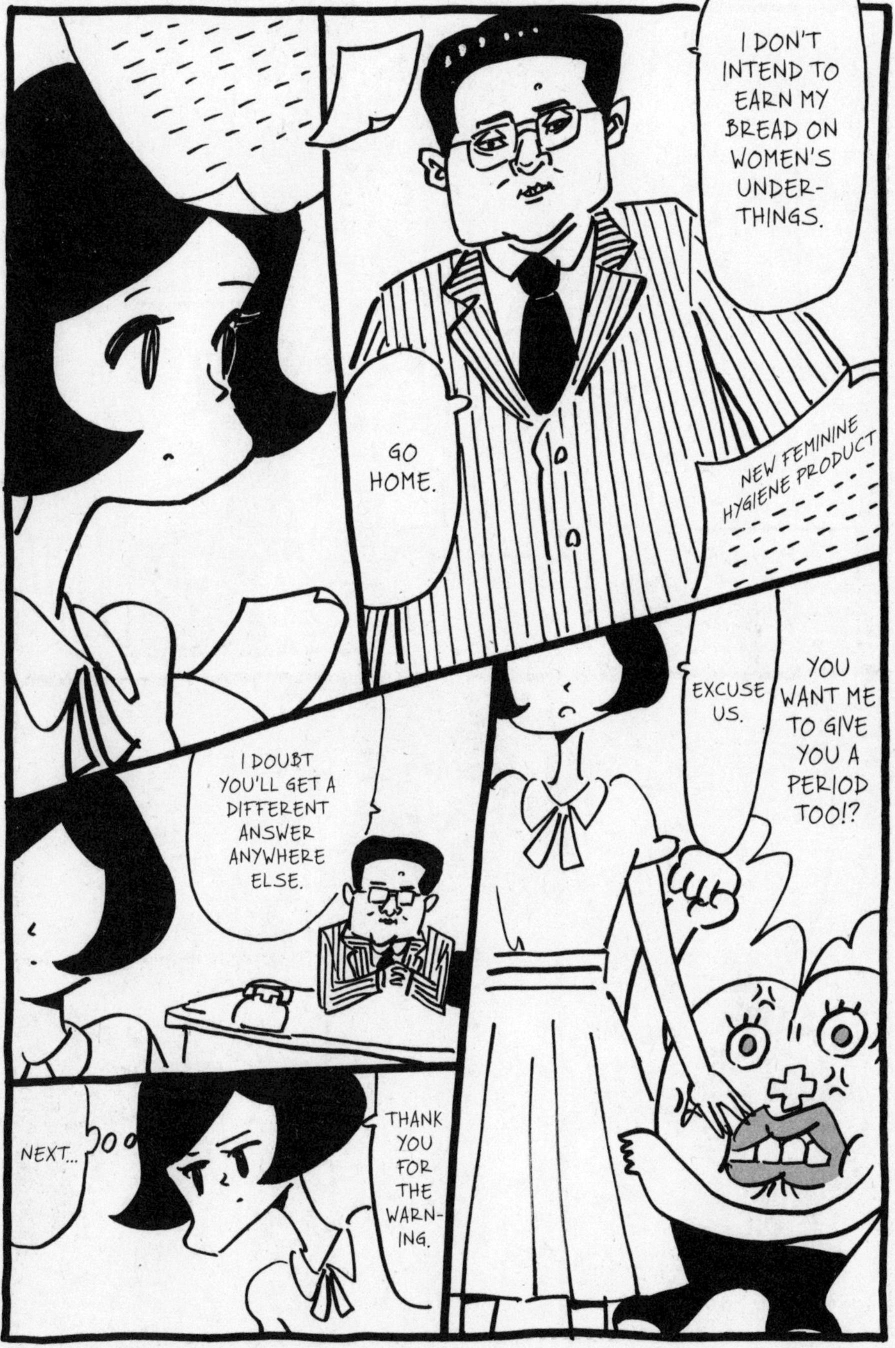
I DON'T INTEND TO EARN MY BREAD ON WOMEN'S UNDER-THINGS.
NEW FEMININE HYGIENE PRODUCT
GO HOME.
YOU WANT ME TO GIVE YOU A PERIOD TOO!?
EXCUSE US.
I DOUBT YOU'LL GET A DIFFERENT ANSWER ANYWHERE ELSE.
THANK YOU FOR THE WARNING.
NEXT...

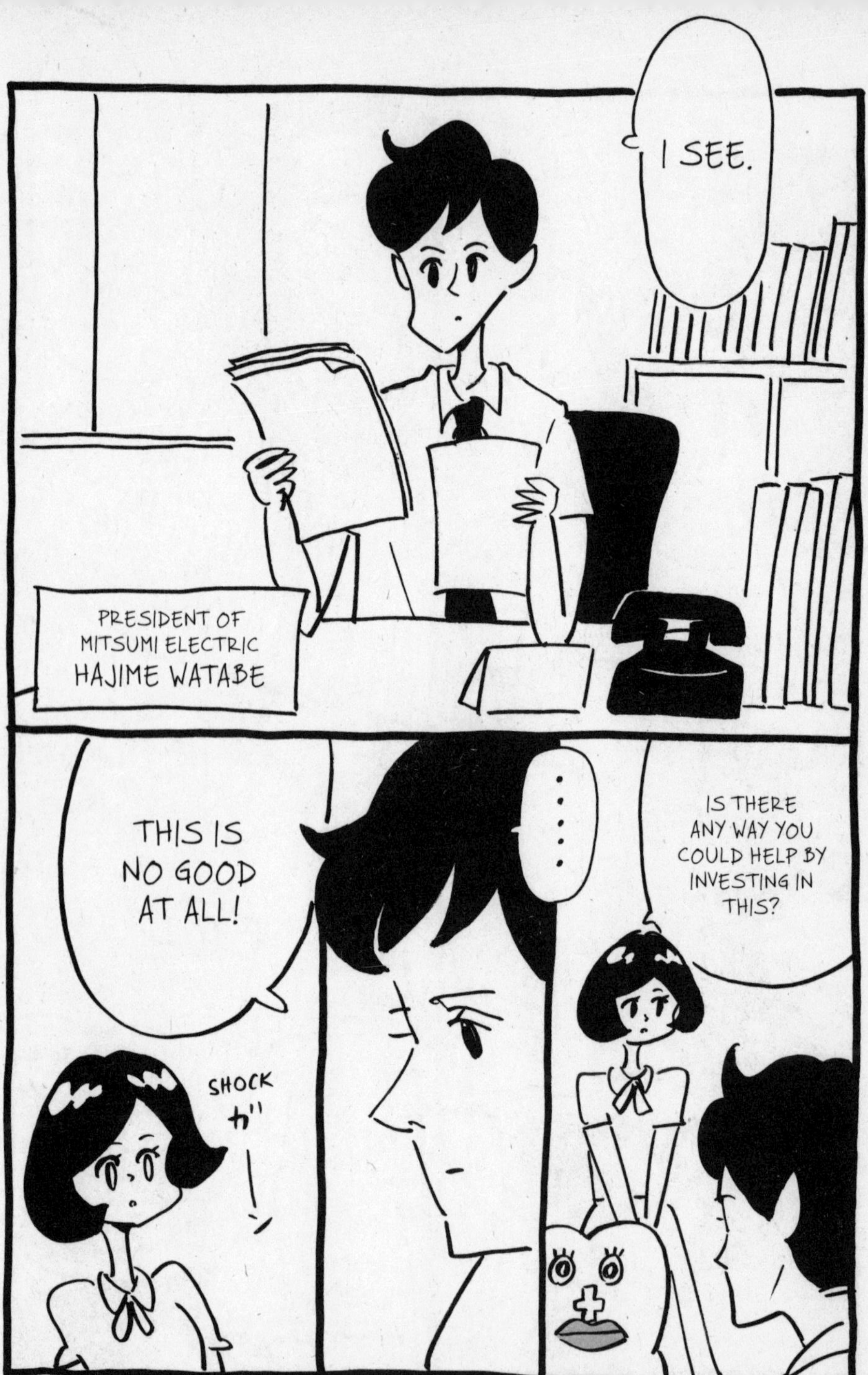
I SEE.
PRESIDENT OF MITSUMI ELECTRIC HAJIME WATABE
IS THERE ANY WAY YOU COULD HELP BY INVESTING IN THIS?
......
THIS IS NO GOOD AT ALL!
SHOCK
ガーン

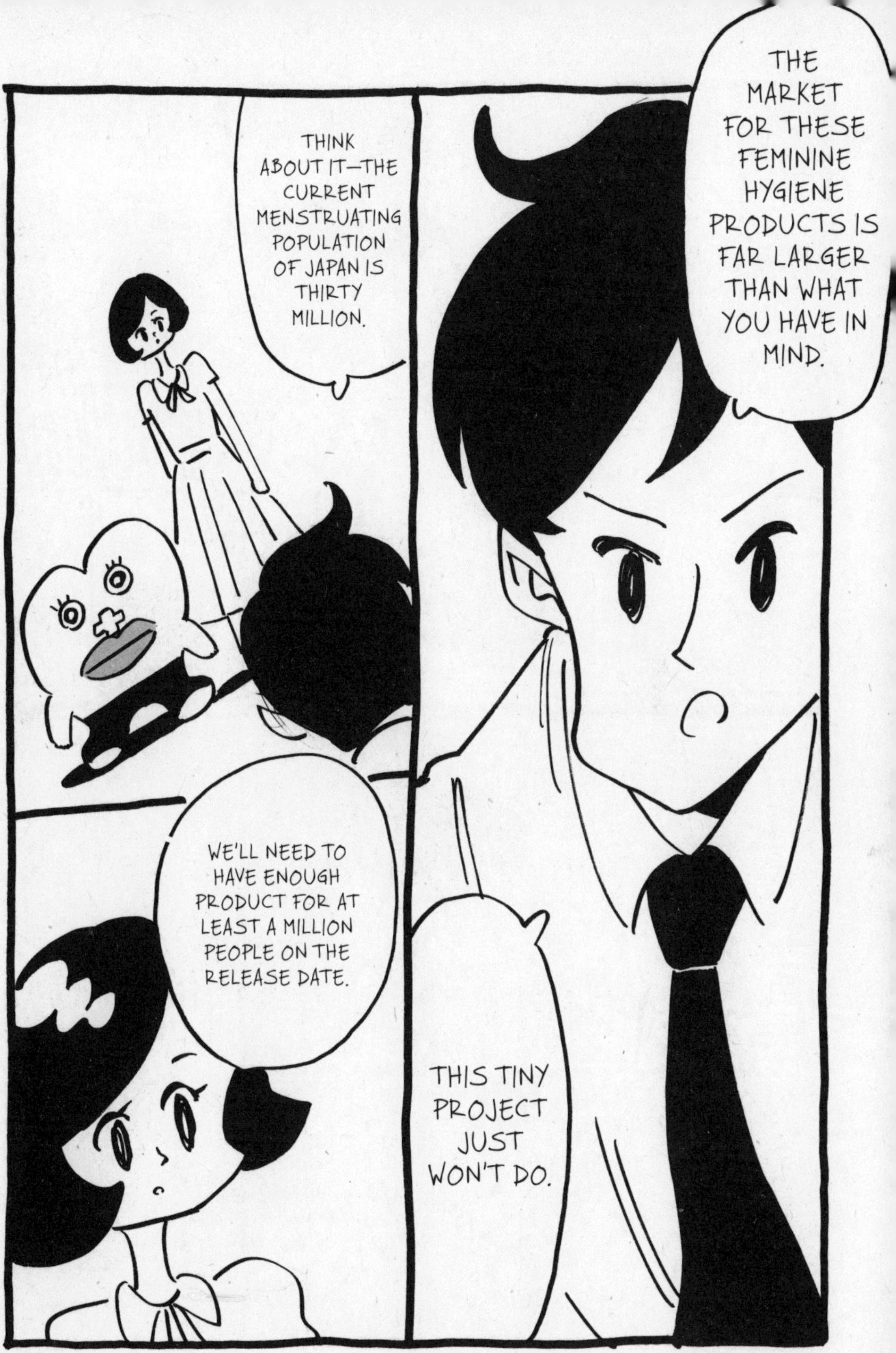
THE MARKET FOR THESE FEMININE HYGIENE PRODUCTS IS FAR LARGER THAN WHAT YOU HAVE IN MIND.
THIS TINY PROJECT JUST WON'T DO.
THINK ABOUT IT—THE CURRENT MENSTRUATING POPULATION OF JAPAN IS THIRTY MILLION.
WE'LL NEED TO HAVE ENOUGH PRODUCT FOR AT LEAST A MILLION PEOPLE ON THE RELEASE DATE.

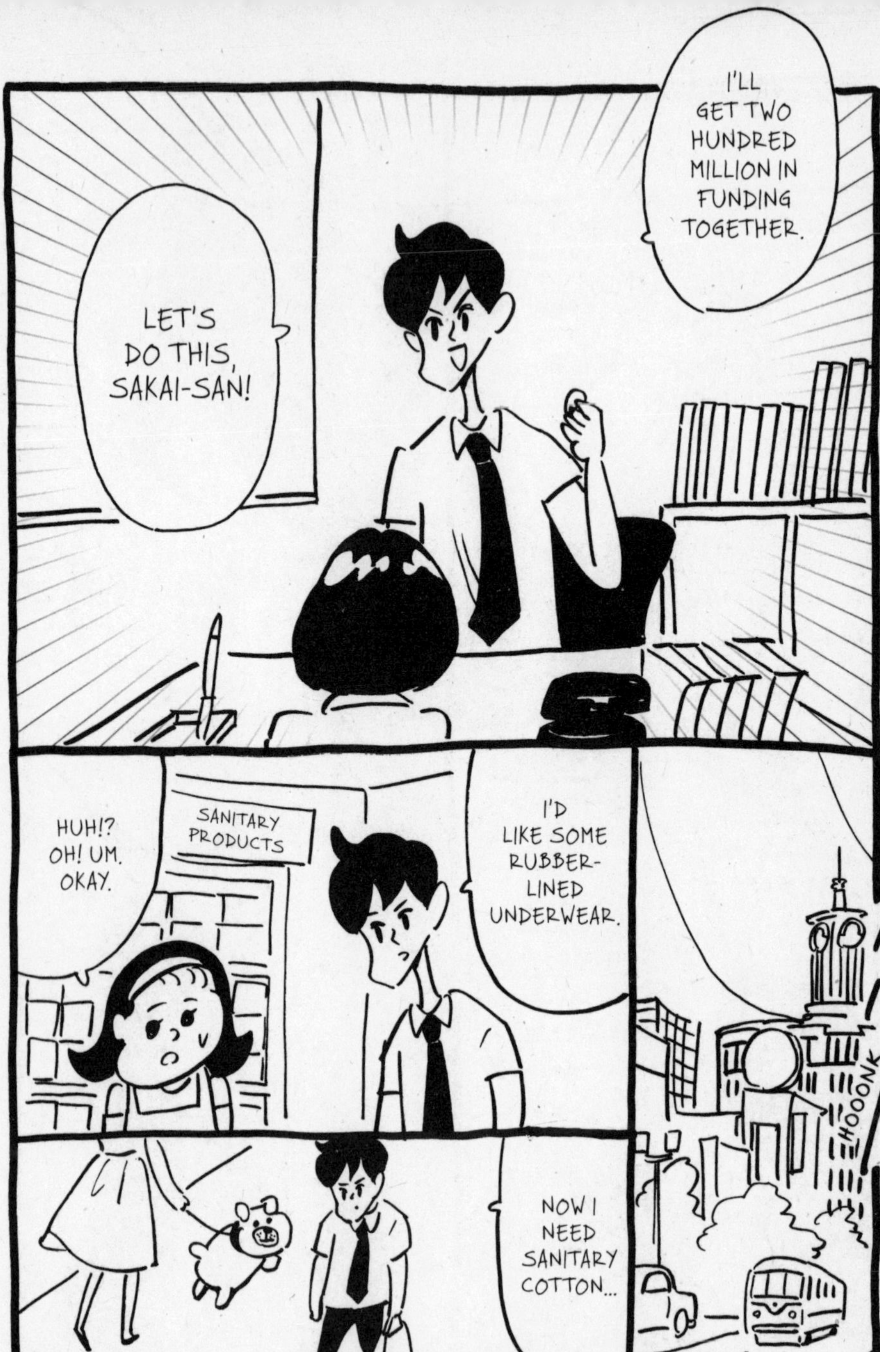
I'LL GET TWO HUNDRED MILLION IN FUNDING TOGETHER.
LET'S DO THIS, SAKAI-SAN!
HOOONK
I'D LIKE SOME RUBBER-LINED UNDERWEAR.
SANITARY PRODUCTS
HUH!? OH! UM. OKAY.
NOW I NEED SANITARY COTTON...

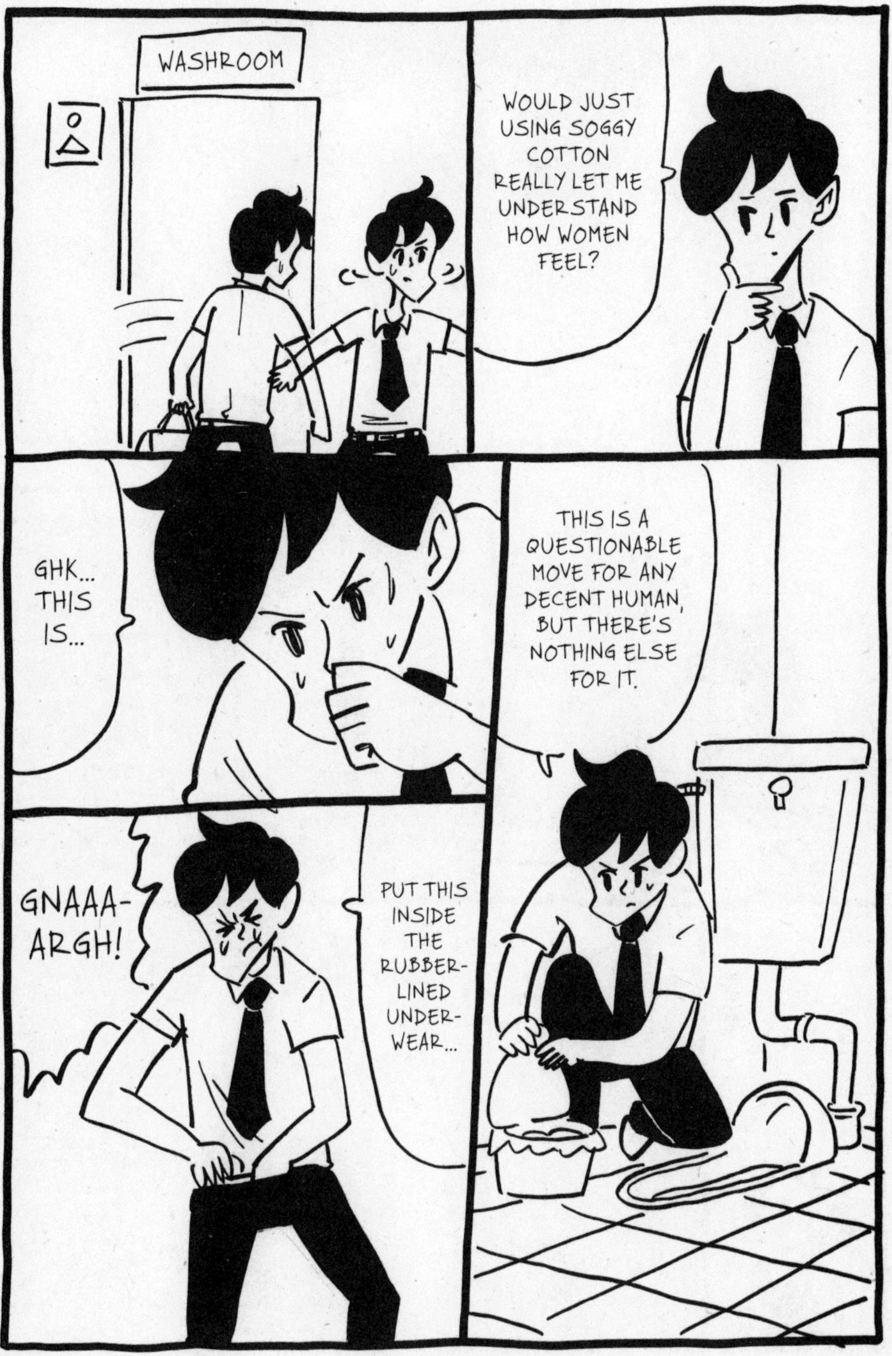
WOULD JUST USING SOGGY COTTON REALLY LET ME UNDERSTAND HOW WOMEN FEEL?
WASHROOM
THIS IS A QUESTIONABLE MOVE FOR ANY DECENT HUMAN, BUT THERE'S NOTHING ELSE FOR IT.
GHK... THIS IS...
PUT THIS INSIDE THE RUBBER-LINED UNDER-WEAR...
GNAAA-ARGH!

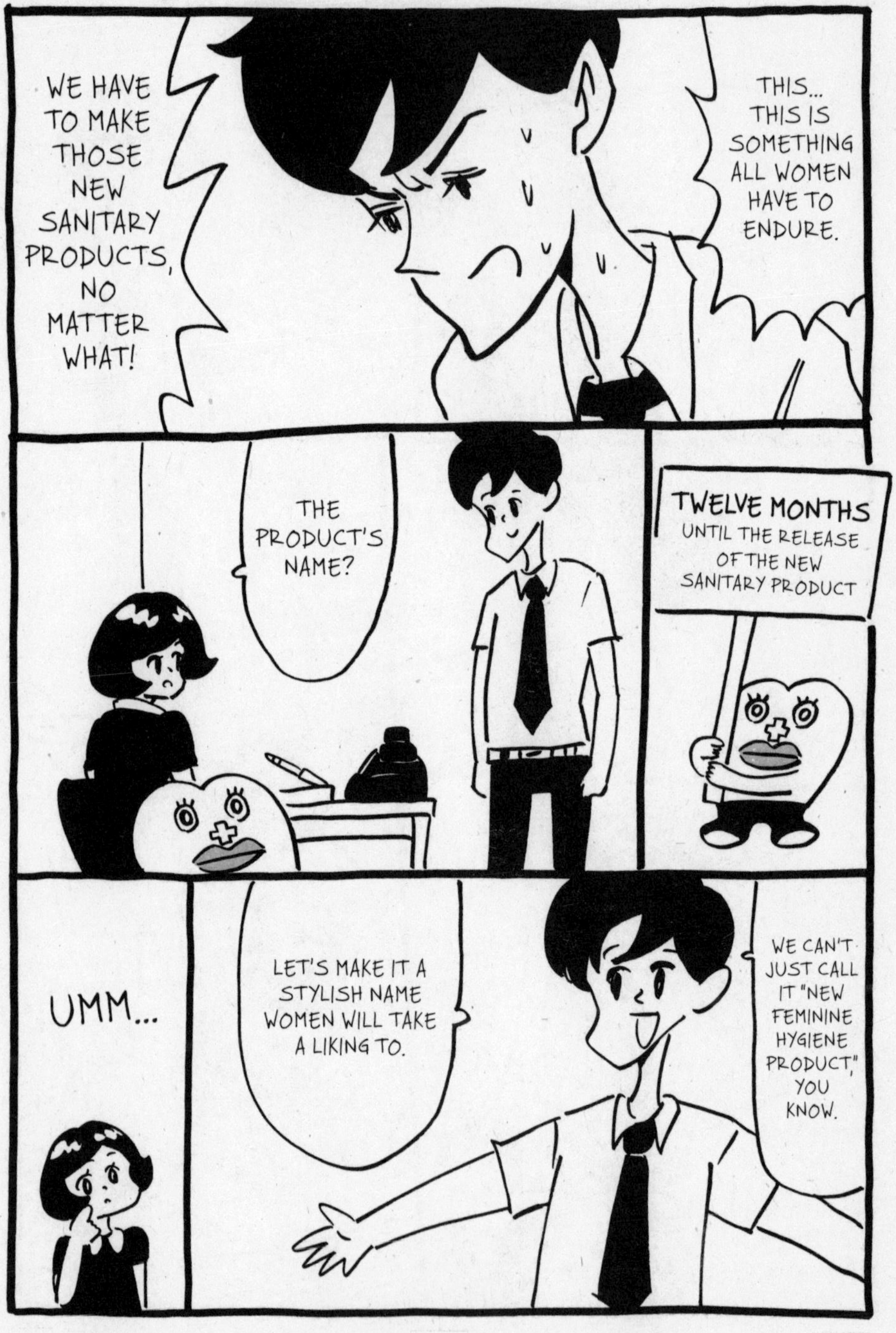
THIS... THIS IS SOMETHING ALL WOMEN HAVE TO ENDURE.
WE HAVE TO MAKE THOSE NEW SANITARY PRODUCTS, NO MATTER WHAT!
TWELVE MONTHS UNTIL THE RELEASE OF THE NEW SANITARY PRODUCT
THE PRODUCT'S NAME?
WE CAN'T JUST CALL IT "NEW FEMININE HYGIENE PRODUCT," YOU KNOW.
LET'S MAKE IT A STYLISH NAME WOMEN WILL TAKE A LIKING TO.
UMM...

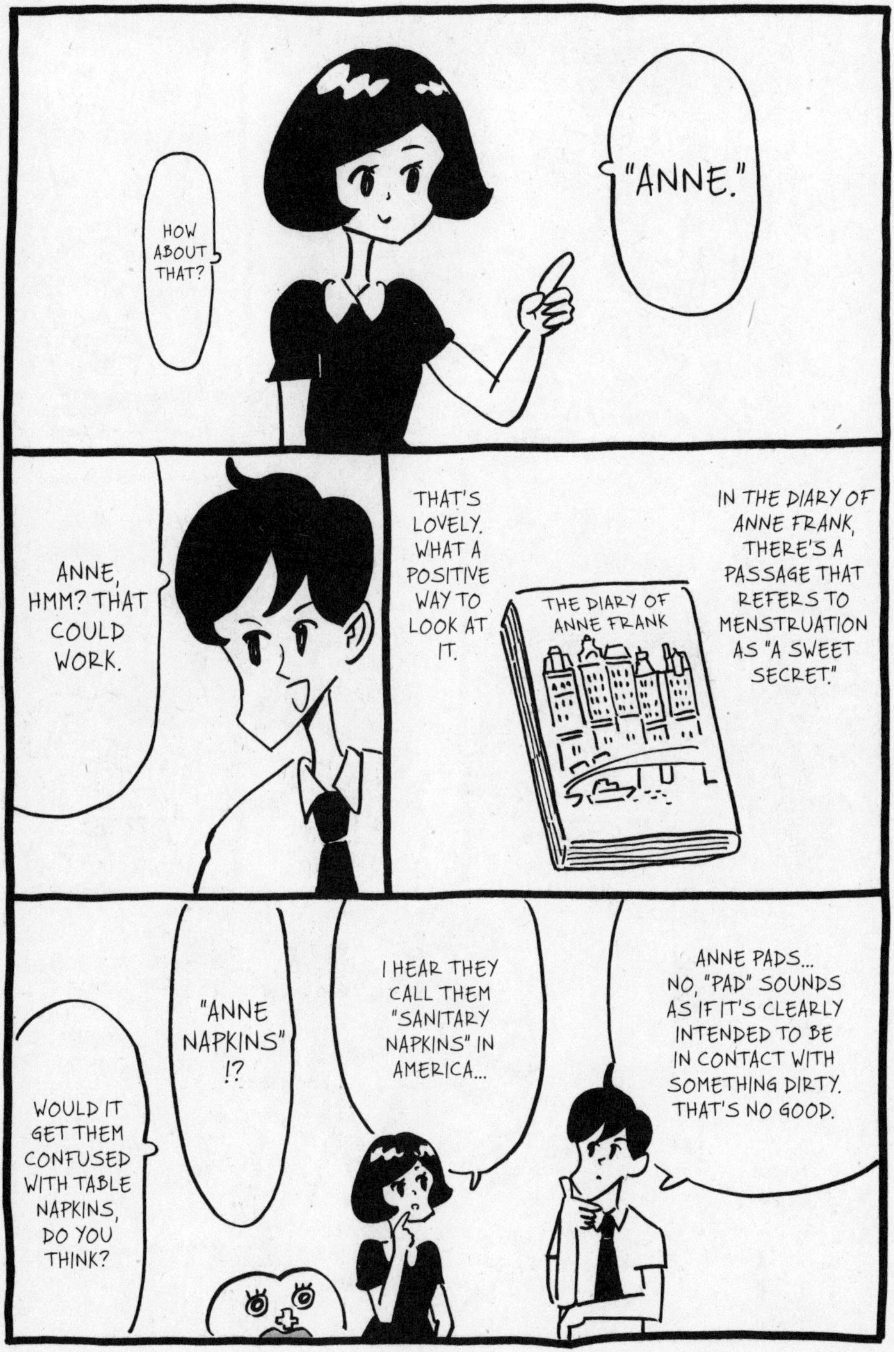
"ANNE."
HOW ABOUT THAT?
IN THE DIARY OF ANNE FRANK, THERE'S A PASSAGE THAT REFERS TO MENSTRUATION AS "A SWEET SECRET."
THAT'S LOVELY. WHAT A POSITIVE WAY TO LOOK AT IT.
THE DIARY OF ANNE FRANK
ANNE, HMM? THAT COULD WORK.
ANNE PADS... NO, "PAD" SOUNDS AS IF IT'S CLEARLY INTENDED TO BE IN CONTACT WITH SOMETHING DIRTY. THAT'S NO GOOD.
I HEAR THEY CALL THEM "SANITARY NAPKINS" IN AMERICA...
"ANNE NAPKINS" !?
WOULD IT GET THEM CONFUSED WITH TABLE NAPKINS, DO YOU THINK?

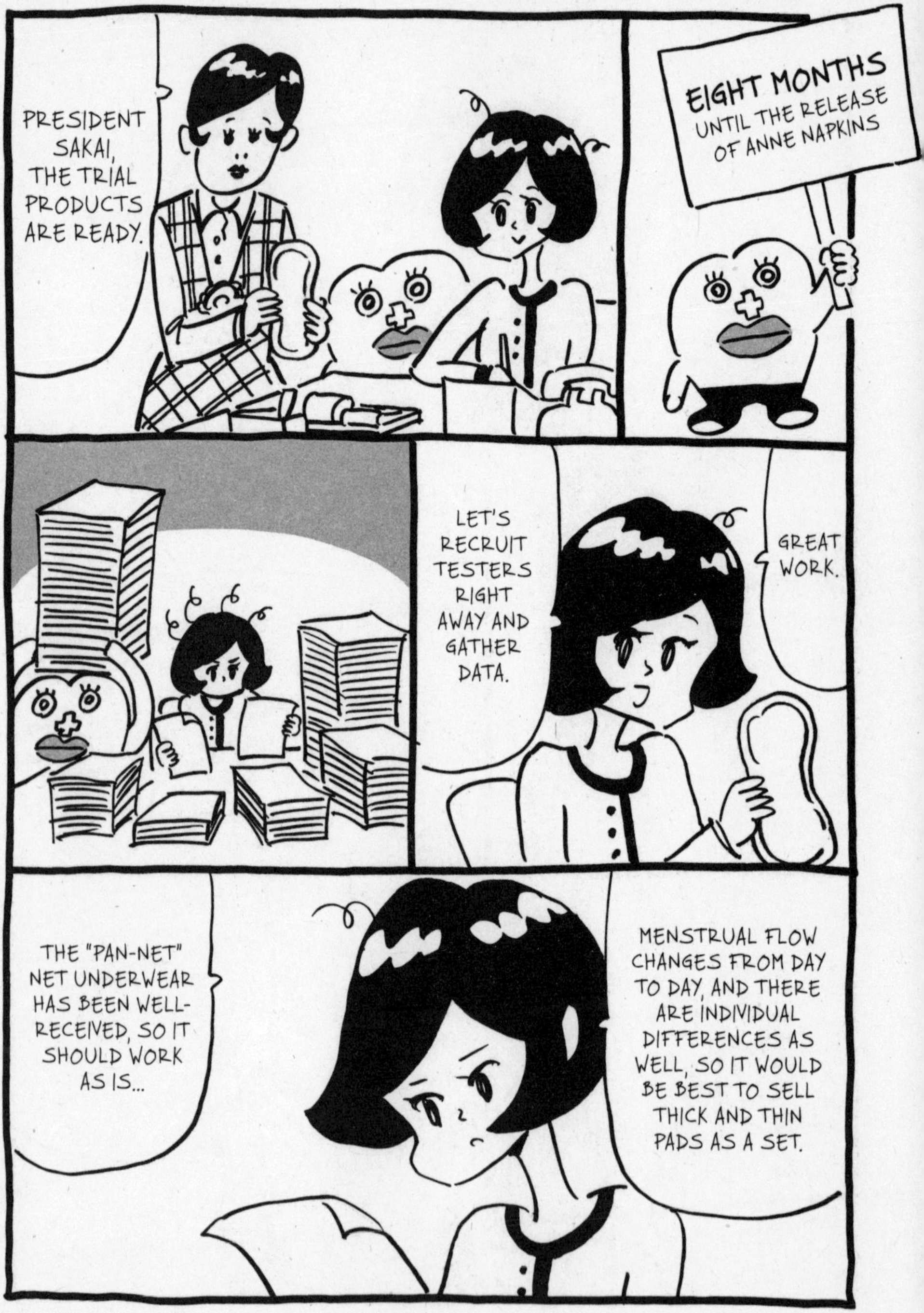
EIGHT MONTHS UNTIL THE RELEASE OF ANNE NAPKINS
PRESIDENT SAKAI, THE TRIAL PRODUCTS ARE READY.
GREAT WORK.
LET'S RECRUIT TESTERS RIGHT AWAY AND GATHER DATA.
MENSTRUAL FLOW CHANGES FROM DAY TO DAY, AND THERE ARE INDIVIDUAL DIFFERENCES AS WELL, SO IT WOULD BE BEST TO SELL THICK AND THIN PADS AS A SET.
THE "PAN-NET" NET UNDERWEAR HAS BEEN WELL-RECEIVED, SO IT SHOULD WORK AS IS...

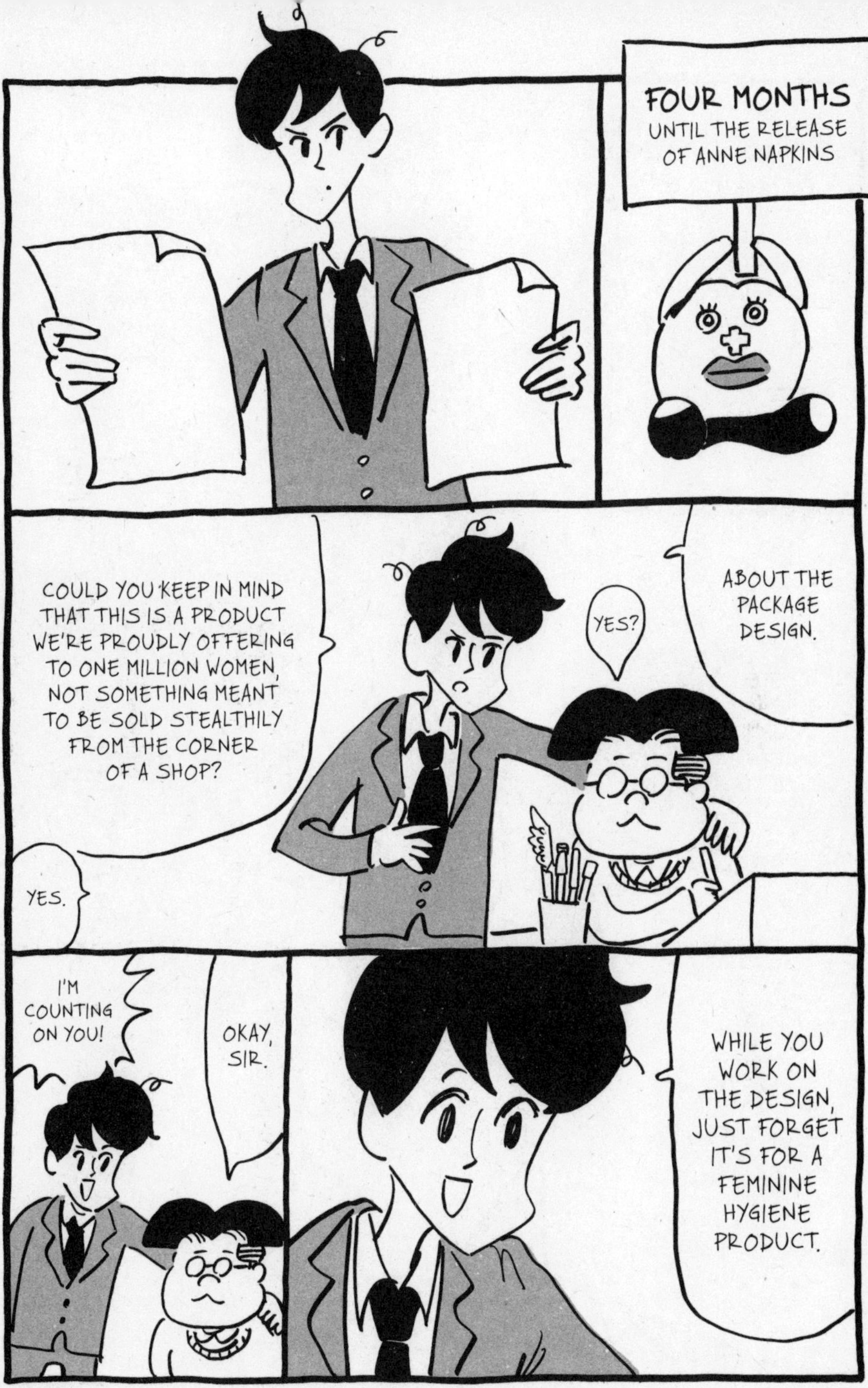
FOUR MONTHS UNTIL THE RELEASE OF ANNE NAPKINS
ABOUT THE PACKAGE DESIGN.
YES?
COULD YOU KEEP IN MIND THAT THIS IS A PRODUCT WE'RE PROUDLY OFFERING TO ONE MILLION WOMEN, NOT SOMETHING MEANT TO BE SOLD STEALTHILY FROM THE CORNER OF A SHOP?
YES.
WHILE YOU WORK ON THE DESIGN, JUST FORGET IT'S FOR A FEMININE HYGIENE PRODUCT.
OKAY, SIR.
I'M COUNTING ON YOU!

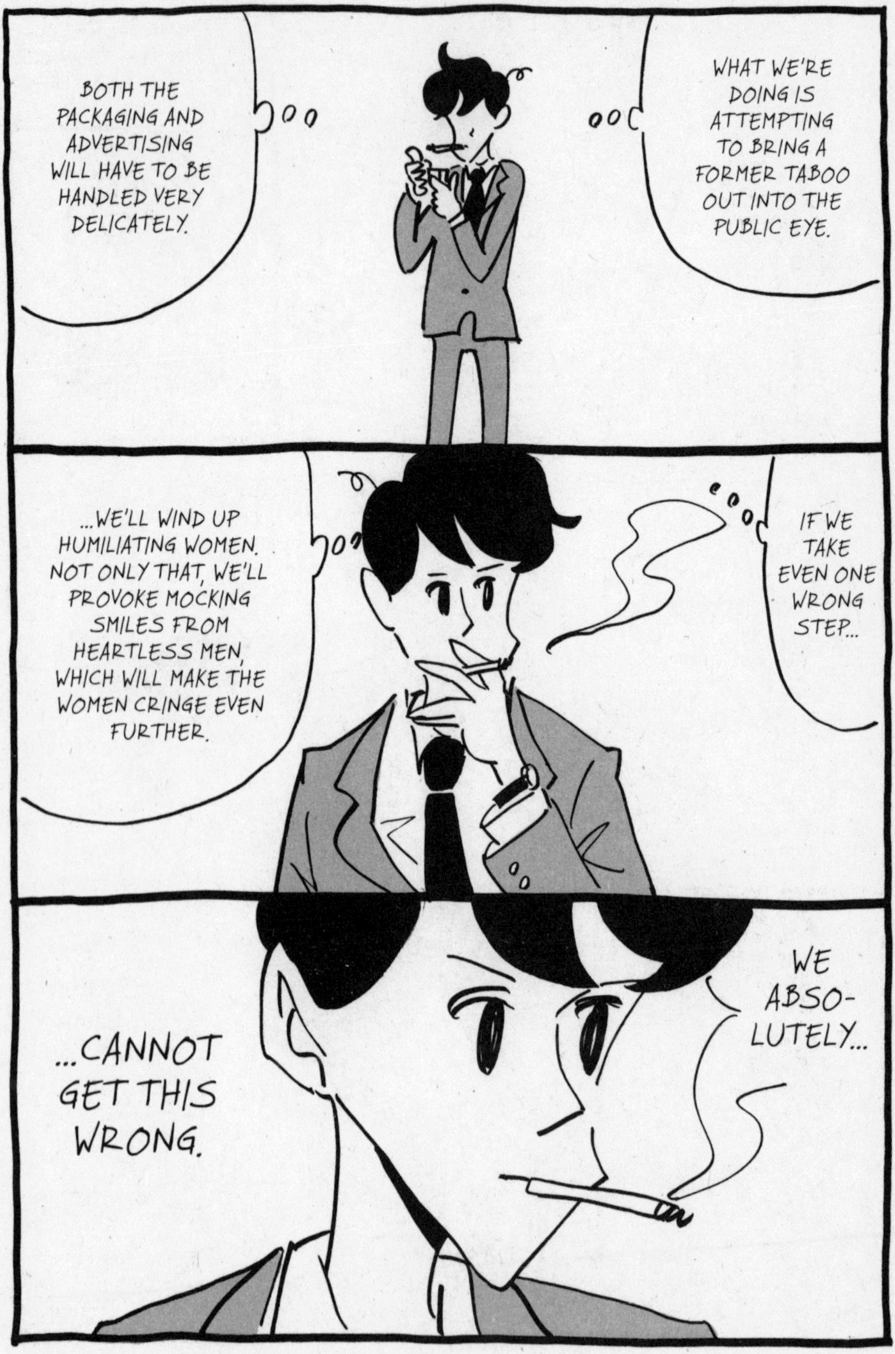
WHAT WE'RE DOING IS ATTEMPTING TO BRING A FORMER TABOO OUT INTO THE PUBLIC EYE.
BOTH THE PACKAGING AND ADVERTISING WILL HAVE TO BE HANDLED VERY DELICATELY.
IF WE TAKE EVEN ONE WRONG STEP...
...WE'LL WIND UP HUMILIATING WOMEN. NOT ONLY THAT, WE'LL PROVOKE MOCKING SMILES FROM HEARTLESS MEN, WHICH WILL MAKE THE WOMEN CRINGE EVEN FURTHER.
WE ABSO-LUTELY...
...CANNOT GET THIS WRONG.

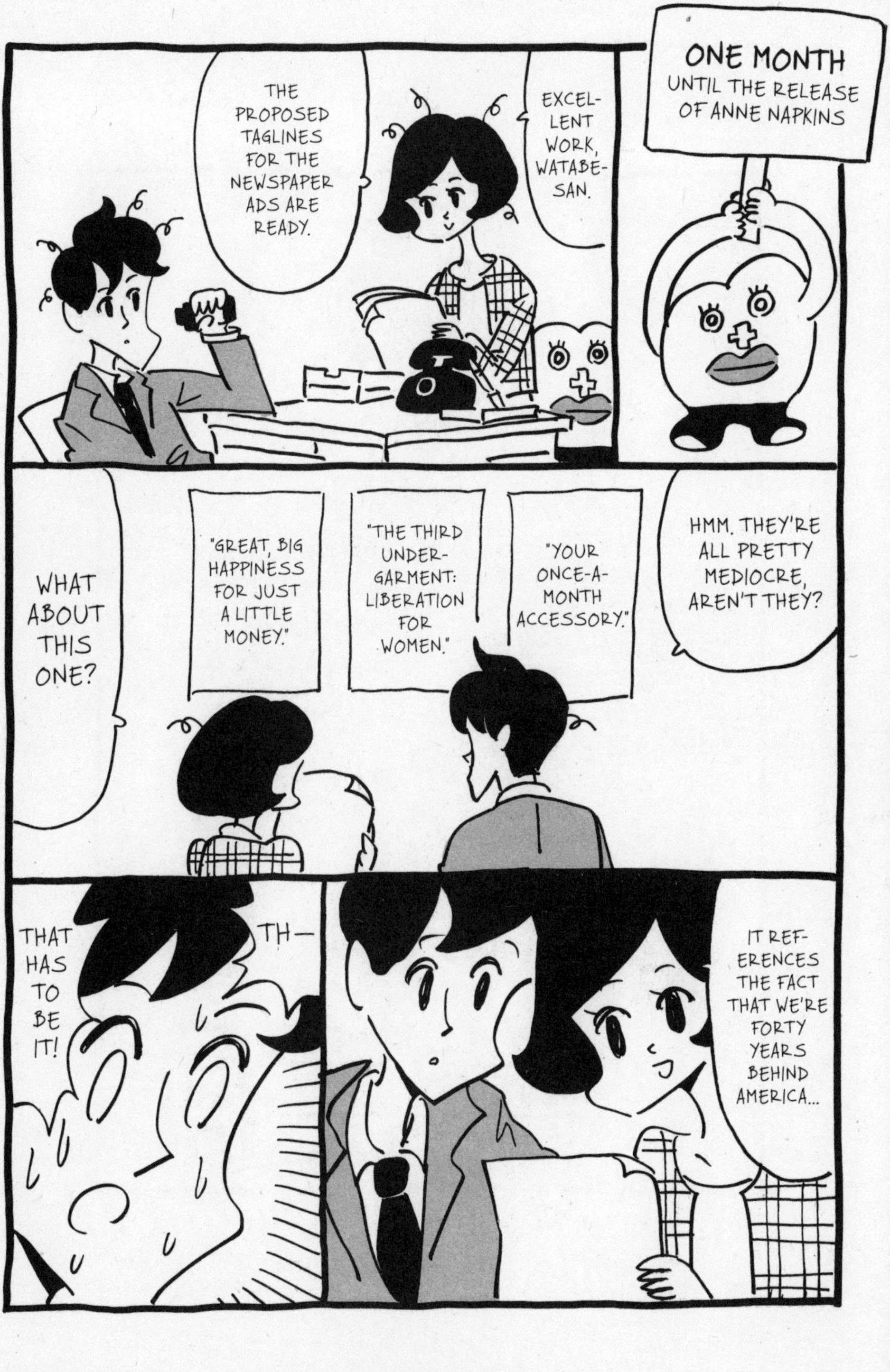
ONE MONTH UNTIL THE RELEASE OF ANNE NAPKINS
EXCELLENT WORK, WATABE-SAN.
THE PROPOSED TAGLINES FOR THE NEWSPAPER ADS ARE READY.
HMM. THEY'RE ALL PRETTY MEDIOCRE, AREN'T THEY?
"YOUR ONCE-A-MONTH ACCESSORY."
"THE THIRD UNDERGARMENT: LIBERATION FOR WOMEN."
"GREAT, BIG HAPPINESS FOR JUST A LITTLE MONEY."
WHAT ABOUT THIS ONE?
IT REFERENCES THE FACT THAT WE'RE FORTY YEARS BEHIND AMERICA...
TH—
THAT HAS TO BE IT!

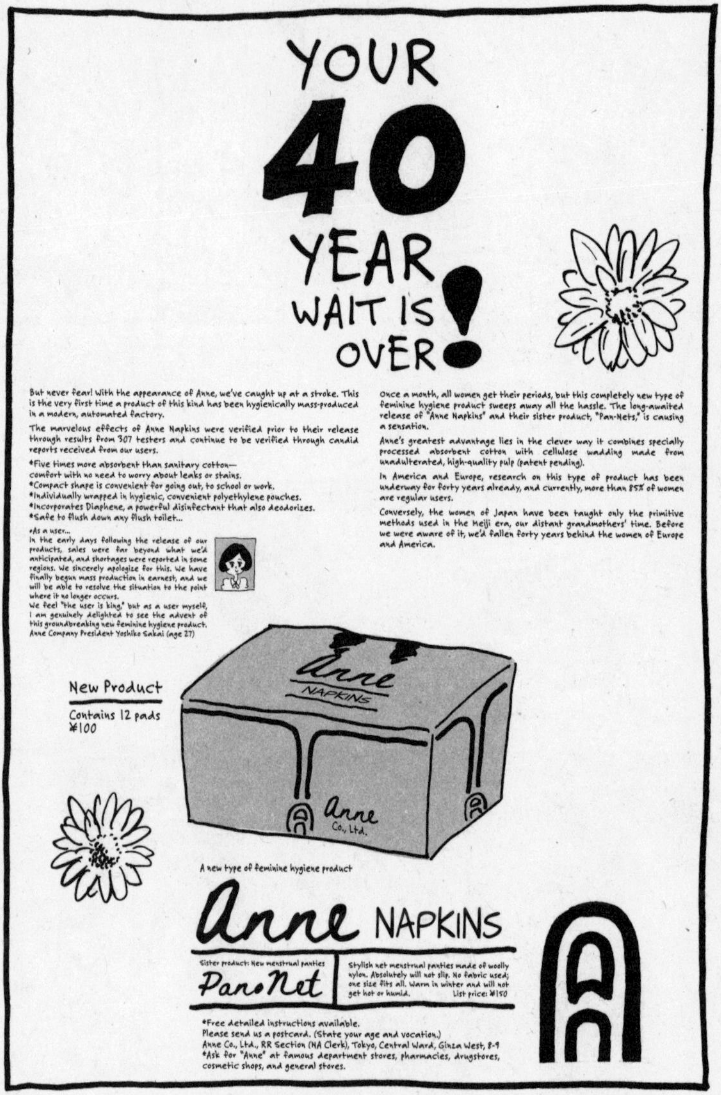

YOUR 40 YEAR WAIT IS OVER!

But never fear! With the appearance of Anne, we've caught up at a stroke. This is the very first time a product of this kind has been hygienically mass-produced in a modern, automated factory.

The marvelous effects of Anne Napkins were verified prior to their release through results from 307 testers and continue to be verified through candid reports received from our users.

*Five times more absorbent than sanitary cotton—
comfort with no need to worry about leaks or stains.
*Compact shape is convenient for going out, to school or work.
*Individually wrapped in hygienic, convenient polyethylene pouches.
*Incorporates Diaphene, a powerful disinfectant that also deodorizes.
*Safe to flush down any flush toilet...

•As a user...
In the early days following the release of our products, sales were far beyond what we'd anticipated, and shortages were reported in some regions. We sincerely apologize for this. We have finally begun mass production in earnest, and we will be able to resolve the situation to the point where it no longer occurs.
We feel "the user is king," but as a user myself, I am genuinely delighted to see the advent of this groundbreaking new feminine hygiene product.
Anne Company President Yoshiko Sakai (age 27)

Once a month, all women get their periods, but this completely new type of feminine hygiene product sweeps away all the hassle. The long-awaited release of "Anne Napkins" and their sister product, "Pan-Nets," is causing a sensation.

Anne's greatest advantage lies in the clever way it combines specially processed absorbent cotton with cellulose wadding made from unadulterated, high-quality pulp (patent pending).

In America and Europe, research on this type of product has been underway for forty years already, and currently, more than 85% of women are regular users.

Conversely, the women of Japan have been taught only the primitive methods used in the Meiji era, our distant grandmothers' time. Before we were aware of it, we'd fallen forty years behind the women of Europe and America.

New Product
Contains 12 pads
¥100

Anne NAPKINS
Anne Co., Ltd.

A new type of feminine hygiene product

Anne NAPKINS

Sister product: New menstrual panties
Pan•Net

Stylish net menstrual panties made of woolly nylon. Absolutely will not slip. No fabric used; one size fits all. Warm in winter and will not get hot or humid. List price: ¥150

*Free detailed instructions available.
Please send us a postcard. (State your age and vocation.)
Anne Co., Ltd., RR Section (NA Clerk), Tokyo, Central Ward, Ginza West, 8-9
*Ask for "Anne" at famous department stores, pharmacies, drugstores, cosmetic shops, and general stores.

THE ANNE CO.'S FIRST NEWSPAPER AD (1961)

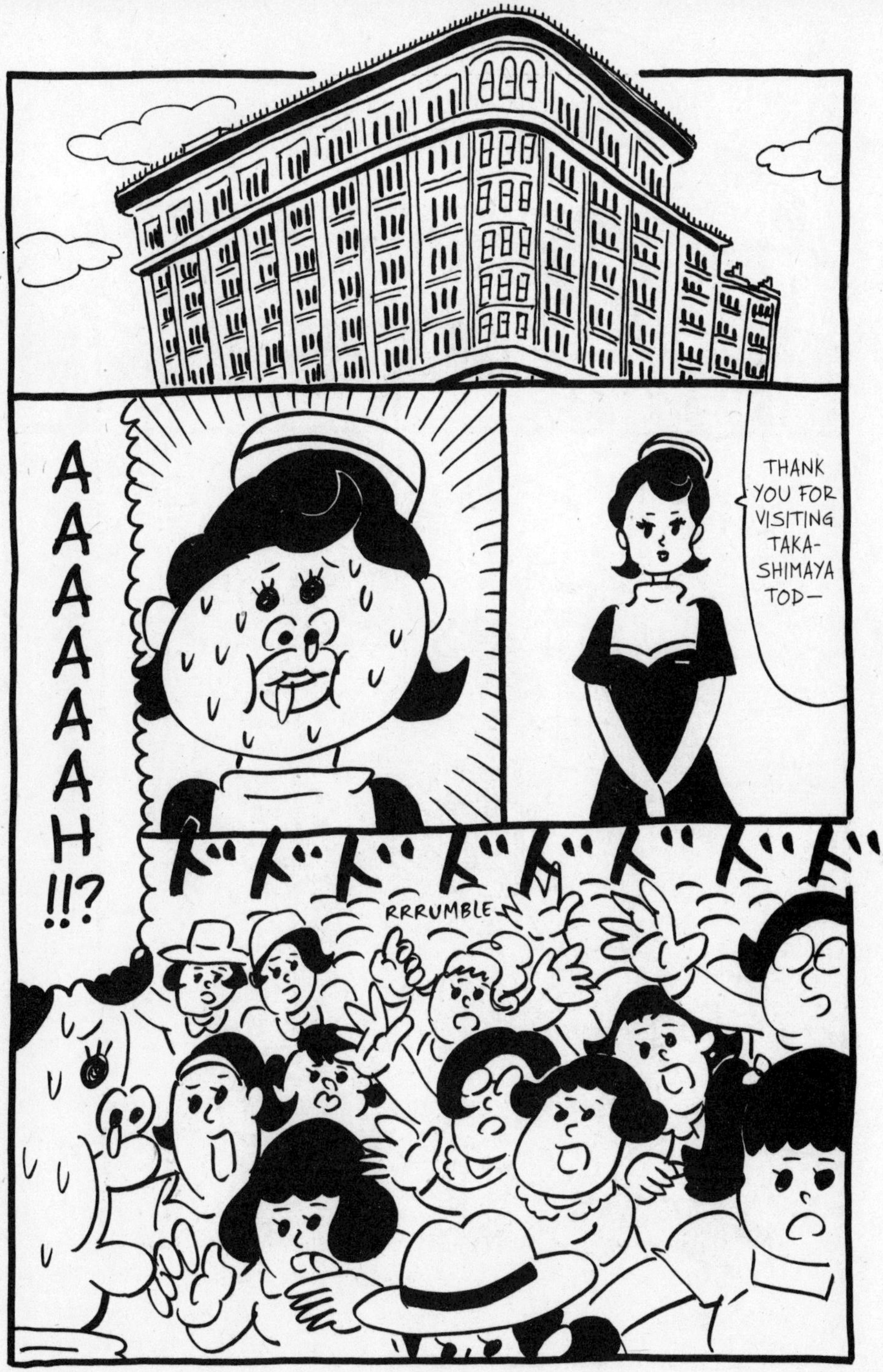
THANK YOU FOR VISITING TAKA-SHIMAYA TOD—
AAAAAAAH!!?
ドドドドドドドド
RRRUMBLE

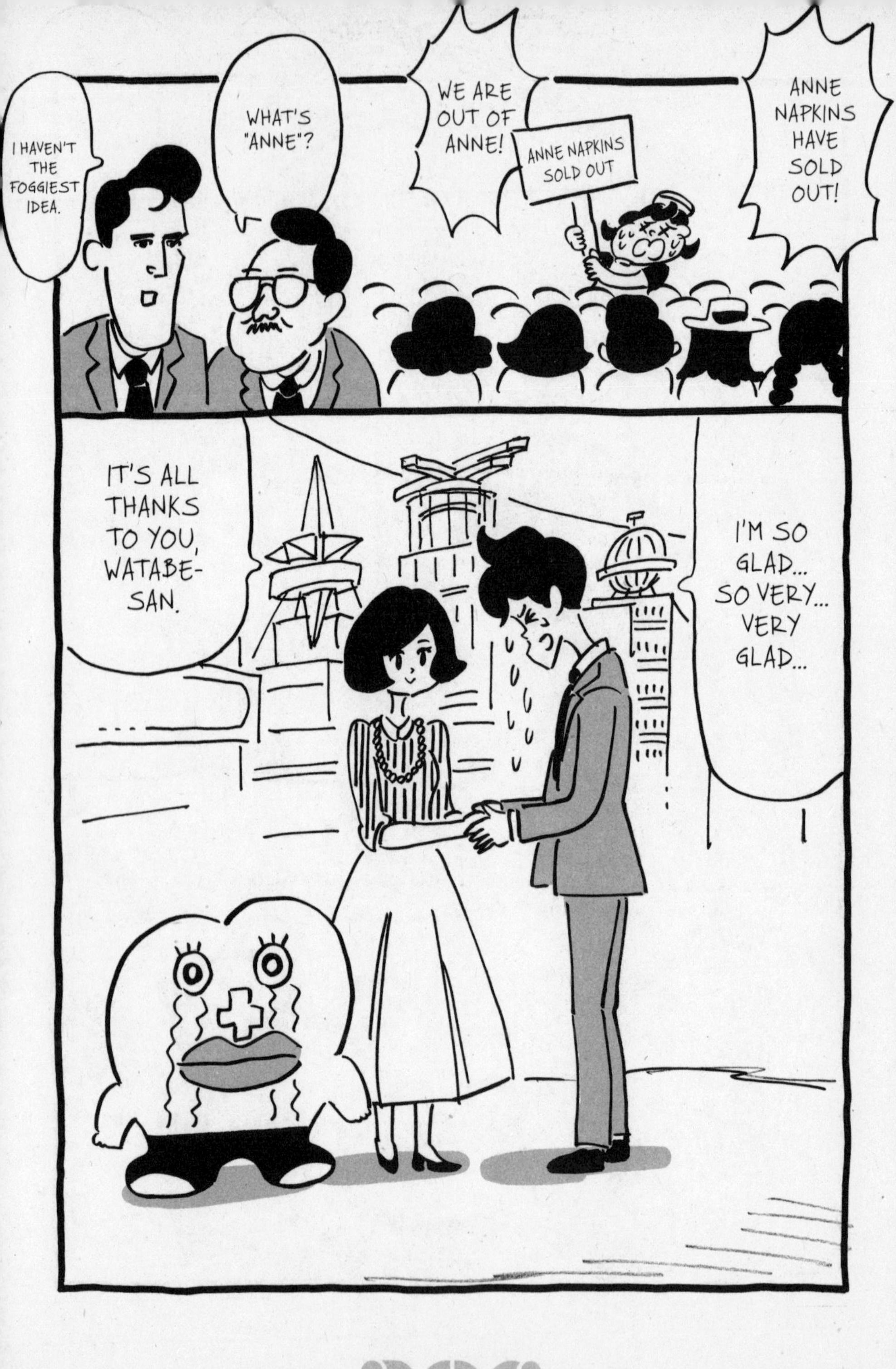
ANNE NAPKINS HAVE SOLD OUT!
ANNE NAPKINS SOLD OUT
WE ARE OUT OF ANNE!
WHAT'S "ANNE"?
I HAVEN'T THE FOGGIEST IDEA.
I'M SO GLAD... SO VERY... VERY GLAD...
IT'S ALL THANKS TO YOU, WATABE-SAN.

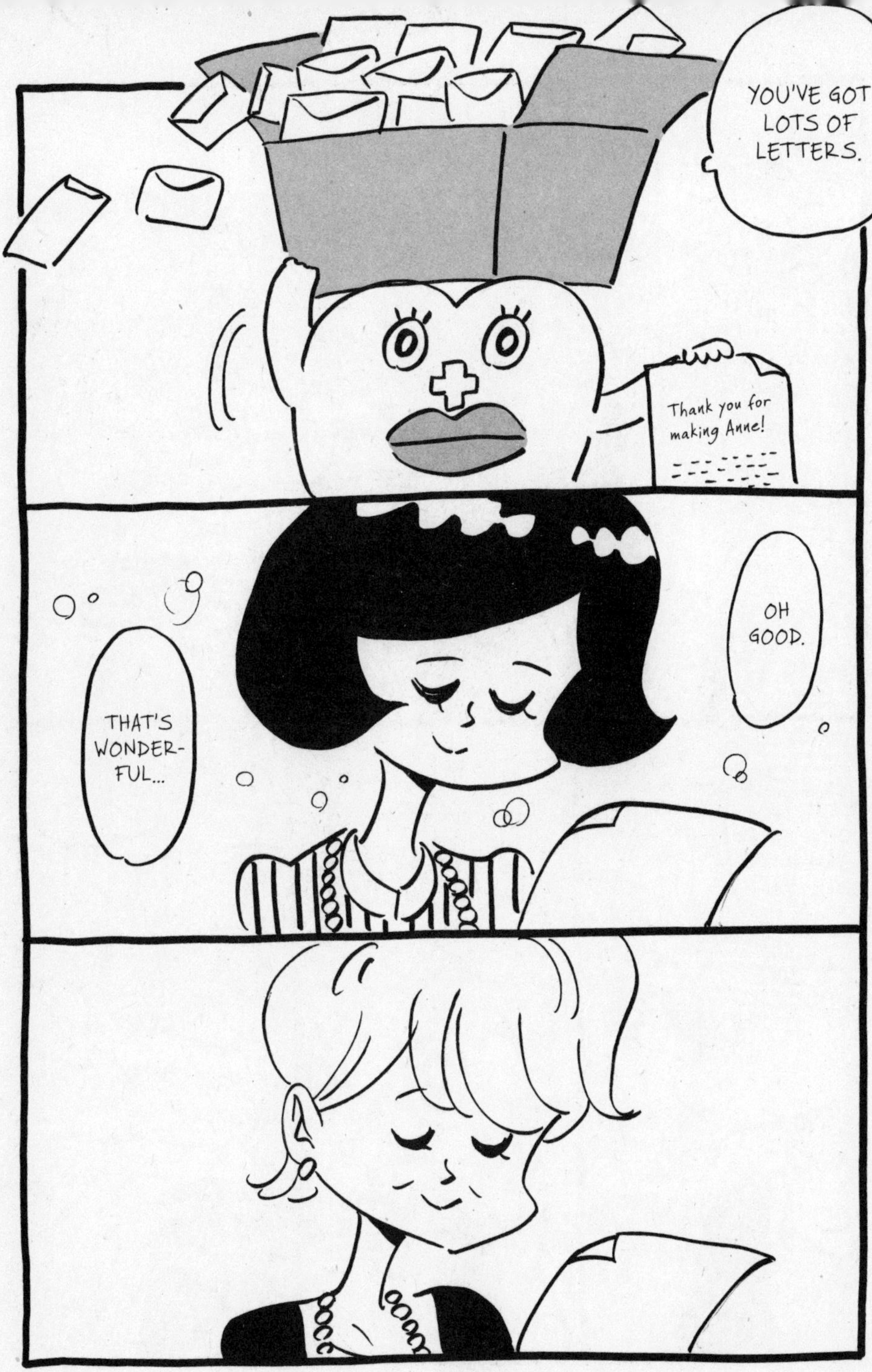
YOU'VE GOT LOTS OF LETTERS.
Thank you for making Anne!
OH GOOD.
THAT'S WONDER-FUL...

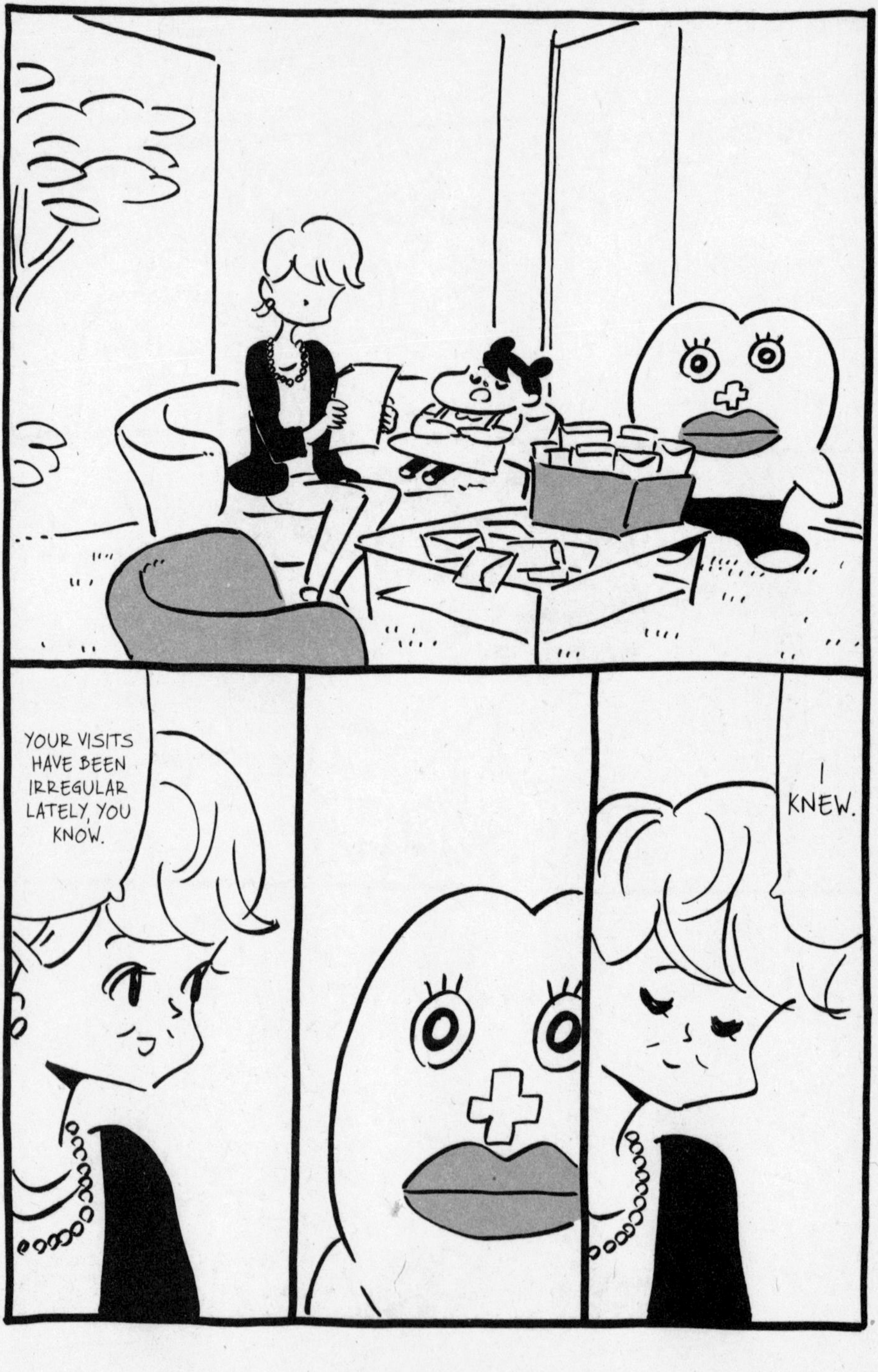
I KNEW.
YOUR VISITS HAVE BEEN IRREGULAR LATELY, YOU KNOW.

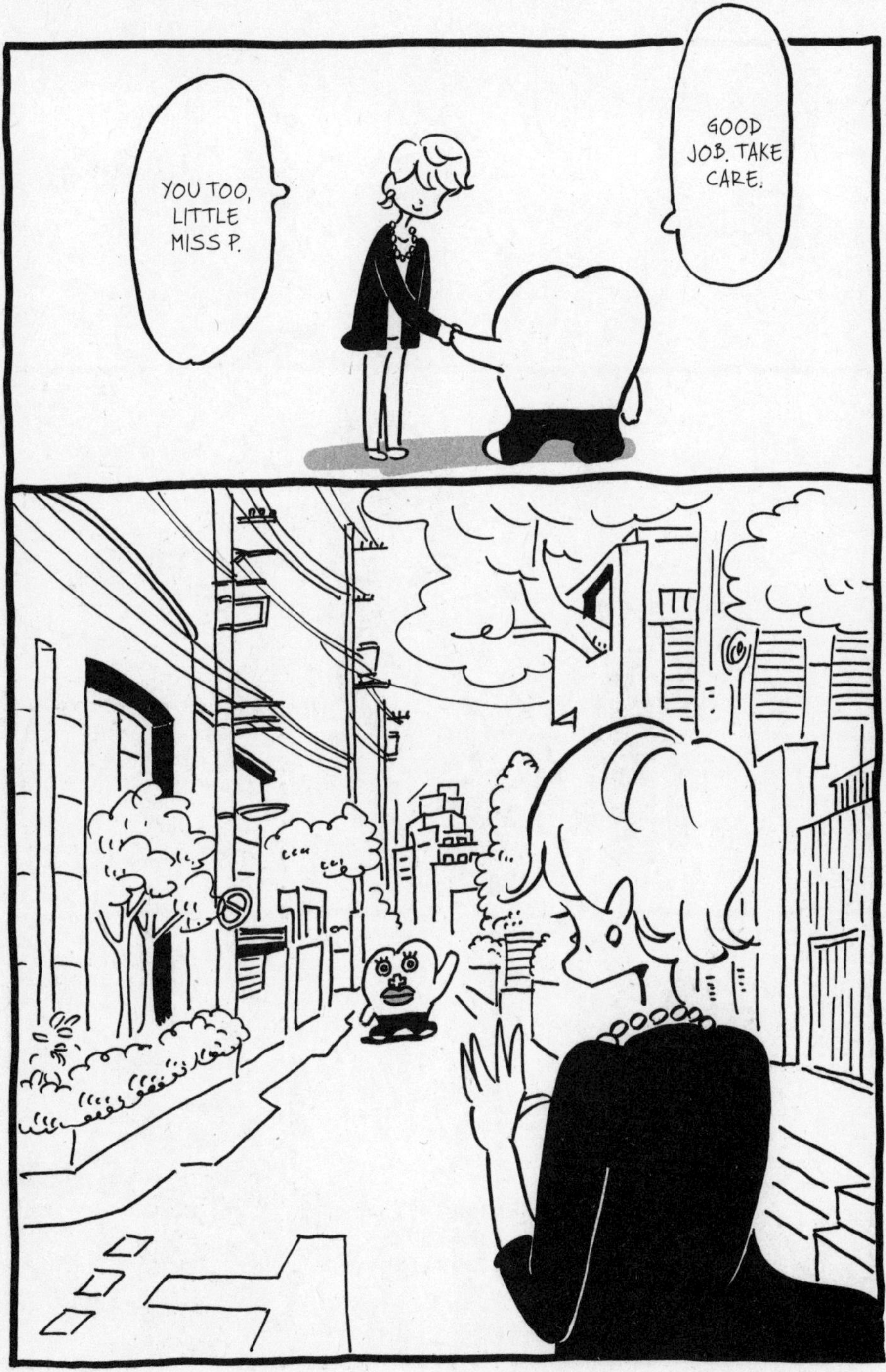
GOOD JOB. TAKE CARE.
YOU TOO, LITTLE MISS P.

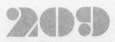

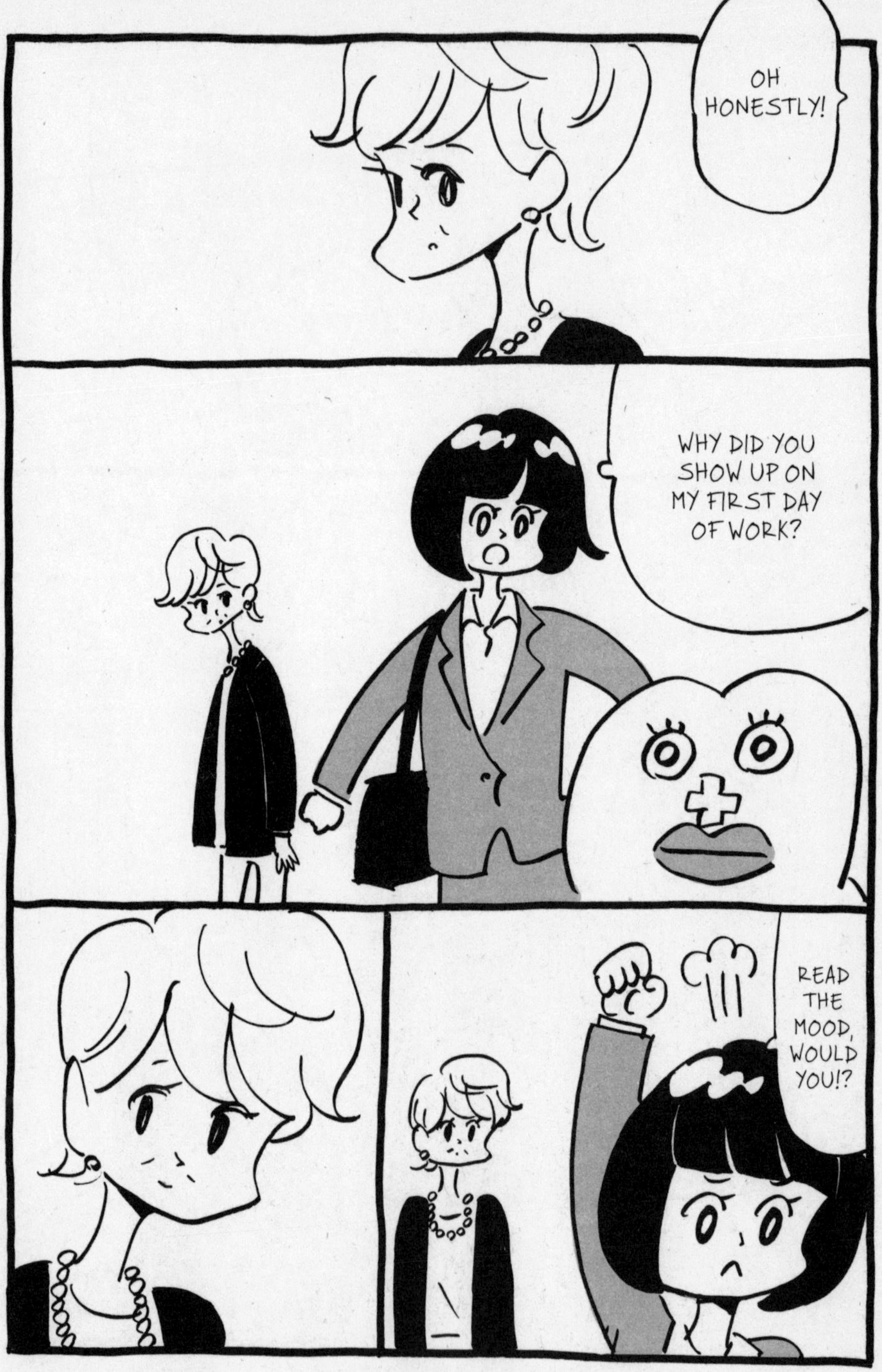
OH HONESTLY!
WHY DID YOU SHOW UP ON MY FIRST DAY OF WORK?
READ THE MOOD, WOULD YOU!?

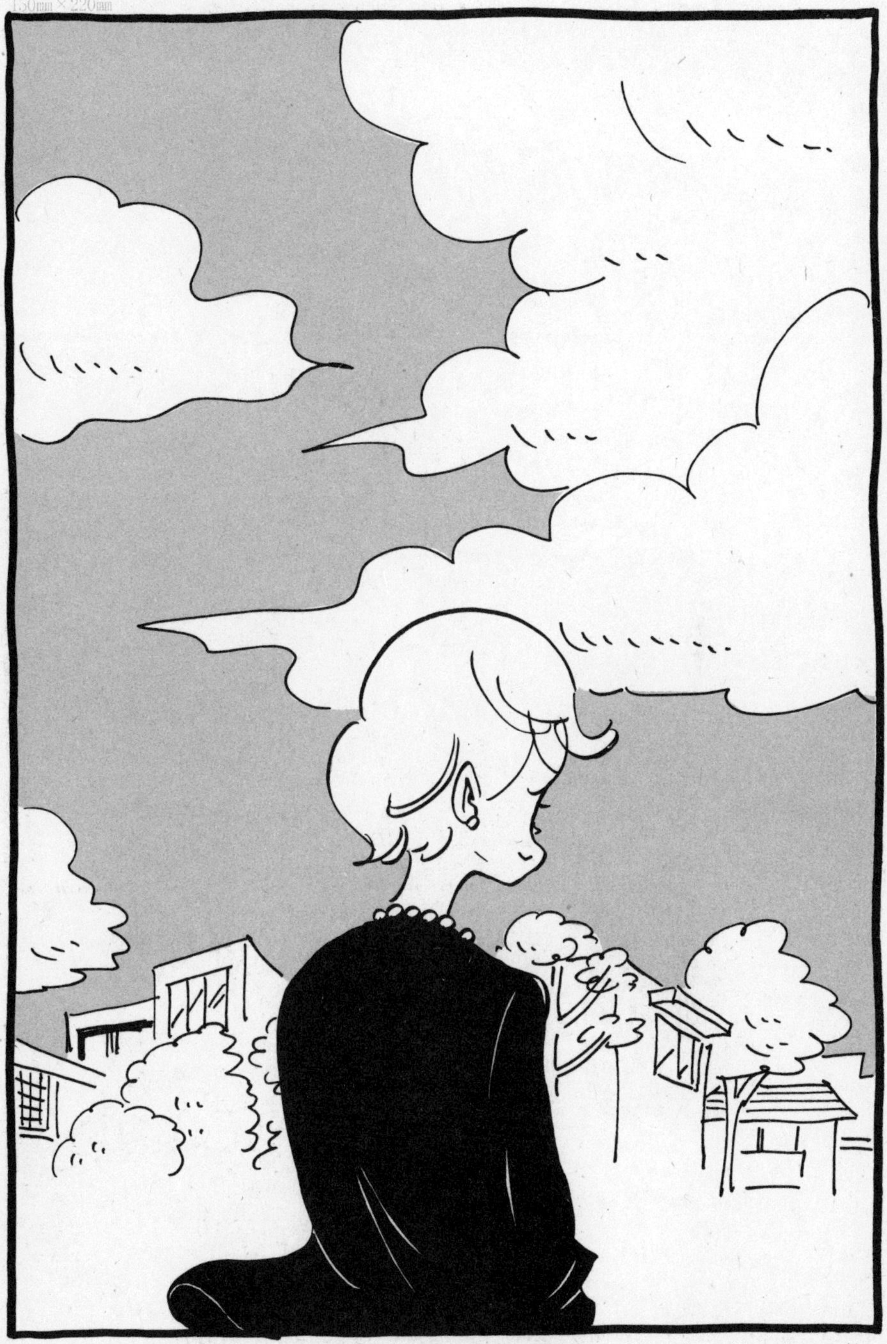

This was a fictionalized story based on the real life of Yoshiko Sakai, developer of Japan's first disposable sanitary napkins.

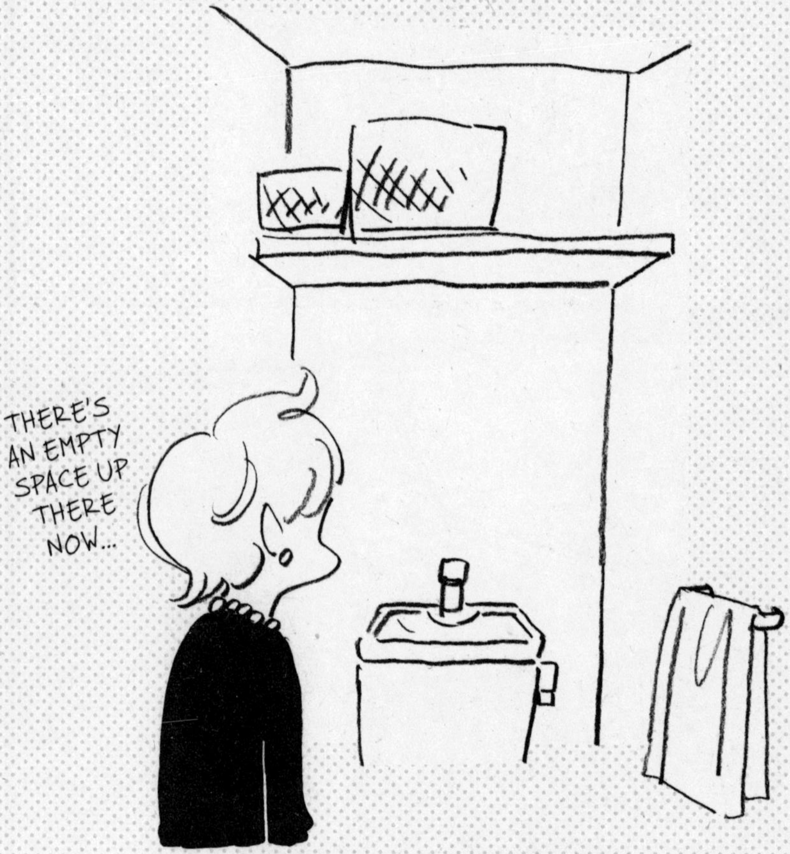
THERE'S AN EMPTY SPACE UP THERE NOW...

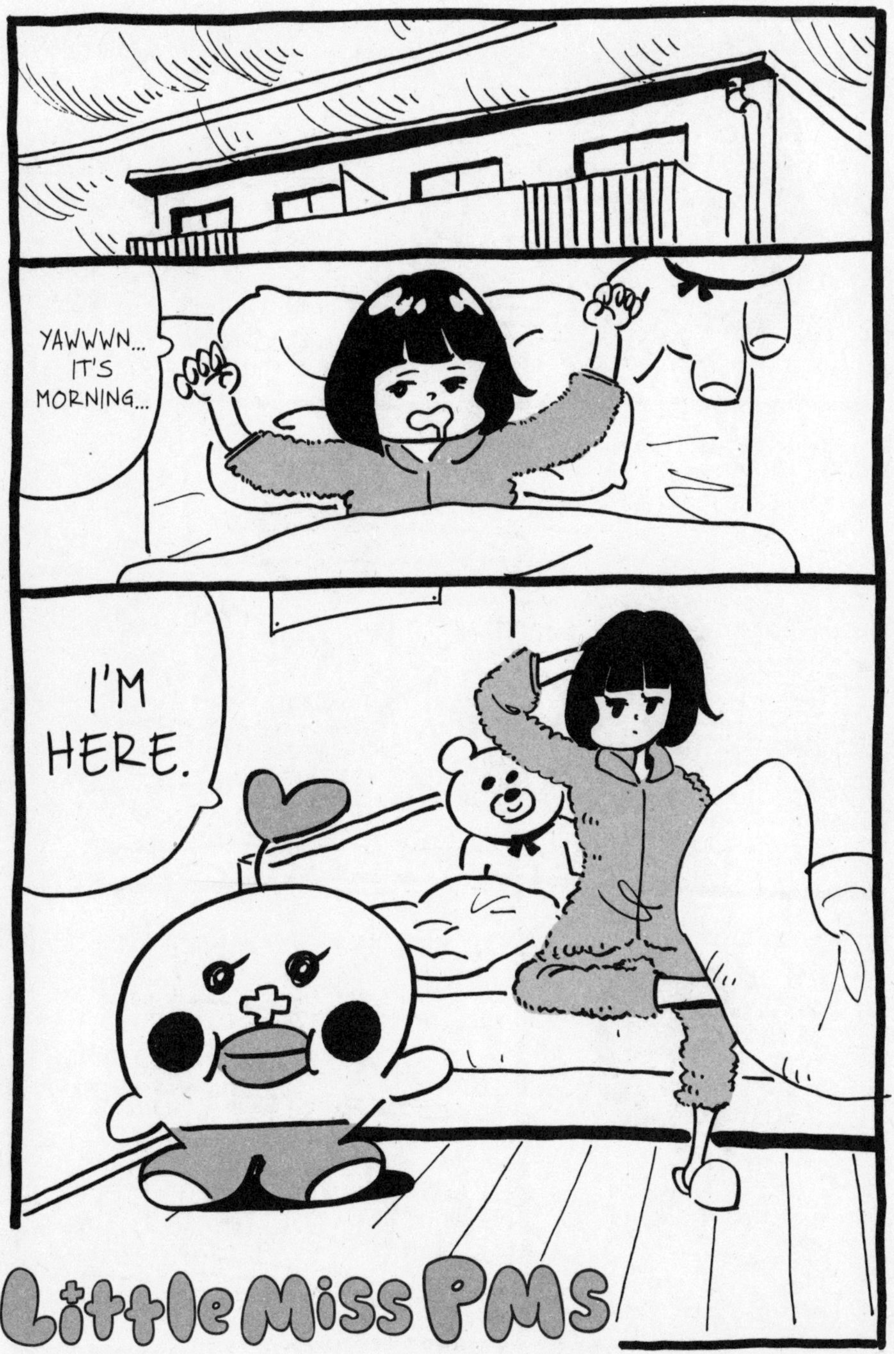
YAWWWN... IT'S MORNING...
I'M HERE.

Little Miss PMS

PMS IS A VARIETY OF UNCOMFORTABLE PHYSICAL AND EMOTIONAL SYMPTOMS THAT OCCUR BEFORE THE BEGINNING OF A PERIOD.

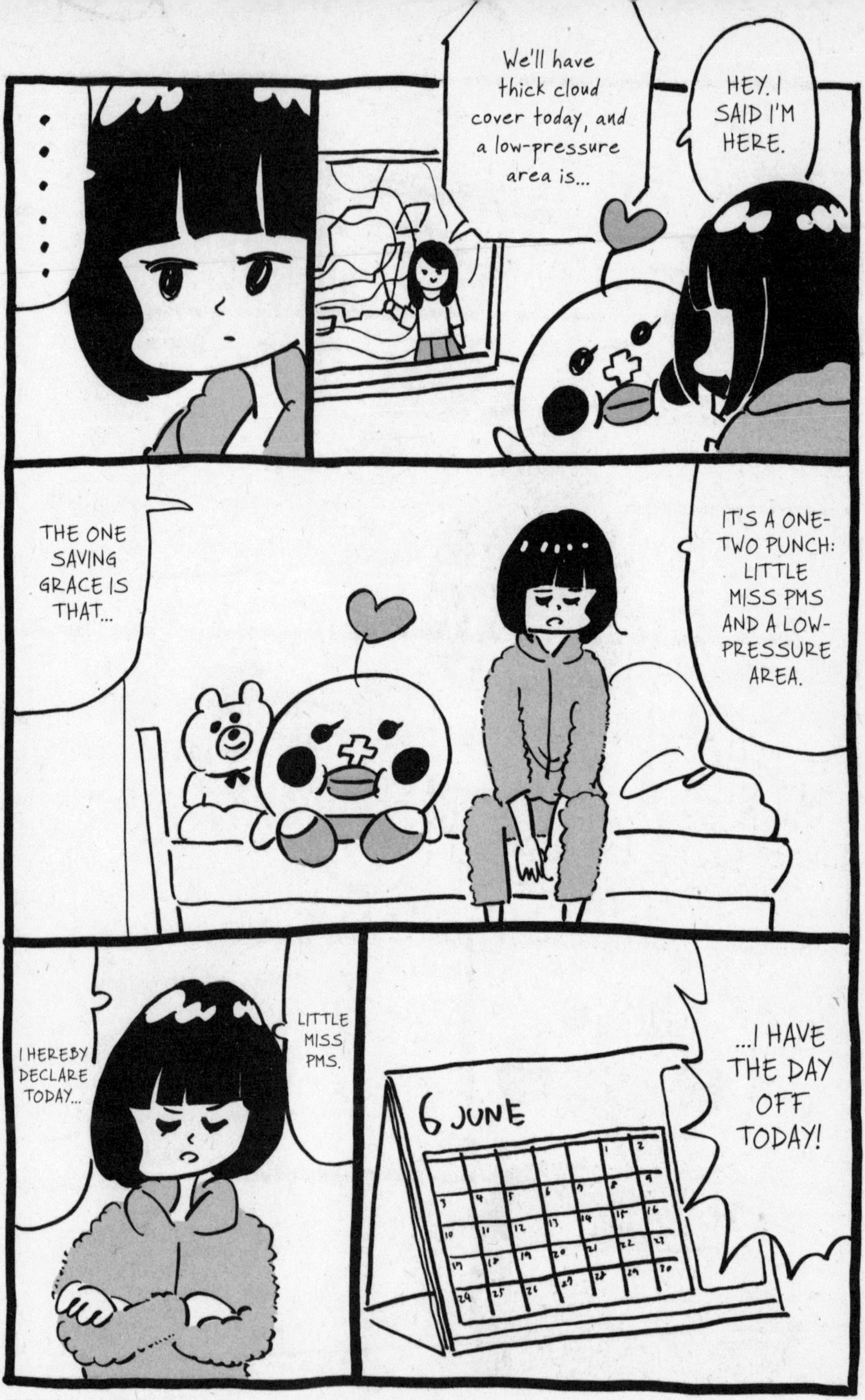
HEY. I SAID I'M HERE.
We'll have thick cloud cover today, and a low-pressure area is...
......
IT'S A ONE-TWO PUNCH: LITTLE MISS PMS AND A LOW-PRESSURE AREA.
THE ONE SAVING GRACE IS THAT...
...I HAVE THE DAY OFF TODAY!
6 JUNE
LITTLE MISS PMS.
I HEREBY DECLARE TODAY...

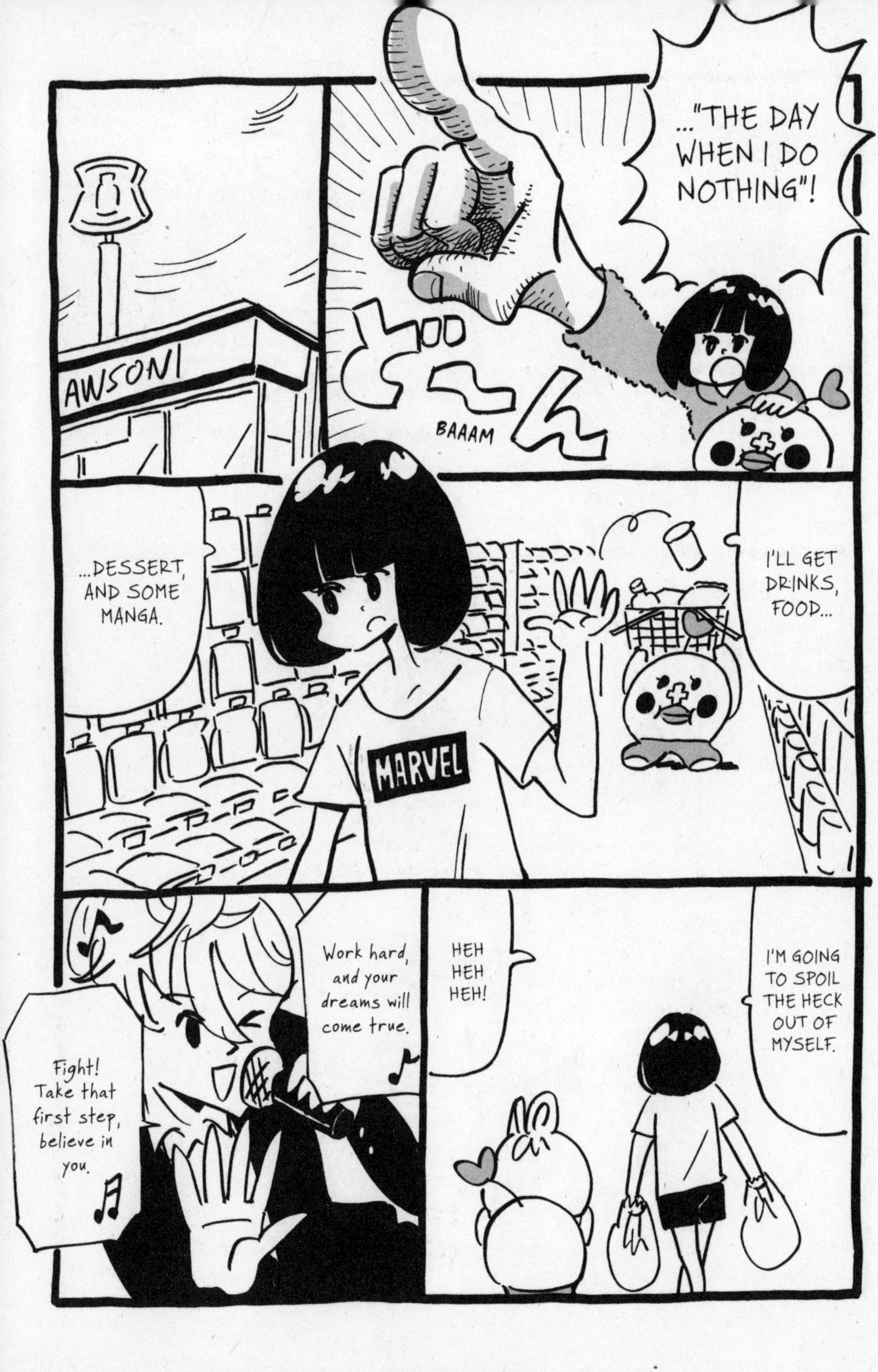
..."THE DAY WHEN I DO NOTHING"!
BAAAM
AWSONI
I'LL GET DRINKS, FOOD...
...DESSERT, AND SOME MANGA.
MARVEL
I'M GOING TO SPOIL THE HECK OUT OF MYSELF.
HEH HEH HEH!
Work hard, and your dreams will come true.
Fight! Take that first step, believe in you.

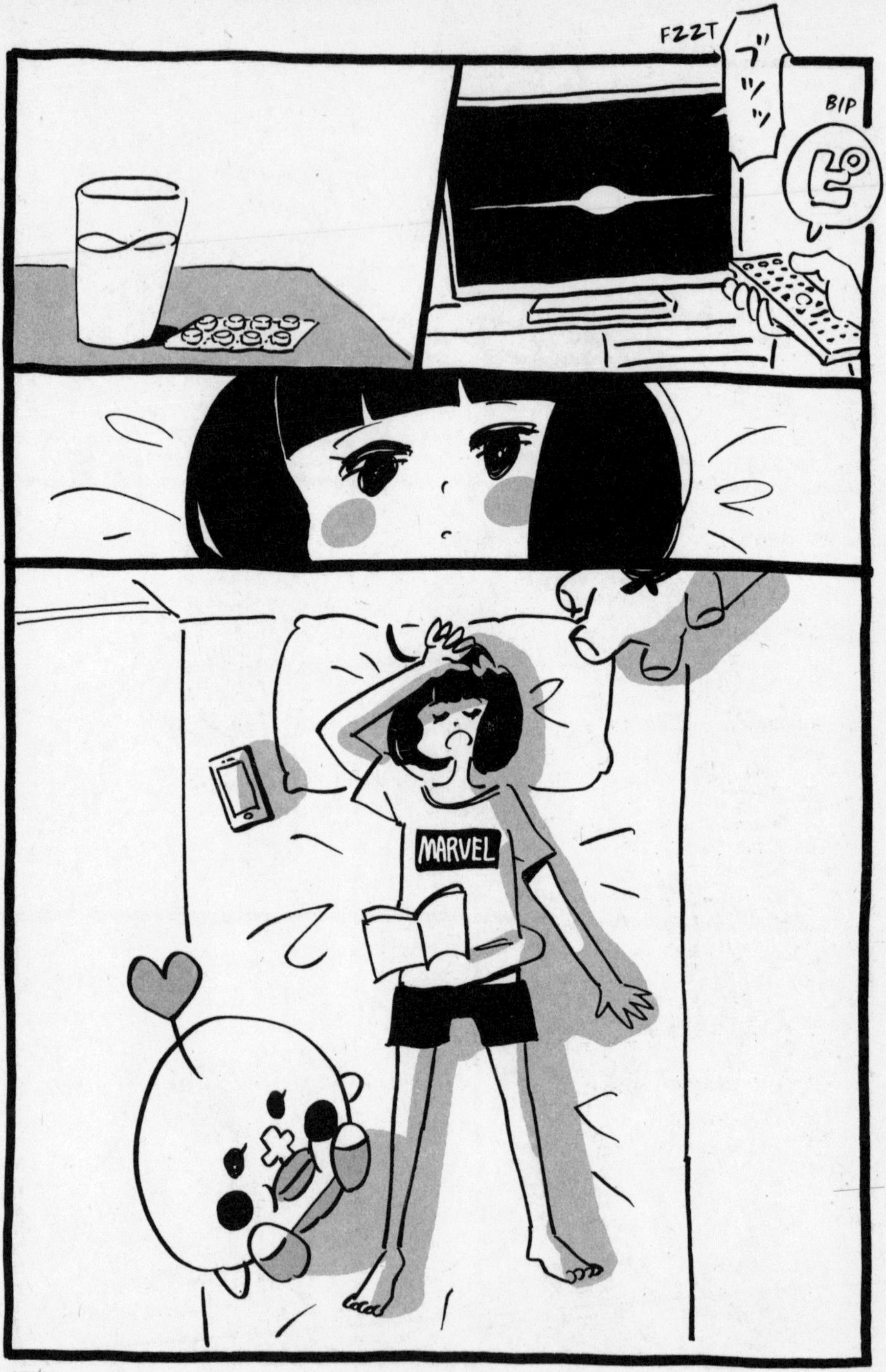
FZZT
ブツッ
BIP
ピ
MARVEL

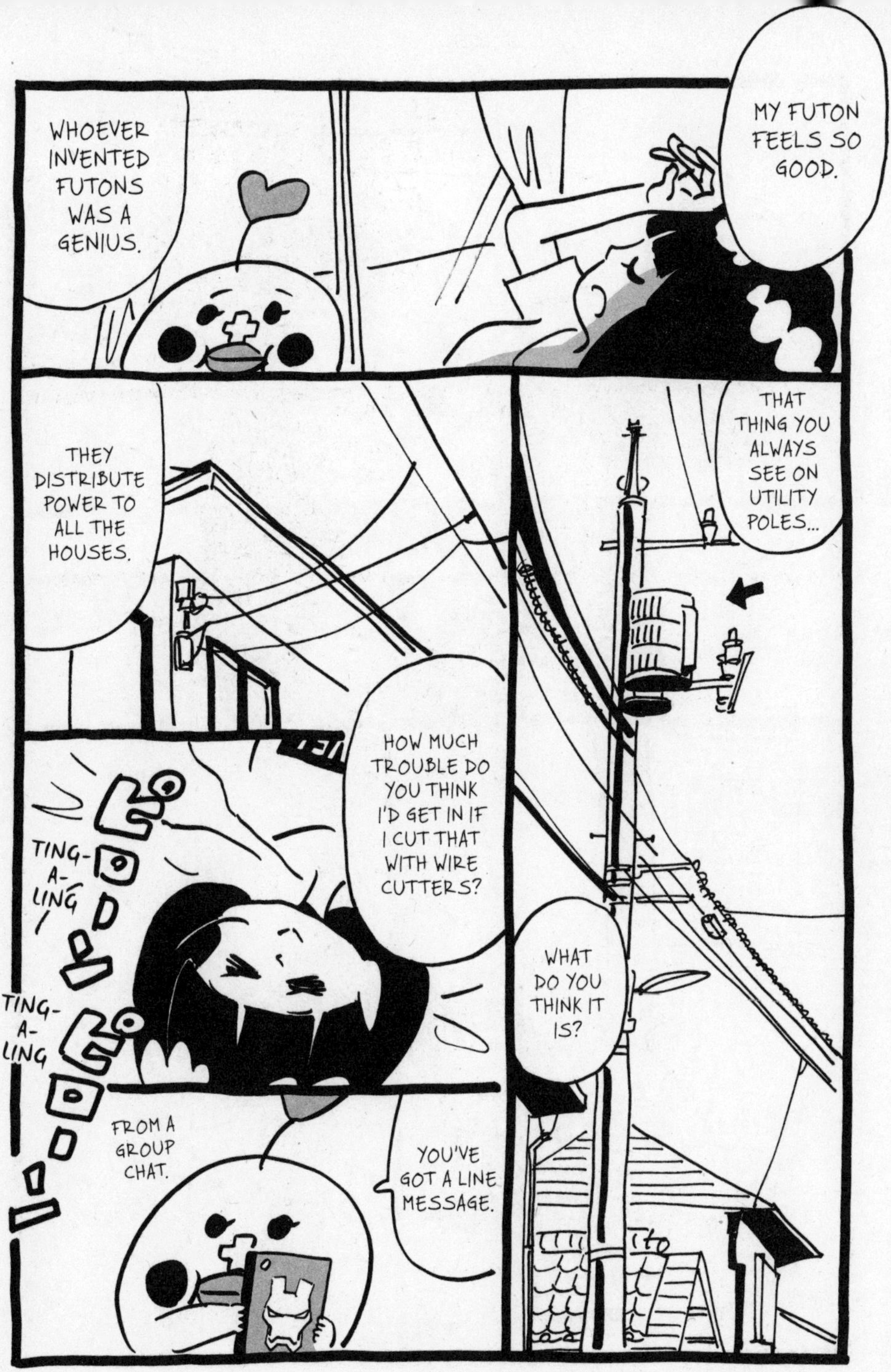
MY FUTON FEELS SO GOOD.
WHOEVER INVENTED FUTONS WAS A GENIUS.
THAT THING YOU ALWAYS SEE ON UTILITY POLES...
WHAT DO YOU THINK IT IS?
THEY DISTRIBUTE POWER TO ALL THE HOUSES.
HOW MUCH TROUBLE DO YOU THINK I'D GET IN IF I CUT THAT WITH WIRE CUTTERS?
TING-A-LING
TING-A-LING
YOU'VE GOT A LINE MESSAGE.
FROM A GROUP CHAT.

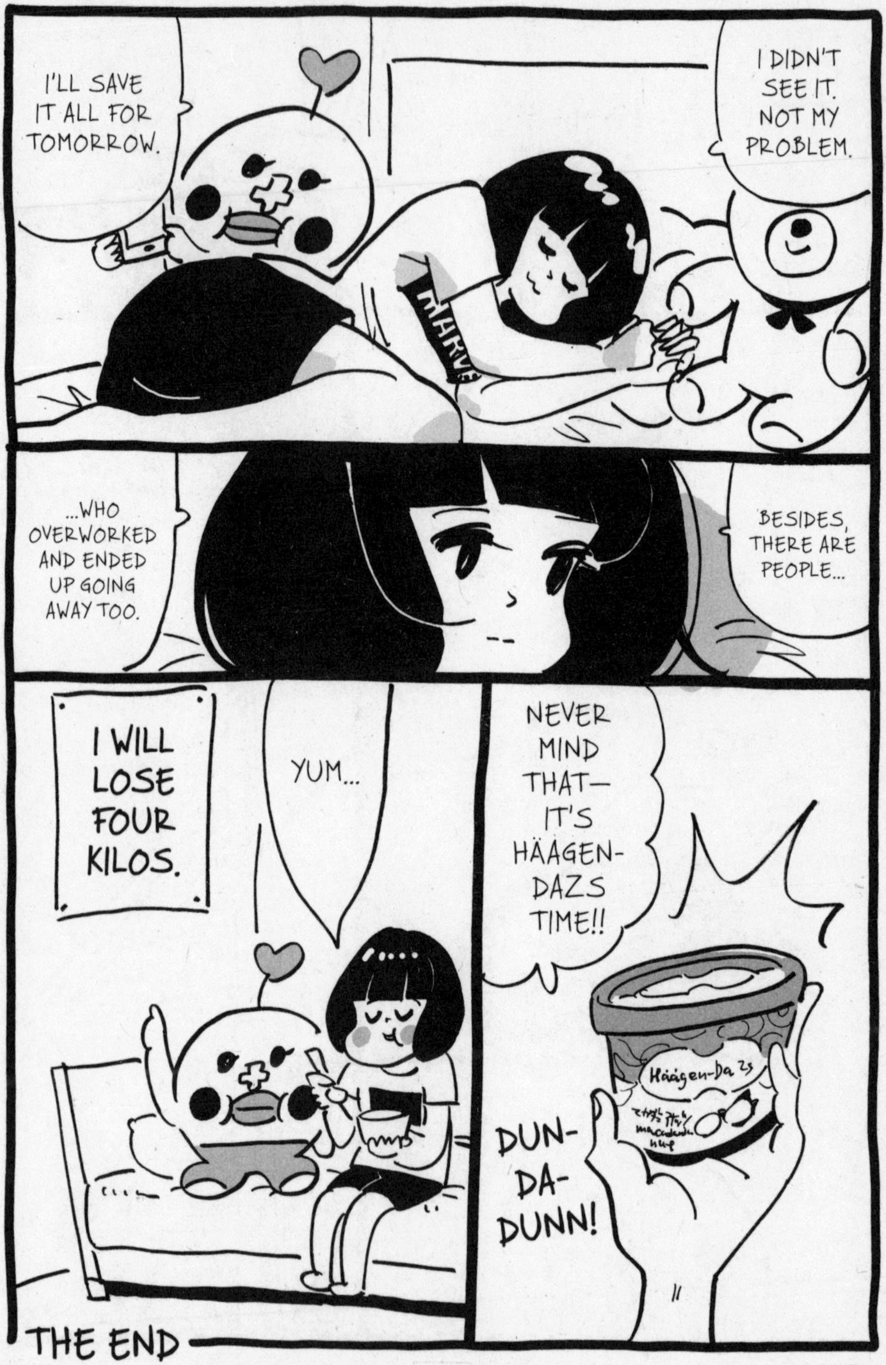
I DIDN'T SEE IT. NOT MY PROBLEM.
I'LL SAVE IT ALL FOR TOMORROW.
BESIDES, THERE ARE PEOPLE...
...WHO OVERWORKED AND ENDED UP GOING AWAY TOO.
NEVER MIND THAT—IT'S HÄAGEN-DAZS TIME!!
DUN-DA-DUNN!
YUM...
I WILL LOSE FOUR KILOS.
THE END

Little Miss P

THE "LET'S DRAW LITTLE MISS P" SONG

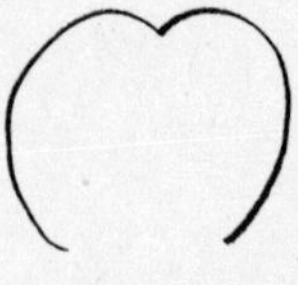

AN OLD GUY WITH A BIG BUTT...

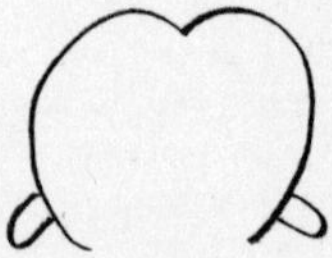

...ATE TWO WIENERS...

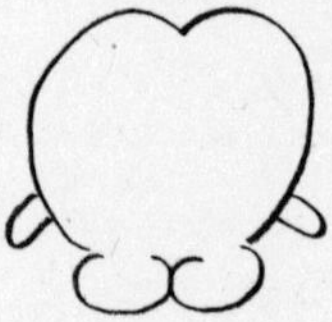

...TWO BEAN-JAM BUNS...

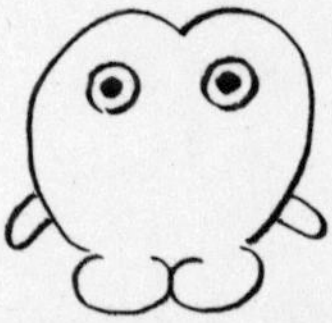

...AND TWO FRIED EGGS. BUT...

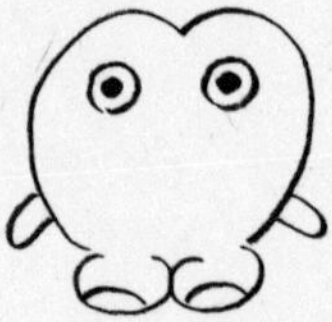

...THE BUNS WERE WORMY...

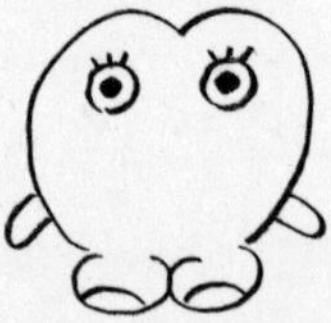

...AND THE EGGS WERE ALL MOLDY. OH NOES!

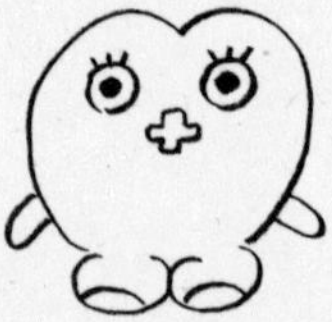

HE GOT INTO AN AMBULANCE, WEEOOOO-WEEEOOO...

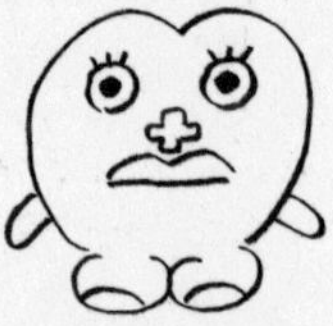

...WENT OVER TWO MOUNTAINS...

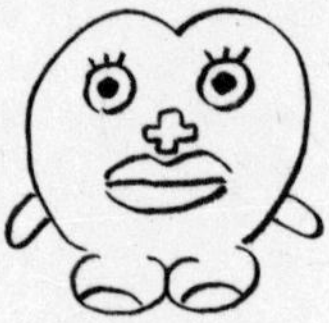

...AND THEN ONE MORE...

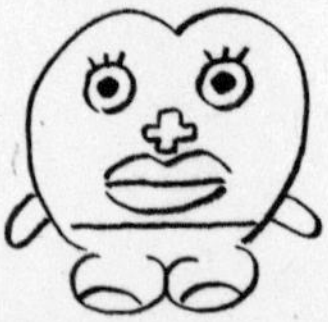

...AND ONCE HE REACHED THE OCEAN, VOILÀ! IT'S LITTLE MISS P.

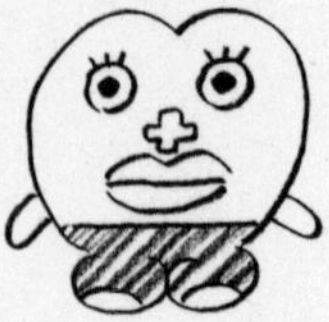

TRANSLATION NOTES

COMMON HONORIFICS

no honorific: Indicates familiarity or closeness; if used without permission or reason, addressing someone in this manner would constitute an insult.

-san: The Japanese equivalent of Mr./Mrs./Miss. If a situation calls for politeness, this is the fail-safe honorific.

-kun: Used most often when referring to boys, this honorific indicates affection or familiarity. Occasionally used by older men among their peers, but it may also be used by anyone referring to a person of lower standing.

-chan: An affectionate honorific indicating familiarity used mostly in reference to girls; also used in reference to cute persons or animals of either gender.

-senpai: A suffix used when addressing upperclassmen or senior coworkers.

-sensei: A respectful term for teachers, artists, or high-level professionals.

CURRENCY CONVERSION

While conversion rates fluctuate daily, an easy estimate for Japanese yen conversion is ¥100 to 1 USD.

PAGE 24 The food being eaten on this page is *sekihan*, or "red rice," rice cooked with red *adzuki* beans. It's traditional to serve it on the day of a girl's first period. The red isn't meant to be a reference to blood; the variety of rice eaten in ancient Japan was naturally red, and it was also too expensive for most people to eat every day, so it was reserved for special occasions. Since that type of rice isn't commonly grown anymore, when rice is served specifically as a celebratory dish, *adzuki* beans are cooked with the grains to give it a similar color.

PAGE 27 *Little Miss P* was originally published on a site called *Omocoro*; *Omokero* is a parody.

PAGE 29 Beta-kun may be a humorous reference to 大喜利β (@ogiribeta), an AI Twitter account set up by *Omocoro* writer Takenouchi-san.

PAGE 33 Matsumoto Kiyoko is a riff on Matsumoto Kiyoshi, a national Japanese drugstore chain. Changing *Kiyoshi* to *Kiyoko* turns the name from masculine to feminine.

PAGE 34 Inochi no Haha (literally "Mother of Life") is a vitamin supplement intended to alleviate the physical symptoms associated with periods.

PAGE 37 Hakata Salt is an actual brand name, although "Hakata" is usually written with different characters. Scattering salt is a Shinto ritual intended to purify a space and drive out evil. While salt isn't generally hurled at unwanted guests, the "Begone and don't come back!" message is the same.

PAGE 40 "Technobreak" is a made-in-Japan word for dying from masturbating too much.

PAGE 46 Thirty million yen is commonly quoted as the amount of money you need to have saved by the age of sixty in order to retire in comfort in Japan. It's roughly equivalent to three hundred thousand USD.

PAGE 52 LINE is a popular messaging app used in Japan.

PAGE 53 The inclusion of the station name, Sakuragicho, identifies the location of the story as Yokohama, one of Japan's most populous cities.

PAGE 62 Periods are sometimes referred to as "the messenger from the moon," and Japanese youth culture has naturally picked up on the *Sailor Moon* parallels, hence our magical girl team depicted in this chapter.

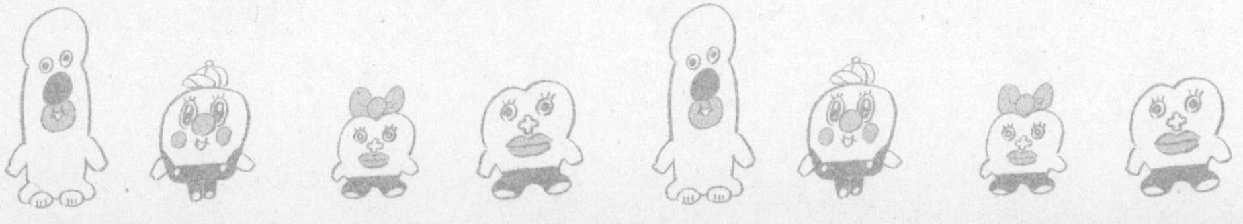

PAGE 64 Tonari's waking lines mimic the first line of "Asa no Rirei," or "Morning Relay," a poem by Shuntarou Tanikawa. His poem begins, "While a young man in Kamchatka / Dreams of a giraffe / A young girl in Mexico / Waits for the bus in the morning haze." A *qilin* is a horned beast of Chinese myth said to appear with the arrival or departure of prominent leaders or thinkers. At some points in history, it was associated with the image of a giraffe.

PAGE 75 The author's road sign confusion is a pretty easy, completely understandable mistake: The signs are nearly identical, but "Do Not Enter" signs have a white background, while "No Parking" signs have a blue one.

PAGE 86 Hokusai Katsushika is an incredibly famous *ukiyo-e* painter who lived during the Edo era, from 1760 to 1849. Several of his woodblock prints—particularly *The Great Wave off Kanagawa* and *Fine Wind, Clear Morning*—turn up on souvenirs very, very frequently. Hokusai actually did publish a manga work consisting of fifteen volumes. However, the pictures aren't connected to one another and don't tell a story, so it doesn't bear much resemblance to modern manga and could be translated as "sketches" instead.

PAGE 88 In many cultures, women were (and, in a few places, still are) considered "unclean" during their periods and were supposed to spend those days in huts built away from the areas where most people lived. In Japan, these were called *imigoya*, or "taboo huts," and they were also where women went to give birth. It was believed that women's *qi*, or "life force," was weaker at times like these, and the isolation was intended to keep the *qi* from being subjected to any further strain.

PAGE 89 Ooi Katsushika, Hokusai's daughter, was a very accomplished painter in her own right. She lived from approximately 1800 to about 1866. She's also the subject of the recent anime film, *Miss Hokusai*, adapted from the manga of the same name, which ran from 1983 to 1987.

PAGE 93 At seventy-four, Hokusai famously said he didn't think he'd drawn anything worthwhile until he was seventy, and didn't expect to be really good until he was one hundred.

PAGE 94 The scars on Yui's back are from moxibustion, a treatment related to acupuncture in which small lumps of pulped mugwort (thought to be beneficial to the subject's health) are burned on certain parts of the body, sometimes to the point where the skin is scarred, in order to cure or prevent diseases. Yui's scars are most likely from a preventative treatment rather than an attempt to cure active syphilis.

PAGE 121 *Yarukkya Knight* is the title of a 1980s school comedy manga that's heavy on *hentai* elements. A live-action movie was made in 2015.

"That porn pool" refers to a heated pool in the Hanazono Room, a luxury studio in Shinjuku. Although it's also used as a location in TV dramas, it's more widely known for its use in adult videos. It shows up in them so frequently, it's said all men have seen it at least once and will immediately think of it when they hear "that one pool," though they may have no idea what or where it actually is.

PAGE 124 Loxonin is a brand name for the anti-inflammatory drug loxoprofen; it's in the same family as ibuprofen.

PAGE 143 The board behind Aoko in the bar features common drink options, two being *shochu* and *chu-hi*. *Shochu* is a traditional hard liquor made with grains and vegetables. Common base ingredients are sweet potato, barley, rice, buckwheat, and cane sugar. *Chu-hi*, commonly found canned, is a mixed drink made from *shochu*, carbonated water, and lemon juice.

PAGE 145 PAIRS is a popular Japanese dating app. It caters to women looking to date online, frequently with long-term relationships in mind.

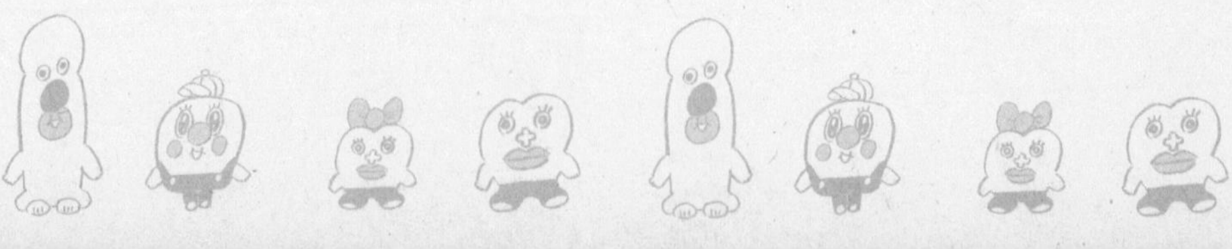

PAGE 147 Wool underwear are knitted underwear, generally with a high waist, designed to keep your lower body warm and ease cramps. Some types also have a pocket over the stomach for a hot pack.

Utamaro is a brand of soap designed to get stubborn stains out of fabric.

Sanitary panties are leakproof underwear designed to be worn during a woman's period. Some have mesh pockets meant to hold pads in place, while others come with padded crotches and can be worn instead of traditional pads. Materials vary, but all are washable and either water-resistant or waterproof.

PAGE 154 The signs behind Aoko describe a variety of pub food offerings. *Moro-kyu* is sliced, raw cucumbers topped with *moromi-miso*, a salty, "chunky" soybean paste that's meant to be eaten as a condiment rather than used in cooking. *Shiokara* is a dish made from various marine animals, consisting of small pieces of meat in a paste of the same animal's salted, fermented viscera. *Gesoyaki* is spicy squid legs. *Motsuni* is stewed organs or giblets and can be made from cow, pig, chicken, or horse organs. *Kimchi* is Korean spicy fermented cabbage and other vegetables.

PAGE 164 In the original, Kuroe's lines are written in *katakana* characters to indicate she speaks fluently but with an accent.

PAGE 165 Kuroe's introductory caption actually refers to her as "double"; it's a recently introduced Japanese alternative to calling individuals of mixed parentage "half." The change reflects the attitude that such people are full-fledged members of both races or nationalities, not incomplete members of anything.

PAGE 178 The R-19 Literature Award is a send-up of the R-18 Literature Award, a writing competition limited to women and judged exclusively by women.

PAGE 179 The spider sculpture pictured here is called *Maman* and is a copy of the original work created by the French-American sculptor Louise Bourgeois. The piece is located outside the Mori Art Museum in Roppongi, Tokyo.

PAGE 185 "Anne's Day" was a Japanese euphemism for periods back in the 1960s and 1970s, taken from the name of the sanitary pad company discussed in this chapter.

PAGE 194 The real-life man who partnered with Yoshiko Sakai to create Anne Napkins was Hajime Moribe; his relatives are still in charge of Mitsumi Electric.

PAGE 200 Pan-Net underwear is made of light nylon mesh and has a tubular crotch that's designed to hold a sanitary pad. From the ad poster given later in this story, Pan-Net was released around the same time as the napkins.

PAGE 205 The building pictured in the first panel is the Takashimaya Nihonbashi department store; it was constructed in 1933 and is currently listed as an important cultural property.

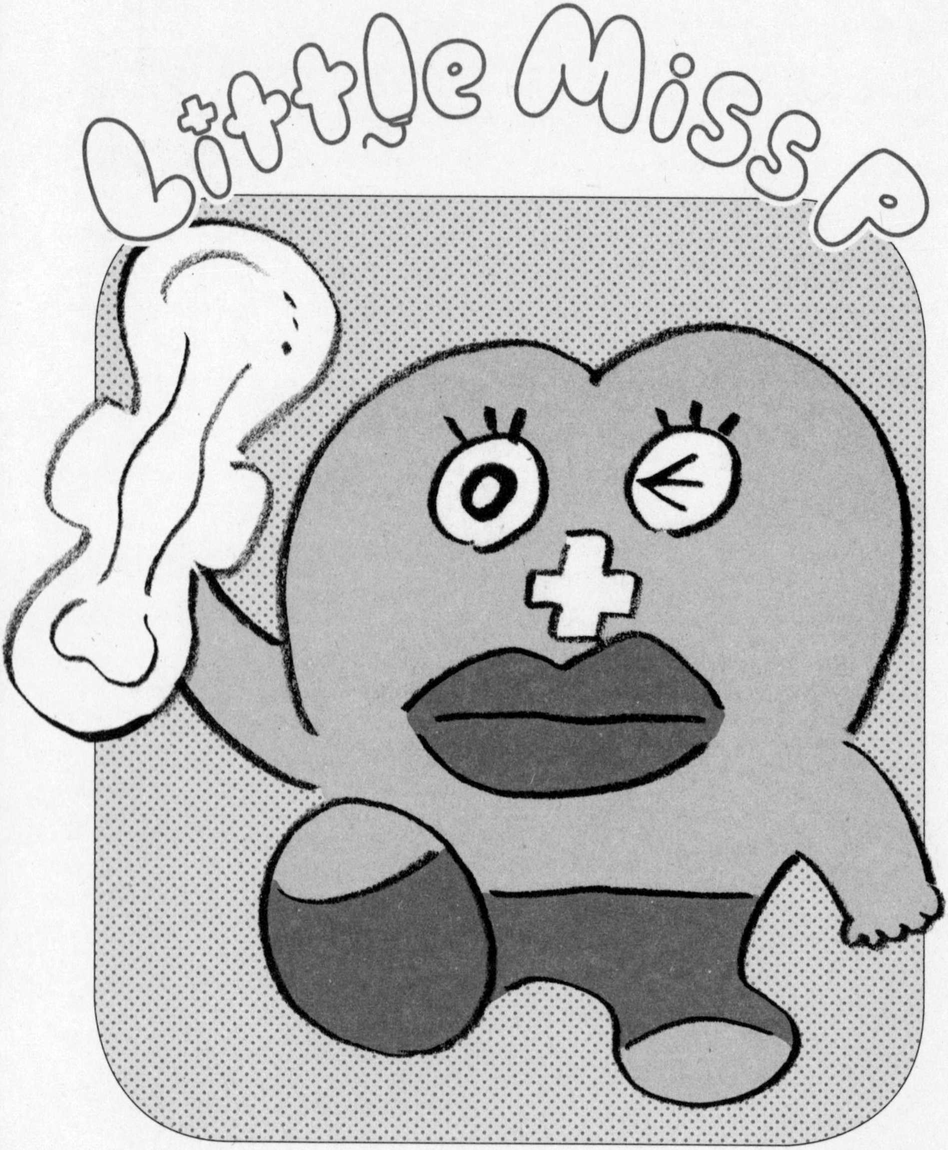
Little Miss P

KEN KOYAMA

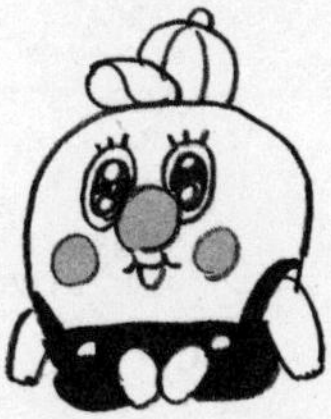

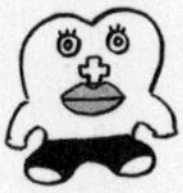

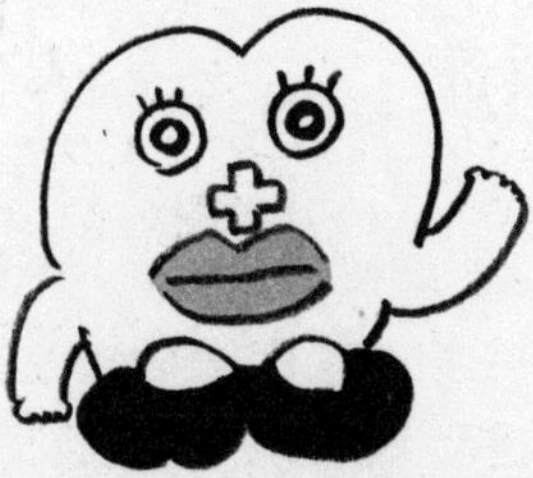

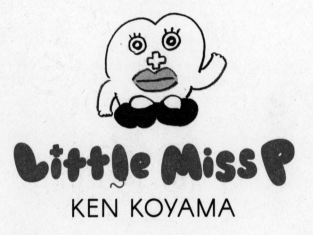

Little Miss P

KEN KOYAMA

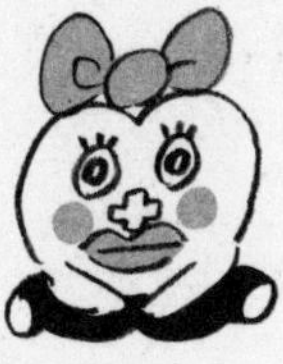

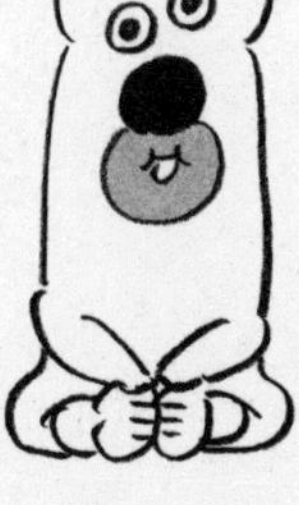

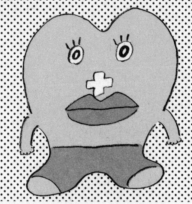

LITTLE MISS P: CHAPTER 1

LITTLE MISS P: NOW

LITTLE MISS P
ANATOMICAL CHART

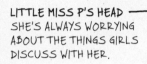

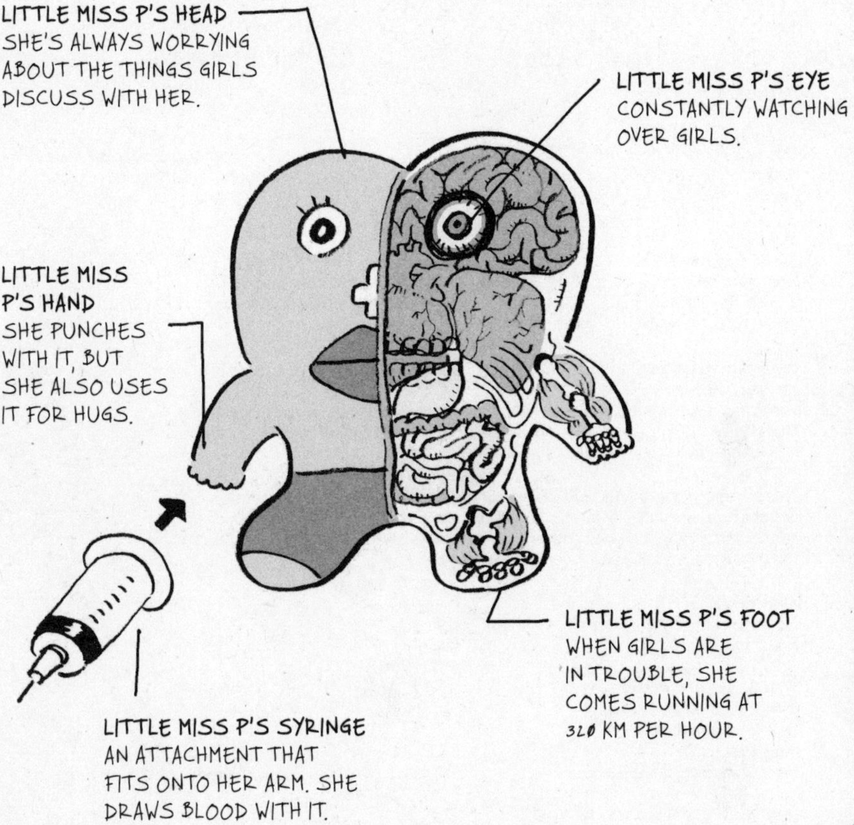

LITTLE MISS P'S HEAD
SHE'S ALWAYS WORRYING
ABOUT THE THINGS GIRLS
DISCUSS WITH HER.

LITTLE MISS P'S EYE
CONSTANTLY WATCHING
OVER GIRLS.

LITTLE MISS P'S HAND
SHE PUNCHES
WITH IT, BUT
SHE ALSO USES
IT FOR HUGS.

LITTLE MISS P'S FOOT
WHEN GIRLS ARE
IN TROUBLE, SHE
COMES RUNNING AT
320 KM PER HOUR.

LITTLE MISS P'S SYRINGE
AN ATTACHMENT THAT
FITS ONTO HER ARM. SHE
DRAWS BLOOD WITH IT.

Little Miss P

KEN KOYAMA

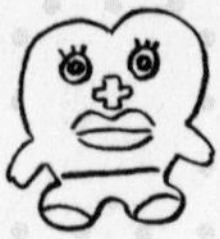

Translation:
Taylor Engel

Lettering:
Abigail Blackman

SEIRICHAN

First published in Japan in 2018 by KADOKAWA CORPORATION, Tokyo.
English translation rights arranged with KADOKAWA CORPORATION, Tokyo through TUTTLE-MORI AGENCY, INC., Tokyo.

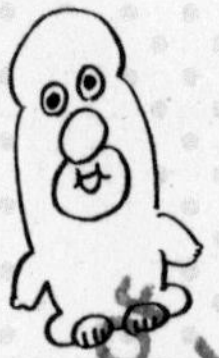

Yen Press
1290 Avenue of the Americas
New York, NY 10104

Visit us at yenpress.com
facebook.com/yenpress
twitter.com/yenpress
yenpress.tumblr.com
instagram.com/yenpress

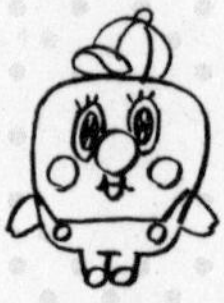

First Yen Press Edition: June 2019

Yen Press is an imprint of Yen Press, LLC.
The Yen Press name and logo are trademarks of Yen Press, LLC.

The publisher is not responsible for websites (or their content) that are not owned by the publisher.

Library of Congress Control Number: 2019934212

ISBNs: 978-1-9753-5708-5 (paperback)
978-1-9753-5709-2 (ebook)

10 9 8 7 6 5 4 3 2 1

WOR

Printed in the United States of America

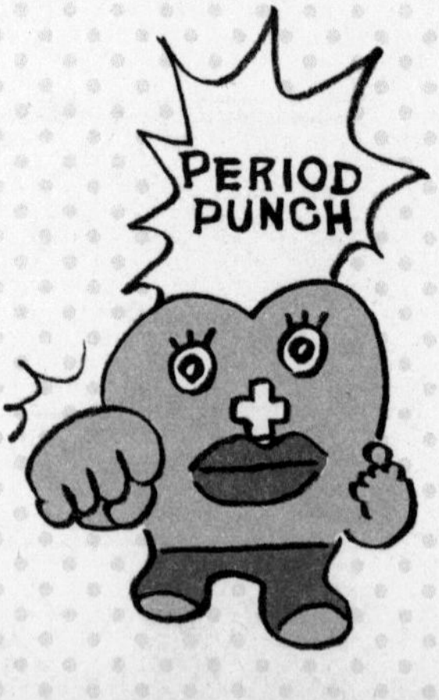
PERIOD PUNCH